The Anthropologist as Curator

The Anthropologist as Curator

Edited by
Roger Sansi

LONDON AND NEW YORK

First published 2020 by Bloomsbury Academic

2 Park Square, Milton Park, Abingdon, Oxon OX14 4RN
605 Third Avenue, New York, NY 10017

Routledge is an imprint of the Taylor & Francis Group, an informa business

First issued in paperback 2021

Copyright © Roger Sansi and contributors, 2020

Roger Sansi has asserted his right under the Copyright, Designs and
Patents Act, 1988, to be identified as Editor of this work.

Cover design: Tjaša Krivec
Cover image: *The only emergency is the absence of emergency*. Filippo Minelli Smoke
performance. Site-specific. Part of *Venturing Beyond* at Somerset House
curated by Rafael Schacter, Somerset House 2016.

All rights reserved. No part of this book may be reprinted or reproduced or utilised in any
form or by any electronic, mechanical, or other means, now known or hereafter invented,
including photocopying and recording, or in any information storage or retrieval system,
without permission in writing from the publishers.

Notice:
Product or corporate names may be trademarks or registered trademarks, and are used
only for identification and explanation without intent to infringe.

Publisher's Note
The publisher has gone to great lengths to ensure the quality of this reprint
but points out that some imperfections in the original copies may be apparent.

A catalogue record for this book is available from the British Library.

A catalog record for this book is available from the Library of Congress.

ISBN13: 978-1-3500-8190-1 (hbk)
ISBN13: 978-1-03-217605-5 (pbk)
DOI: 10.4324/9781003086819

Typeset by Deanta Global Publishing Services, Chennai, India

Contents

List of figures	vi
List of contributors	viii

1 Introduction: anthropology and curation through the looking glass
Roger Sansi — 1

2 Curatorial designs: Act II *Tarek Elhaik and George Marcus* — 17

3 The recursivity of the curatorial *Jonas Tinius and Sharon Macdonald* — 35

4 Whose stories about Africa? Reflexivity and public dialogue at the Royal Ontario Museum *Silvia Forni* — 59

5 Facing the 'curatorial turn': anthropological ethnography, exhibitions and collecting practices *Ivan Bargna* — 73

6 Ethnographic Terminalia: co-curation and the role of the anecdote in practice *Stephanie Takaragawa, Trudi Lynn Smith, Fiona P. McDonald, Kate Hennessy and Craig Campbell* — 97

7 Coming together differently: art, anthropology and the curatorial space *Judith Winter* — 115

8 From Of, to With, to And? Anti-disciplinary exhibition making with art and anthropology *Jen Clarke* — 133

9 Curating the intermural: graffiti in the museum 2008–18 *Rafael Schacter* — 147

10 The curator, the anthropologist: 'presentialism' and open-ended enquiry in process *Alex Flynn* — 173

11 Between automation and agency: curatorial challenges in new terrains of digital/visual research *Eva Theunissen and Paolo S. H. Favero* — 195

12 Anthropological sound curation: from listening to curating *Noel Lobley* — 211

Index — 227

Figures

5.1 Stefano Arienti, *Books of African Arts*. Exhibition *Wonders of Africa: African Arts in Italian Collections*, Palazzo Ducale, Genova, 2011. Photo: Ivan Bargna   81

5.2 Professor Kaptué Lazare's villa entrance hall: collected objects and paintings, pictures, decor and architectural ornaments make up a scene to impress the guests. Bandjoun, Cameroon, 2008. Photo: Ivan Bargna   86

6.1 Ethnographic Terminalia, New Orleans, Louisiana, 2011. Installation view. Photo: Craig Campbell). Floor plan preparation. Photo: Fiona P. McDonald   100

6.2 'Seeing ethnography', 2013. Installation view. American Museum of Natural History, New York. Photos: Fiona P. McDonald   101

6.3 Anecdote-ing at Microsoft Research, Cambridge, Massachusetts, 2016. Photos: Fiona P. McDonald   103

6.4 Ethnographic Terminalia, Philadelphia, Pennsylvania, 2009. Installation view of wall text. Photo: Craig Campbell   104

6.5 Ethnographic Terminalia, Denver, Colorado, *Aeolian Politics*, 2015. Installation view of wall text. Photos: Trudi Lynn Smith (top) and Fiona P. McDonald (bottom)   105

7.1 Robert Smithson, *Glue Pour*, Vancouver, British Columbia, December 1969. Smithson with Dennis Wheeler, Ilya Pegonis and Lucy Lippard Photo: Christos Dikeakos. Copyright © Holt/Smithson Foundation/ licensed by VAGA, New York   118

9.1 Map of the *Walking Tour*, part of the exhibition *Street Art* at the Tate Modern, London, 2008. Copyright © Rafael Schacter   152

9.2 *Signs*, London, Eltono and Nuria, fifty hand-painted signboards, site-specific part of the *Walking Tour*, for the exhibition *Street Art* at the Tate Modern, London, 2008, curated by Rafael Schacter   154

9.3 *Paris Verticale, Series 3*, Honet Giclée on cotton paper 118.9 cm by 84.1 cm. Exhibited at Somerset House, London, 2015, for *Mapping the City*, curated by Rafael Schacter   159

9.4 *C'est à la nature toujours qu'il faut demander conseil* (It is in nature, always, that one should seek advice). Ken Sortais, latex wall hanging and latex, acrylic, foam and wood sculpture, 285 cm by 220 cm (wall hanging), 96 cm by 41 cm by 23 cm (sculpture). Exhibited at Somerset House, London, 2015, for *Mapping the City*, curated by Rafael Schacter   161

9.5	*Cache*, Brad Downey, wall plugs, screws, size variable. Exhibited at Somerset House, London, 2016, for *Venturing Beyond*, curated by Rafael Schacter. The frontispiece work, by the artist Saeio, has here been removed	163
10.1	The exhibition *Cartoneras: Releituras Latino-Americanas*, São Paulo, Brazil, 2018. Photos: Filipe Berndt	185
10.2	The workstation of the public programme team, *Cartoneras: Releituras Latino-Americanas*, São Paulo, Brazil, 2018. Photo: Filipe Berndt	186

Contributors

Ivan Bargna is Full Professor of Aesthetic Anthropology, and Media Anthropology at University of Milan Bicocca, and Visiting Professor of Cultural Anthropology at Milan Bocconi University. He is director of the post-degree programme of specialization in Anthropology of Art and Heritage at University of Milan Bicocca. Since 2001, he has been carrying out his ethnographic research in Cameroon's Grassfields, where he studies arts, visual culture and food practices. Curator of several art exhibitions, he was a member of the scientific board creating the Museum of Cultures of Milan (MUDEC). He is the author of *African Art* (J Milan 1998; St. Léger Vauban 1998; New York and London; 2000; Madrid 2000) and *Africa*, (Milan 2007; Berlin 2008; Los Angeles, 2009), *Biografa plurale. Virginia Ryan: Africa, Art, and Elsewhere* (2018).

Dr Jennifer Clarke is Lecturer in Critical and Contextual Studies at Gray's School of Art, Aberdeen. With a background in the arts and a Ph.D. in Social Anthropology, her research, teaching and public work combine and explore the borders of anthropology, art and philosophy. Her primary areas of expertise are in interdisciplinary contemporary art practice and ecological thinking, and she has significant interest in and experience working in Japan.

Tarek Elhaik is Associate Professor of Anthropology at the University of California, Davis. His research is focused on aesthetic anthropology, philosophies of the image, curatorial practice and conceptual artists' modes of thinking. He is the author of *The Incurable-Image: Curating Post-Mexican Film and Media Arts* (Edinburgh University Press, 2016), a book based on participant-observation in Mexico City's contemporary art scene and intellectual life. He is currently finishing a new book entitled *States of Cogitation*. He is also the founder of AIL: the Anthropology of the Image Lab.

Paolo S. H. Favero is Associate Professor in Film Studies and Visual Culture at the University of Antwerp, Belgium. A visual anthropologist, he has devoted his career to the study of visual and digital culture in India. His core interest is the role of images (new and old) in human life. He is the author of *The Present Image: Visible Stories in a Digital Habitat* (Palgrave Macmillan 2017).

Alex Flynn is Assistant Professor in the Department of Anthropology at Durham University, UK. His research focuses on aesthetics and politics, and he has conducted ethnographic research with artists and activists in Brazil since 2007. Alex is the author of the books *Anthropology, Theatre and Development* (Palgrave, 2015) with Jonas Tinius and *Claire Fontaine: em vista de uma prática ready-made* (GLAC, 2016) with Leonardo Araujo, and is the co-founder of the network Anthropologies of Art [A/A], a platform that seeks to expand contemporary perspectives on the interstices of these two fields. Alex is also the recipient of the São Paulo Association of Art Critics Awards 2016 APCA Trophy for his curatorial practice in the Residência Artística Cambridge programme.

Silvia Forni is Senior Curator of African Arts and Cultures at the Royal Ontario Museum, Toronto, Canada. She is also Associate Professor of Anthropology at the University of Toronto. Among her recent publications are the volumes *Africa in the Market: Twentieth-Century Art from the Amrad African Art Collection* (2015), co-edited with Christopher B. Steiner, and *Art, Honor, and Ridicule: Fante Asafo Flags from Southern Ghana* (2017), co-authored with Doran H. Ross.

The **Ethnographic Terminalia Collective** (est. 2009) functions as a leaderless cooperative. We make decisions on a consensus basis and share duties and obligations equally. We are held together by a mutual interest in the intersections of ethnographic epistemologies, creativity, artistic expression and exhibition. Where possible we curate, write and make things together in shared and equal authorship. While we each maintain individual research, art and curatorial programmes, we aim to operate with a collective voice.

Craig Campbell is Associate Professor of Anthropology at the University of Texas, Austin. His research is concerned with making as well as theorizing modes of description and evocation, with a special focus on exhibition and the ethnographic encounter. He is author of *Agitating Images: Photography Against History in Indigenous Siberia* (2014) . He is one of the co-founders of the Ethnographic Terminalia Collective.

Fiona P. McDonald is Assistant Professor of Visual Anthropology and Media at the University of British Columbia (UBC), Okanagan Campus. She leads the Collaborative & Experimental Ethnography Lab (CE2 Lab) at UBC. Her research interests are water rights, material and visual culture, oral histories, curatorial theory, performance theory, sensory ethnography and cold climate housing (www.fiona-p-mcdonald.com). She is one of the co-founders of the Ethnographic Terminalia Collective.

Kate Hennessy is Associate Professor specializing in Media at Simon Fraser University's School of Interactive Arts and Technology, British Columbia, where she leads the Making Culture Lab. Her research and art practice explore the role of digital technology in the documentation and safeguarding of cultural heritage, and the mediation of culture, history, and objects in new forms. She is one of the co-founders of the Ethnographic Terminalia Collective.

Trudi Lynn Smith (Ph.D.) is trained as an artist and anthropologist and is currently Artist in Residence in the School of Interactive Art and Technology at Simon Fraser University, British Columbia, and Adjunct Assistant Professor in the School of Environmental Studies at The University of Victoria, British Columbia. She works with cultural practices of media and the archive (https://www.trudilynnsmith.com/) and she is one of the co-founders of the Ethnographic Terminalia Collective.

Stephanie Takaragawa is Associate Dean of the Wilkinson College of Arts, Humanities and Social Sciences, California, and Associate Professor of Sociology at Chapman University, California. Her research interests focus on issues of representation in film, mass media, art, performance, and cultural display, with an emphasis on racial formation in the United States. She is one of the co-founders of the Ethnographic Terminalia Collective.

Noel Lobley is an ethnomusicologist, sound curator and artist who works across the disciplines of music, anthropology sound art and composition to develop a series of experiential sound events and international curatorial residencies. He is currently Assistant Professor of Music at the University of Virginia, United States.

Sharon Macdonald is Alexander von Humboldt Professor of Social Anthropology at the Institute for European Ethnology, Humboldt-Universität zu Berlin, Germany. She founded and directs the Centre for Anthropological Research on Museums and Heritage (CARMAH): www.carmah.berlin.

George E. Marcus is Distinguished Professor of Anthropology, University of California, Irvine, and founding director from 2005 of the Center for Ethnography there. Most recently, he is co-author with Luke Cantarella and Christine Hegel of *Ethnography by Design: Scenographic Interventions in Fieldwork* (Bloomsbury, 2019).

Roger Sansi was born in Barcelona, Spain, in 1972. After studying at the universities of Barcelona and Paris he received a Ph.D. in Anthropology at the University of Chicago, United States (2003). He has worked at Kings College and Goldsmiths College, University of London. Currently he is Professor in Social Anthropology at the University of Barcelona, Spain. He has worked on Afro-Brazilian culture and art, the concept of the fetish and on contemporary art in Barcelona. His publications include the books *Fetishes and Monuments* (Berghahn, 2007), *Sorcery in the Black Atlantic* (edited with L. Nicolau, Chicago University Press, 2011) and *Art Anthropology and the Gift* (Bloomsbury, 2015).

Rafael Schacter is an anthropologist and curator based at University College London, working on issues related to both public and global art. He has published three books, *Street to Studio* with Lund Humphries (2018), *Ornament and Order* with Routledge (2014), the award-winning *World Atlas of Street Art and Graffiti* (Yale University Press). Schacter has also participated in numerous exhibitions, curating the *Walking Tour* at the Tate Modern's *Street Art* exhibition, in 2008; *Mapping the City* and *Venturing Beyond* at Somerset House in 2015 and 2016; and *Silver Sehnsucht* in London's Silvertown district in 2017. His most recent project was the exhibition *Motions of this Kind*, featuring eleven artists working in or on the Philippines and emergent from his British Academy Postdoctoral Fellowship (2014–2017).

Eva Theunissen is a Ph.D. candidate at the Visual and Digital Cultures Research Center (ViDi) at the University of Antwerp, Belgium. Conducting online and offline ethnography, her doctoral research focuses on the roles digital images play in the everyday lives of socially marginalized individuals.

Jonas Tinius (Ph.D. Cantab) is an anthropologist of art and currently a postdoctoral research fellow at the Centre for Anthropological Research on Museums and Heritage at the Institute of European Ethnology, Humboldt-Universität zu Berlin, Germany. His research addresses cultural institutions (theatres, museums, contemporary art spaces) and their negotiations of subjectivity, identity and alterity amid growing nationalist sentiments in Europe. He is founding convenor (with Roger Sansi) of the Anthropology and the Arts Network of the European Association of Social Anthropologists.

Judith Winter (born 1966, UK) is curator, writer and Lecturer in Critical and Contextual Studies at Gray's School of Art (Robert Gordon University, Aberdeen). She studied sculpture at Central/St Martins School of Art and Sculpture Studies at the University of Leeds, UK. She has had a distinguished career as an arts professional, most notably as inaugural curator of Middlesbrough Institute of Modern Art (mima) and Head of Arts, Dundee Contemporary Arts (DCA), Scotland, where she has facilitated solo exhibitions by contemporary international artists including: Thomas Hirschhorn (Switzerland); Martin Boyce (Scotland and Venice Biennale); Johanna Billing (Sweden); Matthew Buckingham (US); and Manfred Pernice (Germany). She is currently working on a major solo exhibition: Edward Allington (1951–2017) *Things Unsaid*, Henry Moore Institute, Leeds. Since 2013 she has been working with Professor Tim Ingold as a researcher on the project *Knowing from the Inside: Anthropology, Art, Architecture and Design*, and from 2016 as a guest researcher at the Bauhaus Dessau Foundation, Germany.

1

Introduction: anthropology and curation through the looking glass

Roger Sansi

More than two decades ago, Hal Foster's seminal essay 'The Artist as Ethnographer' opened a wide-ranging discussion on the relations between contemporary art and anthropology (Foster 1995; Gell 1996; Marcus 2010; Sansi 2015; Schneider and Wright 2005, 2010, 2013). However, the question of 'The Anthropologist as Curator/the curator as anthropologist' has not received the same attention. There is an enormous literature on the anthropology of museums and collections (Clifford 1997; Edwards, Gosden and Phillips 2006, Karp and Levine 1991; Karp and Kratz 2007; Kirshenblatt-Gimblett 1998; Lonetree 2012; Basu and MacDonald 2007; to name a few), but not so much has been written on the experience of anthropologists as curators. Yet many anthropologists have worked as curators or have organized exhibits, not just in ethnographic museums, but also in contemporary art settings. Meanwhile, curators in the last decades have reached great pre-eminence in the art world, becoming leading figures in art discourse. Some of them have used anthropology and ethnography as a central inspiration of their work. This double movement opens an interesting space of exchange that so far has been only partially explored. The objective of this volume is to bring together the experience of anthropologists who have been involved in different curatorial projects and have reflected upon the relations between curation, anthropology and ethnography. How does the practice of curation help anthropologists rethink their practice, their work and the concerns of contemporary anthropology? This is the central question of this book. But perhaps, before going further, we could start by the opposite end: the curator as ethnographer.

The curator as ethnographer

The renowned contemporary art curator Okwui Enwezor formulated the analogy in these terms:

> In his own hunt for art, might the travel of the curator – in which he scours the global scenes of contemporary art in search of artistic forms and signs through their

various embodiments in objects, systems, structures, images and concepts – be propelled by [a] similar sense of intellectual vertigo that afflicts the ethnographer? Is the curator a co-traveller with the ethnographer in the same procedures of contact and exploration? What distinguishes the practices of curatorial fieldwork from those of ethnography? In the course of this process, it seems even clearer that the path of curatorial fieldwork, while lacking the certainties of the ethnographic discipline, nevertheless shares in some measure a fascination for the tenuous and speculative; the psychic and the spiritual; the cognitive and the symbolic. Like the ethnographer, the contemporary curator is a creature of wanderlust, except in the present instant, the path begins from a series of detours, disorientations and disarticulations of cultural geographies that are being remapped in the face of rapid global reconfigurations. How does the work of contemporary curating engage with this process of cartographic disorientation? In the last half-century, increased mobility and migration have forced the revision of the rules of proximity, eroding cultural borders, exacerbating the relationship between guests and hosts. Rather than practices of good neighbourliness and shared space, greater proximity – that is to say active, unceasing contact between different cultural communities – have instead led to spatial and temporal disjunctions. This means that contemporary societies need to define how to manage conflict, live with cultural dissent within conditions of hostility and non-recognition. (Enwezor 2012: 21)

Enwezor did not identify the ethnographer with the traditional authority figure who provides a totalizing narrative of a particular culture. On the contrary, he departed from the postmodern critique of this authority figure, where the ethnographer is the 'creature of wanderlust' that operates montages between the strange and the familiar, presenting a world of disjuncture and erosion of cultural borders. This text can be found in the catalogue of an exhibit, *Intense Proximity: An Anthology of the Near and the Far* (2012), where ethnographers appeared as these ambiguous but fascinating figures of mediation between collapsing worlds.

Enwezor's proposal has many similarities with Foster's 'artist as ethnographer' (Foster 1995). Foster coined the expression 'the ethnographic turn', pointing to the growing interests of artists in issues of identity and its representation in the 1990s. He described the relationship between artist and anthropologist as a kind of mirroring, in which both look at each other as an image of how they would like to see themselves, as an object of envy. Anthropologists want to be artists, they envy their freedom and openness, while artists want to be anthropologists, they envy their critical perspective and direct access to cultural alterity. However, since these images are a construction of desire, they do not project a very realistic image of the 'other'. If we replace the artist with the curator, will we fall into the same trap?

Why do curators want to be anthropologists – and the other way around? What does this desire tell us about the contemporary situation of both curators and anthropologists?

To address these questions we should start by tracing the outcomes of the 'ethnographic turn' in art practice. The attraction of anthropology for contemporary art practitioners in the 1990s was premised on the assumption that it could offer a critical take on the politics of representation, a less ethnocentric and elitist approach to art and culture than that of modern art. One could ask if, twenty years later, the art world is less ethnocentric and elitist. The answer would be ambivalent: the international art world is certainly elitist, that is constitutive of its very structure as an institution, but at the same time the number of art centres, festivals, events, biennials and practitioners of contemporary art have multiplied around the globe to an unprecedented level (Gielen 2010), engaging new artists, art worlds and publics. The question would be if this globalization of contemporary art is just an extension and consolidation of its institutional imperialism or, on the contrary, if it could generate structural transformations. In the meantime, 'Decolonization', as we will see in several chapters of this book, has become the *mot d'ordre* in contemporary art, following and extending the concerns with postcolonialism at the end of the twentieth century. On the other hand, in these two decades, the interest of contemporary art in anthropology has not waned, quite the opposite. Beyond questions of representation and identity, central to Foster's argument, many art projects not only have engaged with 'difference' as a concept, but also have used anthropological methods and theories in their practice. Many participative art projects are based upon fieldwork and are inspired by anthropological theories of exchange to reflect upon social practice (Sansi 2015). In other terms, contemporary art practice not only discusses identity politics, but also enacts forms of social practice using anthropological methods and ideas. Art critics such as Foster (1995) and Bishop (2012) may question the artistic 'quality' of many of these projects, but the 'quantity' cannot be ignored, and hence their social significance: they have become so widespread that they have become a genre in their own right, sometimes called 'social practice' (Sholette 2012).

Participatory curation

The work of curators has also substantially changed in the last two decades. The multiplication of art spaces and events increasingly requires the figure of the curator as a mediator between the multiple agents involved in the process of producing and showing art: from 'representing' ideas through visual texts, to engaging with publics and communities, producing events, mediating social communities, even creating experimental social situations. The new roles of the art curator are multiple.

Just like in art practice, participatory curation has a big precedent in the 1970s, when new museological practices emerged in community museums and ethnological museums (Vergo 1989). But it would be in the 1990s that these practices would become widespread in contemporary art curation, acquiring a new dimension, from the periphery to the centre of cultural production: participation was not just a marginal form of practice – it became a dominant paradigm. The work of Hans-Ulrich Obrist is a famous example of this turn to participative curation. The project 'Do it' (1992), for example, was premised on the idea of offering 'written instructions by artists, as a point of departure, each of which could be interpreted anew every time they were enacted'.[1] Marcel Duchamp's statement 'art is a game between all people of all periods' is often quoted as the driving force behind the exhibition. After its initial enactment, 'Do it' has been featured in at least fifty different locations worldwide.

Still, like the 'relational art' forms that they often worked with, these participative projects could be accused of limiting participation to the ephemeral temporalities of the contemporary art world. But we should also make reference to the multiplication of 'durational' approaches to curation (O'Neill and Doherty 2011). Durational approaches start from acknowledging the significance of engaging audiences and encouraging research-based outcomes that are responsive to their specific contexts, audiences and locations over time. This emphasis on long duration, site-specificity and research brings curatorial practice very close to what anthropologists call fieldwork.

The curatorial laboratory

The contemporary drive to participation is connected to another important aspect: the interest in experimentation in the wider sense of the term, attempting to connect experimental art with other forms of speculative practice, such as experimental science as well as social experiments. Basu and Macdonald pointed to 'exhibition experiments' (2007), in the double sense of the term, as both a tentative curatorial proposal and a laboratory that creates new knowledge. Again, Hans-Ulrich Obrist appears as a precedent to this development, with the *Laboratorium* show (Obrist and Vanderlinden 2001), whose ambition was to stage the relations between scientists, artists, dancers and writers. The objective was to open up spaces of dialogue, not from a central institution that interpellates its subjects, but between the different collectives themselves. Thus the activities of each group were opened up for the others to see and question: the artists were invited to the scientific laboratories, the scientists to the process of artistic production. The museum itself shifted its spaces, displacing the museum offices to the exhibition area for all the public to see.

The collaborations between art, science and social practice have become widespread in recent decades. Inspired by authors in science and technology studies, such as Rheinberger (1997) and Latour (2005), these collaborations are premised on the notion that, in spite of their radically different cultures, experiments in science, art and politics have one point in common: they do not only attempt to represent reality, but also to make it concrete, to perform it. Furthermore, experimentation is defined essentially as a participative event; departing from the model of the traditional scientific laboratory as a closed space, in which humans might control nature in order to better understand it, contemporary approaches define experimentation as a social process rather than a knowledge site (Corsín Jiménez 2013: 2). The new 'collective experiments' for Latour are happening outside the traditional laboratories – on us, with us, we are all participating in them (Latour 2005).

In this context, the borders between scientific, artistic and social experimentation are becoming blurred. This expanded model of experimentation would not be based solely on scientific research labs, but also on open software, design labs, media labs (Rabinow et al. 2018) and artistic collaborative practices in general (Marcus 2010).

Corsín and Estalella underscore the centrality of hospitality in this model, as opposed to the radical strangeness and separation between objects and subjects of the traditional 'pure' science lab (Corsín and Estalella 2010).

What would be the role of the curator in these new 'laboratories'? More than a doorkeeper in charge of a closed space, the curator would appear as a mediator whose role it is to facilitate collaboration and experimentation, the exchange between the different actors involved in the experimental space. Obrist again exemplifies this shift: he notes that the term curator comes from the Latin *curare*, meaning taking care, curing, helping, rather than doorkeeping (Obrist 2014).

The anthropologist as curator

The relationship of the ethnographer with the curator can be seen precisely from the prism of this interest in experimentation. So far, I have talked about how a curator can be seen as an ethnographer. But what about the anthropologist as curator? That question has started to be addressed by some anthropologists in recent years. In *The Incurable-Image: Curating Post-Mexican Film and Media Arts* (2016), Tarik Elhaik, who is himself a film curator and anthropologist, starts from this parallelism: at the same time that we see curatorial work that is increasingly similar to what anthropologists call fieldwork, anthropologists start to question what constitutes this 'work' of ethnography. In what they have defined as the 'anthropology of the contemporary', Rabinow et al. (2008) propose notions such as 'assemblage-work' to replace 'field-work'. The object of study of anthropology is no longer a given singular community, located in a singular space for a particular time, but an assemblage of different parts: people, places, objects, concepts and agencies of different sorts that constitute contemporary assemblages. This notion of assemblage-work is related to Marcus's para-site (2000) – participatory spaces where multiple divergent agents and agencies discursively interact across geographic, temporal and disciplinary boundaries. The model for the para-site would be the design lab, as an open process that does not just represent the world as it is, but produces and tests new experimental objects. The anthropologist as curator would have the role of mediator in the production of these experimental objects.

One of the examples used by Elhaik is the curatorial collective Teratoma, who made a remontage of Eisensteins's *Que Viva México!* (1931–32) and then a recreation of its filming at its specific site, Tetlapayac. As a curator himself, Elhaik organized a programme of films, 'Yo soy Mexico', which were dealing with of the 'post-Mexican' condition in similar ways to Teratoma's project, adding recursive layers to this experimental object.

Nikola Ssorin-Chaikov's proposal of 'ethnographic conceptualism' starts, like Elhaik, from a questioning of traditional notions of fieldwork. For Ssorin-Chaikov, fieldwork does not only represent reality but also is a part of its fabrication; it is a form of social intervention. Ethnographic conceptualism proposes to use the performative and conceptual methods of contemporary art as ethnographic methods. In 2006, Ssorin-Chaikov curated an exhibition, *Gifts to Soviet Leaders*, at the Kremlin

Museum of Moscow. This exhibition displayed the presents given to former Soviet leaders. But the curators gave great importance to the comments in the exhibition's visitors' book, which offered all possible views across the political spectrum as well as reflections on the values and meanings of the objects displayed – and which eventually became a part of the exhibit. For the curators, the exhibition was both an end and a means of research, a post-Soviet artefact and a tool in the ethnography of post-Soviet Moscow; the exhibition both displayed and performed post-socialist society. In this case, ethnographic conceptualism was an ethnographic research and a conceptualist depiction of this exhibition's organizational infrastructure (Ssorin-Chaikov 2013: 7–8).

We could say that the notion of the anthropologist as curator incorporates elements of the approaches we have seen before, like the 'montage' of Enwezor and the participatory laboratory of some of Obrist's projects. But the question returns. What distinguishes curatorial work from ethnographic work? If we insist on the mediations, on the relations, on the connections, then the specificity of these different kinds of work is diluted. Does that mean that their value is also diluted? Some of the chapters in this book express concern with this possibility. Is there a point in maintaining these distinctions, in detaching the curator from the ethnographer? And if 'contemporary societies need to define how to manage conflict' and 'live with cultural dissensus', as Enwezor says, are either the curator or the ethnographer well placed to manage this conflict?

The expanded field of the curatorial

At this point we need to consider in wider terms what are we defining as curation. The literature on the 'curatorial' in the last few years has been very prolific (Balzer 2015; Bismarck et al. 2012; Lind 2012; Martinon 2013; Obrist 2014; O'Neill 2012; Smith 2012). The 'curator' has become an all-encompassing term: the curator as everything else (the curator as ethnographer, the curator as mediator and so on). This 'expanded field' of the curatorial is built upon the expanded field of art. As modern and contemporary art rejected the academy and professionalism, and embraced experimentation, chance and deskilling, artists started to take upon themselves many different roles: travellers, scientists, narrators, thinkers, ethnographers, social mediators, political agitators, and so on. The curator is in the same puzzle as the contemporary artist, whose practice is always something more and something other than art. What would be the difference between artist and curator then? For Irit Rogoff (2013) the problem of the expanded mode of art is that it appears simply as a celebration of multiplicity, confusing infinite expansion of the museum with inclusion and compensation. For Rogoff, rather than just a celebration of multiplicity, what is interesting about this expanding field is that it manifests an epistemological crisis, and the curatorial would be in a privileged position to address it. The role of the curatorial would be to bring together knowledge, sensibilities and insights, assembling them together and enacting the event of knowledge rather than illustrating them (Rogoff 2013: 43).

Introduction 7

But again, who gives to the curator this privileged position of bringing others together? Or better, what allows this encounter to happen? What is behind this 'epistemological crisis'? The privileged position of the curator may be just a sign of our current mode of production. Carolyn Christov-Bakargiev, the artistic director of 'Documenta X', said that 'the curator is the most emblematic worker of the cognitive age' (Balzer 2015: 3), an age based in the production of discourse, values, relations. The omnipresent figure of the curator as a mediator simultaneously occupies multiple roles: author, interpreter, communicator, administrator, impresario, diplomat, but in any of these roles, the curator does not really produce anything per se, but writes narratives, exchanges information, builds relations, generates value. At the same time the role of curator is deprofessionalized: many 'star' curators are not professionally trained as such, while, paradoxically, curatorship courses proliferate. But curators do more than curating art: they delocalize exhibits, research, interview, debate, do ethnography, multiply events. All these different activities are developed without necessarily being professionally trained in these tasks, like in the case of contemporary artists that approach different media and tasks without being trained in them . But in opposition to or separation from the contemporary artist, the curator cannot embrace chance and process as method so explicitly; the curator has to provide the discourse that brings things together and has to make ends meet. In these terms, curators may indeed be the model for the workers of the cognitive age, as Christov-Bakargiev says, workers that produce contents, discourses and values, because they are the ones with the responsibility of turning an art event into accountable value. The role of the curator would be to bring to light the project beyond the art event: the project in the terms of Boltanksi and Chiapello, as a stabilization of processes and connections, in order to make them irreversible, a pocket of accumulation that can be justified, that generates value (Boltanski and Chiapello 2005: 105).

In these terms the figure of the curator appears closer to that of a manager, a manager of relations, discourses and aesthetic value, but a manager nonetheless. It may seem that we are very far from the ethnographer who would appear to be a more romantic or critical figure. But really? Isn't the task of the ethnographer to manage difference, to mediate? Can the ethnographer learn from the managing skills developed by curators, in terms of the micropolitics of mediating between institutions, communities and all kinds of different agents? Some authors in this volume point in this direction.

These are very broad questions, indeed. But the proposal of this book is to ask these questions openly and without prejudice. The academic reaction to these comparisons, to the 'expanded field' of art and curatorship, for example, is often built on arguments of purity and detachment (Sansi and Strathern 2016). By separating ourselves from the flow, or the avalanche of cognitive capitalism embodied by the curator, anthropologists and other academics aspire to maintain a critical distance instead of getting their hands dirty in the network of value relations. Is this detachment indeed possible? This volume does not intend to simply celebrate interdisciplinarity and experimentation, but nor are we interested in withdrawing from thinking what anthropology can become beyond its traditional academic fences. On the contrary, we think that these exchanges, these experiments are interesting, provoking thought, reactively, about

8 *The Anthropologist as Curator*

what constitutes the work of ethnography and anthropology in general terms. But our aim is not to build yet another theory of the 'curatorial' or to propose a 'curatorial turn' in anthropology. Our objective is much more modest: it is to take a close look at the experience of anthropologists who have worked as curators, describing their working processes ethnographically, their intellectual and material constraints, the very detail of their infrastructures and processes, starting with the anecdotes. These descriptions can be crucial in order to think together where this relationship can take us, which new perspectives can be opened up.

The chapters

The purpose of this book is precisely to address all these questions from a variety of viewpoints, examples and experiences. In 2016, a workshop on the 'Anthropologist as curator' was held at the Pirelli Hangar Bicocca art centre in Milan as part of the larger European Association of Social Anthropologists (EASA) conference. Out of our discussion several questions emerged: the range of forms of curation; the different media; the relation between exhibitions and archives; the forms of participation and mediation, and the politics of curatorship; the position of the academic anthropologist in regard to these forms of mediation; the long-standing, contentious history of anthropological practices of curation, before the recent interest of contemporary art curators; and the figure of the 'curator' as a model of and model for the cultural worker, and the worker in general, in our times. The workshop produced a landscape that, at that time, we were only able to start mapping; and the idea for this edited volume emerged at that event. Some of the contributions to this volume are a result of that workshop and some have been added in the ongoing discussion that followed. The purpose of the book is to bring together different anthropologists who have worked as curators in a contemporary art context, to address these issues from their experience.

After this introduction, Chapters 2 and 3 build up the frame of the general discussion of the book from different points of view. Chapter 2 is a conversation between Tarek Elhaik and George Marcus. The point of departure is the 'writing culture' debate of the 1980s, led by Marcus among others, and the legacy of its call for experimental methods. From there, the two authors discuss the possibility of developing new forms of anthropological practice beyond traditional fieldwork, towards more experimental models of research, such as Marcus's notion of the 'para-site' and Elhaik's book, *The Incurable-Image* (2016), in which Elhaik explores the parallelism between curatorship and ethnography. Elhaik tentatively proposes the curatorial as a third mode of anthropological work: after the 'comparative method' of nineteenth-century evolutionism, and the site-specific 'ethnographic method' of twentieth-century cultural relativists, might curation emerge as a new method for the twenty-first century? For Elhaik, curation reframes the Boasian critique of the comparative method: with curation, the anthropological problem shifts from a concern with the comparison of facts and objects from different places to 'a concern with assembling a wilder kind of difference that is far from being whimsical' (Elhaik, Chapter 2, this volume). Curation as practice appears also in contrast to the classical Boasian and

Malinowskian 'ethnographic method' understood as a direct representation of a single site, a 'field', precisely because curation would be concerned with the assemblage of different elements rather than the representation of a single field. The practice of curation can be seen, in these terms, as a method that corresponds to the new kinds of sites that anthropologists work with, as described by Marcus, characterized by multiplicity (the multisite), excess and ambiguity between the object and the subject of representation (the para-site).

However, Elhaik and Marcus point out that they are not proposing yet another 'turn'. The engagement with curation continues the invitation to experimentation of previous generations of anthropologists, to propose new modes of inhabiting the world and using their discipline, and to work playfully in terms of montage, design and assemblage, understanding anthropology as a 'minor science', an empirical mode of thinking that deterritorializes conventional methods and categories. Then, like now, these experimental, playful and tentative proposals met with resistance, which Elhaik identifies with the current call of ontologically oriented anthropologists for a 'perpetual decolonization'. This apparently revolutionary call may, paradoxically, question the legitimacy of experimentation, by putting the emphasis back on representation.

This very paradox of representation is central to the chapter that follows. Chapter 3, 'The recursivity of the curatorial' by Jonas Tinius and Sharon Macdonald, addresses one of the issues discussed in this introduction, the expanded field of curatorship. Confronting the notion of the curator as an all-encompassing mediator, they argue that there are multiple forms of curation that cannot be accounted for by this emergent model, in particular the traditional model of the professional curator as a museum-based caretaker of objects. The authors start from a clear position of *not desiring* to become the other – appreciating the proximity, but without blurring the boundaries (and thus also the differences) between the curator and the anthropologist.

Tinius and Macdonald are working on the project *Making Differences in Berlin: Museums and Heritage in the 21st Century* in collaboration with museums, where they struggle to maintain their autonomy as anthropologists. Macdonald addresses the awkward negotiation of her position as a researcher in a context where her participation takes different forms, from being a formal member of an advisory board to a more informal role as 'accompanying' or 'following' the process of exhibition-making, in a context where 'participation' and 'transparency' are the watchwords. Tinius, on the other hand, presents a collaborative project with the curator Bonaventure Soh Bejeng Ndikung, entitled 'Relexification Dialogues', a set of conversations around concepts that address the relation between anthropology and curation. The aim of these dialogues is not to write a dictionary, but to experiment with a long-term exchange and joint recalibration of perspectives. One of these concepts is 'recursivity', that is, in very general terms, the quality of a figure that draws upon itself. A mirror reflecting a mirror reflecting a mirror would be an iconic example of recursivity. The argument of the recursive emerges in this context to describe the process of mutual mirroring of anthropology and curation: not only does curation mirror anthropology, but, as Tinius realized, his fieldwork also mirrors in style and content some of the models and formats of curation. Could this process of mutual reflection become 'the staging ground for the development of an idea' (Rogoff 2013:16)? More than a dialogue between anthropology and curation, could it be the enactment of an event of knowledge? The authors are uncertain about this possibility. What if rather than a mirror reflecting a mirror, the image of recursion, the mirrors are broken, as Ndikung says? What if the mirrors are turned back to each other and they only reflect themselves, as in Foster's 'ethnographer's envy'? The fear of being absorbed by the other, of getting lost in the mirror reflections, of being trapped and losing agency, authority, representation, is present in this and other chapters in this volume. The description of the relation between art and anthropology as an 'uneven hermeneutics' (Schneider 2018), referenced in this chapter and also in Flynn's chapter in this volume, starts from an ontology of representation, where they each occupy clearly delineated subject positions, and one may fear being absorbed, incorporated or cancelled by the other. But hermeneutics, interpretation, dialogue and reflexivity, are not the same thing as recursivity. The recursive is not an exchange between two given subjects, but a self-constitutive relation. Recursivity prefigures a relational ontology, where relations take precedence over entities (Sansi 2015). If we discuss the relation between art and anthropology in terms of recursivity, we are not introducing a dialogue between given subjects, but the prefiguration of a third subject, beyond the 'representation' of anthropology and/or art; we project the relation towards a prefigured future, rather than representing a given past.

On the other hand, the question of the past, of representation, cannot be easily dismissed, but is recurrent (if not necessarily recursive!) in recent years in the form of the debate on decolonization, as many authors in this book demonstrate. Even if the art world has become relatively more globalized, perhaps we are not very far from the identity politics that Foster was discussing in the 1990s as a source for the 'ethnographic turn'. For example, in his chapter in this volume, Flynn proposes to think in terms of a redistribution of the sensible, after Rancière(2004) and Strohm (2012), to question *who* discusses representation and identity (Flynn, this volume). And yet, for Rancière, the distribution of the sensible that aesthetics proposes is precisely built in contraposition to the regime of representation. The task of art in the aesthetic regime for Rancière would be to enact new subjects, rather than represent the given world more or less fairly. The open question at this point would be whether the ongoing debates on representation, which still seem inevitable in the second decade of the twenty-first century, may in fact be in contradiction with the claims to experimentation and prefiguration in anthropology and art.

The two chapters that follow explicitly engage with these questions of representation. Chapters 4 and 5 are written by anthropologists Silvia Forni and Ivan Bargna, who have both worked in ethnographic museums on African art and contemporary art projects. Building on their experience as curators they reflect upon how contemporary art curation and anthropology have influenced each other. Forni is a curator at the Royal Ontario Museum, and her chapter addresses the complicated history of its African collections. The exhibit *Into the Heart of Africa*, in 1989, proposed an experimental reading of this collection, highly influenced by the then current (1980s) postmodern critiques of the museum. However, the exhibit faced the backlash of the African-Canadian community that understood the exhibition as an expression of liberal white privilege. A quarter of a century later, the museum has apologized for this exhibit and proposed to develop a long-term, multi-platform project *Of Africa*, led by Forni, the art historian Julie Crooks and the curator Dominique Fontaine. *On Africa*, like *Into the Heart of Africa*, proposed to challenge the traditional strategies of museum display in ethnographic museums, but in a very different manner: this time around, counting on the active collaboration of the African-Canadian community.

Bargna has worked both in participatory art projects and with ethnographic collections, and in Chapter 5 he discusses some of his curatorial projects, in particular the exhibit *Wonders of Africa: African Art in Italian Collections* (Bargna 2012), where he had the collaboration of artist Stefano Arienti. For Bargna there is a fundamental difference between anthropological and contemporary art curation: 'unlike curatorship in the world of contemporary art, which tends to suck the world inward towards the exhibition space, anthropological ethnography takes the exhibition space out into the world, making of it a space for fieldwork, tracing an unbroken web of cross-references between interior and exterior' (Bargna, this volume). In these terms, the anthropologist sees the exhibition not as a final outcome but as a research space.

Chapter 6 presents the trajectory of the curatorial collective Ethnographic Terminalia in their own terms. The collective was formed in 2009 to organize a parallel space of exhibition during the American Anthropological Association (AAA) meetings. During the last decade, Ethnographic Terminalia has experimented with different formats. In this chapter they describe their exhibitions as prototypes (Boyer 2011): open processes where the act of curation stands as a kind of performance. Particularly interesting in the case of Ethnographic Terminalia is the relationship between the curators and the public: the public for the AAA events were, ultimately, the colleagues of the curators, anthropologists like themselves, and hence the 'participatory' feedback, the 'recursive' loop, between the public and the curator has a very specific meaning.

Chapters 7 and 8 are authored by Judith Winter and Jennifer Clarke respectively, both researchers on the project *Knowing from the Inside: Anthropology, Art, Architecture and Design* (2013–2018), led by Timothy Ingold at the University of Aberdeen, UK. One of the main objectives of the project has been to foster working relations between anthropologists, artists, architects and designers, and produce outcomes that are not limited to written texts but include the production of exhibitions and installations. Winter has a long-standing career as a curator in different contexts. Her chapter describes how the figure of the contemporary curator emerged in a context of practice, rather than as a clearly delimited academic figure. The contemporary art curator, in opposition to the classical keeper of collections, carries out a critical practice and mediates a lived experience; and for Winter, in these terms, the common discursive space between contemporary art and anthropology is self-explanatory. Drawing from the thought of Roy Wagner and Maria Lind, Winter addresses anthropology and art curation as digressive and speculative practices, rather than academic knowledge with the task of containing and contextualizing life.

Clarke, on the other hand, is trained as an anthropologist. In her chapter, Clarke focuses on two exhibitions in which she has participated, within her larger research project in *Knowing from the inside*, which emphasized the potential of anthropology working *with* art: producing research not only in the form of academic output, but with artistic practice. This 'working with' operates in an ambiguous terrain that, for Clarke, has had uneven results, in some cases more successful than others. In the chapter,

Clarke points out what she learned about artistic practice as a professional practice, with its explicit and implicit assumptions, and the conflicts and contradictions she encountered in working with professional artists and curators, precisely because her project operated from an ambivalent terrain, in terms not only of her position but also of its final results. Clarke has come to think of art anthropology and curation as an 'ecology of *practices*', a 'mode of questioning' that situates the relevance and limits of one practice in relation to the others, considering how knowledge gleaned from one field might be brought to bear on others (Stengers 2005; Clarke, this volume).

The notion of an ecology of practices is interesting. Stengers does not defend the 'preservation' of practices in their uniqueness and pristine autonomy ('art' or 'anthropology'), placing them above the risk of decreasing differentiation, a general 'expanded' model of practice, capitalist management or 'the curatorial'. An ecology of practices is not about describing different practices as they are, but as they might become in relation to each other. To think in terms of this ecology in relations means thinking in terms of mutually constitutive and interdependent differences. In these terms, as Clarke says, divergent practices '*impinge upon*' one another, a relational approach not unlike Marcus's (2008) (Clarke, this volume).

Chapters 9 to 12 address different fields, forms and contexts of curation that exceed the conventional framework of the fine arts, from street art to film and sound. Starting with Rafael Schacter, an anthropologist and contemporary art curator, who has worked in particular with graffiti and street art, forms of practice that are often placed outside the sphere of contemporary art and that resist being exhibited and curated in conventional ways. From his initial, collaborative curatorial work with street artists, Schacter has moved to work as a curator in a wider field of contemporary practice. In this process, he has learned to work on exhibitions not just as a method to enable his research, but as a means of generating research.

In Chapter 10, anthropologist Alex Flynn emphasizes some interesting parallelisms and differences between ethnography and curatorial practice. On one hand, Flynn discusses the 'presentialism' of some forms of curatorial practice, in which the curator accompanies the practice of artists well beyond the exhibition space, in a shared life that he compares with ethnography. On the other hand Flynn contrasts ethnography with expography, meaning exhibition design. Working on 'expography' involves a number of material, practical and administrative concerns that may not be apparent in ethnography: from wide-ranging questions such as 'how to occupy a space?' to apparently insignificant decisions, like where to exhibit – on a table, floor or wall? The curatorial process is, in this plain sense, 'three-dimensional', materialized, grounded, in ways that ethnographic practice hardly considers. Although there are important points of encounter between the curatorial and anthropological processes with regard to conducting research, it is on the detail of how this research is carried out and aestheticized, materialized, situated that we must focus. Engaging with curatorial practice in this horizontal manner, thinking through infrastructures, can facilitate a rethinking of anthropological processes of knowledge production.

The final two chapters address the extension of practices and theories of curation to other media. In Chapter 11, 'Between automation and agency', Theunissen and Favero argue that the role of the visual researcher is increasingly being defined as a form of curation. At a time when more and more people produce, edit and distribute images, the visual researcher has become a 'curator' of these ready-made projects, rather than a 'film director' or 'producer'. This extension of the practice of curation beyond the realm of visual arts towards all practices of image production, moving or still, is recursively redefining the practice of both fine art curators and visual anthropologists in the conventional sense. But, on the other hand, they also note that overall, a great deal of the curatorial 'labour' is automated and algorithm-driven. In these terms, we should question the extent to which the digital infrastructures on which we rely do in fact also 'participate' in, and even co-create the material that we, as researchers, collect and exhibit.

Finally, in the last chapter, Noel Lobley illustrates what could be an anthropology of sound curation, exploring a series of ongoing curation projects designed to link major ethnographic collections from sub-Saharan Africa with contemporary local and international artists and communities.

All these different chapters show the multiple ways in which curatorial practice, ethnography and anthropology are intertwined today; the different forms of collaboration, conjunction, mimesis, 'uneven hermeneutics', reversibility and recursivity, bringing into question not only the limits of the 'curatorial', but also the transformations of anthropological practice in the last few decades. In these terms, the objective of this book is not only to make a contribution to the literature on the relations between art and anthropology, but also to make a wider contribution to the rethinking of what the labour of anthropology has become, and how it can help to reshape and recast other forms of practice in the contemporary world. The extensive transformations that the work and status of the curator has undergone in recent decades and its extension to other many fields, including anthropology, can help anthropologists rethink the future of their discipline, not just in terms of the new theories and 'turns' that may emerge, but in particular how these changes are intimately connected to the kind of work we do, the infrastructure of our labour.

Is the figure of the curator an opportunity for anthropologists to exit the shambles of the institutional crisis of academia? It would be limiting and also contradictory to see it in these terms. On the one hand, it seems to coincide with managerial requirements for justification, because curatorial practice has a wider public repercussion, a wider 'outreach'; but, on the other hand, curatorial practice is difficult to justify in the increasingly bureaucratized hierarchy of academic production as a 'scientific output'.

However, it is also limiting to reject or withdraw from engaging with the 'expanded field' of the curatorial, waiting for the tide to recede, because this is not a passing fad but a significant condition of the contemporary world. In a 'relational' society, where value is measured by the capacity to build networks, establish links and assemble, the only possible, realistic answer is to engage with the network, to plunge into the expanded field, to multiply the relations, rather than withdrawing (Sansi and Strathern 2016).

The different chapters in this book take very different positions in regard to this game of mirror reflections between the anthropologist and the curator: from Elhaik's strong proposal to see curation as a third method for anthropology, to the defence of autonomy of many anthropologists who fear being cannibalized by curation, to more dynamic proposals to define these relations within an ecology of practices. At a wider, practical level, all the chapters show how working with, on, as, through and even against curators has become part of the work of many anthropologists, simply because ethnography starts from the social practices and discourses it encounters. And if curation has become a keyword for contemporary global society, it has to become a topic of discussion for contemporary ethnography, and also a form of practice through which fieldwork is carried out. Schacter's and Flynn's chapters, among others, show very explicitly how curatorial and ethnographic practice can become intertwined and mutually enlightening.

But more specifically, all the chapters express a concern with the agency of anthropologists, a concern that is a late result of the protracted crisis of representation that we still suffer; from being the self-attributed producers of legitimate representations of the other to becoming just one more agent in an fluid platform of multiple images and discourses. The claim to 'curation' seems to reflect the aspiration to manage this flux, give it a purpose and a value through assemblage and montage. And yet, as Theunissen and Favero show in Chapter 11, the flux of images and discourses that surrounds us is not only overwhelming and difficult to manage but it is also increasingly, *recursively*, self-curated through algorithms. The real challenge, at this point, is not just the 'extended field' of curation but the engagement with this third agent, the self-curating, self-assembling digital infrastructures that surround us. How are we 'participating', 'collaborating', working with this third agent, is probably the most urgent question we should start to address right now.

Note

1   http://curatorsintl.org/special-projects/do-it

References

Balzer, David (2015), *Curationism: How Curating Took Over the Art World – And Everything Else*, London: Pluto Press.

Bargna, Ivan (2012), *Wonders of Africa, African Art in Italian Collections*, Milan: Silvana Editoriale.

Basu, P. and S. MacDonald (2007), *Exhibition Experiments*, London: Blackwell.

Bishop, Claire (2012), *Artificial Hells: Participatory Art and the Politics of Spectatorship*, London and New York: Verso.

Bismarck, Beatrice von Jörn Schafaff and Thomas Weski, eds. (2012), *Cultures of the Curatorial*, Berlin: Stenberg Press.

Boltanski, L. and E. Chiapello (2005), *The New Spirit of Capitalism*, London: Verso.

Boyer, Dominic (2011), 'A Gallery of Prototypes: Ethnographic Terminalia 2010, Curated by Craig Campbell, Fiona P. McDonald, Maria Brodine, Kate Hennessy, Trudi Lynn Smith, Stephanie Takaragawa', *Visual Anthropology Review*, 27 (1): 94–6.

Clifford, James (1997), *Routes: Travel and Transformation in the Late Twentieth Century*, Cambridge, MA: Harvard University Press.

Corsín Jiménez, A. (2013), 'Introduction: The Prototype: More Than Many and Less Than One', *Journal of Cultural Economy*, 7 (4): 381–98.

Corsín Jiménez, A. and A. Estalella (2010), 'The Prototype: A Sociology of Abeyance', Available online: http://limn.it/issue/00/ (accessed 29 July 2019).

Edwards, E., C. Gosden and R. Phillips, eds. (2006), *Sensible Objects: Colonialism, Museums and Material Culture*, London: Bloomsbury.

Elhaik, T. (2016), *The Incurable-Image: Curating Post-Mexican Film and Media Arts*, Edinburgh: Edinburgh University Press.

Enwezor, O., ed. (2012), *Intense Proximity: An Anthology of the Near and the Far [La Triennale 2012]*, Paris: Artlys.

Foster, H. (1995), 'The Artist as Ethnographer?' in G. Marcus and F. Myer (eds), *The Traffic in Culture: Refiguring Art and Anthropology*, Berkeley: University of California Press.

Gell, A. (1996), 'Vogel's Net: Traps as Artworks and Artworks as Traps', *Journal of Material Culture*, 1 (1): 15–38.

Gielen, P. (2010), *The Murmuring of the Artistic Multitude: Global Art, Memory and Post-Fordism*, Amsterdam: Valiz.

Karp, I. and S. Levine, eds. (1991), *Exhibiting Cultures: The Poetics and Politics of Museum Display*, Washington, DC: Smithsonian Institution Press.

Karp, I. and C. Kratz (2007), *Frictions: Public Cultures / Global Transformations*, Durham, NC: Duke University Press.

Kirshenblatt-Gimblett, Barbara (1998), *Destination Culture: Tourism, Museums, and Heritage*, Berkeley: University of California Press.

Latour, Bruno (2005), *Making Things Public: Atmospheres of Democracy*, Cambridge, MA: MIT Press.

Lind, M., ed. (2012), *Performing the Curatorial – Within and Beyond Art*, Berlin: Sternberg Press.

Lonetree, Amy (2012), *Decolonizing Museums: Representing Native America in National and Tribal Museums*, Chapel Hill: University of North Carolina Press.

Marcus, G. E., ed. (2000), *Para-sites: A Casebook against Cynical Reason*, Vol. 7, Chicago: University of Chicago Press.

Marcus, George (2010), 'Contemporary Fieldwork Aesthetics in Art and Anthropology: Experiments in Collaboration and Intervention', *Visual Anthropology*, 23: 263–77.

Martinon, Jean-Paul, ed. (2013), *The Curatorial: A Philosophy of Curating*, 41–8, London: Bloomsbury.

Obrist, H. U. (2014), *Ways of Curating*, London: Macmillan.

Obrist, H.-U. and Vanderlinden, B. (2001), *Laboratorium*, Cologne: DuMont.

O'Neill, P. (2012), *The Culture of Curating and the Curating of Culture(s)*, Cambridge, MA: MIT.

O'Neill, P. and C. Doherty, eds. (2011), *Locating the Producers: Durational Approaches to Public Art*, Amsterdam: Valiz.

Rabinow, Paul, George E. Marcus, James D. Faubion and Tobias Rees (2008), *Designs for an Anthropology of the Contemporary*, Durham, NC: Duke University Press.

Rancière, Jacques (2004), *The Politics of Aesthetics: The Distribution of the Sensible*, New York: Continuum.

Rheinberger, H.-J. (1997), *Towards a History of Epistemic Things*, Stanford: Stanford University Press.

Rogoff, Irit (2013), 'The Expanded Field', in Jean-Paul Martinon (ed.), *The Curatorial: A Philosophy of Curating*, 41–8, London: Bloomsbury.

Sansi, Roger (2015), *Art, Anthropology and the Gift*, London: Bloomsbury.

Sansi, Roger and Marilyn Strathern (2016), 'Art and Anthropology after Relations', *Hau*, 6 (2): 425–39.

Schneider, A. (2018), 'Between Uneven Hermeneutics and Alterity: The Dialogical Principle in the Art – Anthropology Encounter' *Field. A Journal of Socially-engaged Art Criticism*, 11-Fall 2018.

Schneider, A. and C. Wright, eds. (2005), *Contemporary Art and Anthropology*, Oxford: Berg Publishers.

Schneider, A. and C. Wright, eds. (2010), *Between Art and Anthropology: Contemporary Ethnographic Practice*, Oxford: Berg.

Schneider, A. and C. Wright, eds. (2013), *Anthropology and Art Practice*, London: Bloomsbury.

Sholette, Gregory (2012), 'After OWS: Social Practice Art, Abstraction, and the Limits of the Social', *E-flux Magazine*. Available from: https://www.e-flux.com/journal/31/68204/after-ows-social-practice-art-abstraction-and-the-limits-of-the-social/ (accessed 28 September 2018).

Smith, Terry (2012), *Thinking Contemporary Curating*, New York: Independent Curators International.

Ssorin-Chaikov, N. (2013), 'Ethnographic Conceptualism: An Introduction', *Laboratorium*, 5 (2): 5–18.

Stengers, I. (2005), 'Introductory Notes on an Ecology of Practices', *Cultural Studies Review*, 11 (1): 183–96.

Strohm, Kiven (2012), 'When Anthropology Meets Contemporary Art Notes for a Politics of Collaboration', *Collaborative Anthropologies*, 5: 98–124.

2

Curatorial designs: Act II

Tarek Elhaik and George Marcus

Bloc 1: Critique / then and now

Marcus: We might presume that readers of this new dialogue have read our previous one (Elhaik and Marcus 2010) and know something of your work (and mine), but it is safer, just at the beginning not to presume this. So, let us begin at the beginning and go rapidly from there to where we were headed.

Elhaik: In our previous conversation, we framed curation by specifically engaging the legacy of writing culture and the futures of the experimental moment in the human sciences. I think we began by claiming anthropology's status as a *minor* science: an empirical mode of thinking that deterritorializes the 'royal' and dominant sciences, their conventional methods and categories, their traditional expressive modes and stratified ways of articulating the relation between form and matter.[1] A task of anthropology as a minor science is to reconfigure but not abandon the hylomorphic model. We do not need to revisit all of it here, directly at least. Yet, I would like to underscore that moment's continued significance in relation to some of the trends that have since emerged, less as an expression of a melancholy science than as an affirmation of the subterranean productivity and radioactivity of those years. It is therefore not unreasonable to claim that this radioactivity is precisely what is being neglected today by *majoritarian* tendencies, within both disciplinary anthropology and in the global art world. These neglectful tendencies and trends are often expressed in the idiom of 'turns'. I mention this as a kind of Baudelairean caution to the reader who might be tempted to capture 'curation' as an entrepreneurial opportunity, an exchange value that would oil the political economy of an emerging curatorial turn, a methodological road map to settle new territories in a competitive academic market.

Curation became of interest to me then as a tool that could extend and reconfigure the project of anthropology as critique, as you and Michael Fischer famously put it (Fischer and Marcus 1986), as well as to recast, in an idiom borrowed from curatorial practice, Michel Foucault's plea for a critical ontology of ourselves (Foucault 1984).

The experimental moment in the human sciences also established a provocative link to a notion of experimentation as failure. It was a plea to the anthropological community to generously welcome the inevitable shortcomings and failures in the work of many anthropologists who were grappling with thinking beyond representation and who were creating new modes of inhabiting the world and their discipline. The experimentation you and Fischer spoke of was not uttered in the language of ancestors, the founding fathers of the discipline. The effect was a salutary loosening of generational loyalties. For some of us at least, a dwindling population it seems, it nicely located experimentation within anthropology's modernist legacy, a legacy that would be connected to a larger archaeology of the human sciences, of modernity, and of modes of subjectivation that would later be reconfigured by a new generation of contemporary anthropologists.

As today and as then, there were resistances, from Edward Said's critique of Orientalism (Said 1979) to today's call by ontologically oriented anthropologists to carry out a 'perpetual decolonization' (Viveiros de Castro 2012) of the discipline. Positively, the experiments with forms between art and anthropology, initiated in the 1920s and 1930s in many contexts – from France, to Mexico, to Brazil – were reanimated in the 1990s on, a reanimation that took pride in proposing playfulness, pleasure and curiosity as ethical substances and antidotes to historical debts and obligations. Thus earlier metaphors and tropes – such as montage, assemblage and design – were rendered available as new media for anthropological thinking, ethnographic writing, participant-observation-based enquiries and so on. A bit later you proposed a non-metonymical mode of fieldwork practice designated by the term 'multisited research practice (Marcus 1996)'. Multisited research practice was attractive, especially if understood as an invitation to overexpose the advantages and limitations of Franz Boas' critique of the comparative method (Boas 1896) under the light of curation. With curation, the anthropological problem shifts from a concern with the 'comparability of the collected material [that] must be proved and tested' (Boas 1896: 5–7) through geographical, cultural and regional areas towards a concern with assembling another kind of difference that is far from being whimsical. Moreover, if the commentary indexed the mode of thought of scholastics and medieval thinkers (e.g. Averroes, known as the commentator of Aristotle's corpus), and if the comparative did characterize the geo-cultural thought image of nineteenth-century and twentieth-century moderns, then perhaps curation might currently be indexing the attitude and mode of thought of late moderns and their contemporaries.

Marcus: Thanks for this interesting prolegomenon. I think the most pressing theoretical problems remain methodological – though perhaps we should avoid the latter term. As important to me now as when I wrote the book with Mike Fischer are certain enduring problems signalled but not taken up in my 1995 piece on multisited ethnography (Marcus 1995). There were a number of people writing on a decentred, mobile anthropological practice in the 1990s (perhaps in reaction to globalization visions and theories, and post-Cold War ruptures in theories – like Marxism – that had contextualized so much anthropological work), but mine was focused on how ethnography, or its updated version, was to be done. I settled on a 'following' metaphor, which was very effective in communicating the idea of multisited ethnography and its implications (and it appealed to ordinary ideas about processes, commodity chains, networks, etc. in the world), but buried in that piece is a more difficult and creative idea – that 'what was related to what' in a research project as it unfolded was determined more by suturing, juxtaposition and connecting sites (montage!) not literally in contact. Of course this was an aesthetic ideal in how to frame and contextualize ethnography going forward, amply expressed in *Anthropology as Cultural Critique* (*ACC*) by Fischer and me. But there were not yet (and maybe still not) any convincing discussions and theories about this (we tended to point to interwar documentary experimentation in different Euro-American places). The exception is probably the dominance of actor-network theory primarily in science studies, which Latour has an interesting history (which we need not examine) of owning and disowning. And, of course, it touches on the arenas in which Paul Rabinow reoriented his work after 2000 and influenced several generations of extremely talented students.

Also at the core of these hard problems of multisitedness were basic issues about the fate of comparison in anthropology – which, though strong ideologically (comparative purpose is in the genomics, so to speak, or lifeblood of the discipline), died as specific organized projects that once formed and justified major anthropology departments in the US during the post-Second World War expansion of universities – the science historian Rebecca Lemov is interesting to read here (Lemov 2015). You end your comments with the issue of practising comparison in anthropology, which I think is basic. In so doing, you also raise the figure of Boas, and his shackling of notions of the comparative suitable for work today. Could you expand a bit more on this? I think the Boasian tradition is very redeemable, given Boas' personal practice. An article by Matti Bunzl (Bunzl 2004) is important here, where he makes Boas Foucauldian in an original way. For me, the Foucault is less important than thinking about Boas as a fieldworker who wants to create material from fieldwork with curation (in the museum context) in mind. In this way, moments/scenes of shared construction in fieldwork that Bunzl evokes in his Boas essay foreshadow the idea of para-sites in multisited research, which are conjuring spaces for collaborative concept work in a project that will crucially play out in its productions – be they textual, in the tradition of ethnographic writing, or, increasingly, performative and multimodal.

If you trace my lineage from *Anthropology as Cultural Critique* (*ACC*), through the multisited paper of the mid-1990s, to my recent concerns with intermediate forms that anthropologists produce before 'docking' in disciplinary authority, and my own moves towards and within the anthropology of art (where you and I intersect), then we find a rich terrain of engagement – which you have developed in the name of curatorial design and practice. You have a thoroughly thought-out, richer vision of and theoretical engagement with how anthropologists can connect things (and become comparative in a more systematic or collective way) that appeals to me very much, as well as a sense that studio practices can develop these ideas.

Regarding the question of the human, there are a number of strains in anthropological thinking (and the philosophy that has influenced it) about this that are worth reviving, but given its past recent history, I see that addressing this question anew needs to proceed in alliance with knowledge of what is going on in science (bioscience and now environmental science) and technology (artificial intelligence). Anthropological thinking can exceed or be different from science and technology studies (STS) in this regard, but the most challenging thinking has come out of engagement with this arena from the 1990s onwards. This is not a faith in or deferral to science and technology, just that it helps to know and acknowledge what is going on there, before reviving or innovating long-standing humanistic options about discussing the human, or post-human, or the transcending of the nature–culture divide. I thought Rabinow's *Anthropos Today* (2003) provided a stimulating direction, in which the dominant (US) tradition of cultural anthropology might move, at the level of the terms and design of the practice of enquiry itself. But it and later publications have failed to have, for whatever reasons, a direct broad influence, though this thinking had foundational effects on the creativity and originality by which several generations of remarkable students who he has mentored produced research in a number of arenas, including the anthropology of art, which is the broad context for our conversation.

Another very general point occurs to me – today I look over the table of contents of long-standing, leading anthropological journals (mainly US but really international, including *HAU*) – and I marvel at the range of topics and interests that anthropologists, particularly younger ones (of course) are pursuing. There is no theoretical or 'turn' framework that the discipline currently provides that encompasses the range of thinking and conceptual artifice that is in this diverse literature. It is eclectic in a good way – one can see the disciplinary outlines that hold projects together, but really they are each on their own in different kinds of worlds – marked by themes that represent anthropology in the long view – but do not have easy or convincing specific theoretical programmes that you could point to.

My view is that the strains for theory in framing distinctive conceptual schemes are not the answer for vitalizing disciplinary perspective – but instead, such vitality is in the kind of theory that produces 'method' experiments – like, I think, curatorial design and the plea for intermediate forms before docking in the harbor of academic debate, prestige, and reward. There is indeed an emblematic and conventional theory of method in anthropology, and method itself is a rather boring word of constraint, but what creates perspectives within the guild is the rethinking of how analytic schemes take shape in projects of fieldwork and then circulate in rather unstable and ephemeral ways. I am very interested in the contemporary ways and means of this circulation, which are not much reflected upon explicitly by anthropologists. Curatorial design does not essentialize the theoretical but re-embeds it in a distinctive set of connective practices. In a recent collection edited by Dominic Boyer, Jim Faubion and me – *Theory Is More Than It Used to Be* (2015) – we try to articulate this condition in which 'theory' serves the multitude of diverse curiosities that have come to define the range of research projects being pursued in anthropology and that all share the norms of post-1980s expectations of field research as well as of ethnographic writing (practices/norms of reflexivity and a declared politics perhaps being the most discussed, and aesthetic effects and controlled speculation being the least discussed). The distinctive elaboration of the idea of curatorial practice that you continue to articulate exhibits a methodological originality that also resets what critical and speculative analytics should emerge from a contemporary anthropology of art. Maybe we can explore this further in our conversation.

Well, this may, and should, all seem rather obvious – on reflection – to any practitioner of contemporary anthropology – but I marvelled at the variety in the table of contents of a number of anthropology journals. They register an expansive field of operation for anthropology for which an authoritative disciplinary assessment (through its theoretical fashions and turns of the moment) can only be very partial. Here is where curation comes in, in that it provides a far more diverse and wide-ranging framework for the 'projects' in fieldwork that ethnographers and their subjects undertake. It provides just enough of the contrary kind of authority that anthropologists need in order to explore concepts or inventions that will not be corralled by disciplinary interests or ambitions at any given moment or interval. The concept of curation, while problematic (in a good way), provides these degrees of freedom and potentially organizes more diverse responses or receptions to research within a project's duration, for which the anthropologist has to account. In the name of 'method', anthropologists might infiltrate studio practices authoritatively into their fieldwork so as to creatively and flexibly give voice and presence to these intermediate receptions.

Elhaik: I agree with you that STS, AI and the anthropology of art (our concern here) continue to be stimulating fields of inquiry with a potential to provide resources for thought, matter to be curatorially designed, and ultimately restore belief in anthropology both as a disciplinary and post-disciplinary horizon. Post-disciplinary in two senses. First, as an invitation to think about the dangers and opportunities associated with new global circuits (finance, the art market) and new media assemblages where 'control' overlaps with and erodes disciplinary power (Deleuze 1992). Second, in the sense of that which is productive of complex 'liaisons' and modes of collaboration (Biagioli 2009). In both cases, the 'post' refers to a line of flight through, alongside, and within a given discipline, steering clear from the facile interdisciplinary 'fieldwork' and intercultural research praised in contemporary art curatorial practice and in the academic humanities.

Bloc 2: So, what is curation?

Marcus: The term curation, 'to curate something', is profligate by now. I see books on it in London shops (mainly!), and often leaf through them. In my ethnographies seminar, it arose several times among students as a term of contemporary practice, useful and meaningful to them, injected within traditional expectations of 'performing' ethnographic research and writing. But you are an innovator in its usage in the art–anthropology domain specifically, out of the milieu of your graduate experience in the group of students influenced by Paul Rabinow, and particularly from your experiences in Mexican art and social theory circles (the influence of Roger Bartra among others).

So, can you give a baseline account of the evolution of your interest in the concept, what its boundaries of practice are in anthropology that moves in art during the, what? Early 2000s? And obviously connecting your thinking about curation specifically to *The Incurable-Image* (Elhaik 2016) and the implication of this wordplay. And though you make this very clear in the earlier chapters of your book, I think we need to make especially clear – especially for anthropological readers – what is to be admired, and criticized, in the whole regime of relational aesthetics, participatory art movements and site-specific installations. For example, when I first read *Artificial Hells* (Bishop 2012) I was quite excited by it and I still feel it is a very useful text for anthropologists, yet when I based a talk on it in Australia, anthropology/art world types were very critical of it, but I didn't quite get why. I find the writings of Grant Kester (Kester 2004, 2011), sometimes in contest with Bishop, also quite simpatico – I manage not to pay much attention to the art-writing polemic aspects of it. So, what's not to like here for anthropologists?

I just finished a book with Luke Cantarella (a scenographer) and Christine Hegel (an anthropologist, also artist) about some projects we have done over the past five years – called *Ethnography-by-Design: Scenographic Collaborations in Fieldwork* (Hegel, Cantarella and Marcus 2019). Because I resisted writing a strong chapter on ethnography, the scenic design features took over the book and reshaped what were scenes of ethnographic work. Actually, I found this energizing and gave into it easily. Yielding the ethnographic stance (or authority) to the play of something like site-specific installation was an interesting and pleasurable process. But it's not over. Somehow now the ethnographic significance begins – but among receptions – anticipated and unanticipated. While the book tracks our 'atelier' history over five years, the book itself as a product of what we did is very artefactual. Anyhow, this was an interesting experience of my becoming a little passive as studio and art production took over spaces/places that had been ethnographically explored through and through. The value added was in the emergence of 'internal publics' in each of the projects, which added ethnographic opportunity, depth and dimension (variously exploited).

With my own experience in mind of what I consider differential aesthetic curations by interventions of scenographic arts in relation to specific ethnographic projects under way, completed or emergent, I would ask you to say something, first, about the rise of curation as something that anthropologists might practice, while resisting its perhaps tempting simplification as an enhancement or tweaking of ethnography that has to manage a multisited space/scope of operation (for example, it won't save you from the 'incurable image' that ethnography dwells in). And, second, about why the installation-oriented/artificial hells-type project is, or is not, ultimately what the anthropologist is after? (For example, do they – participatory art projects – fail concept-work in the discursive ways that anthropologists as ethnographers require?) Or, does such art seem to fulfil (as I tend to think) methodologically the required thickness of culture ripe for interpretation? But, finally, are we after something else far from the Geertz era, even though in some of Geertz's most famous passages (as in the Balinese Cockfight essay, for example), he evokes images and ideas congenial to the interpretive and critical art-writing around participatory works and site-specific installations? Some basic laying out of positions/thinking along these two axes might be our way to move forwards on this occasion.

Elhaik: From the standpoint of critical philosophy the range of application of the term curation is perplexing. The new range of application has certainly exceeded the boundaries of its initial museographic and gallery context. This excess is, of course, not a bad thing. It is welcome. Yet, I do not think that the form it is currently taking will provide us with tools to grapple with whatever comes after modern art and modernist aesthetics. For instance, land art's recruiting of the desert and the landscape as a canvas (e.g. Robert Smithson) is still on the side of the Kantian sublime. Land art also still relies on the referent of painting, its interesting cultivation of three-dimensionality and architectural forms notwithstanding. On the side of anthropology, the curatorial and the artistic are unduly attached to venues, forms and modes borrowed from the art world. 'Biennale' is such a vexing floating signifier, for example. The ongoing universalization and democratization of these venues, modes and forms find particular expression in the exaltation of so-called community, public and social art practices, the main objective of which is often to mirror real-time temporal dynamics in the 'real world' and give visibility to so-called peripheral geographical logics. From my participant-observation-based conversations with curators, conceptual artists and anthropologists in Mexico City, I have tried to embark on an enquiry that invites us to pause and ask: but how is curation, with its attendant excess, an anthropological problem that complicates the vigilance of critical philosophy?

My training in the Rabinow circle and Bartra's notion of a 'post-Mexican condition' (Bartra 2002) were both helpful in tackling this difficulty. They also led me to ask how can and should contemporary curation reconfigure the life, language and labour of the New Man imagined by Mexicanist aesthetics and the historical avant-garde. While my book (Elhaik 2016) concluded with the understanding that the curation of *anthropos*, of the human, could be likened to an *ars curatoria* in search of an anthropology to come, I recently began to question whether a contemporary mode of curation is necessarily indexing a figure, *tout court*. Why not something abstract and non-figurative? Contemporary curation, I thought, would contribute to de-anthropologizing anthropology? By this I want to suggest that anthropologists can and should find ways to curate futures less and less illuminated by the historical avant-garde's new humanism and its attendant utopian imagination. Our task is to create a mode of curation that problematizes what comes after the New Man of the historical avant-gardes of the 1920s and of the political modernisms of the 1960s.

In my view, curation could also be useful to anthropologists if we find ways to elevate it (as I think you tried to do with montage) to the status of a human faculty and power activated by forces encountered in the undisciplined zone between art history and anthropology. Because it was first designed and later modified in the fragmentary conditions of modernity and late modernity, curation belongs at once to critical philosophy, anthropology and art history. We should therefore not be discouraged by Latour and the ontologists, who see critique (and faculty theory) as something that never happened or too negative as a result of its subject/object design. We should also not lose sight of the fact that critique, with its diagnostic dimensions and mode of vigilance, is 'withering'. We need to think Kant, and the anthropology of art, after Duchamp (Deleuze 1993; De Duve 1996; Rabinow 2014). The most obvious move would be to place curation on a par with the faculty of the imagination, something internal to the non-legislative faculty of the sensible. It is, alas, what sensory ethnographers and relational aestheticians are doing when they overflow art (my solidarity here with museum-based artists!) by extending aesthetics to 'the whole of human relations and their social context, rather than an independent and private space' (Bourriaud 1998: 113). Instead, it would be interesting to look at curation as an intermediary faculty, neither exalted as an alternative to nor lamented as a subordinate to reason (as anthropologists do when they speak of 'imaginative horizons' (Crapazano 2004)). We could think of the location of this curatorial power or faculty as an intermediary, or rather as a complex junction between imaginative horizons and the anthropology of reason (Rabinow 1996), legislating anthropology and its problems somewhere between the imagination, the understanding and speculative reason. I have recently referred to that power as one of 'cogitation' (Elhaik 2018).

I also think that relational aesthetics and social art practice are not useful when they amplify an already existing anti-aesthetic orientation in anthropology, one to be found in Alfred Gell (Gell 1998), for instance. I still see value in the modern spectatorial relation, its afterlife in contemporary life, the contemplative modes of engagement and art-writing they inspire and so on. This is not necessarily auratic, if by aura we mean an affinity between the mode of enchantment of sacred objects and that of unique artworks under the current aesthetic regime of reproducibility. To care for and reconfigure the separation advocated by modern aesthetics is to reorient its traditional focus on the beautiful and the sublime towards new moods, states of animation, ethical struggles and '*états d'âme*' with cogitative powers exceeding the various agendas of autonomizing and emancipating alienated spectators (Berardi 2009; Ranciere 2009).

I think curation operates as a relational barometer of an expanded and expanding field of artistic practices. To curate is to be attentive to and evaluate this expansion. For this reason, curation's ethical substance is the image and image-work. These are the images that artists and art experts (including anthropologists of art) share with architects, urbanists, designers and other image-workers. 'Image-worker' is the umbrella term under which curation makes sense to me, not the other way around. Montage shares with curation this form of attention towards image-work. It understands images as a relation to thought and thinking, images as the medium through which we think the unthinkable, through which we can undo not only our 'dogmatic' but also our 'critical' image of thought (Deleuze 1968). Eisenstein's deployment of montage, intellectual montage in particular, was meant primarily as a 'shock to thought'. The faculty of curation has the capacity to shock us too. This happens with full force when we move alongside the image-work of urbanists, visual artists, architects, photographers and so forth.

A final point. I think most anthropologists tend to prefer and value the concrete over the abstract, at times dogmatizing concreteness, at others accentuating anthropology's figurative bias, and certainly echoing the demonization of abstraction in most[2] contemporary art. I certainly hope for another kind of relation between art and anthropology. We will need 'to read these relations backwards' (Strathern 2014) and design fieldwork mises-en-scène in contemporary abstraction, lest we repeat Lévi-Strauss's misguided suggestion in the first chapter of the Savage Mind that we are *only* scientists of the concrete (Lévi-Strauss 1966). In my view, abstract and artificial hells, in the museum, the gallery, in our classrooms, studio-based or designed for the contemplative spectator and learner might perhaps be as stimulating as the emancipatory objectives sought out by relational aesthetics and community art. As the dream of the emancipated New Man of the avant-gardes further withers and fragments, and as new modes of abstraction and concreteness put increasing pressure on our previous montages and play of faculties, we are left with the task of curating what can be called 'concrete abstractions'. Concrete abstractions are the kind of compositions that emerge when the participant-observer moves alongside the new objects, environments and moods created by intellectually driven artists and other image-workers.

Marcus: Well, we have our work cut out for us, so to speak – curation and montage are so deeply associated with method in the way they have been borrowed by anthropologists, and are limited by the bias against, and suspicion of, abstraction as a mode or object of thought, as you point out. It is good that we show something else – as composition – a kind of analytic keyword for what we are about. So, we have 'montage' and 'curation' beyond comparison, and curation and montage as twins of sorts. Plus a contrary embracing (for the anthropologist, but not the art historian or critic!) of abstraction as a mode of analytic thinking closely entwined with the empirical and concrete of observation and thinking within fieldwork. If we are not interested in questions of representation or method, then in what senses are we interested in these terms – curation and montage? As the making of situated abstractions? And if we reintroduce abstraction so exiled from anthropological discourse, we need a language or vocabulary for its use.

Since I am less knowledgeable than you about contemporary art world discourse, how is what we are doing different from that, not simply a kind of art criticism? Aside from trips to studios and exhibitions, and interviews, what makes our treatment of made abstractions fieldwork? It may not be important to retain the idea of ethnography, but it definitely seems important to retain the notion of fieldwork. It means what? Some sort of engagement with modes of composition?

Anyhow, I am just shooting in the dark here mostly. There is something declarative of the doctrinal that we need about 'composition' rather than 'method' to re-cognize curation and montage for readers.

Elhaik: Thinking takes a long time to settle. It requires patience, waiting for certain ideas, concepts, experiences, demons and experimentations to become stabilized. I think ethnography played a certain role in my first book (Elhaik 2016) , as one medium within a larger intermedia mode of inquiry and composition. By this, I mean I was observing the way my informants, intercessors, interlocutors and epistemic partners were curating the breakdown of Mexicanist aesthetics, cultural forms and historical figurations of society and national culture – the racialized ethnos, subject, political community – imagined by the avant-garde. It was not ethnographic in compositional terms. I was not writing Mexican culture. Yet, it was nonetheless informed by the experimental moment in the human sciences and the emphasis on writing opened up during those years. I think *The Incurable-Image* is in the tradition of the anthropological essay, quite illustrious in Mexico (Bartra, Paz) and Germany (Adorno), for instance, but alas valued cautiously in American anthropology and social sciences. I also introduced a fieldwork mode I termed 'curatorial work'. This mode is the medium that enabled me to make sense of my dialogues with and observations of my interlocutors' image-work and concept-work. As a result, 'incurable-image' was the concept created in order to account for the intermediary space between image and concept that Lévi-Strauss had too hastily filled with 'concrete entities' called signs. Hyphenated, the incurable-image emerged as an image-concept, one that immediately begged for a special kind of care, of curation, beyond semiotics and linguistics, beyond culture and society. The curation of these image-concepts would take place, I thought, and continue to think, in a wild intermediary territory untamed by signs, symbols and imagined communities. As I just said, this gradually led me to think beyond the 'science of the concrete'.

Yet, the problem-space I am working on would not have been possible without the more or less classical version of participant-observation I carried out when I was in Mexico City: two years of full immersion, travels only within the Latin American context, fluency in the linguistic and symbolic registers of my interlocutors, learning Mexican Spanish and so on. Must this be a ritornello, something that all anthropologists ought to rehearse and repeat? I do think so, as I am fond and biased towards *dépaysement* and would recommend it. Not as a principle set in stone, but as an option for those who take difference in the direction of non-identity. So, the methodological refrain of *dépaysement* opened up new routes and perspectives I have enjoyed and learned much from, indeed getting lost each time their horizons began to recede. The concern with and interest in 'aesthetic' questions also lives on from that first fieldwork. Equally strong, is the commitment to the creation of non-ethnographic fieldwork modes out of participant-observation. *But*, I have neither the pretension nor the desire to speak on behalf of the entire discipline and what comes before, alongside and beyond ethnographic methods. The questions I grapple with emerged and are specific to the border zone where art history and anthropology enter into a 'disciplinary cannibalism' (Dufrêne and Taylor 2010). There, the anthropologist can create a free play between field-work, image-work and concept-work. Participant-observation could then be read, aesthetically and conceptually, as a playful movement between the sensible, the imagination and cogitation.

Marcus: And, what about the passage from the first fieldwork to your new research mise-en-scène?

Elhaik: Well, there are differences and important lessons learned. Certainly, concerns with what comes after ethnos, after Mexican society, concerns with long-term residence and commitments to a society or culture, have left the research mise-en-scène. Of course, fieldwork still consists in artist studio visits; guided tours with art historians and curators; research collaboration and membership in curatorial teams, which often result in book anthologies and programming (e.g. the Getty Initiative, Pacific Standard Time, MOCA)[3]; observing and dialoguing with other kinds of 'image-workers', such as architects, as is the case with my ongoing collaboration with the Biennale d'architecture d'Orléans around the public and monumental sculptures of the late Mexico City-based artist Mathias Goeritz; my own activities in Anthropology of the Image Lab (AIL), a space for monthly conversations between art scholars, curators, artists and anthropologists at University of California, Davis.

Curatorial Designs

In the book I am currently working on I am particularly interested in questions of aesthetic anthropology, the aftermath of earlier discussions on the subject. I'm thinking of Jacques Maquet's work (Maquet 1986), which still yields interesting insights if read in a post-ethnos key. Compositionally, this new book revisits an older tradition, that of the essay, in particular essays inspired by encounters with artists and cities. Michel Leiris on Francis Bacon (Leiris 2008), of course, but also Georg Simmel's beautiful book on Rembrandt (Simmel 2005) or his essays on Rome, Octavio Paz's brilliant book on Marcel Duchamp (Paz 1978).

Bloc 3: Having been modernist

Marcus: Your self-possession as an unabashed modernist gives you several advantages in thinking freely that are inhibitions for otherwise estimable thinkers for whom modernism is passé, out of fashion, and so on, with no current vogue (as far as I can perceive) to replace it.

So, experiments with form, for you, mean compositions expressed through the essay. We might have explored this a little more, and what you mean by image-work, what core work it does for you in your own explorations? I see this in your interest for the figure of Averroes – since it seems to be your preoccupation and that of some of the artists/intellectuals in whom you are interested. What is the relation of image-work to concept-work – must the relation be made?

Say more about Simmel, and Simmel and his essays on Rome as an inspiration – he, more than other references of inspiration, has come up repeatedly.

As I say, scenography has been my central referent experience recently and its relationship to ethnography (as conventionally conceived), and the 'retreat' of ethnography into it! Scenography at the level of craft is definitely image-work, though subordinated to the demands of design craft in the context of theatre.

Elhaik: I think the description of a recent visit to Mexico City might show why the modernism I speak of is neither mere re-modernism nor an expression of a sense of unease with the ever-elusive yet necessary term 'contemporary'. I've been going to Mexico City to research archival material and visit various architectural sites and monumental public sculptures that defined Mexican modernity and mid-century modernism, structures built at the threshold between abstract expressionism and minimalism between 1953 and 1968. The sites I was looking at were all designed and curated by the German émigré (artist and art historian) Mathias Goeritz (1915–90). He had also completed some of these projects in collaboration with modernist architects such as Luis Barragan, Pablo Ramirez Vasquez and Ricardo Legoreta. Some of these sites can be experienced through long walks in the area called Espacio Escultórico on the beautiful UNAM campus, near the new Museo de Arte Contemporáneo (MUAC). Other sites can only be experienced through a long drive along the controversial 1968 Ruta de la Amistad, the sequence of nineteen monumental sculptures by international artists, including one by Goeritz himself, arranged and 'curated' alongside the Periferico Sur highway. Similarly, a fieldworker in movement is required to study the colourful prismatic Torres Satellite in the north of the city. Goeritz's instructions to experience these 'highway sculptures' were very clear: they were designed for a moving spectator, indeed a participant-observer, riding in an automobile. The aesthetics, the sensation one gets during these drives, are hinged on kinetic pleasure. These theatricalized highway sculptures are abstract, conceptually sophisticated, unabashedly modernist, yet with one foot already in a minimalism in the making. They synthetize many architectural forms, from different periods and places (e.g. medieval towers in Tuscany, pre-Columbian pyramid, Manhattan's skyline, the Alhambra and so forth). They are the effect of a transcultural montage in which original places and forms nonetheless get lost. They shock our way of thinking. Referentiality is suspended.

We can also play with these sculptures, like a child would. In fact, on another visit the next day, this time to the Museo Experimental del Eco (1953), Goeritz's masterpiece, I was pleased to notice how children were gluttonously playing with these minimalist and abstract shapes. It was quite beautiful to observe them jump and play around colourful monoliths, triangular prisms and other sun-illuminated geometrical figures projecting two-dimensional shadows on minimalistically designed walls, with imperfect angles and that rarely run parallel to each other. Goeritz's instructions and curatorial mode, I began to wonder, complicate recent arguments regarding the 'end of flânerie' or concomitant revitalization of the figure of the walker (Bull 2016). What I really enjoyed, indeed took pleasure in while looking at these late modernist public artworks, from the perspective of an automobile, is the unsustainability of the opposition between tactility and opticality, and its attendant sacralization of the Heideggerian language of dwelling, walking and abode one sees in the current demonization of automobile and machinic capitalist culture. I realized that these fieldwork encounters enabled me to reconfigure the conceptual persona of the flâneur, perhaps a new kind of flâneurie is brewing through these drives. In this sense, fieldwork on Mexico City's mid-century modernism both draws from and exceeds the commodity criticism and aesthetic analyses derived from capitals and capitalisms of the nineteenth century. Anthropologists need and can find help here, the kind of help that Georg Simmel had provided, paradoxically, in his *faux-pas footnote* against the 'ugly modern' side of Rome (Simmel 2006).

In his little-read essay on the Eternal City, Simmel was repeating, in his own words, the fascination of generations of German intellectuals during their voyage to Italy. His was a romantic take on Rome. The sociologist of modernity and psychologically inclined theorist of the blasé not only wanted to see what Freud had already seen (a topological model of the mind), but he was also interested in the 'miracle' of the cityscape of Rome as an effect of a montage that puzzled him, what he called an 'unintentional beauty'. Rome is notoriously *uncurated* for Simmel, as it is for those of us who are familiar with the city, today. Beauty is accidental. Rome is incurable, according to Simmel's 'aesthetic analysis' (the subtitle of his essay). Its miraculous beauty arises when fragments form together in ways that 'they do not deserve by themselves'. Rome is submitted to a Kantian aesthetics in such a way that the play between sensation and analysis, between image and concept, reaches a climax, a romantic one to be sure, that elevates us. It elevates us just as Goeritz's public sculptures 'lift us spiritually'. A *sensus communis* emerges. We are psychologically reconciled with our inner sense, not unlike the kind of inner sense Simmel saw at work in his book on Rembrandt.

Fieldwork here opens us up again to cities understood as works of art (the afterlife of a modernist trope), in the same way Kant and, later, nineteenth-century aesthetic thinkers, saw an analogy between nature and art. Simmel is a German romantic, of course, and he searches for a totality in the assemblage-work carried out by cities. This is an interesting modernist paradox, one that we can do much with. While Simmel, the great critic of modernity, strangely flirts with a counter-modernist aesthetics, Goeritz never envisages it, his critique of Le Corbusier and functionalism notwithstanding. The task for me is to figure out how fieldwork can and should look through a remediation of the figure of the flâneur, all the while remaining committed to the legacy of modernism as it becomes historical, yet not having exhausted its aesthetic appeal. I think it is important to recognize modernism's enduring capacity to generate moods and sensations of complex resemblances and affinities. These complex resemblances and affinities, the outcome of image-work, are in dire need of montage, curation and concept-work.

Bloc 4: Laboratory curation

Marcus: I would like in part to focus on what you are trying to do with your lab studio space at Davis. These kinds of experimental space, as labs or centres, are more frequently being created within and alongside anthropology departments now. For example in October 2018 I learned of the formation of a Center for Experimental Ethnography at the University of Pennsylvania, Philadelphia; in my own department, with the arrival of new faculty, we have just renewed the Center for Ethnography, established in 2005; there are many other examples, and the number is growing, of such initiatives. In my own history, it goes back to the Rice Circle (a title we took with some self-effacing levity, but in the years and decades since, we now take both more seriously and nostalgically) and the Late Editions project of the 1990s (a Rice-based collective of varying composition, which produced a University of Chicago Press series of eight annual volumes, the experimental side of which was to document the *fin de siècle*, in an era when the critique of documentary representation was prime) and then to the design-oriented discussions with Paul Rabinow of the 2000s, ending with ideas for labs and studios (summarized in the short dialogic volume, *Designs for an Anthropology of the Contemporary* (2008). Now the term 'multimodal' is everywhere as the practice space for experiments in anthropology. Why this trend? Is it intersecting congenially with things we are talking about? Or just as this sort of anthropology comes into being – is it in fact the same thing we are talking about? – are we growing out of it?

Multimodal anthropology is the alternative to the return to the rich archives of historic ethnographic work as area studies of the ontology turn. Or more sympathetically it encompasses the latter's concern with some sort of evolution out of the idea of modernity (ontology over epistemology) that we refuse to give up, or at least want different thinking about than anthropology has been able to provide.

Anyhow let's maybe get into these issues for our last conversation about the centres adjacent to, or within, long-established departments of anthropological disciplinary authority, and that we are now especially interested in working within.

Elhaik: Yes, AIL, or the Anthropology of the Image Lab, is both a venue and an online curatorial platform I have set up at UC Davis. Its main objective is to engage the challenges posed by contemporary image-workers to both anthropological thinking and art curatorial practice. However, AIL is not a media lab in the way often thought of. Although we welcome media artists and professional curators, our objective is neither to produce experimental media-works nor to exhibit fieldwork data. Of course, when necessary and when the opportunity arises, we also curate (in the traditional sense of the term) programmes for art or film institutions. In a sense, AIL is an unusual kind of gallery populated not only by image-workers but also by the 'incurable' conceptual personae they uneasily stand for: the architect, the artist, the curator, the archivist, the librarian, the anthropologist and so forth. Through conversations and Podcast Series[4] we conjure up, host and welcome – well, we curate – the intrusion of the figures and personae we encounter during fieldwork.

In AIL we also challenge 'cultural difference' as having become a dogmatic image of thought. We are interested in generating another kind of difference, one that moves alongside a contemporary anthropology – contemporary art axis, specifically. This motion is not friction-free, drawing its intellectual energy from a vibrant and unstable triptych: (1) a continuation of the fascinating experimental moment in the human sciences, its critical vocation and reconfiguration of anthropology's modernist legacy; (2) a re-evaluation and an overcoming of the so-called 'ethnographic turn in contemporary art'; and (3) a commitment to concept-work alongside critical artists and art experts.

The acronym, AIL, was carefully chosen. It is a wordplay on the clinical and ethical registers of the term 'curation': care, cura, curare, curate and the incurable. I believe that the curation of images and image-workers is a matter of health. It animates us, it is good for the soul. Of course, not in the sense that it can cure, signal a utopian future or return us to pre-existing times when we have never been modern. However, I do believe that the curation of conceptual personae and images of thought is a complex form of reconceptualization that could become one of the twenty-first century's foremost and vital forms of care. Our current and future health depends on it.

Marcus: I think this extended comment by you connecting curation to image and image-workers (as 'epistemic partners, so to speak) is a good place to end. Image and image-working, so basic to the discourses of art history and art-writing, are very challenging to anthropologists who have been involved for a very long time in exploring the visual by applying the norms and virtues of ethnographic method to filmmaking and photography. I see that the curation of images is something else. There is a deep phenomenology to it to which anthropologists have been quite accustomed in practising the ideals and arts of fieldwork, but interpreting images means delving into abstractions that seem far from the empirical and the social, and this might make them allergic. You however through your discussion of Simmel, for example, your critique of a Lévi-Straussian expression of a science of the concrete in one of his most influential works, and your account of the ethnographic movement in the art world,

Curatorial Designs 31

you demonstrate the worth and power of attending to images as abstraction. However, you do this, not by delivering or shrouding them in equally abstract analytic discourses of connoisseurship, but in a quite conventional way (for anthropologists) by drawing on the experiences of fieldwork and its associations as a curatorial task – not directly for the museum and its controls and habits as a public space, but for those occasions that emerge as opportunities for staging receptions and responses in the course of fieldwork. This is not by any means offering a new method (insistently so), but adapting our culture of enquiry to a kind of 'structure of feeling' that we thought we had left behind in modernism. Especially, in a comfort with the contemplation of and dwelling within abstraction. In a sense, it is highly original repair work, in order to rescue and preserve the project of critique towards which anthropology had so productively turned in the preceding era. To show this as fieldwork, as a complex, participatory practice both within and on the edges of contemporary art-making, both sympathetic to and suspicious of the latter's own socially situated, self-critical reflexive capacities, is a worthy project for creating a non-obvious, or instantly attractive understanding of curation, as something other than a practice so easily conceived as akin to ethnography in a world of fragmented, multisited subjects. You have shown me something of how 'anthropology as cultural critique' might be vitally practised today—otherwise.

Notes

1 'Minor' or 'nomadic' science belongs to the conceptual repertoire of Gilles Deleuze and Felix Guattari.
2 There are exceptions to this rule, of course, and contemporary abstraction is on the rise again.
3 https://www.lafilmforum.org/ism-ism-ism/
4 http://www.antimagelab.com/podcast-archives/

References

Bartra, Roger (2002), *Blood, Ink, and Culture: Miseries and Splendors of the Post-Mexican Condition*, Durham: Duke University Press.
Berardi, Franco (2009), *The Soul at Work: From Alienation to Autonomy*, Semiotexte: Foreign Agents Series.
Biagioli, Mario (2009), 'Post-disciplinary Liaisons: Science Studies and the Humanities', *Critical Inquiry*, 35 (4): 816–33.
Bishop, Claire (2012), *Artificial Hells: Participatory Art and the Politics of Spectatorship*, London: Verso.
Boas, Franz (1896), "The Limitations of the Comparative Method of Anthropology", *Science* New Series, 4 (103): 901–8.
Bourriaud, Nicolas (1998), *Relational Aesthetics*, 113, Dijon: Les Presses du Reel.
Boyer Dominic, James D. Faubion and George E. Marcus (2015), *Theory Can Be More Than It Used to Be Learning Anthropology's Method in a Time of Transition*, Ithaca, NY: Cornell University Press.

32 *The Anthropologist as Curator*

Bull, Michael (2016), 'The End of Flânerie: iPods, Aesthetics, and Urban Experience', in Tim Ingold and Jo Lee Vergunst (eds), *Ways of Walking: Ethnography and Practice on Foot*, New York: Routledge.

Bunzl, Matti (2004), 'Boas, Foucault and the "Native Anthropologist": Notes Toward a Neo-Boasian Anthropology', *American Anthropologist*, 106 (3): 435–42, 2.

Crapanzano, Vincent (2004), *Imaginative Horizons: An Essay in Literary-Philosophical Anthropology*, Chicago: University of Chicago Press.

De Duve, Thierry (1996), *Kant after Duchamp*, Cambridge: MIT Press.

Deleuze, Gilles (1968), *Différence et Repetition*, Paris: PUF.

Deleuze (1992), 'Post-Scripts on Societies of Control' *October*, 59: 3–7.

Deleuze (1993), *Essays Critical and Clinical*, Minneapolis: University of Minnesota Press.

Dufrêne, Thierry and Anne-Christine Taylor (2010), *Cannibalismes disciplinaires. Quand l'histoire de l'art et l'anthropologie se rencontrent*, INHA et musée du quai Branly.

Elhaik, Tarek (2016), *The Incurable-Image: Curating Post-Mexican Film and Media Art*, Edinburgh: Edinburgh University Press.

Elhaik, Tarek (2018), 'Cogitation', *Cultural Anthropology*, Fieldsights Series (Open Source).

Elhaik, Tarek and George Marcus (2010), 'Curatorial Designs in the Poetics and Politics of Ethnography Today', in A. Forero and L. Simeone (eds), Armando Publishers.

Fischer, Michael and George E. Marcus (1986), *Anthropology as Cultural Critique: An Experimental Moment in the Human Sciences*, Chicago, IL: University of Chicago Press.

Foucault, Michel (1984), 'What Is Enlightenment?' ('Qu'est-ce que les Lumières ?'), in Paul Rabinow (ed.), *The Foucault Reader*, 32–50, New York: Pantheon Books.

Gell, Alfred (1998), *Art and Agency: An Anthropological Theory*, Oxford: Oxford University Press.

Hegel, Christine, Luke Cantarella and George E. Marcus (2019), *Ethnography by Design Scenographic Experiments in Fieldwork*, London: Bloomsbury.

Kester, Grant H. (2004), *Conversation Pieces: Community + Communication in Modern Art*, Berkeley: UC Press.

Kester, Grant H. (2011), *The One and the Many: Contemporary Collaborative Art in a Global Context*, Durham: Duke University Press.

Leiris, Michel (2008), *Francis Bacon*, Barcelona: Ediciones Poligraf.

Lemov, Rebecca (2015), *Databases of Dreams: The Lost Quest to Catalogue Humanity*, New Haven: Yale University Press.

Lévi-Strauss, Claude (1966), *The Savage Mind*, Chicago: University of Chicago Press.

Maquet, Jacques (1986), *The Aesthetic Experience: An Anthropologist Looks at the Visual Arts*, New Haven: Yale University Press.

Marcus, G. (1995), 'Ethnography in/of the World System: The Emergence of Multi-Sited Ethnography', *Annual Review of Anthropology*, 24: 95–117.

Marcus, G. (1996), *Ethnography through Thick and Thin*, Princeton: Princeton University Press.

Paz, Octavio (1978), *Marcel Duchamp: Appearance Stripped Bare*, New York: Arcade Publishing.

Rabinow, Paul (1996), *Essays on the Anthropology of Reason*, Princeton: Princeton University Press.

Rabinow, Paul (2003), *Anthropos Today: Reflections on Modern Equipment*, Princeton: Princeton University Press.

Rabinow, Paul (2014), 'Strife-Withering of Critique', Berkeley: ARC (Anthropological Research On the Contemporary, blog post).

Rabinow, Paul et al. (2008), *Designs for an Anthropology of the Contemporary*, Durham: Duke University Press.

Ranciere, Jacques (2009), *The Emancipated Spectator*, London: Verso.

Said, Edward W. (1979), *Orientalism*, New York: Vintage.

Simmel, Georg (2005), *Rembrandt: An Essay in the Philosophy of Art*, New York: Routledge.

Simmel, Georg (2006), *Rome: Une Analyse Esthetique*, Paris: Editions Allia.

Strathern, Marilyn (2014), 'Reading Relations Backwards', *Journal of the Royal Anthropological Institute*, 20: 3–19.

Viveiros de Castro, Eduardo (2012), 'Introduction to Post-Social Anthropology', *Hau: Journal of Ethnographic Theory*, 2: 421–33.

3

The recursivity of the curatorial

Jonas Tinius and Sharon Macdonald

Introduction

It has become increasingly evident and is widely attested in museum, contemporary art and other exhibition contexts that 'curating' is a pervasive buzzword. Some might even say we no longer live in an age of the engineer, the bricoleur or the flâneur, but in an age of the curator, whose figure, depending on your point of view, evokes awe, annoyance or anxiety. There is no shortage of art historical, museological and anthropological texts (this one and the volume of which it is part included) speaking of the prominence and pervasiveness of curatorial discourse and practice. The number of workshops and graduate programmes for 'up-and-coming' curators, at which new, or those described as such, theories about art and curating are distributed, is itself both cause and result of this discursive formation that began, arguably, some three decades ago.

Curatorial practices no longer refer primarily to the taking care of an exhibition or the selection and interpellation of (art, ethnographic, etc.) objects and artists, but have expanded beyond museum and exhibition contexts to the questioning of these infrastructures themselves and the arrangement of theories as well as participatory and discursive formats. On the one hand, post-Fordist labour modalities that 'valorise hyper-production' (Rogoff 2013: 41) have led to a proliferation of theories and practices in an expanded curatorial field, in which everyone appears to be a curator and everything appears in need of curation. Or so it seems. Not only does this interpretation appear to suggest that this kind of valorization is the primary driver of such a theoretical advancement; it also downplays the complex range of other processes at play, such as the mobilization of innovation in the creative industries, changing institutional structures in art academies that combine theory and practice, and transforming formats across the arts (e.g. curating in the performing arts), and so on. On the other hand, Rogoff has suggested that the increasing transdisciplinarity of artistic and curatorial production has not just led to a blurring of lines across art or exhibition contexts, but has also, simultaneously, provoked a new set of formats, programmes and conversations that interrogate the meaning of curatorial practice itself (ibid.). The long list of publications addressing the relation between 'curating' and 'the curatorial' attests to this evidently generative phenomenon (see the introduction to this volume).

This chapter starts from the observation that merely pointing out the broadening scope and prevalence of curating as a practice, the curator as a professional role and 'the curatorial' as a theoretical discourse, overlooks some of the nuanced differences and shifts that occur in different exhibition constellations and curatorial fields, and fails to address reasons for the contemporary allure of the curatorial. In fact, the pervasive notion of the curator as a networking broker, who no longer requires connoisseurial competence and skills in handling objects, refers to a particular form of curating that has emerged from a relational and participatory shift in the arts, globalization and deinstitutionalization of the contemporary arts field from the 1990s onwards. It refers to an 'independent curator' no longer based in museums, but instead an initiator of project-based representations and thematic group shows, both gatekeeper of artistic visibility and translator of different epistemological realms no longer confined to one discipline. It also refers to a particular understanding of curatorial practice, less as an object-based and visual form of showing than as a reflection on curating itself as well as on its infrastructures, epistemologies and power relations. Focusing only on this form of curatorship, however, ignores less glamorous kinds of curating. Yet even object-based and more strongly museum-based and non-arts curating can be implicated in new assemblies of objects, relations, ideas and people (see Basu and Macdonald 2007).

Here, we look at the two central conceptual phenomena indicated in the title of this contribution: recursivity and the curatorial, before analysing the ways in which these theoretical distinctions play out and can be made sense of with respect to our own ethnographic field-sites in Berlin. These sites are themselves overlapping and expanded fields of curatorial practice, crossing the sometimes precarious membranes of museums, heritage and contemporary art. As such, they serve not as an illustration of our preceding conceptual analysis, but as themselves ways of thinking of the recursivity of the curatorial. Following from this, we interrogate not just the recursivity of the curatorial, but also its consequences for anthropological practice and theorizing.

The first concept we address is 'the curatorial'. It has been mobilized to open up the infrastructures of curating and curatorial theorizing; not as another term to ground the field professionally and define what curating is, but precisely 'to challenge the very protocols and formats that define it: collecting, conserving, displaying, visualizing, discoursing, contextualizing, criticizing, publicizing, spectacularizing, etc.' (Rogoff 2013: 45). In this sense, as Rogoff has put it, 'the curatorial' is meant 'to become the staging ground of the development of an idea', rather than a choice for another definition of what curating is. The curatorial, then, is a way to describe the reflexivity of the 'expanded field' of curatorial practice on itself. This, it appears to us, is a useful way into understanding the relation of anthropology to curatorial practice, and one to which our ethnographic accounts speak. But it is also a notion that may allow us to address the slightly less easily marketable story about the buzzword 'curating'. Just at that point when everything seems curatable and everyone appears to be curating something or someone, the term – we are not the first to note this (see Balzer 2015 and Obrist 2008) – becomes fuzzy and the boundaries of the practice porous and indecipherable. Instead of curator-envy (to borrow from Hal Foster's take on art and ethnography, see Foster 1995: 304), there is increasing malaise, even doubt, about its critical potential and pervasiveness. In an age of the managerial self-borrowing from social and artistic critique (see Boltanski and Chiapello 2007 [1999]; Bröckling 2007; Gielen and De Bruyne 2012), is the curator yet another mediator in the project dynamics of a post-Fordist labour modality? Unlike the attested mutual fascination with each other's fields (curating and anthropology, respectively), we have also observed sceptical reciprocal interrogations into the practice at the heart of anthropology, leading to exchanges beyond envy and towards criticality. Instead of asking why curators want to be anthropologists and the other way around, we proceed by examining the implications and consequences of *not* desiring this metamorphosis. It is just at this moment, however, that an analysis of and a reflection on these relations of exchange or co-criticality may be helpful, especially for anthropologists who curate, curators who are interested in anthropology, and those trying to understand this precise interrelationship. Thinking recursively about the protocols, formats and infrastructures of how anthropology relates to curatorial practice in our ethnographic sites, we may illuminate some usually overlooked and perhaps generative tensions between both anthropology and curatorial practice.

In this chapter, therefore, we do not restrict our gaze to the independent curator emerging within the field of contemporary art but also consider a wider range of curatorial roles and practices. Our aim is not to rehearse and inscribe a genealogy of curatorial 'types', but rather to elucidate various approaches to, understandings of and reflections upon curating by curators, and to ask what the consequences of these could be for anthropologists in their relation to curating or their role *as* curators. For, to understand the implications of this porousness of the relation between anthropology and curatorial practice and its potential embrace or rejection of anthropological curating and a curatorial anthropology (an anthropology, perhaps, that continually reshapes itself recursively through curatorial practice), means asking about the potential end as well as the future of both.

It is for this reason that we connect a discussion of 'the curatorial' with one about 'recursivity'. The latter term seeks to achieve, we contend, an effect in anthropology similar to that of the former in the curatorial field. In a parallel move to the debate on the ethnographic turn in contemporary arts scholarship and practice (Siegenthaler 2013), which has analysed and often favourably described the overlapping, approximating relationship between artistic and anthropological practice (see Sansi 2015; Schneider and Wright 2005, 2010, 2013), this volume attests to a similar interest in thinking about the similarities and mutual interests that lie between anthropological and curatorial practice. Moreover, art and curating are variously seen as ways to rethink anthropological practice, and vice versa. Anthropology, in many of these seminal writings on the art–curating–anthropology nexus, appears as a source of inspiration for artistic and curatorial work. Roger Sansi (introduction, this volume) invites contributors to this book to ask: 'How does the practice of curation help anthropologists rethink their practice, work, and concerns of contemporary anthropology?' For the curator Okwui Enwezor (2012 et al.: 21), cited in Sansi's introduction, 'like the ethnographer, the contemporary curator is a creature of wanderlust'.[1] Enwezor's curatorial take on the 2012 Paris Triennale, from the catalogue of which his statement is drawn, presented a 'radical break with national approaches' to the renowned curatorial event and introduced a pioneering non-representational, transnational, postcolonial – and, above all, anthropological – frame of reference (see Oswald 2016: 679, 683). Yet, his ascription of 'the curator [as] a co-traveller with the ethnographer in the same procedures of contact and exploration' (Enwezor et al. 2012: 21) lends itself to an all-too-easy methodological, epistemological and, ironically, what some would regard as a colonially connoted equivocation.[2] Rather than regarding the curator and the anthropologist as joint explorative travellers, we would like to highlight the ways in which their conceptual frames, especially in contexts of close collaborations like the ones analysed in this book, operate rather on a recursive level of *ricochet* difference. Ricochet effects do not replicate sameness or present a perfect copy; rather, they introduce refracted, distorted and sometimes accidentally formed perspectives onto an object, person, or practice – and, importantly, they differ depending on one's standpoint. Borrowing from Sarah Franklin (2013), for whom 'the anthropological meanings of both recursivity and reflexivity [...] turn on the question of comparison' (2013: 17), we wish to underscore the way in which the relationship between anthropology and curating can be analysed critically through the lens of generative recursive relationships. Franklin offers a neat image for thinking about the analogy: 'like two mirrors facing each other (a classic image of recursion), the reflections are also ricochets' (ibid.: 21). In the same vein, we are not interested here in showing merely *that* anthropology and curating are intertwined, or that one is *like* the other ('anthropology as curating'), but rather, our focus is on what the 'effects of sameness' (ibid.) *do* to our understanding of each. How can we appreciate the proximity without blurring the boundaries, and thus also the differences, unevenness and scepticism between anthropology and curating?

The two overlapping field-sites presented in this chapter directly speak to the analyses above, while articulating responses to the question of recursivity, anthropology and the curatorial from different fields of curatorial practice. Departing from the multi-researcher project 'Making Differences: Transforming Museums and Heritage' at the Centre for Anthropological Research on Museums and Heritage (CARMAH), Humboldt-Universität zu Berlin, we have been conducting ethnographic research on a variety of different museum, exhibition-making and curatorial contexts in Berlin.[3] While researchers study fields as divergent as the restitution of colonial-era objects (Förster et al. 2018), exhibition-making in museums of Islamic art, social media engagement in memorials to Holocaust victims or data management structures in museums of natural history, to name but a few, these fields are variously bounded and unbounded, overlapping and mutually distinguishing. What we mean by this is that the institutions we study are at times connected through infrastructures of state patronage and funding, or share public presence through events and discourses, while often, simultaneously, situating themselves publicly and discursively as quite different kinds of institutions, fields and practices. We have elaborated how certain concepts – provenance, translocality, engagement, alterity, the post-ethnological – appear and shift meaning across these fields, being both variously understood and mobilized in different institutional fields, as well as sometimes even becoming means of challenging formats and structures of exhibition contexts (CARMAH 2018). Complementing this research, we brought forward a methodological proposition for how to think through the complexity of interlocked and idiosyncratic organizations in this context, without giving up the ethnographic specificity of each context or giving in to the trap of institutional relativism and 'methodological containerism' (Macdonald, Gerbich and Oswald 2018).

Most noticeably, many of the institutions we study in Berlin react in one way or another to the much discussed and contentious Humbolt Forum in the Berliner Schloss (Berlin City Palace) that is nearing completion and meant to open to the public in late 2020. This monumental, partially reconstructed Prussian-era palace, erected on the site of the former GDR's Palace of the Republic, will display objects from the collections of the Ethnological Museum and the Museum of Asian Art, as well as showing other exhibitions, including one about Berlin. While critical debates about the palace and the ambivalent image of German identity and national self-understanding that it might project onto the capital began many decades ago (see Binder 2009), it has more recently become a focus for debates about anthropology, colonialism and German identity (e.g. von Bose 2016). In such a context, the role of curators working inside and outside institutions affiliated with the Humbolt Forum has become one of critical mediators between public discourses and institutional affordances.

The Humbolt Forum presents a provocative research backdrop and, for some members of our team, a direct field-site. Its complex entanglement of curatorial practices and negotiations sometimes concerns the very questions we are also asking ourselves as anthropologists. These questions include those of how to study and describe related museum discourses in a city; how to understand the current reckoning with the arguably problematic role of German anthropology during the country's colonial era; and what curatorial strategies dealing with postcolonial theory in the field of contemporary art in Berlin can contribute to reflecting on such complex museum and heritage developments.

We address these theoretical challenges and ethnographic dilemmas in this chapter by way of two of our field-sites. One of these is the making of the Berlin Exhibition in the Humbolt Forum, whose content is primarily conceived and shaped by a curatorial team specifically assembled for the purpose, drawn from established institutions as well as freelance curators, under the leadership of the Director of the City Museums (*Stadtmuseen*) of Berlin. The curators also work closely with communication and education staff from the cultural educational organization *Kulturprojekte* and the design company *Krafthaus* as well as with many others. The other field-site is of collaborative research with the independent contemporary art project space SAVVY Contemporary in Berlin's northern district of Wedding.[4] These two projects are dealing, in different ways and with different emphases, with the legacy of German colonialism, German identity in the present and migration. But the focus of our analyses in this contribution is the modalities of our engagement as anthropologists with the curatorial team and the strategies and processes of these organizations. In both cases, we have experienced our relationships to be ones of critical, shifting and, at times, even uncomfortable engagements between curatorial and anthropological practice. Given the heightened public and professional attention in recent years to the role of anthropology and the coloniality of ethnological museums, our roles as anthropologists studying curators engaging with these legacies were sometimes ones in which we would face projections of anthropology during our research. We variously experienced pragmatic interest in understanding what each (anthropology/curating) has to offer in rethinking the other's practice and theorizing about museums and heritage, yet we are wary of describing these relations as ones of sameness, equivocation or even enthusiasm, let alone envious and uncritical approximation. Rather, as Arnd Schneider has noted, we found ourselves in relations marked by a 'mutual recognition of difference' (2015: 27) in a generative albeit 'uneven hermeneutic field' (ibid.) between anthropological and curatorial practices. Without assuming that we are already doing the same thing, we wish here to interrogate the kinds of relations made and unmade between these two practices. Based on comparative ethnographic research, we thus explore what kinds of insights each field-site offers for thinking about the recursive relational modalities of anthropology, ethnography and curating.

Anthropology, recursivity and the curatorial

> We wish to talk about curating, because we thought we saw a possibility nestling within its protocols, a possibility for other ways of working, relating and knowing. (Martinon and Rogoff 2013: viii)

'The curatorial' has been one of the keywords in debates on curatorial practices and theorizing during the last ten years (see e.g. O'Neill 2012 and Smith 2012). Meant not as an adjective, but as a noun, it is used to evoke and conjure up a set of different entry points into curating, alternative ways of thinking about curatorial practice and theorizing. Across a wide number of publications and programmes, the term addresses the observation that the 'expanded field of the curatorial is built upon the expanded field of art', as Roger Sansi (introduction, this volume) notes. Just as the meaning of contemporary art – and its possible definitions – have shifted, expanded and blurred into fields beyond the classic confines of modern autonomous art in recent decades (see Canclini 2014), so too has the meaning of curating. What interests us here is the way in which this discussion has arisen not from without, but from within curatorial programmes and curatorial initiatives.

In the preface to the widely cited anthology *The Curatorial* (2013), Irit Rogoff and Jean-Paul Martinon reflect on the origins for their concern about a distinction between 'curating' and 'the curatorial'. They write:

> If 'curating' is a gamut of professional practices that had to do with setting up exhibitions and other modes of display, then 'the curatorial' operates at a very different level: it explores all that takes place on the stage set-up, both intentionally and unintentionally, by the curator and views it as an event of knowledge. So to drive home a distinction between 'curating' and 'the curatorial' means to emphasise a shift from the staging of the event to the actual event itself: its enactment, dramatization and performance. (ibid.: ix)

While Martinon describes the curatorial in his editor's introduction as a 'strategy for inventing new forms of departure' (2013: 4), the distinction he ponders with Irit Rogoff in the paragraph above, from the book's preface, is more reflexive and less performative. As anthropologists we too are not simply concerned with the intricacies of 'putting on an event', but rather with understanding 'the staging ground of the development of an idea or an insight' (2013: 45). In that sense, Rogoff and Martinon's elision and elusion of a definition of 'the curatorial' open up the practice of curating for interrogation. If 'the curatorial' is the 'staging ground or the development of an idea or an insight', rather than being concerned with the practical staging of the event (understood here as, say, an exhibition or a performance), then it begins to question its own beginning and ending, its modalities and premises. It is a notion that operationalizes and marks off elements within curatorial practice as 'set aside', or rather it emphasizes how and where things become framed within a curatorial field. 'The curatorial [...] breaks up this stage, yet produces a narrative which comes into being in the very moment in which an utterance takes place, in that moment in which the event communicates and says, as Mieke Bal once observed, "look, that is how this is"' (Martinon and Rogoff 2013: ix). Put in this way, it is akin to the way in which anthropologist Karin Barber (2007) and performance studies scholars Tracy C. Davis and Thomas Postlewait (2003) have described 'theatricality', namely as ways in which theatre and performance draw attention to their own 'conventions in the moment of its transpiring' (ibid.: 15). 'The curatorial', then, is a way for the curatorial field to refer back to its own conventions, discursive formations and protocols, not just in their moments of enactment, but before and after as well.

Rogoff suggests that there is good reason for mobilizing 'the curatorial' in such a recursive and reflexive way. In her essay 'The Expanding Field' (2013), she suggests that two parallel processes undergird the flourishing of what David Balzar has since coined as 'curationism' (2015). First, as noted above, Rogoff suggests that the expansion of curatorial agency and visibility is directly linked to 'the dominance of neoliberal models of work that valorise hyper-production' (2013: 41), thus rendering the curator a post-Fordist entrepreneur par excellence. Second, she argues that the absence of a stringent disciplinary history of curating, 'or a body of stable empirical or theoretical knowledge' (ibid.: 45), has been to the benefit of the production of knowledge in the field of curatorial practice. Even though the latter claim in particular is arguable and highly contingent on the kind of curating we refer to, it leads to an interesting argument, namely that 'such absences allow for a flexibility of operating and for the possibility of considerable invention, be it of archives or subjects or methodologies' (ibid.).

For Rogoff, thus, 'both curating and the curatorial [...] are largely fields grounded in a series of work-protocols with little cumulative history or a body of stable empirical or theoretical knowledge at their disposal' (ibid.). While this means that their epistemological grounding is unstable, it also affords a flexibility to draw on a variety of archives and methodologies. Neither Rogoff nor Martinon write from a neutral standpoint, of course: situating themselves within programmes that deploy specific discourses, their interventions are situated within particular historical and epistemic formations.[5]

Her own involvement with this programme, as she writes, did not seek to 'determine *which* knowledges went into the work of curating but would insist on a new set of relations between these knowledges' (ibid.). As such, an exploration of the curatorial was less interested in 'ground[ing] the field professionally' than in 'map[ping] the movement of knowledges in and out of the field and how they are able to challenge the very protocols and formats that define it: collecting, conserving, displaying, visualizing, discoursing, contextualizing, criticizing, publicizing, spectacularizing, etc.' (ibid.). These are, at heart, also anthropological questions, or at least ones that would allow for a generative comparison between what 'the curatorial' offers to an anthropology as and an anthropology of curating. What, one might also ask, would it mean to translate the concept of 'the curatorial' into anthropology or ethnographic practice?

It is not our purpose to dwell on a rejection or approval of their theses or analyses of the post-Fordist present. Rather, we wish to take up some of their cues in order to supplement anthropological perspectives on the curatorial as a practice and way of framing. In particular, it is a question for us, as anthropologists engaging with curatorial practices and theorizing, as to what extent this offers potential for a reflexive, recursive analysis of anthropology and curating; a situation that could be seen, as Sarah Franklin puts it, as 'deriv[ing] from the relationship between framing devices, such as models, and their contents – as in the cases of remodelling models, or re-conceiving concepts' (2013: 15). Reframed in the context of our research, we thus ask: What differences and similarities are enacted or performed in recursion, and what kinds of ricochet effects do we notice as anthropologists studying curators who themselves engage in anthropological questions and issues we are facing ourselves? What are the 'generative effects of recursion' (Barnes 1971, 1973, cited in Franklin 2013: 19) of their practice and our study of their practices? And more so, does it offer potential for a continuous reshuffling and rethinking so that we each consequently – perhaps in a series of endless moves – change what we do?

Recursivity differs from reflexivity. Reflexivity refers to reflection on one's own position, and in our research contexts could indicate anthropologists coming to new understandings of themselves through reflecting on others, or other people thinking about anthropologists and thus coming to altered understanding of themselves. Recursivity, however, is about a 'sequence of revelation' in which the relation between two perspectives 'is constantly redefining the partners in the exchange, the objects of exchange, and the very concept of exchange' (Sansi 2018: 123). As such, recursivity is performative and implies action. It refers to an ongoing mutually affecting relationality between things, people, thoughts and forms of knowledge. This is not just a combination of reflexive processes but the generation of something new. More than just anthropologists and curators thinking about each other, recursivity can – perhaps in a long series of additive moves – lead to altogether novel positions. In the context of laboratory stem cell research, Sarah Franklin (2013: 20) points to what is necessary to achieve this:

> Recursion, in this sense – attention to the properties of the equipment you are using to determine, or manage, the properties of something else – is itself an empirical, necessary and pragmatic art.

In our situations, we are not dealing with 'properties of equipment', and we are not interested in 'determining or managing' the properties of something else, but the recursive phenomenon remains similar. What kinds of equipment, here understood in the sense of 'what ways of analysing', do we have at hand for dealing with the protocols of reflexive curating? How do we 'mind the gap' between anthropology studying curatorial practice and problematizing anthropology without either 'evening out' (ibid.) the differences or simply positing a direct symmetry between the two fields? And lastly, how do we avoid turning this process into another exercise of reflexive anthropology, where curating appears merely as an object-mirror, instead of one of two eye-level perspectives? In some sense, it could be argued, as Martin Holbraad (2013: 123) suggests, that

> *all* knowledge is recursive, inasmuch as it always involves calibrating the means of knowledge (empirical and analytical procedures, experimental protocols and tools, scales of measurement, assumptions, concepts – in short, its 'equipment') with the object of knowledge [...] to know something is recursively to adjust one's body of knowledge to it.

Yet, there are specific ways in which this recursive generation of knowledge plays out in different fields. In the case of the relation between anthropology and curating, and to return to the mirror-image metaphor of the ricochet effects of recursivity, we are dealing with a socio-epistemic exchange. As Holbraad puts it, 'if what anthropology strives to "grasp" is itself *another* way of grasping [...], then the anthropologists' attempt can only take the form of a *shift of perspective*' (ibid.: 124). Crucially, he argues, this is not a matter of 'adjusting' to a body of knowledge imagined as logically or epistemically inferior (ibid.: 126), but one of 'epistemic xenophilia' where two points of view, like in the recursive mirror image, 'stand in a relationship of mutual constitution' where one '(recursively) provides the terms with which [the other's] knowledge itself is composed' (ibid.). Recursivity, therefore, describes not the reproduction of difference (alterity) or sameness (mimesis), but the open-endedness of this mutually constitutive relation. An emphasis on it acknowledges 'the injunction to keep constitutively open the question of what any given object of ethnographic investigation might *be* and, therefore, how existing concepts and theories have to be modulated in order the better to articulate it', as Holbraad and Pedersen (2017: x) have suggested in the context of the ontological turn. Thinking recursively about the curatorial from an anthropological point of view, then, means engendering, or allowing the contexts of our fieldwork to engender, 'transformational [...] conceptual landscapes' (Holbraad 2012: 47). This then leads to the questions of how such a recursive perspective might 'help to sustain [...] the transformation of anthropology itself, and what ... this transformation [would] entail?' (ibid.).

In the following, we explore some of the ways in which our field-sites offer ethnographic inroads into these conversations. We ask, among other things, what happens when anthropology is not a desired 'co-traveller' (Enwezor) to curating, but an invited, critical commentator: or, indeed, something more akin to a 'sparring partner' (Tinius, forthcoming and 2017)? What are some of the generative differences and discrepancies between the protocols of curators and anthropologists reflecting on their practices? And what kinds of transformations do these different kinds of differences in such co-critical, recursive and collaborative relations between anthropologists and curators entail for the possible recalibration of each position, especially for the anthropologist?

Berlin's recursive curatorial fields

As part of our joint research project, we have been conducting a multi-researcher ethnographic study of the transformations of museum institutions and discourses on exhibition-making in the city for over two years now.[6] In frequent research meetings, our team comes together to exchange our experiences and compare perspectives. Several among us who have been trained as anthropologists (or who have been trained in ethnography in a related discipline, such as sociology) have also been involved in the curation of exhibitions in ethnological museums, historical museums and museums of art. Most of us are actively engaged in participant-observation in exhibition-making in an even broader range of institutions, ranging from large and well-known public institutions to smaller and often project-based initiatives across the city of Berlin, and sometimes beyond it. Many of these ethnographic projects address in some ways the institutions and the practices of curating, including, for instance, through concerns with visitor engagement, modes of display or the social routines of exhibition-making procedures, ranging from *jours fixes* to public symposia and publications. Moreover, many of us have constructed joint activities, often in explicit co-funded frameworks and with collaborative aims, in which our interlocutors may also include other professional anthropologists who work in the field themselves. These projects are thus not just about anthropologists studying curators and creating broad descriptions about their practices, but are also about creating new practices, methods and understandings of anthropology and curating, attempting to create and rethink through each collaborative and critical inquiry, and thus, in a move not unlike that of the ethnographic conceptualism proposed by Ssorin-Chaikov (2013), creating new forms and social realities as part of our research.

Our collective project thus offers a broad set of possible routes into the recursivity of curatorial practice, but we have deliberately chosen two particular instances. One, drawn from Sharon Macdonald's research on the making of the Berlin Exhibition in the Humbolt Forum, concerns the development of modes of participatory curation. As Roger Sansi writes in the introduction to this book, the move towards participatory curation has become widespread, and clearly entails curators working, in some sense at least, ethnographically. What they do, however, is not simply a version of anthropological activity but a mode of engagement with its own motivations, constraints and possibilities. As he observes, the role of such curators can be rather managerial, acting as mediators between different agents. This is a rather different figure of the curator from the artistic freewheeler that is often privileged in anthropologists' 'curator envy', as we discussed above. Indeed, as Sansi notes, from the perspective of the more managerial curator, it is the ethnographer who may seem to be the relatively unfettered and creative agent. In the brief discussion here, what we want to focus upon, however, is not so much the views that the anthropologist and the curators held of each other's form of work but, rather, the shared yet distinct enterprise in which both were engaged of trying to figure out what might be meant by and entailed in participatory approaches. In particular, we draw attention to moments in which the approaches of each were recursively shaped by the other, or in which they might further be so.

Let us here say something first about the idea of 'participation' in our own multi-researcher ethnography, as well as in the Berlin Exhibition ethnography. Written into our project's shared set of methodological premises was that we would aim to find modes of engaging ethnographically that were not restricted to a 'distanced observer' role and that would welcome and even seek active participation beyond the more usual 'going along with' positions of established 'participant-observation'. We often talked about this as 'collaborative', and some of our colleagues chose to use variations of the term 'observant-participation' (see Macdonald, Gerbich and Oswald 2018: 148) to indicate the desired greater emphasis on participating than in more conventional fieldwork.

In the case of the Berlin Exhibition, Sharon Macdonald took on roles of various kinds and degrees of participation at different moments – a process that was sometimes awkward to negotiate.[7] The role that was clearly flagged as 'ethnographer' was mostly described by the curators, and by herself, as one of 'accompanying' or 'following' the exhibition-making – though all also emphasized that this was a role in which she would also have input, drawing on her experience as a museologist, especially if, as the curators put it, she detected possible 'mistakes being made'. While at the regular meetings of the curators she was mostly occupied primarily with listening and writing notes; she also joined in to varying degrees, depending on the topics being discussed. There, as well as in other meetings or via email, she made suggestions for possible content or contacts – such as providing ideas for people, including some of our own research team (Jonas Tinius among them), who might help mediate with the diverse communities in Berlin; and she commented on content and text. In addition to accompanying the exhibition-making process as an intermittently intervening ethnographer, Sharon contributed to the shaping of the exhibition in a more formal capacity, as a member of the exhibition's Advisory Board. Despite the fact that the remit of the Advisory Board was partly the same as that of the participating ethnographer, namely to help the curators avoid making errors and to contribute to improving the exhibition, switching to the more formal position could feel awkward. One instance of this was at the first meeting of the board, when she automatically went to sit next to the curators, only to be told by them, 'No – you are supposed to sit at the other end of the table'. There were other role switches or blurrings of boundaries too, such as when curators came to events organized at our research centre, CARMAH, or sought out Sharon's advice on ideas for their Ph.Ds, or shared experiences of dealing as a foreigner with German bureaucracy, or discussed anthropology – as some curators had studied it, including within our own university department.[8]

It is worth noting, as we discuss in the conclusion to this chapter, that the work of the Berlin team was highly discursive, with extensive debates among the curators – and later with others, including the Advisory Board members and further interlocutors known as 'critical friends' – about the approach that they would take. Early discussion led to decisions that the exhibition would not be 'object-based' or 'object-led' but, rather, that it would be highly 'participatory' and 'multivocal'. Discussion often focused on concepts that would be deployed in shaping the exhibition, with this sometimes drawing on anthropological and other theoretical sources, as in relation to 'migration' and 'colonialism', for example. Curators brought in examples from museums and exhibitions elsewhere, sometimes including ones that our anthropological team were looking at or had expertise in. As in our own research team, much thought was given to the contested site of the Humboldt Forum itself, and the ethnological collections in particular. However, while we, as a team of anthropologists, also needed to figure out where we stood in relation to it, for the curators this was a more constantly pressing and practical matter, as well as one that had even more weighing upon it politically, than was the case for us. Not only did the extensive discussion among the curators guide the internal planning of the exhibition, it also created a basis for presentations to politicians, press and public, in numerous talks and interviews, especially with the exhibition's chief curator, Paul Spies. Particularly significant was a document produced by the curators called *Berlin und die Welt. Konzept der Ausstellung des Landes Berlin im Humboldt Forum* ('Berlin and the World. Concept of the Exhibition of the Berlin City-State in the Humboldt Forum') that was presented to press and public in July 2016. Although profiled as a guiding concept, it was far from representing the end of the extensive discursive work – rather, in its own recursivity, it was not so much a blueprint for a next stage of practical work as a basis for continued reflection, development and revision.

Within the overlapping contexts (see also Macdonald 1997) of the work of the Berlin Exhibition curators and our 'Making Differences' research, what we want to briefly focus upon here is the ethnographer's participation in the curators' development of participatory approaches, the similarities and differences between the results of this involvement, and the recursive effects of such work for thinking about ethnographic research within the 'Making Differences' project. It was decided early on in the making of the Berlin exhibition that 'participation' would be fundamental to its approach. Precisely what this meant, however, needed to be worked out, not least as it was sometimes evident in early meetings that there were different assumptions in play – some curators regarding it as primarily relating to providing interactive opportunities within the exhibition, and others as entailing various degrees of involvement of 'communities' (as it was usually expressed) and relinquishment of curatorial authority. A series of meetings was established in order to draw up what the participatory approach would be. Sharon joined these, sharing some of her museological knowledge. Nina Simon's classification of different kinds of participation – ranging from 'contributing' to 'hosting' and 'co-creating' (2010) – became part of the regular curatorial discourse as the curators figured out which particular combination of participatory modes they would seek to achieve in different parts of the exhibition. As well as this contributing to a general rationale of how they would proceed – in particular, how they would attempt to avoid what they called a 'top-down' approach – they also addressed what it would mean in practice. Sharon took part in these discussions as well, and additionally contributed by writing a report in which she drew on her anthropological and museological knowledge about issues that needed to be considered when working with communities. Some of the points that she made, such as about the risk of communities feeling 'used' and even abandoned after a project had finished, played directly into the planned practices of the curators, and helped them to argue their case for a dedicated member of staff who would carry out this work.

In some ways, the discourse of 'participation' among the curators was similar to that within our own research team. In particular, it tended to be seen as 'more democratic', as allowing for 'a greater range of voices' and, thus, as making for a livelier product. It was also, however, in several respects more carefully worked out and far reaching than that of the ethnographers. Even though Sharon had introduced to the curators the issue of long-term engagement and what might happen after a project formally ends, this had not at that time been something discussed within our own research project. Furthermore, there was a level of detail of discussion about matters such as the payment of community participants, and of the kinds of contracts that they would sign, that did not have a close ethnographic parallel (though it might have done so – and a recursive effect could prompt it). Likewise, what some see as the most radical of Simon's forms of 'participation', namely 'hosting' – in which an institution gives up its space for a community or other group to do with it what they will – was contemplated by the curators, and later was instantiated. At that time, however, nothing similar had been attempted within our team's fieldwork, and what it might mean within an ethnographic research project was, thus, a question that the curatorial practice raised – and one that we have only begun to contemplate. 'Co-creation' – which some see as more radical than 'hosting', as Simon herself seems to do – was also much discussed by the curators, and is also part of the exhibition that is in the making. In this case, there was more within our research centre that could be seen in this light,[9] though the tendency has been for the co-creation to be within the realm of exhibitions and public engagement rather than anthropology as such. An exception to this, however, is the work of Jonas Tinius described below. Intimated here, then, are not simply reflections by curators and ethnographers about each other's practice or ideas, but also ways in which those practices can recursively 'bounce back' and reshape the ensuing ways of doing things by both parties.

One aspect of Jonas's 'Making Differences' research involves a collaborative project between the anthropologist and the curator Bonaventure Soh Bejeng Ndikung with the working title 'Relexification Dialogues'. The project is based on a year-long series of one-hour or longer conversations around an alphabet of key concepts that address the relation between anthropology and curating in general (e.g. 'exhibition-making' or 'coloniality'), and also draw on specific projects curated by Bonaventure and accompanied as part of his broader ethnographic project by Jonas (e.g. 'b' for 'beer', referring to artist Emeka Ogboh's brewing project as part of the 2017 Kassel-Athens exhibition documenta 14). Relexification is a term borrowed from linguistics, which refers to processes during second-language acquisition 'whereby one language [...] seeds a creole' by having some of its vocabulary replaced with vocabulary from another language, 'while almost everything else in the original language remains unchanged' (DeGraff 2002: 323). Bonaventure and Jonas understand this notion as a description of processes complementary to those in our proposition about recursivity – indeed, around the time of writing this article, they conducted a conversation on the concept for the letter 'r'. As such, these dialogues bring into conversation two ways of speaking and thinking that are not predicated on sameness, or even on a mutually shared interest: instead, they aim to experiment with a long-term exchange and recalibration of perspectives, conceptual and discursive, but always in response to ongoing fieldwork and shared experiences from phases of participant-observation with the exhibitions curated by Bonaventure and his team at SAVVY Contemporary. They do not seek to define words or create a new joint language, but to perform resonances, creating, as was formulated in an initial project plan, 'an anthropological and curatorial 'jargon' [...] using and inserting changes into established conceptual definitions, helping each other unlearn associations and references, and substituting old vocabularies with new meanings' (Ndikung and Tinius 2017). The conversations are nearing completion at the time of writing, but their aim is to serve as a published reference point for a deliberate emphasis on the ambivalent and shifting terrain between anthropology and curatorial practice, thus allowing it to feed back into the very conceptual and socio-epistemic field from which it arose.

'Bonaventure, let's start these dialogues with the letter 'a' to talk about anthropology' – Jonas opened their first joint session on a 2017 October morning in the subterranean exhibition and office rooms of the SAVVY project space in Berlin's northern district of Wedding. As a starting point in this first conversation on anthropology, Jonas chose to refer back to their first meeting in the project space. Almost an entire year earlier, in September 2016, as Jonas was starting his ethnographic fieldwork project as part of the 'Making Differences' research outlined above, he had already begun visiting exhibitions and had read up on the history and conceptual framework of SAVVY Contemporary. Introducing himself to Bonaventure for the first time as an anthropologist, however, the curator responded 'I am sceptical of anthropologists', thus already initiating a tension inherent in the exchange.

The encounter across two very different, rather than similar or mutually attractive standpoints, initiated their joint fieldwork conversations in 2016. Over the ensuing months, they continued to articulate different standpoints, recognizing a generative scepticism about each other's positions, often aimed at the history and disciplinary presence of anthropology (voiced by Bonaventure), or at simplified representations of anthropology in artistic and curatorial contexts today (voiced by Jonas). These included conversations about exhibitions or large curatorial projects in which Bonaventure was involved, such as documenta 14 in Kassel and Dakar in 2017 or the Dakar Biennale in 2018 in Senegal, both of which contained curated sections and artworks addressing various aspects of the history or practice of European anthropology. In the latter case, Bonaventure had even conceived an exhibition with members of his SAVVY Contemporary project (co-curated by Kamila Metwaly and Marie Hélène Pereira) for the Dakar Biennale 2018 around the work of Egyptian ethnomusicologist Halim El-Dabh (1921–2017) entitled 'Canine Wisdom for the Barking Dog / The Dog Done Gone Deaf', the opening and set-up of which Jonas accompanied as part of his research.[10]

But back to the first letter/dialogue. A few minutes into the conversation on the letter 'a' and concept of 'anthropology', Bonaventure said:

> You know very well that I come from a family, not completely of anthropologists, but my father is an anthropologist. I observed that very early. Although in his time, and his people [in Cameroon], in the 1970s, were very much interested in studying

The Recursivity of the Curatorial

their own people, their own cultures, but they studied, I mean he studied, within a framework and science that was made to study him. Do you understand where I'm getting to? (Ndikung and Tinius 2017)

What Bonaventure was indicating, as he continued to explain, was the question about the production of difference in anthropology and his curatorial work as a way to counter or produce alternatives to an anthropological knowledge formation. Anthropology, he argued, implies for him a construction of cultural difference to a culturally 'other' understudy in order to reflect on the anthropological self; a 'necessity to be able to create an Other in order to be able to create yourself', as he put it. This, for Bonaventure, 'comes into play when I say that I am sceptical of anthropologists and anthropology as a discipline [...] and so a lot of my practice is about how we take certain things and people out of that 'savage slot', out of where they have been placed, by some anthropologists'. Confronted with such a scepticism, and a self-description that so strongly rejects anthropological knowledge formation, one can hardly speak of an invitation or a desire on the part of the curator to be an anthropologist, as discussed by Sansi in the introduction to this book. However, Bonaventure responded to Jonas's suggestion for a sustained series of conversations around shared concerns between anthropology and curatorial practice, because he recognized that the project was an attempt at dialogic thinking rather than a hierarchical researcher–informant fieldwork relationship. Instead of trying to co-curate, or co-ethnographize each other's practices, they sought to articulate both an anthropology and a curatorial practice that each enacts its knowledge co-production in dialogue, rather than doing so on behalf of the other. Over the course of the next twelve months, they continued conversations on letters including 'b' (blackness/beer), 'c' (coloniality), 'h' (Humboldt Forum), 'm' (masculinity), and so on, to name a few, talking about both their immediate surroundings and the specific projects they have done; also always addressing and referring back to conversations they had conducted before.

As such, the dialogues themselves became reference points for future conversations, generating concepts and terms that recurred in later dialogues. As such, while recursivity is not an evident outcome of any dialogue, the conversations were conducted with the deliberate intention of drawing on aspects of this generated archive. In that sense, they both engaged, and reminded themselves in doing so, in generating discourse about curating and anthropology *through* conversations, rather than from a single perspective of analysis and writing about the other. Moreover, their aim was to generate not only conversations for the purpose of, say, having an archive of dialogues for publication or research, but also as a resource to refer back to in future projects. In other words, they engaged in the creation of a dialogic, non-definitive encyclopaedia that would continue shaping their positions as well as feeding back into their future thinking. Referring to their modalities of speaking as 'rehearsed improvisations' (personal communication), they prepared conversations in loose ways – roughly agreeing to about one hour per letter, and with a few shared notes and reference points for each conversation – but keeping the conversation spontaneous and unplanned in its content, while rereading and returning to that which had already been said and transcribed.

In a recursive analytical move, we, the authors of this chapter, contend that the way Bonaventure and Jonas set up the dialogues in itself tells us something about both anthropology and curatorial practice, in the general and in the specific. Specifically regarding curatorial practice, Bonaventure and Jonas conducted a dialogue on 'e' (exhibition-making) that illustrates this point. Asked how Bonaventure regards exhibition-making and what the role of writing 'concepts' (project proposal sketches, or curatorial statements that often served as the basis for discussion), he responded that for him,

> [w]riting a concept becomes a very significant part of exhibition-making, because I create this kind of a discursive context in which I can work with artists and other curators. Even if I am working from the artist to the exhibition, I try to create a conceptual context within which we want to move. It is like creating a playground, and from there we go on to see how we can dialogue. *The important thing is that the exhibition doesn't become an illustration of the concept, but an extension of it.* If we stick to the allegory of the ground, it is like tilling the soil. The concept becomes the soil; the exhibition becomes the possibility of tilling that soil. How do we work, how do we farm, harvest on that soil? To me, an exhibition is hardly ever about answering a question, but finding ways of posing the right questions. So it's really about looking for that possibility of expressing something for which I don't have the answer yet, and which may be answered by a visitor, or another, in different and multiple ways that I may or may not agree with. 'How is the question posed?' then becomes the task. (Ndikung and Tinius 2017; emphasis added)

As such, the 'Relexification Dialogues' themselves function as a way to think about the 'conceptual context' within which Bonaventure as a curator wants to move. It is, in the rehearsed spontaneity modality mentioned earlier, an attempt at finding the right modes of asking questions. Indeed, for him, 'very important for understanding exhibition-making is the creating of a context, which in my practice generally has to do with, first, writing a concept'. In the same discursive modality, Bonaventure described a central difficulty of exhibition-making for him being the effort to avoid that it merely illustrates an idea, but instead performs it so that curating becomes a 'performative gesture' (Ndikung and Tinius 2017). In some ways, this description of curatorial practice as the translation from concept to context to the creation to performative staging of an idea reflects Rogoff's definition of the curatorial: 'the staging ground for the development of an idea'. In other ways, however, it may also conjure up questions about the relation between how anthropologists conceptualize their own fields, and the move from methodology to fieldwork to writing-up and theorization. Perhaps it is indeed, as Sharon has put it elsewhere, 'this dialogic nature of the ethnographic *process* that is one of the most important aspects of, and reasons for doing, ethnography' (2003: 162), and one in which the ethnographer is not just an author, but equally open to recursive interpretation by their interlocutors.

Conclusion: the recursivity of the curatorial

In this chapter, we have proposed a series of analytical and ethnographic discussions about the intersection of recursivity and the relation between anthropological fieldwork and curatorial practice. Our choice to mobilize 'recursivity' and 'the curatorial' as both ethnographic and analytical terms has itself had a performative reason. For both of us, researchers on a project with overlapping field-sites, an analysis of our fieldwork often produces a series of recursive moves, whereby we may end up reading texts by our interlocutors, or analyses from journalists 'within our field' whose concepts we reframe for our own analysis.

In the Berlin Exhibition, Sharon was confronted, among other things, with the various meanings of 'participation' mobilized by the curatorial team, including those of her own forms of participation in the exhibition's making and the ways in which our own research project – and the various forms of engagement of our researchers – would operate. Jonas produced a mode of fieldwork that itself also mirrored in style and content some of the models and formats of exhibition-making he was interested in studying. Both of our research projects, therefore, operate at a recursive level, but they also try to analyse the discursive and recursive nature of these curatorial fields. Moreover, besides discussing some of the theoretical references of this text with interlocutors in our field – Jonas conducted a 'Relexification Dialogue' on 'recursivity' after completing a first draft of this paper with Sharon – 'the curatorial' as a concept that emanated from curatorial theorization also became a point of reference in Jonas' fieldwork.

In *Talking Contemporary Curating* (2015), Terry Smith's sequel to his seminal *Thinking Contemporary Curating* (2012), he writes that '[p]erhaps the most significant development in curatorial practice in the last decade is that the field has become markedly more discursive in character' (Smith 2015: 13). More than that, 'discourse' for him is now 'upfront and at the center of curatorship' (ibid.,: 14). Unpacking his observation, he notes:

> Curators now talk more often, and more publicly, about what they do and how they do it. They also talk less guardedly, and in more depth than ever before, about *why* they do it. They speak more searchingly about curating as a practice that is as grounded in processes of conceptualisation, and as committed to the production of new knowledge, as it is in its more traditional pursuits: the pragmatics of caring for collections, planning programmes, working with artists, mounting exhibitions, attracting viewers and educating them. (ibid.)

If, for Smith, this is a result of a dialogue between curators and conceptual artists who increasingly took over the 'theoretical accounting' for their own work (ibid.: 15), the 'Relexification Dialogues' attest to a different, albeit related, phenomenon. Indeed, some of the most contentious points of the dialogues could be described as struggles about the epistemic jurisdiction of anthropological practice. How do you conduct a conceptual reflection, for instance, on the notion of 'Heimat' or 'hospitality' without simply rehearsing an anthropological reference corpus, but instead allowing a curatorial take to unpack an anthropological introduction to a dialogue? This might seem like a trivial question. Dominic Boyer, however, in his analysis of the relationship of anthropologists to their expert interlocutors, suggests that not every venture 'into other domains of expertise' is an innocent encounter of interdisciplinary endeavour (2008: 42). Rather, 'every intellectual profession ideologically imagines its expertise as occupying the centre of knowledge (even when individual experts have their doubts), and thus exploring and coordinating other epistemic jurisdictions are important professional work that confirms the universalist ambitions of one's own jurisdiction'. (ibid.)

With this critical position in mind, the question of a dialogue between anthropology and curatorial practice that touches on both in a recursive manner becomes more challenging. In what sense is one position interested in confirming their ambitions of epistemic jurisdiction over the other? If, for Bonaventure, the 'Relexification Dialogues' serve as a published archive for future projects, incorporating an expansive personal and professional discursivization of his curatorial thought, they might equally well be conceptualized as forms of fieldwork on Jonas's part, and thus again be incorporated into the field of academic anthropology and publishing formats such as this book chapter. Therefore, Bonaventure and Jonas attempted to maintain and attune to a tone of conversation, and a general intention throughout these dialogues, which aims at a recursive outcome – namely, an attempt to alter their positions and thinking about their own and each other's practice by *talking* about shared concerns (encapsulated in keywords, concepts, places, reference points) from often shared fields (e.g. Berlin, Athens, Dakar) and experiences (e.g. shows they have seen together).

Besides these recursive moments of our overlapping curatorial fields, we would like to draw out a set of further observations from our above analyses. First, an obvious question is about the kinds of curatorships we are dealing with in our ethnographic contexts. There are certainly some overlaps – in particular, neither is what we might term 'traditional curatorship', especially in that neither begins from an existing collection of objects that is 'cared after' and put on show. Both exist in some ways outside established structures, the Berlin Exhibition team having been created specifically for this one purpose and existing only temporarily as an organizational structure, and SAVVY being an independent yet publicly funded institution encompassing a broad range of activities encompassing artistic, but also activist, academic, even spiritual or anthropological, realms. Moreover, both – and especially their charismatic directors, Paul Spies and Bonaventure Soh Bejeng Ndikung respectively – position themselves, albeit in different ways, in what might even be called an 'ethnographic' stance of critically reflecting on Berlin and its institutions, including the Humboldt Forum. At the same time, however, the Berlin Exhibition, as part of the Humboldt Forum, remains more within those structures; what feels 'radical' or 'critical' here is not identical with how the same ideas are perceived at SAVVY. In addition, SAVVY draws mostly from the context of artistic practices, discourses and objects, and sees its position as contributing primarily to creating different protocols and parameters from this field of publishing and theorizing, whereas the curators of the Berlin Exhibition position themselves more within participatory exhibition development aimed at wider publics, including artistic practice within this, rather than as a self-referential field in itself. To achieve the former, individual curators at SAVVY are encouraged to articulate their own positions in the kinds of concept papers Bonaventure mentions in his dialogues with Jonas; whereas curators at the Berlin Exhibition were encouraged to draw on individual strengths and creativity to contribute to what became a collective project that will result in a single, albeit multivocal, exhibition.

Second, what generative consequences do each of these fields then have for our possible ways of thinking of a curatorial anthropology, that is, one that explores the protocols of exhibitions and modes of display, viewing curating as 'an event of knowledge' (Martinon and Rogoff 2013: ix)? For us, curatorial practice thus conceived undoubtedly offers a modality of engaging with wider audiences, as alternatives to the predominantly wordy modes of anthropological expression. Moreover, a recursive curatorial anthropology that would pay greater attention to the protocols of its discursive formation and to the development of ideas, to their 'staging', in Rogoff's words – not as a reflection on method, but as a way of doing anthropology – might have the effect of producing generative tensions across the still widely entrenched discrete stages of research design, fieldwork, writing-up and theorizing. It would also allow for an opening-up of formats and protocols of communication – moving perhaps closer to a conceptual ethnographic enterprise as outlined by Nikolai Ssorin-Chaikov (2013). But perhaps some of this is already happening, and we may just need to reframe our way of looking at our own practices. Some of the museums we are studying in Berlin, for instance, are after all 'not only … part of a familiar Western cultural framework, [but] it also offer parallels and overlaps with ethnography's own institutional context, politics and practices'. In other words, they 'mirror … and collide … with aspects of the ethnographic endeavour itself' (Macdonald 1997: 161), thus offering a possibility for a 'parallel context' (ibid.) or a recursive curatorial ethnography in dialogue with debates on an anthropology at home.

Our proposal might seem to move back from curatorial practice to anthropology, but we also detect another possibility. Instead of analysing what curating can do for anthropology, we would like to see the prospect of a recursive curatorial field for anthropology in an invitation for anthropology to transgress itself. As Roger Sansi (2018: 124) has suggested in relation to the recursivity of the gift, maybe we can also, in this context, shift the focus towards seeing the relation between the curatorial and anthropology as a possibility for a mutual becoming of something else. But rather than speculating on abandoning anthropology or declaring it at an end (Jebens and Kohl 2011), we prefer to think of the recursivity of the curatorial as a field that invites anthropology to attend to possible metamorphoses or transgressions of itself without becoming unrecognizable. This means retaining recognition of the distinct nature of our respective endeavours while not seeing these as completed or immutable. In conversation about the concept 'recursivity' Bonaventure once asked: 'What if one were to have a broken mirror facing another broken mirror?' Acknowledging that our respective projects are incomplete and riddled with cracks – that is, as productively rather than fatally 'broken' – is precisely what can allow for an energizing experimentation with anthropological formats, practices and concepts in a recursive relation with the curatorial.

Acknowledgements

We thank those in our research fields at the Berlin Exhibition and at SAVVY for their discussion and input. In particular we are grateful to the following for their

54 *The Anthropologist as Curator*

contribution and feedback on earlier drafts of this article: Bonaventure Soh Bejeng Ndikung; Pia Chakraverti-Wuerthwein; Brinda Sommer; and Paul Spies. Our colleagues at CARMAH are an ongoing source of lively discussion and inspiration. We also acknowledge the Alexander von Humboldt Foundation for funding our research as part of Sharon Macdonald's Alexander von Humboldt Professorship. None of those mentioned here bear responsibility for any shortcomings of our work.

Notes

1 The French version of the sentence reads: 'Comme l'ethnographe, le commissaire contemporain est une créature vouée a l'errance, hormis a l'instant present […]'. (Enwezor et al. 2012: 21).

2 French version: 'Le commissaire est-il un compagnon de voyage de l'ethnographe, partageant ses procédures de mise en contact et d'exploration?' (ibid.).

3 For an overview of the project, visit www.carmah.berlin (last accessed 9 October 2018).

4 For more information on SAVVY Contemporary and the Berlin Exhibition, see Tinius 2018 and https://www.stadtmuseum.de/humboldt-forum (last accessed 4 December 2018), respectively.

5 Indeed, at the time of a first draft of this chapter (October 2018), the 'Curating/ Knowledge' Ph.D. programme at Goldsmiths, University of London, from which the cited volume arose, celebrated its 12th anniversary with a conference on the relationship between curating and knowledge – thus perhaps offsetting to some slight extent Rogoff's own earlier observation that there is little cumulative or at least discursively reflected history on curating and the curatorial. A brief description of the event *C/K12* at the Department of Visual Culture of Goldsmiths, University of London (11 October 2018), which included a talk by Ndikung, can be found here: https://www.gold.ac.uk/calendar/?id=11832 (last accessed 5 December 2018).

6 This was initiated in 2015 by an Alexander von Humboldt research professorship granted to Sharon Macdonald. For further details see http://www.carmah.berlin/ making-differences-in-berlin/ (last accessed 9 December 2018).

7 From this point we use our first names, as those are how we refer to each other and are how we were primarily referred to in our field-sites.

8 The Institute of European Ethnology in which CARMAH is located.

9 In particular, a notion of 'creative co-production' – originally developed by Tal Adler – is central to the TRACES (Transmitting Contentious Cultural Heritages with the Arts: From Intervention to Co-Production), funded as part of the Horizon 2020 *Reflective Society* programme. That project's work package 5, *Contentious Collections,* led by Sharon Macdonald, is based in CARMAH, as are Tal Adler and Anna Szöke, who also work on the project's *Dead Images* creative co-production. Creative co-productions are teams of artists, researchers and cultural institution staff who work on a problem, jointly developing techniques to tackle it, over a long period of time. See http://www. traces.polimi.it (last accessed 14 October 2018).

10 For more information on the project, visit: https://savvy-contemporary.com/en/projec ts/2018/the-dog-done-gone-deaf/ (last accessed 14 October 2018).

References

Balzer, David (2015), *Curationism: How Curating Took Over the Art World and Everything Else*, London: Pluto.

Barber, Karin (2007), *An Anthropology of Texts, Persons, and Publics*, Cambridge: Cambridge University Press.

Basu, Paul and Sharon Macdonald, eds. (2007), *Exhibition Experiments*, London: Wiley-Blackwell.

Binder, Beate (2009), *Streitfall Stadtmitte. Der Berliner Schlossplatz*, Cologne: Böhlau.

Boltanski, Luc and Ève Chiapello (2007 [1999]), *The New Spirit of Capitalism*, Trans. Gregory Elliott, London; New York: Verso.

Bose, Friedrich von (2016), *Das Humboldt Forum. Eine Ethnografie seiner Planung*, Berlin: Kadmos.

Boyer, Dominic (2008), 'Thinking through the Anthropology of Experts', *Anthropology in Action*, 15 (2): 38–46.

Bröckling, Ulrich (2007), *Das unternehmerische Selbst. Soziologie einer Subjektivierungsform*, Frankfurt: Suhrkamp.

Canclini, Néstor García, (2014), *Art beyond Itself: Anthropology for a Society without a Storyline*, Durham, NC: Duke University Press.

CARMAH (2018), *Otherwise: Rethinking Museums and Heritage. CARMAH Paper #1*. Berlin: Centre for Anthropological Research on Museums and Heritage (open-access publication) DOI: http://www.carmah.berlin/wp-content/uploads/2017/10/Carmah_Paper-1.pdf (last accessed 8 October 2018).

Davis, Tracy C. and Thomas Postlewait (2003), 'Theatricality: An Introduction', in Tracy C. Davis and Thomas Postlewait (eds), *Theatricality*, 1–39, Cambridge: Cambridge University Press.

DeGraff, Michel (2002), 'Relexification: A Reevaluation', *Anthropological Linguistics*, 44 (4): 321–414.

Enwezor, Okwui (2012), 'Intense Proximité: de la disparition des distances', in *Intense Proximité. Une Anthologie du Proche et Du Lointain. La Triennale 2012*, 18–36, Paris: Éditions Artlys.

Förster, Larissa, Iris Edenheiser, Sarah Fründt and Heike Hartmann, eds. (2018), *Provenienzforschung zu ethnografischen Sammlungen der Kolonialzeit. Positionen in der aktuellen Debatte*, e-publication, Berlin: Humboldt. DOI: https://doi.org/10.18452/19029 (last accessed 6 October 2018).

Foster, Hal (1995), 'The Artist as Ethnographer?' in George Marcus and Fred Myer (eds), *The Traffic in Culture: Refiguring Art and Anthropology*, 302–9, Berkeley: University of California Press.

Franklin, Sarah (2013), '*In Vitro Anthropos*: New Conception Models for a Recursive Anthropology?' *Cambridge Anthropology* 31 (1): 3–32.

Gielen, Pascal and Paul De Bruyne, eds. (2012), *Teaching Art in the Neoliberal Realm: Realism versus Cynicism*, Amsterdam: Valiz.

Holbraad, Martin (2012), *Truth in Motion: The Recursive Anthropology of Cuban Divination*, Chicago; London: The University of Chicago Press.

Holbraad, Martin (2013), 'Scoping Recursivity: A Comment on Franklin and Napier', *Cambridge Anthropology*, 31 (2): 123–7.

Holbraad, Martin and Morten Axel Pedersen (2017), *The Ontological Turn: An Anthropological Exposition*, Cambridge: Cambridge University Press.

Jebens, Holger and Karl-Heinz Kohl (eds) (2011), *The End of Anthropology?* Canon Pyon: Sean Kingston Publishing.

Macdonald, Sharon (1997), 'The Museum as Mirror: Ethnographic Reflections', in Andrew Dawson, Jenny Hockey and Allison James (eds), *After Writing Culture: Epistemology and Praxis in Contemporary Anthropology*, ASA Monographs 34. London; New York: Routledge.

Schneider, Arnd (2015), 'Towards a New Hermeneutics of Art and Anthropology Collaborations', *EthnoScripts*, 17 (1): 23–30.

Macdonald, Sharon, ed. (1997), *The Politics of Display: Museums, Science, Culture*, London; New York: Routledge.

Macdonald, Sharon, Christine Gerbich and Margareta von Oswald (2018), 'No Museum Is an Island: Ethnography beyond Methodological Containerism', *Museum & Society*, 16 (2): 138–56.

Martinon, Jean-Paul (2013), 'Introduction', in Jean-Paul Martinon (ed.), *The Curatorial: A Philosophy of Curating*, 1–13, London: Bloomsbury.

Martinon, Jean-Paul and Irit Rogoff (2013), 'Preface', in Jean-Paul Martinon (ed.), *The Curatorial: A Philosophy of Curating*, viii–xi, London: Bloomsbury.

Ndikung, Bonaventure Soh Bejeng and Jonas Tinius (2017), 'Introduction', in *Relexication Dialogues: Across Anthropology and Curating*. Unpublished manuscript.

Obrist, Hans-Ulrich (2008), *A Brief History of Curating*, Paris: Les Presses du Réel.

O'Neill, Paul (ed.) (2012), *The Culture of Curating and the Curating of Culture(s)*, Cambridge, MA: MIT Press.

Oswald, Margareta von (2016), 'La Triennale: Entre Négociations et volontarisme', *Cahiers d'Études Africaines*, LVI (3), 223: 679–98.

Rogoff, Irit (2013), 'The Expanding Field', in Jean-Paul Martinon (eds), *The Curatorial: A Philosophy of Curating*, 41–8, London: Bloomsbury.

Sansi, Roger (2015), *Art, Anthropology, and the Gift*, London: Bloomsbury.

Sansi, Roger (2018), 'The Recursivity of the Gift in Art and Anthropology', in Gretchen Bakke and Marina Peterson (eds), *Between Matter and Method: Encounters in Anthropology and Art*, 117–30, London: Bloomsbury.

Sansi, Roger (2020), 'Introduction', in Roger Sansi (ed.), *The Anthropologist as Curator*, London: Bloomsbury.

Siegenthaler, Fiona (2013), 'Towards an Ethnographic Turn in Contemporary Art Scholarship', *Critical Arts: South-North Cultural and Media Studies*, 27 (6): 737–52.

Schneider, Arnd and Chris Wright, eds. (2005), *Contemporary Art and Anthropology*, Oxford: Berg Publishers.

Schneider, Arnd and Chris Wright, eds. (2010), *Between Art and Anthropology: Contemporary Ethnographic Perspectives*, London: Bloomsbury.

Schneider, Arnd and Chris Wright, eds. (2013), *Anthropology and Art Practice*, London: Bloomsbury.

Simon, Nina (2010), *The Participatory Museum*, Santa Cruz: Museum 2.0.

Smith, Terry (2012), *Thinking Contemporary Curating*, New York: ICI.

Smith, Terry (2015), *Talking Contemporary Curating*, New York: ICI.

Ssorin-Chaikov, Nikolai (2013), 'Ethnographic Conceptualism: An Introduction', *Laboratorium*, 5 (2): 5–18.

Tinius, Jonas (2017), *Sparring Partners: An Introduction to the Gallery Reflections Series*, Berlin: ifa-Galerie.

Tinius, Jonas (2018), 'Awkward Art and Difficult Heritage: Nazi Art Collectors and Postcolonial Archives', in Thomas Fillitz and Paul van der Grijp (eds), *An Anthropology of Contemporary Art*, 130–45, London: Bloomsbury.

Tinius, Jonas (forthcoming), 'The Anthropologist as Sparring Partner: Collaborative Fieldwork, Curatorial Practice, and Postcolonial Critique', *Berliner Blätter. Ethnologische und Ethnografische Schriften.*

4

Whose stories about Africa? Reflexivity and public dialogue at the Royal Ontario Museum

Silvia Forni

Since its inception as an academic discipline, anthropology has been linked in many ways to museums. This connected history has been shaped by disciplinary paradigm shifts whereby collections inspired by positivistic scientific goals were progressively deconstructed as expressions of the power relationships at the root of collecting practices rather than as an 'objective' representation of 'other' cultures (Stocking 1985; Shelton 2006). The mid-1980s were a moment of reckoning in the social sciences that deeply shaped curatorial practice in ethnographic museums in the latter part of the twentieth century. The self-reflexive theoretical shift, questioning the objectivity of anthropological accounts (Clifford and Marcus 1986; Marcus and Fischer 1986), was echoed by scholars taking a critical look at museums and collections and their role in civil society (Ames 1986; Vergo 1989; Karp, Kreamer and Lavine 1991). Far from being *heterotopias* (Foucault 1972, 1986) removed from the flow and messiness of social life and biological rules, museums, particularly those with world-ranging collections, had to come to terms with the deeply colonial premises of their institutional foundations and the contemporary legacies of these beginnings (Clifford 1988:189–251). While the pace and the depth of change varied greatly from institution to institution, by the end of the 1980s it was clear that the authoritative voice of the museums was increasingly scrutinized and challenged by politically active members of communities that claimed historical connections with the materials exhibited in the museums' public galleries or held in their seemingly inaccessible repositories. The Royal Ontario Museum (ROM) in Toronto was the theatre of one of the oft-quoted museum confrontations of this era.[1] In this chapter, I explore some of the complications that anthropologists as curators face when moving from the theoretical domain of academic debate, to the much more complex sphere of public engagement. Through the case study of the ROM's African section, where I have been working as a curator since 2008, I address the difficult path of developing new forms of exhibitions and programmes that can address concerns relevant to museum audiences and communities in the twenty-first century, while also engaging in serious and respectful ways with the materiality of collections. As an anthropologist working in a museum, I am well aware of the fraught history that lies at the origin of the encyclopaedic museum, and the lasting power imbalances that are still present in the dialogic and collaborative museum projects of the twenty-first century.

Yet, as proposed by Sharon Macdonald, Henrietta Lidchi and Margaret von Oswald, I also believe it is possible, or at least worthwhile, to work on projects that can contribute to more convivial relationships in the complex cosmopolitan societies in which we live. While museums are not outside society's power dynamics, they can be places of experimentation that can 'contribute toward more cordial forms of social relations across past and existing divides' (Macdonald, Lidchi and von Oswald 2017: 103)

Authoritative museum positioning gone awry: *Into the Heart of Africa*

The ROM's African collection was never a museum highlight, despite being part of the institutional encyclopaedic vision since its founding in 1914. Without the oversight of a specialized curator, the ROM's African holdings grew over the years through donations from donors who spent part of their lives on the African continent as military, missionaries, volunteers and academics, and individuals who had become fascinated with African aesthetics and collected works through galleries and dealers. For the first seven decades of the life of the museum, the African collection was assigned as a secondary field to anthropology curators specializing in other regions of the world.

In the mid-1980s, anthropologist Jean Cannizzo was hired as contract curator to develop an exhibition that would highlight this sizeable but rarely displayed material. After surveying the collection, and assessing its strengths but also its numerous gaps, Cannizzo decided to approach the project as an opportunity to experiment, in the gallery space, with the insights of current theories. When conceiving the display, she envisioned a three-pronged presentation that, at one level, explored the imperial history of museum collections and reflected on the constructed nature of ethnographic truths; at a second level, experimented with different forms of exhibition design, highlighting how this dimension could affect the way we perceive and appreciate an object; and at the third level, provided insight into the ethnographic context of production of the artworks themselves.

The title of the exhibition, *Into the Heart of Africa*, was changed shortly before the opening from *Into the Heart of Darkness*. In both versions, it was a clear reference to Joseph Conrad's famous novel *Heart of Darkness*, but also to the less known, yet similarly historically situated, 1874 account by Georg Schweinfurth, *The Heart of Africa*. Positioning the gaze and the interpretation strictly on the side of the European colonial agents and collectors unmistakeably singled out the first thematic prong – addressing the colonial history of collections – as the driving theme of the exhibition. And it is precisely this approach that became violently contentious.

The first galleries of *Into the Heart of Africa* were intended to challenge the authoritative positioning of the museum as a privileged location for telling stories about 'others' and turn the reflection to 'ourselves' by questioning the colonial origin of the collection and exposing the uneven and violent power dynamics that framed the colonial encounter and shaped museum collections. In the catalogue, that provided a clear statement of the theoretical framing of the exhibition, Cannizzo reflected on 'the transformational power of context [which] suggests that the meaning and significance of an object change according to the circumstances in which it appears and is understood' (1989: 12). Aware of the open-ended communicative potential of exhibitions where 'the meaning of the collections is generated in the interaction between the curator, the object, and the visitor', Cannizzo saw museums as 'negotiated realities ... crucial to understanding one's cultural self as well as the ethnographic other' (ibid.). Yet, despite the cutting-edge theoretical framing, which echoed the most recent calls for a different type of museology expressed, among others, by James Clifford (1986) and Brian Durrans (1988), the curator and the museum were quite unprepared for the backlash that occurred when members of the African-Canadian community responded to the invitation to approach 'the museum as an artefact' and read the 'collections as cultural texts' (Cannizzo 1989: 92). The postmodern approach used in the exhibition, which used quotation marks as an ironic framing and distancing device from the outrageous quotes extracted from colonial and missionary sources, was seen by the protesters as an expression of liberal white privilege, completely out of touch with the complex reality of racism and injustice still very much alive in Canadian society.

After the opening, protesters from the local African-Canadian community challenged the tone and approach chosen by the institution and criticized both the vision and the authority of the curator. The pickets in front of the museum, led by a group called the Coalition for the Truth about Africa (CFTA), called for a dismantling of the display, which they read as a highly problematic extension of the power imbalance at the core of the colonial enterprise. By enlarging racist colonial images on its walls and reproducing verbatim the words of militaries and missionaries, without taking a clear critical stance, the museum was, in the eye of its critics, reproducing racist stereotypes that continued to undermine the agency and humanity of African people. As poignantly pointed out by NourbeSe Philip (1991) in her thoughtful and lucid critique of the exhibition, one of the main epistemological impasses resulted from the way the museum reacted to the protesters. By completely dismissing their critiques and hiding behind the smoke wall of academic authority, the museum failed to acknowledge that the claims of the young people picketing the museum were in fact a request by the African-Canadian 'readers' to be able to share in the interpretation of this 'cultural text' from a different perspective. As an experiment in self-reflexivity, *Into the Heart of Africa* intended to be an opportunity to reflect on 'the complexities of cross-cultural encounters' (Cannizzo 1989: 92), but only according to parameters established by the institution itself. 'Very much in keeping with that now notorious picture of the white missionary woman teaching African women how to wash clothes, the cross-cultural encounter that the curator saw as a possibility, could only happen if it went in one direction – from the repository of knowledge and power – the ROM – to the subject people – irrational and emotional African Canadians' (Philip 1991: 74).

The events surrounding *Into the Heart of Africa*, highlighted the very different impact that postmodern reflexivity can have when put into practice outside the walls of academia. Indeed, self-reflexivity, shared authority and the notion of culture as 'contested, temporal and emergent' (Clifford and Marcus 1986:19) were, by the 1980s, widely accepted theoretical and methodological foundations of anthropological research and writing. Yet in the making of the exhibition and in its public presentation, these insights were mostly lost in the reiteration of the authoritative voice of the museum. Despite the sensitive theoretical framing of the catalogue, both the display and the handling of the protesters on the part of the ROM's management clearly positioned cultural authority squarely in the museum's field, dismissing alternative perspectives and refusing to recognize the Black protesters at their doorstep as legitimately sharing in the construction of the cultural significance of the objects and the stories put on display

As highlighted by many of its critics, this exhibition failed on several different levels. The choice to use irony rather than expressing a clear critique was seen by Linda Hutcheon as being 'postmodernly deconstructive' without being 'postcolonially oppositional' (1994: 222). Also, despite its intention to be multi-pronged and despite its claim of presenting multiple perspectives rather that a single interpretation or a grand master narrative, the exhibition did not engage in the 'postmodern dialogic museum mode' (Hutcheon 1994: 224). No African voices or counter-narratives were included in the display. The only voices that could be heard loud and clear were those of the missionaries or colonial agents, while the African perspective was left to be decoded from the artworks on display, though even these were presented through pretty standard Western museological conventions and framed as objects of art or ethnography based on Western taxonomies. In addition to the exhibition's shortcomings, no real dialogue was entered into with the protesters, whose knowledge and 'truth' were dismissed and judged as ungrounded and irrelevant from an academic standpoint.

After its time at the ROM, *Into the Heart of Africa* did not travel to any of the other venues that had originally requested to host it. While the exhibition itself imploded, it had long-lasting effects of the life of many individuals involved in these events, from the curator to the leaders of the protest, some of whom were arrested and targeted by the police long after the end of the picketing. It also left a lingering strain in the relationship between the museum and the Black community of the greater Toronto area, something that was still being felt over two decades later.

Opening space and accepting failure: a journey towards decolonization

Despite its self-reflexive intentions, by refusing to engage in a serious dialogue with the protesters, the museum unquestionably positioned voice and authority in the realm of white-dominated academic discourse. As a public institution it failed to listen to the constituency it claimed to want to engage, and, in doing so, had perpetuated the fundamentally racist and exclusionary attitudes prevalent in the so-called multicultural Canadian society of the late 1980s.[2]

The degree to which the events surrounding *Into the Heart of Africa* were still an unresolved issue in the relationship between the ROM and the Black community did not become fully apparent to me until a few years into my tenure at the museum. Since the protest, the ROM could count a number of projects that were done in collaboration with Black partners and, on the surface, the protest seemed to be ancient history. Yet, as projects would encounter obstacles, tensions would easily arise and the ghost of the past would re-emerge, tainting communication and outcomes. This continuing resurfacing of the memory and, in the case of people who were involved or present at the time of the protest, the trauma generated by the dismissal and silencing operated by the museum in 1989, were significant obstacles in changing the way people from the Black community would engage (or not) with the museum. Certainly, the museum had not fully acknowledged its responsibility in the debacle and had never responded to the protesters' demands. This was not forgotten by many of the members of the local Black community who, quite understandably, refused to see the institution as a place where their stories could be heard.

As an outsider to the community, I was very aware that the only way to attempt to break this vicious cycle was to ground every project in dialogue and collaboration, expecting no miracle or quick answer, and being prepared for failure. As aptly observed by Ivan Karp, 'collaboration is an opportunity to fail in the most splendid way' (quoted in Silverman 2015: 1). Indeed, collaboration is often not a solution. Collaborative projects have high potential of failing or falling short of expectations, of becoming a new, potentially conflictive, 'contact zone' (Pratt 1992: 6–7, Clifford 1997: 192). Collaboration is messy, difficult to control and direct. In addition, museum collaboration usually still occurs in situations of unequal power relationships where the institution ultimately remains in control of the final message delivered to the public (Bennet 1998; Boast 2011). Yet, engaging in this process of itself has the potential to generate outcomes that can contribute to shape and transform institutional practices.[3]

While the projects that I initiated at the ROM since 2008, were all developed through some level of consultation and collaboration with community partners, in 2013, thanks to the willingness of independent curators Julie Crooks and Dominique Fontaine to engage longer term with the museum, we were able to develop an initiative explicitly directed at rethinking and redressing some of the issues that had continued to haunt the museum since 1989.

Of Africa, as the initiative was called, took impetus from a number of exchanges with colleagues and community partners and was grounded in the initial concept presented to the ROM by Julie Crooks and Dominique Fontaine. Starting in 2014, Crooks, Fontaine and I worked on the development of a multi-year and multi-platform project addressing issues of presentation and representation of Africa and its diaspora in mainstream museums that would also take into account the specific history and challenges that the ROM needed to address. I will not enter in the details of the project that has been discussed elsewhere (Forni 2017; Forni, Crooks and Fontaine 2019). Here I would like to focus on some of the elements *Of Africa's* methodology that more closely connect to recent concerns at the core of critical museology and more recent museum anthropological theorization.

Unlike typical museum projects, *Of Africa* did not start with predetermined outcomes, but more as a conceptual umbrella under which to organize our activities and engage various partners and advisers in dialogue and assessment. Working with an advisory committee of academics, artists, curators and educators, we were able to narrow down a few important issues that needed to be addressed in order to start

64 *The Anthropologist as Curator*

building a different foundation for the relationship between the museum and the Black community.

In the first year we identified three paths of action: on the one hand, we decided to organize a few smaller exhibitions that would intervene and complicate the narrative of the museum's permanent displays; on the other, we pursued public programmes that would present a variety of points of view on issues relating to African and diasporic art and history.[4] Alongside these public-facing initiatives, we also decided to attempt to contact some of the protesters of 1989, and see if there was a willingness to resolve the issues that had been lingering for over two decades.

The choice to rely not only on exhibitions and lectures, but to create public spaces of dialogue to open up space to the voices that were not heard in the late 1980s was a purposeful attempt at a decolonial move. Although we were working within the strictures of the institution, the relatively low budget and the open-endedness of the project allowed us to move one step at a time, allowing the possibility for different forms of enunciations as the dialogue proceeded. I am using here the concept of 'enunciation' as theorized by decolonial thinkers Walter Mignolo and Rolando Vazquez (2013), for whom the decolonial option is enacted not through representation, but through enunciations that are uncoupled from colonial logics.

The 2014 two-day symposium entitled *Of Africa: Histories, Collections, Reflections* was prefaced by a private event where the leaders of the CFTA were invited to meet with the museum director and senior staff and reflect on the incidents of twenty-five years earlier. That event, and the first day of the public symposium, were marked by palpable tension and pain. At the same time, this coming together for the first time in over two decades also opened up the possibility of a dialogue and for different forms of enunciations to be heard. The exchanges that followed this first encounter continued to highlight the tensions between the desire of the institution to be in control and the demands that the CFTA brought to the fore on behalf of the Black community. And this ultimately was not a surprise. More than fifty years ago, Frantz Fanon had described the process of decolonizing and bringing change to the established order as 'a program of complete disorder [that] … cannot come as a result of magical practices, nor of a natural shock, nor of a friendly understanding' (1963: 36). Yet the desire of both parties to stay in the conversation and figure out a way forward finally resulted in an official apology on the part of the museum that was publicly accepted by three of the leaders of the CFTA on 9 November 9 2016.[5] In many ways, the dialogic process initiated by *Of Africa* helped to put in motion the necessary work of exposing the historical wound that affected the relationship and, in doing so, hopefully to make it possible for a process of healing to begin.

The positive response to the apology, even after so many years, highlighted the importance of acknowledgement and dialogue as the foundation for an engaged museum practice, which not only encompasses exhibitions but also every other aspect of museum work. In the last part of this chapter, I focus on two of the more recent manifestations of the *Of Africa* initiative as concrete examples of outcomes of this vision and process.

The exhibition, *Here We Are Here: Black Canadian Contemporary Art* that opened at the Royal Ontario Museum on 26 January 26 2018 is in many ways the culmination of the process started four years before. It featured the work of nine Canadian artists, Sandra Brewster, Michèle Pearson Clarke, Chantal Gibson, Sylvia D. Hamilton, Bushra Junaid, Charmaine Lurch, Esmaa Mohamoud, Dawit L. Petros and Gordon Shadrach, who reflect on the history and contemporary presence of Blackness in Canadian society. Rather than selecting pre-existing works from these artists, we decided to request that each submit a proposal and develop the exhibition, allowing time and space for the artists to share their ideas and interact with one another.[6] During two workshops, one at the beginning, and one half-way through the development, we met to discuss the ideas underlying the exhibition and the individual works as well as the technical challenges encountered during the production. Though each artist worked in a different medium and with a very personal agenda in mind, the workshops created a shared understanding of the exhibition, which in many ways enhanced the dialogue between the artworks. Positioned in an open rectangular gallery, in a high-flow area of the museum, *Here We Are Here* gave prominent space to a conversation that had never before been enunciated at the ROM.

The placement at the core of the encyclopaedic museum, was quite noticeable as it created a visible rupture in installation style. The exhibition did not follow the factual and authoritative style of the galleries surrounding it. It avoided strong overarching narratives or cathartic solutions. Most of all, it strived to introduce a sense of doubt, a moment of reflection, a space to pause. Significantly, the exhibition was framed on either end by sound pieces: on one side the almost haunting chant of names of enslaved Africans, free Black Loyalists from the American Revolutionary War, and free Black Refugees from the War of 1812 living in Nova Scotia at the turn of the twentieth century recovered by Sylvia Hamilton's archival research; on the other side, the hissing sound of Michèle Pearson Clarke's *Suck Teeth Composition (After Rashaad Newsome)*, a gesture of frustration, disappointment and disbelief shared by Black people on both sides of the Atlantic. Different in tone and aesthetic, these two pieces provided an effective framing for the show by claiming a space of enunciation, of re-humanization and of frustration for the continued denial of presence and belonging to people of African descent from the Canadian historic narrative, but also from the permanent displays of its museums. While all the pieces in the exhibit claimed presence in different ways, they also connected through a variety of other thematic threads: violence of history, memory of slavery, emotional cartographies, family histories, self-fashioning, political engagement. The result was not a unified narrative, but a space of interrogation, of questioning and of reflection, guided by different artistic voices and perspectives. *Here We Are Here,* did not wrap things up in a neat and 'feel good' way. It created a space where that wound of the continual denial of Blackness in White Canada could be exposed, as the starting point for possible reparation and healing.[7]

Reparation and healing were also at the core of another important event that was part of the programmes offered alongside the exhibition.[8] On 10 April 2018 Canadian poet NourbeSe Philip performed her poem *Zong!* in the historic entrance of the museum, the same entrance that was picketed by the protesters in 1989. *Zong!* is one of Philips's best known poetic masterpieces. A long poem composed from the fragments of the trial records known as the *Zong* case. This trial reflects the legal battle between the insurance company and the owner of the slave ship *Zong*, who, on November 29 1781, threw overboard 150 live enslaved Africans somewhere in the Atlantic Ocean between the coast of West Africa and the Island of Jamaica. As described by Philip,

> *Zong!*, the poem, is composed entirely from the words of the found text, Gregson vs. Gilbert. Through fragments of voices, shreds of memory and shards of silence, *Zong!* unravels the story that can only be told by not telling. It is participatory and ritual; an interplay between noise and silence. *Zong!* performs even as it unperforms ideas of history and memory, haunting a space where Ancestral voices join with ours through spoken word, music, video, movement and improvisation to create a polyvocal, counterpointed soundscape immersed in the amnesia of history and memory. (http://www.nourbese.com/zong/ consulted on 30 October 2018)

While every *Zong!* performance is an immersive improvisation that works as cathartic memory and healing ritual, the ROM event had an added layer to it. For months before the performance NourbeSe and her crew (Vivine, Amai, Kobena and Y) visited with objects from the collection, many of which were part of the *Into the Heart of Africa* display. The relationship established with the objects was integrated in the performance, which took place in their presence. Set on tables right by the drummers, the objects were present as witness and as material extensions of those ancestors whose lost memory acts as a continuing haunting presence in the diasporic experience.[9] This framework is a recurrent feature in Black literature and theory. In Black studies, *hauntology* is a discursive trope referring to the way in which haunting, spectres and ghosts have been used to recall the constant presence of the past, namely the transatlantic slave trade, and to express how that trauma continues to 'haunt' the present (McDougall 2016: 50). In the ROM performance, the trauma re-enacted in the presence of the spirit of the ancestors was twofold: the mourning of the victims of the *Zong* massacre and the memory of the trauma generated by *Into the Heart of Africa*. Once more the performance did not offer a solution, nor did it absolve anyone. Yet, it created a space of deep emotional connection, energy, vulnerability and strength that made it possible for those present to participate in the pain and aspire to move beyond. NourbeSe Philip's performance also strongly affirmed the relevance of the African collection in the life of diaspora Africans living in Canada. In this context the objects were not just spoils of colonialism, they became material anchors of ancestral memories, fellow displaced beings, travel companions in a journey of re-signification and rediscovery.

Months after the performance, the visitation continues. As new material and emotional relationships are being forged, the possibility of new forms of display and interventions in the museum space are being generated. It is our hope that this slow and uncertain process will be able to account for the ongoing affective presence of displaced material in the museum context, and inspire displays that can account for the multiple truths about Africa that museum objects embody and elicit.

As pointed out by Raymond Silverman 'there are multiple epistemologies, multiple "ways of knowing", that often meet and coalesce in the objects upon which various meanings have been inscribed' (2015: 3). Understanding these different meanings, learning about these different knowledges is a process grounded in communication and respect. While these dialogic or 'interrogative' (Karp and Kratz 2015) processes do not guarantee successful outcomes, they nevertheless attempt to challenge the 'declarative, indicative, or even imperative' curatorial modalities associated with a type of museology grounded in academic authority (Thomas 2010: 10). The inability of the ROM to release control and truly embrace the postcolonial theoretical orientation that it claimed created a controversy with a long-lasting legacy. *Of Africa* proposed to counter this with a more open-ended approach that would present issues and questions rather than offer solutions. The cautious yet positive response to this approach on the part of the local Black community has been an encouragement to keep moving in this direction. While this dialogic approach will not undo the past, nor erase the still-present power imbalance of the relationship between the museum and the community, it may however be a worthy pursuit. As recently pointed out by Sharon Macdonald, Henrietta Lidchi and Margareta von Oswald, this critically optimistic approach may be an effective counter to the 'fear of otherness, and … troubled relationship across alterity, that so often characterizes the postcolonial' (2017: 95). Inspired by the critical humanism and 'demotic cosmopolitanism' of Paul Gilroy (2004), this approach offers a path to reanimate colonial collections in a way that can imbue new meaning and relevance to the vestiges of a problematic past.

Acknowledgements

This article reflects many years of discussion and collaboration with a large number of people. It is impossible for me to list all of those who have contributed to the ideas and project addressed in this chapter. Nevertheless I wish to acknowledge and thank a few key individuals. I am grateful to Julie Crooks and Dominique Fontaine who made *Of Africa* possible. The thoughts in this article are in many ways the result of our collective thinking. Yaw Akyeaw, Jean Augustine, Josh Basseches, Cheryl Blackman, Sandra Brewster, Shelley Butler, Michèle Pearson Clarke, Afua Cooper, Warren Crichlow, Wayne Dunkley, Pamela Edmonds, Mark Engstrom, Andrea Fatona, Rebecca Frerotte, Elizabeth Harney, Arlene Gehmacher, Chantal Gibson, Sylvia Hamilton, Sharon Irving, Francis Jeffers, Rostant Rico John, Karin Jones, Bushra Junaid, Erin Kerr, Cara Krmpotich, Charmaine Lurch, Connie MacDonald, Esmaa Mohamoud, Ken Montague, Geraldine Moriba, Ajamu Nangwaya, Chiedza Pasipanodya, NourbeSe Philip, Dan Rahimi, Gordon Shadrach, Gaetane Verna, Wendy Vincent, Rinaldo Walcott, Klive Walker, Genevieve Wallen, Natalie Woods, Jamea Zuberi were advisers, critics and collaborators in different phases of this project. This article reflects personal views and perspectives that may not be shared by all those mentioned above, yet the process and events discussed could not have been possible without their contribution. I also wish to acknowledge the critical financial support of the Royal Ontario Museum to the *Of Africa* initiative.

Notes

1 The controversy surrounding *Into the Heart of Africa* has been analysed by many scholars from a variety of disciplinary perspectives. Some of the more extensive references may be found in Ames 1991; Butler 1999, 2008, 2013; Cannizzo 1991; Clifford 1997; Crean 1991; Da Breo 1989; Forni 2017; Hutcheon 1994; Mackey 1995; Philip 1991; Riegel 1995; Schildkrout 1991; Shelton 2008.

2 The policy of multiculturalism was officially adopted by the government of Canada under Pierre Trudeau during the 1970s and 1980s. While the acceptance of this idea as a solution to racism is very strong among the white population of Canada, racism is a very common reality for members of the Black community. See, for example, Nelson and Nelson 2004. Racial tension in Toronto was very high at the time of the *Into the Heart of Africa* protest. Almost three decades later the Black Lives Matter movement highlighted the persistence of racial inequality and anti-Black violence in Canadian society in terms that were not so dissimilar to the ones being raised in the 1980s.

3 There is a vast literature on collaboration in museums, highlighting both the successes and the failures of these projects, as well their potential to obscure the persistence of patronizing colonial dynamics. My practice and the reflections in these pages have been influenced by the work of many, including: Karp, Kreamer and Lavine 1991; Peers and Brown 2003; Karp et al. 2006; Basu and Macdonald 2007; Boast 2011; Phillips 2011; Golding and Modest 2013; Krmpotich and Peers 2014; Bennet et al. 2017.

4 Many of the exhibitions and programmes realized under the *Of Africa* umbrella are described in Forni 2017 and Forni, Crooks and Fontaine 2019.

5 The content of the apology was discussed over several meetings by a committee composed of senior museum administrators and five members of the leadership of the CFTA. The final text condemned in very explicit terms the events of 1989:

> The Royal Ontario Museum produced the exhibition *Into the Heart of Africa*, which opened at the Museum in November 1989. This exhibition was intended to critically examine the colonial relationships and premises through which collections from African societies had entered museums. The exhibition displayed images and words that showed the fundamentally racist ideas and attitudes of early collectors and, in doing so, unintentionally reproduced the colonial, racist and Eurocentric premises through which these collections had been acquired. Thus, *Into the Heart of Africa* perpetuated an atmosphere of racism and the effect of the exhibition itself was racist. The ROM expresses its deep regret for having contributed to anti-African racism. The ROM also officially apologizes for the suffering endured by members of the African-Canadian community as a result of *Into the Heart of Africa*.

The ROM and the CFTA issued a joint press release on the day of the event, which was taken up by many mainstream and community publications, see https://www.rom.on.ca/en/about-us/newsroom/press-releases/royal-ontario-museum-and-the-coalition-for-the-truth-about-africa.

See also, for example, https://www.thestar.com/news/gta/2016/11/09/rom-apologizes-for-racist-1989-african-exhibit.html and http://www.theglobeandmail.com/news/toronto/royal-ontario-museum-offers-apology-for-racist-african-exhibition/article32784266/

6 This exhibition, like the broader project, was curated by Julie Crooks, Dominique Fontaine and myself. Dawit L. Petros's work *Sign* was the only piece that was not created expressly for the exhibition. The work was already part of the ROM collection and it was included in the exhibition for its thematic relevance.

7 This aspect of the exhibition was remarked upon in the many thoughtful reviews that appeared in newspapers and magazines. See, for example, Chris Rattan's piece in *Now Magazine* https://nowtoronto.com/culture/art-and-design/the-rom-here-we-are-here-pushes-back-narrow-views-blackness/; Murray White's review in the *Toronto Star*, https://www.thestar.com/entertainment/visualarts/2018/01/28/new-show-returns-rom-to-african-canadian-issues-and-scores-a-provocative-success.html; Felicity Tayler's piece in *Esse*, http://esse.ca/en/emeka-ogboh-power-plant-here-we-are-here-black-canadian-contemporary-art-royal-ontario-museum (last consulted on 30 October 2018).

8 A more complete list of programmes offered alongside the exhibition can be found on the museum's website, https://www.rom.on.ca/en/exhibitions-galleries/exhibitions/here-we-are-here-black-canadian-contemporary-art (last consulted on 30 October 2018).

9 A recording of the 10 April performance can be seen on YouTube https://www.youtube.com/watch?time_continue=16&v=BSp9UTU8YZo (last consulted on 30 October 2018).

References

Ames, M. (1991), 'Biculturalism in Museums', *Museum Anthropology*, 15 (2): 7–15.

Ames, M. (1986), *Museums, the Public and Anthropology*, New Delhi: Concept; Vancouver: UBC Press.

Basu, P. and S. Macdonald (2007), 'Introduction: Experiments in Exhibition, Ethnography, Art, and Science', in S. Macdonald and P. Basu (eds), *Exhibition Experiments*, 1–24, Oxford: Blackwell.

Bennett, T. (1998), *Culture: A Reformer's Science*, London: Sage.

Bennett T., F. Cameron, N. Dias, B. Dibley, R. Harrison, I. Jacknis and C. McCarthy (2017), *Collecting, Ordering, Governing: Anthropology, Museums, and Liberal Government*, Durham: Duke University Press.

Boast, R. (2011), 'Neocolonial Collaboration: Museum as Contact Zone Revisited', *Museum Anthropology*, 34 (1): 56–70.

Butler, S. R. (2013), 'Reflexive Museology: Lost and Found', in Andrea Witcomb and Kylie Message (eds), *The International Handbooks of Museum Studies*, 159–82, London: John Wiley & Sons.

Butler, S. (2008), *Contested Representations: Revisiting into the Heart of Africa*, Peterborough: Broadview Press.

Butler, S. R. (1999), *Contested Representations: Revisiting into the Heart of Africa*, Amsterdam: Gordon & Breach..

Cannizzo, J. (1991), 'Exhibiting Cultures: "Into the Heart of Africa"', *Visual Anthropology Review*, 7 (1): 150–60.

Cannizzo, J. (1989), *Into the Heart of Africa*, Toronto: Royal Ontario Museum.

Clifford, J. (1985), 'Objects and Selves – An Afterword', in G. Stocking (ed.), *Objects and Others: Essays on Museums and Material Culture*, 586–95, Madison: University of Wisconsin Press.

Clifford, J. (1988), *The Predicament of Culture: Twentieth-Century Ethnography, Literature, and Art*, Cambridge, MA: Harvard University Press.

Clifford, J. (1997), *Routes: Travel and Translation in the Late Twentieth Century*, Cambridge, MA: Harvard University Press.

70 *The Anthropologist as Curator*

Clifford, J. and G. Marcus (eds) (1986), *Writing Culture: The Politics and Poetics of Ethnography*, Berkeley: University of California Press.

Crean, S. (1991), 'Taking the Missionary Position', *This Magazine*, 24 (6): 23–8.

Da Breo, H. (1989–1990), 'Hazel A. Da Breo Interviews Dr. Jeanne Cannizzo', *Fuse*, 13: 36–7.

Durrans, B. (1988), 'The Future of the Other: Changing Cultures on Display in Ethnographic Museums', in R. Lumley (ed.), *The Museum Time-Machine: Putting Cultures on Display*, 144–69, London: Routledge.

Fanon, F. (1963), *The Wretched of the Earth*, New York: Grove Press.

Forni, S. (2017), 'Engaging Dialogues: Re-framing Africa at the Royal Ontario Museum', *Museum Worlds: Advances in Research*, 5: 197–210.

Forni S., J. Crooks and D. Fontaine (2019), 'Activism, Objects and Dialogues: Re-engaging African Collections at the Royal Ontario Museum', in R. Janes and R. Sandell (eds), *Museum Activism*, 186–96, London: Routledge.

Foucault, M. (1972), *The Archaeology of Knowledge*, trans. A. M. Sheridan Smith, New York: Pantheon.

Foucault, M. (1986) 'Of Other Spaces: Utopias, and Heterotopias', *Diacritics*, 16: 22–7.

Gilroy, P. (2004), *Postcolonial Melancholia*, New York: Columbia University Press.

Golding, V. and Modest, W., eds. (2013), *Museums and Communities: Curators, Collections and Collaboration*, London: Bloomsbury Academic.

Hutcheon, L. (1994), 'The Post always Rings Twice: The Postmodern and the Postcolonial', *Textual Practice*, 8 (2): 205–38.

Karp, I. and C. Kratz (2015), 'The Interrogative Museum', in Raymond Silverman (ed.), *Museum as Process: Translating Local and Global Knowledges*, 278–98, London: Routledge.

Karp, I., C. Kratz, L. Szwaya and T. Ybarra-Frausto (2006), *Museum Frictions: Public Cultures/Global Transformations*, Durham and London: Duke University Press.

Karp, I., C. M. Kreamer and S. Lavine (eds) (1991), *Museums and Communities: The Politics of Public Culture*, Washington, DC: Smithsonian Institution.

Krmpotich C. and L. Peers (2014), *This Is Our Life: Haida Material Heritage and Changing Museum Practice*, Vancouver: UBC Press.

Macdonald, S., Lidchi, H. and von Oswald, M. (2017), 'Special Section: Engaging Anthropological Legacies', *Museum Worlds: Advances in Research*, 5(1): 95–223.

Mackey, E. (1995), 'Postmodernism and Cultural Politics in a Multicultural Nation: Contests over Truth in the *Into the Heart of Africa* Controversy', *Public Culture*, 7: 403–31.

Marcus, G. and M. Fischer (1986), *Anthropology as Cultural Critique: An Experimental Moment in the Human Sciences*, Chicago: University of Chicago Press.

McDougall T. M. (2016), '"The Water Is Waiting": Water Tidelectics, and Materiality', *Liquid Blackness*, 3 (6): 50–62.

Walter M. and R. Vazquez (2013), 'Decolonial AestheSis: Colonial Wounds/Decolonial Healings,' in *Social Text-Periscope*, Available online: http://socialtextjournal.org/perisc ope_article/decolonial-aesthesiscolonial-woundsdecolonial-healings/.

Nelson, C. and C. A. Nelson, eds. (2004), *Racism, Eh? A Critical Inter-Disciplinary Anthology of Race and Racism in Canada*, Concord: Captus Press.

Peers, L. and A. Brown, eds. (2003), *Museums and Source Communities: A Routledge Reader*, London: Routledge.

Philip, M. N. (1991), 'The White Soul of Canada', *Third Text*, 5 (14): 63–77.

Whose Stories about Africa?

Phillips R. (2011), *Museum Pieces: Towards the Indigenization of Canadian Museums*, Montreal: McGill-Queens University Press.

Pratt, M. L. (1992), *Imperial Eyes: Travel, Writing, and Transculturation*, London: Routledge.

Riegel, H. (1995), 'Into the Heart of Irony: Ethnographic Exhibitions and the Politics of Difference', *The Sociological Review*, 43 (S1): 83–104.

Schildkrout, E. (1991), 'Ambiguous Messages and Ironic Twists: *Into the Heart of Africa* and *The Other Museum*', *Museum Anthropology*, 15 (2): 16–23.

Shelton, A. (2006), 'Museums and Anthropologies: Practices and Narratives', in S. Macdonald (ed.), *A Companion to Museum Studies*, 64–80, Oxford: Blackwell.

Shelton, A. (2008), 'Foreword', in S. Butler (ed.), *Contested Representations*, 1–3, Peterborough, ON: Broadview.

Silverman, R. (2015), 'Introduction: Museum as Process', in Raymond Silverman (ed.), *Museum as Process: Translating Local and Global Knowledges*, 1–18, London: Routledge.

Stocking, G., ed. (1985), *Objects and Others: Essays on Museums and Material Culture*, Madison: University of Wisconsin Press.

Thomas, N. (2010), 'The Museum as Method', *Museum Anthropology*, 33 (1): 6–10.

Vergo, P. (1989), *The New Museology*, London: Reaktion.

5

Facing the 'curatorial turn': anthropological ethnography, exhibitions and collecting practices

Ivan Bargna

My thoughts about the anthropologist as curator start from a number of general considerations about the points of affinity and divergence between ethnographic practices in anthropology and those of the curator in the world of contemporary art. Then I will discuss my research experience as a full-time university anthropologist who, occasionally, but not accidentally, finds himself taking on the role of curator. My focus is on curating and ethnographic practices in the field of collections and collecting practices, inside and outside museums.

As an anthropologist of art and scholar of African art, I have done research both in the field and with collections. My work in Cameroon on the art and visual culture of the Grassfields has involved research on local community museums and artistic–ethnographic projects with contemporary artists. In Italy, I have worked on public and private collections of African art, and have curated several exhibitions including *Wonders of Africa, African Arts in Italian Collections* (Bargna and Parodi da Passano 2010), on which I will focus a part of my analysis. I was a member of the advisory planning committees for the Museum of Cultures of Milan (MUDEC) and the Pavilion Zero, one of the main exhibition pavilions at the 2015 Milan Expo. Finally, I have collaborated with contemporary art curators on exhibition and artistic–ethnographic projects in socially sensitive contexts (Bargna 2012, 2014, 2018; Bargna and Coccia 2018). In all, a rather heterogeneous assortment of fields and researches, but one that is held together by the recurrent intersection of the figures of the anthropologist and curator. In these pages, however, I will consider only the Africanistic part of my research, going back and forth between Cameroon and Italy.

Curatorship and collecting of cultural diversity

The growing affinity between the figure of the contemporary art curator and that of the anthropologist is the product of certain changes in the world. With the end of

East–West bipolarity and the future-fixated ideologies of the nineteenth and twentieth centuries, a geopolitical picture has emerged that has the postmodern condition and postcolonial reality woven into its very fabric, and questions of cultural diversity and social inclusion at its heart (O'Neill 2012). Against this background, we see the emergence of global art (Belting and Buddensieg 2009), the proliferation of museums and art biennials in the southern hemisphere (Belting, Buddensieg and Weibel 2011), and contemporary art curators' invocation of ethnography as a form of cultural critique (Enwezor 2012).

Cultural diversity, once the preserve of ethnographic museums, has become a popular territory in the world of contemporary art, where it sheds any residual image of folkloristic archaism and becomes instead a necessary condition of creative innovation. Museums have also been transformed. These temples of conservation have become motors of the cultural economy and urban regeneration capable of driving tourism and property investment – processes of gentrification that, in turn, make exhibits of our very cities and encourage the transformation of culture in the heritage of material and non-material culture, thus facilitating a sort of museification of reality.

On the one hand, heritage 'is created through metacultural operations that extend museological values and methods (collection, documentation, preservation, presentation, evaluation and interpretations) to living persons, their knowledge, practices, artefacts, social worlds, and life spaces' (Kirshenblatt-Gimblett 2006: 161), while, on the other, the cultural differences are co-opted in the global market by the international art system – making them equivalent and consumable – mostly through an 'inclusive approach using unconnected fragments of other cultures which are held to have an inherent aesthetic value that makes contextual background unnecessary' (O'Neill 2012: 58).

In such a context, where the recognition and commoditization of culture intertwine – though not without ambiguity – we have seen museums and curatorial practices become more culturally sensitive, participative and interactive. The popularization of the anthropological notion of culture also has a role in this process, especially insofar as it critiques the dichotomy of high and low culture, a stance that helps to expand the scope of what we consider 'heritage' and of what can be collected (Boltanski and Esquerre 2017: 45).

In an age marked by the proliferation of objects and their accelerated obsolescence, the widespread cultural phenomenon of 'the collection' somehow both reinforces (you can collect anything) and rejects (you cannot collect everything) the anomie of mass consumerism, shifting the emphasis from the useful to the significant, from the fulfilment of needs to the intensification of desires, from 'use value' to 'staging value' (Böhme 2017).

If there is a difference between the collector and the serial hoarder or compulsive consumer, it lies in the capacity for discernment, for selecting objects according to certain criteria and presenting them in a meaningful order that condenses a view of the world and a way of life. In a similar fashion, the curator is the one who – faced with the proliferation of art works engendered by the revolutionary conceptual decoupling of art and technical ability – asserts their personal role as gatekeeper and mediator, applying the filters that are essential to the creation of a differentiated hierarchy of value. Such

Facing the 'Curatorial Turn' 75

processes are common to both the level of the celebrity – the great collectors and star curators who set the trends – and the anonymity of everyday practice.

We can ask whether, in addition to reacting by intensifying their role as refuges for intimacy, the collections of the future will also adopt the model of seasonal duration we have come to know from fashion: collections that are put together to last for a short time and are then abandoned. Collections could take the form of shopping, setting trends rather than gathering memories. The relationship with the past is reduced to the fleeting emotion of a revival or a vintage flavour (Lipovetsky 2013: 252–6). This is a form of collecting that responds to emotions, based on fluid bonds, and that no longer needs stable collections and memorial monuments.

Once this has been said, we can also ask ourselves whether, in this context, the permanent collections, which are increasingly seen as a burden, do not constitute, precisely because of their outdatedness and their tough materiality, an obstacle to the cultural cannibalism that often guides temporary and ephemeral exhibitions.

With the curatorial turn, exhibitions have become increasingly attuned to subjects of topical interest, with the focus shifting from permanent museum collections towards temporary exhibitions. Museums themselves have been compelled to follow suit with short-lived exhibits that are revised periodically every few years, to the point – with the emergence of new, immersive and interactive technologies – that we now find them embracing the concept of the museum without collections, or even objects (Conn 2010). Contemporary art curators create exhibitions without artists or artworks, but based instead on dialogue with artists and the audience, The outcome does not need to be an exhibition in the traditional sense. This is a process of dematerialization engendered by a critique of the commoditization of art, but this same process, paradoxically, opens the way for a more pervasive commodification of everyday experiences in consonance with an economy increasingly centred on immaterial goods and services (Pine and Gilmore 1999; Rifkin 2000).

The shift driven by the curatorial turn, from conservation to the development of cultural projects, paves the way for museums to reinvent themselves as open, flexible multifunctional spaces. But it also risks leaving them as little more than empty containers, brands that are called on to project their aura on to whatever event they happen to be hosting (weddings, conventions, product launches). We witness this phenomenon, in particular, in the increasingly close interrelationship between the worlds of art, fashion and luxury goods, wherein art is incorporated seamlessly in the production of an ever-more intangible set of cultural commodities, its aura transferred to brands that increase the value of, and instil a kind of 'soul' in, a range of infinitely reproducible products (Lipovetsky and Serroy 2013; Geczy and Karaminas 2013; Amselle 2016).

Viewed against this backdrop, the practices of curatorship become a model for a cultural economy in which creativity is essential to the capacity for innovation demanded by globalized competition. In such an environment, cultural diversity – both past and present – becomes a form of cultural deposit, lying ready to be exploited by 'creative' uses and forms of easy consumption that erase the very otherness they convey (Landry 2006: 400–4).

The cultural mediation and participative practices of curators and artists (and to some extent anthropologists) converge in an unceasing process of narrativization

76 *The Anthropologist as Curator*

that – through shared or negotiated modes – contemporizes cultural heritage in terms of the pressing issues of the present, but that, in doing so, risks descending into anachronism and chatter, whereby objects merely recite what their users want to hear: an economy of signs (Baudrillard 1972), in other words, creating value by associating new narratives with existing objects.

In the 'current general culturalization and musealization of society [...] the discursive ground has moved into the museum, rather than the curator having left the museum' (Lind 2012: 12).The reference made by many curators (e.g. Enwezor 2012 and Gioni 2013) to anthropological ethnography by seeking to focus on relationships, contexts and situations, seems little more than rhetorical posturing, which is to say that ethnography is declared by but not practised, that it exists in the museum but lacks a 'field'. This is the risk anthropologists need to guard against.

If there is one thing that sets the anthropological approach to curatorship apart, it is the nexus it establishes with the field. Unlike curatorship in the world of contemporary art, which tends to suck the world inwards towards the exhibition space, anthropological ethnography takes the exhibition space out into the world, making of it a space for fieldwork, tracing an unbroken web of cross-references between interior and exterior.

The exhibition as an ethnographic field

Building on the discussion in the previous pages, in this second section I analyse the path taken by my own research on 'traditional African arts'. By following a common thread – the collecting practices – this analysis redrafts the link between an ethnographic 'exhibition experiment' (Basu and MacDonald 2007) I curated in Italy (*Wonders of Africa*) and research I have carried out in the Grassfields region of Cameroon.

Wonders of Africa: African Arts in Italian Collections was held in Genoa in 2010 and 2011 (Bargna and Parodi da Passano 2010). The venues were two municipal spaces, the Palazzo Ducale and the Museum of Culture at Castello d'Albertis, which, together, funded the exhibition. The team of curators comprised the anthropologist Giovanna Parodi da Passano, the artist Stefano Arienti and myself.

The exhibition provided the opportunity for an ethnographic research about the collecting of African arts in Italy through a participatory process, making the exhibition a catalyst or a 'para-site' (Marcus 2000) in which the cultural dynamics at work are not only displayed but (per)formed. At the same time, we were engaged in a self-reflexive process, deconstructing the very apparatus we were using to reveal its limits and artificial character.

An exhibition is never merely the realization of some authorial figure's vision. Rather, it is the product of a collective work that requires the mediation of viewpoints and diverse interests. One good example is the genesis of the name *Wonders of Africa*, which we can find as a rather trite title, with more than an echo of outdated, exoticized stereotypes.

African Arts/Italian Collections would have more faithfully captured the curators' own outlook, but the Palazzo Ducale marketing office and the catalogue publisher (who also oversaw the bookshop and the merchandizing operation) judged it to be lacking in appeal, a sure prelude to a flop: if we were to achieve our target of 40,000 visitors, we would need something more evocative, more engaging. Faced with these non-negotiable demands, I suggested *Wonders of Africa* with the subtitle *African Arts / Italian Collections*. This was consequently transmuted into *African Arts in Italian Collections*, losing – along with the slash – the contrastive relationship between the two terms and reducing the phrase to a simple indication of the objects' provenance.

In the visual promotional materials, the exoticizing note was tempered through elegant graphics and the picture of a Baule statue from the Ivory Coast, a 'classical', harmonious carving guaranteed not to disturb the viewer – a typically Italian marriage of primitivism and classicism, pleasant, easy on the eye.

If we want to consider our exhibition itself as an ethnographic field, however, we must consider these events not as impediments to the creation of a personal project, but as indicators of a set of culturally significant circumstances. If the exoticizing stereotype implied by Africa's 'wonderfulness' was desirable from a marketing viewpoint, it was therefore also interesting in anthropological terms, insofar as it intersected with the common conceptions that are the building blocks of culture. It is also important to remember that the image that people in Italy have of Africa is more diverse and complex than this suggests. The potential audiences for the exhibition are therefore equally varied, even though the brand chosen seems to have selected a specific target group, that is, people who habitually attend art exhibitions.

The marketing operation was seeking to intercept and draw momentum from a number of important anniversaries and events taking place around the time of the exhibition: the football World Cup in South Africa, the 50th anniversary of the independence of numerous African states and the 150th anniversary of the unification of Italy. It also served to embed the exhibition in the wider media environment. Bear in mind that all this was taking place in a country in which migratory flows, second-generation African Italians and the phenomena of reception and rejection were helping to reshape what it meant to be 'African' or 'Italian'.

Devising the structure of the exhibition meant working on the gap between the expected and the eventual audience, taking the publicized image of the exhibition/product and the expectations it generated and trying to reorient them, not only by incentivizing the shift from 'wonder' to 'resonance' (Greenblatt 1991), from aesthetic engrossment to critical distance, but also by encouraging the visitor to transfer this sense of wonder to another recipient. Indeed, the first thing that should have made the visitor marvel was the fact that the artefacts were not found in Africa, but in the homes of Italians.

If the objects on display did not arise out of nothing (as the neutral, suspended space of the *white cube* might imply), they did not come from Africa either (as a more classic ethnographic contextualization could lead us to believe). Even if they were created there – in Africa – today their homes are in the residences of Italian collectors, where they would return, moreover, at the end of the exhibition. All this needed to be taken into account: the sense of surprise could offer a foothold for promoting greater self-reflexivity, at least in some of the visitors.

Above all, it was matter of disregarding the expectations implied by the heterotopic space of the museum, that we could eliminate the distance and transport ourselves to Africa. It was for this reason that we arranged for visitors to be welcomed by a video on a large screen that forced them to take stock of where they were actually standing, of the fact that everything they were experiencing was taking place in Genoa, in Italy, and not in Africa. The screen displayed the homes of the Italian collectors, the places from which the exhibits actually came from, and to which they would return, thus making visible the material conditions that allowed the objects to be exhibited.

It was a case of evidencing the collectors' role as agents of cultural mediation, the way they have contributed to shaping our view of Africa through the appropriation and aestheticization of certain objects. The Africa that appears to us through the filter of art is very different to the one we receive from television coverage of humanitarian disasters, not necessarily any less stereotypical, imaginary or emotional, but different none the less. It says something about Africa, and a great deal about 'us'.

Thus we focused, at one and the same time, on both people (Africans and Italians) and objects (African, yet also Italian), outlining or evoking their respective stories wherever they intersected. For instance: the documents that might accompany an object (catalogues, family photos, customs records, proofs of purchase, certificates of authenticity and so on) were presented not in the form of supporting information, as external to the object, but as parts of an extended existence that was spread through time and space, and as parts of the lives of the people with whom the objects had come into contact (Gell 1998). Thus, in the exhibition, where it was most meaningful and visually effective, these documents were treated as integral parts of the exhibitory apparatus, valued for their nature as objects.

As we know, in themselves, African objects do not, for the most part, start out as works of art, that is, springing from an artistic intention; they become works of art when they arrive in the West. Instead of treating this trajectory as a deviation (the rejection of their original identity in their appropriation by the West) or as their fate (the acknowledgement of art's universal human value once it is stripped of the burden of its cultural particularism), we could map out the movements through space and the semantic and relational changes that objects and people undergo by reconstructing the genealogy of their journey.

This approach gives the lie to the old, but never extinguished, idea of the opposition between the ethnographic and the aesthetic perspectives, the first of which puts the object back into the context of its origin (the cultural matrix), while the second decontextualizes it to enhance its uniqueness (the artistic masterpiece).

The drawback of this approach is its one-sidedness: we end up, on the one hand, with objects that have no context (valorized for what they are, for their formal characteristics); on the other hand, we get contexts without objects, in which case the uniqueness of the object is lost in its typicality, or the classification by type, or the general coordinates of the culture of which the object constitutes a document. Instead, our starting point is the fact that the objects are here, in Italian collections.

Conventionally, exhibition objects are displayed with the collectors very much kept in the background, being treated as lenders and nothing more (with the partial exception of the 'solo shows' built around a collector's biography or even just his name). To the opposite, and complementary, extreme, in some cases it is collecting itself that is on display, as an example of a cultural practice rooted in the West, with the individual objects now taking a back seat.

The *Wonders of Africa* show had a different focus: it was the relationship between 'African arts' and 'Italian collections', considering them to be intertwined and exhibiting them as such, each seen through the other: if the art is indeed African, the collections are nevertheless Italian.

After all, putting the focus on the collections does not mean treating the objects in a decontextualized fashion. A collection is composed of objects, true, but is also defined by the context in which they are placed: the relationships between the individual objects, and between the objects and the places and the people that have assembled them, both from the material and the symbolic point of view. This means that a collection understood as a product must be seen as the ever-provisional and ever-evolving result of the practice of collecting, itself understood as a process with a social, cultural and individual orientation. For that matter, the exhibition itself can be considered a temporary collection: a transitory collection of collections, which will leave a more lasting trace in the catalogue.

Following these considerations, it was decided to seek the collectors' contribution in realizing the exhibition, which took the form of collaborative and participatory planning. And although the selection criteria for the works were those that corresponded to the curators' aims, the curators avoided imposing their own judgements according to their personal tastes and deferred to those of the collectors themselves.

At the castle d'Albertis, the interaction with and between the collectors was made visible through a performative installation: a Yoruba maternity statue from Nigeria was placed on the summit of a stepped pedestal. The collectors were then invited to arrange their own *ibeji* figurines around it (figures of twins, sculpted in the event of the death of one or both children, which are treated as hosting the soul of the deceased, and which the mothers therefore nurture as though they were living children). However, they were given a condition: each of the various figures was to be placed at a different distance from the top of the pedestal, and thus from the mother, in accordance with the quality attributed to it. To make this possible, the collectors had to reach an agreement by discussing their assessments and criteria. The idea was to videotape the process so it could be screened during the exhibition on a monitor on one side of the installation. In the event, however, the collectors refused to express a consensus, a withdrawal no less significant than any positive enunciation, although a switched-off television (even one accompanied by a notice explaining the reason) clearly has less visual impact than a video.

However, before getting to the stage of selecting individual works, there was the matter of selecting the collectors. Even if inclusiveness was one of the factors involved (the largest possible number of collectors), it is also true not only that many collections were left out, but also that a certain kind of collecting was preferred. What kind? We could simply define it as 'quality collecting', of the sort that assembles 'authentic works' of 'elevated aesthetic value'. Bearing in mind, however, that this is not an appraisal of objects that are endowed with specific properties, the existence of which need merely to be acknowledged, but the discursive product of a community of practice that elaborates its own expert pool of knowledge, the status of which is socially recognized.

80   *The Anthropologist as Curator*

In other words, Italian collectors of African art constitute a community and not an aggregate of separate individuals – a community that participates in a broader 'art world' (that of 'African', 'tribal' or 'ethnic' art) as well as in the transnational culture to which they belong, holding different positions and playing different roles (some of them dangerously blurred): collectors, dealers, auction houses, anthropologists, museologists and publishers (Price 2010).

We asked the collectors to accompany the works in a variety of ways: recording video interviews in their homes, providing additional objects from their domestic environment and even conducting tours of the exhibition as guides. Their stories revealed their motivations, the real or imaginary relationships they, and we, have with Africa, the internal logic that guided the development of their collections, or the impact of chance events, the emotional relationship they have with the pieces, the way they came into their possession and the memories they carry (Bargna 2013).

Certain stories took us to Africa. But this was the Africa of Italians, the Africa that mattered to them, and the Africa with which their lives have coincided: an Africa in which Africans, themselves, appear only fleetingly. With others, we remained in Italy, or else found ourselves in other European countries (France in particular, the main port of call for many Italian collectors).

In order to tell these stories, Giovanna Parodi da Passano and I turned to the co-curator with whom we had designed the exhibition, artist Stefano Arienti. Our intention was to build a device that would enable the visitor to understand the objects by somehow experiencing them. This was not a matter of setting works of contemporary art alongside the traditional African pieces and trying to make something of the affinities and parallels between them, as a modern primitivist approach might entail, nor of handing the artist carte blanche in order to obtain a different or 'freer' perspective on the situation. Rather, it implied working together on a shared curatorial project, in which each person's skills and knowledge could serve the group as a whole.

The artist therefore joined anthropologists in the two-year genesis of the exhibition, studying and meeting collectors and their collections all over Italy. The videos recorded in the collectors' homes were included in the exhibition together with certain objects considered representative of their way of life, which were situated in little 'salons' designed to evoke the particular character and context of the collection in question. In the videos, the visitor would find the same works that were exhibited before them, but captured at a different moment in their social existence, the intimate, everyday environment of the home added to the more public space of the exhibition.

Books and catalogues of African art were positioned on the tables, as though they were reference texts provided for the use of visitors. These were actually works by Arienti, even though this was – by design – not immediately apparent (unless the visitor was already familiar with the artist): we did include cards with the name and title of the work, but set these at a certain distance.

Arienti had 'interfered' with the books, drilling into them to make holes that ranged from the tiny to the enormous. In some cases, these would pierce the eyes of the masks on the covers and pass from one side of the book to the other (see Figure 5.1). In others, they would follow the outline of the image, reproducing it on the interior of the book

Figure 5.1 Stefano Arienti, *Books of African Arts*. Exhibition *Wonders of Africa: African Arts in Italian Collections*, Palazzo Ducale, Genova, 2011. Photo: Ivan Bargna.

in such a way that it was superimposed on the text and illustrations, only to fade gradually as the reader approached the final pages.

Despite being, to all intents and purposes, works of contemporary art, these books legitimized their own presence as integral parts of the exhibitory apparatus. In the world of the art collector, the role of books and catalogues extends far beyond that of providing supplementary information; they are authoritative sources that establish canons and repertoires, that create icons and pedigrees. Indeed, some collectors of African art only collect published works. Images educate and direct the gaze, transforming the act of viewing the object into the recognition of something already known. The book is part of the extended existence of the art object. The exhibition's own *Wonders of Africa* catalogue had a part to play, too.

The visitor who approached Arienti's pieces supposing them simply to be books (as they had been allowed to believe) would be hindered in their desire to read and understand; instead of finding answers, they would find themselves asking questions about an everyday object that had suddenly revealed itself as enigmatic and unusable. The book, by the very fact of its being mistreated, by being put out of commission, appeared to the visitor in all its materiality, yet also – at the same time – in all the sacrality that comes from being recognizable as a book for its aesthetic appearance, regardless of what was written in it. Subsequently – though not always – the visitors, in their surprise, would become aware that what they had in their hands was a work of contemporary art. The artefact thus acquired a multiple, stratified identity that would be activated differently on each occasion by a different visitor.

At its heart, the practice of curatorship is concerned with the use and interpretation of specific spaces with things and words. The vaulted atrium of the Palazzo Ducale, one of the exhibition venues, offers a large space divided into numerous 'rooms'. Used, historically, as a depository for the Palazzo's food stores, today – repurposed, in the frame of the heritage polices – it appears to us almost like a three-bay cathedral nave with massive pillars and adjoining spaces. In the main room, the African objects were arranged on a long, white platform in the central 'bay', taking care to employ all the scenic artifices (lights, stands, distances) required for the sophisticated, rarefied atmosphere that collectors seem to think is necessary to bring out all the aesthetic qualities of their pieces, elevating artefacts to the status of artworks. The sacral appearance of the venue, in all its historical gravity, helped to reinforce this celebratory aspect of the exhibition. But the 'salons' arranged along one of the side bays, despite not interfering directly with the view of the works in the centre, did impinge somehow on the aura of the suspended exhibition space and bring the works within it back into the world, into the everyday.

With this deconstructive approach, we aimed at encompassing the world view of the 'native' (in this case Italian collectors) while keeping to a suitable distance from it, as befits participant-observation. This approach was also manifested in the decision to present some objects in clusters: rather than seeking out and isolating 'masterpieces', in an attempt to define or reaffirm a canon by referring to a prototype, we chose to underline variabilities, variants and changes, thus generating a network of cross-references between the objects. In some cases, these clusters represented individual collections, which were set out as such in the display. In this way, the discourse of the curators was therefore able to assume a level of critical autonomy in relation to the collections and collectors, albeit it remained in dialogue with them.

To engage with (partially) shared conceptions of 'common sense' means not only to consider the ideologies that have sedimented in our linguistic codes, but also the ethnocentrism embodied in sensorial forms of experience, and in particular the traditional pre-eminence of sight in Western culture, a primacy on which, until recently, the museum itself was modelled. This issue becomes more pressing as the cultural distance between the visitor and the object increases. We therefore need to start asking questions about the diversity and specificity of the sensorial and aesthetic codes that might direct the production of objects and images in another culture, and – by moving beyond the dichotomy of aesthetic universalism and cultural relativism – to attempt a culturally differentiated aesthetic experience of objects. On this question, it is worth considering the distance between our visual aesthetic (by now largely in decline), with its denial of corporeity, and the African appreciation of proprioception and kinaesthesia, that makes the objects, in their practical and ritual handling, less a correlation of the gaze as a function of the movement of the body.

In order to make this distance more evident (and to some extent traversable), a mask – an elephant Bamileke mask of Cameroon – was displayed with a video alongside (with a set of earphones), placed at the eye level of both the visitor and the mask. The sounds and images were those of the dancing mask, not from the point of view of the spectator of either the exhibition or the performance, but from that of the mask itself, to which an action camera was attached to follow the movements of the body. It was a clear shift in perspective that, nonetheless, did not allow for any sort of identification with the mask: to feel like the mask, it is not enough merely to participate. You have to believe.

Albeit in an entirely different context, a similar distance separates the visitor from the collector's tactile, olfactory and deeply intimate experience of his or her objects.

Whereas in Africa, such objects are destined for certain uses and actions (ritual, therapeutic, sacrificial, etc.), when an object becomes part of a Western collection, its future is generally one of immobility, and the denial of any form of tactile usage. Its fate is to be contemplated. This transformation is effected, largely, with display cases.

In Genoa, however, there were no showcases, unless the collectors put them as a condition of the loan. Where we did use them, we sought to tear away the inherent 'obviousness' that makes them so invisible, and show how, by increasing the status of the objects they are meant to protect and separating them from the surrounding space, they act (much like a picture frame or plinth) as intermediaries in our experience. To highlight the material presence of the showcases, Stefano Arienti glued on them silhouettes of the objects they contained, evoking the play of shadows in Plato's cave and bringing to light the opaque nature of transparency.

The majority of the objects were placed on platforms that both encouraged and (for security reasons) obstructed a tactile engagement with them: it felt like you could reach out and touch them, but the sloping wall of the platform prevented you from doing so, while sirens admonished anyone who stretched out a hand to behave in a more orderly fashion. We hoped that this, deliberately created, frustrating situation would encourage a more tactile gaze, the sort solicited by the three-dimensionality of sculpture and by the material character of sacrificial layers and the patinas of use. These are ambiguous experiences: moving beyond a purely contemplative gaze means taking a step closer, solicited by the cultural agency of the object; yet it can also be an expression of the sort of liberties that we would never allow ourselves with other works of art, with which we would maintain a respectful distance. The spectator's relationship with the bodies of the statues, meanwhile, is not unlike the one we have with other people's bodies: through processes of personification of (attractive, seductive) objects and the reification of people (who are made accessible, available), the behaviours that we exhibit in regard to one are transferred, to some extent, to our interactions with the other. In this, our colonial legacy most likely still carries a certain weight.

This engagement with questions of shared conceptions was particularly acute in the room dedicated to *nkisi* figures from the Democratic Republic of Congo, and other figurines commonly labelled as 'fetishes'.

The question of 'fetishism' when talking about traditional African art is a particularly sensitive one, as it impacts not only on the collector, but also on the African populations whose world views have often been disqualified by being labelled in this way. The term 'fetish' has long been applied to African statues (Pietz 1985, 1987). It subsequently fell out of favour as the perception of fetishism progressed from being a characteristic of African cultures to a consequence of Eurocentric appraisals that, mistakenly, accused Africans of being incapable of appreciating the difference between the object's material and the spiritual entity it represented. As a result, the term 'fetish' has been abandoned, although many Africans still continue to use it, at least when speaking in the languages of the former colonial powers.

More recently, anthropology has revived the notion of 'fetishism', freeing it of its discriminatory connotations and using it as a term suitable for describing the materialism to be found in African religions (Augé 1988) or to acknowledge a characteristic that is not just African, but amply transcultural. This means that 'fetishism' is not just the distinctive trait of a certain cultural system or an individual psychological disposition any more, but a universal, normal attitude, so common that it can be adopted as a methodological principle of anthropology itself, that is, recognizing a certain agency of things and not only people (Gell 1998; Latour 1996; Miller 2005). This approach no longer treats the object as a recipient, mirror and reflection of independent and external social dynamics, but as an agent that contributes to directing them, an actor with whom almost personal relations can be established, in a perspective that leads in due course to recognizing that things can have a social life and a biography (Appadurai 1986). From this angle, it is then possible to reconnect 'Africa' and Italy, making collectors into a bridge.

The collector's relationship with the collection is, in part, mediated by senses, feelings and affects: to learn anything about an object, you need to get to know it, spend time with it, bind yourself to it in a relationship that treats objects as animated entities, as near-human beings. Seen in this light, collecting is not so much a borderline practice as a place where ordinary everyday practices (our animistic relationship with objects: the car, mobile phone, sofa, etc.) take on a more reflexive, clearly visible form. If anything, this reasoning applies even more so to collecting traditional African art, whose masks and statues already function in a framework of a conceived and ritualized 'animism' (or 'analogism' – Descola 2005: 280–320) when they are still in Africa. There is no evidence that many collectors have converted to the cults whose objects they possess, but many of them feel and say that they entertain an 'animistic' relationship with them that links them to their origins. When they are transferred from Africa to the West, these objects do not simply mutate into signs (works of art or ethnographic objects), but somehow remain presences that act. The words used to describe these relationships are the ones familiar to love affairs, to family affections and to friendship ('they keep me company'). Many collectors tend to consider themselves and to live their relationships with their collections not as a question of property, but as a life spent together, prioritizing 'the desire of what you possess' over the mere desire to possess.

In a love affair, the initiative is attributed to the object that entrances, seduces and conquers: sparks can fly when there is an elective affinity. The statement that the collector does not possess objects but is possessed by them is a commonplace that is largely shared by collectors of 'primitive art' (Derlon and Ballini 2008: 60–1). The proprietary dimension of possession is converted into a 'magical' dimension that, as this is about Africa, becomes something more than a metaphor and is anchored to the object's real or imaginary previous life.

Given these considerations, we were faced with creating an exhibition device that, starting with common notions of African 'fetishism', would facilitate a reworking of these very ideas, providing a bridge between self and other, making it possible for the audience to translate the far-off and distant in their own terms, but without reducing it to themselves. For all that these figures – conduits for ambivalent forces – can be employed to bring harm to others, they are often given a far more therapeutic function.

Yet rather than simply stating or explaining, our task was to enable the perception of this aspect.

With this in mind, we gathered the fetishes in a large cube at the centre of the room. They were 'protected' by tall panels of toughened glass but with large openings at the corners allowing anyone who so wished to reach in an arm and almost touch the objects. Or perhaps it was to allow the fetishes to escape from their box. In other words, the panels were a protective apparatus but with escape routes that leave the question of who needs protection from whom far from clear. At the centre of the cube, Arienti had arranged a pile of cushions that, split open, had spilled their feathers outwards, some even floating down to the floor. Completing the display, there was a screen displaying photos of the sacrifice of a chicken, whose blood was splattered on to the head and body of a sick woman, and – in a small display case – a 'voodoo doll to placate your wrath' with large needles bearing legends such as 'wear lingerie more often', 'sexy slave', 'shut up!' and so on (a toy I had picked up in Milan that had images of 'African' masks on the packaging).

With this reversal of roles, the 'voodoo doll' served, in ironic fashion, to evoke the question of ours and other people's fetishes, and the nexus between the real and imaginary, between 'them' and 'us'. A less immediate, but perhaps more profound, physical and emotional association was the one we sought to engender between the feathers of the cushions (an apparent interloper) and those of the sacrificed bird. We were attempting to facilitate the transfer between the sensations evoked by a recognizable, personal, intimate object – the one on which we rest our heads and fall asleep at night – and those inspired by the sacrificial images of blood, which, beyond any repulsion they might provoke, also expressed the joy and serenity of the sick person restored to health. I could not say precisely what effect this apparatus actually produced; with the central role played by the senses and emotions, it was an experience that would not necessarily reach the level of full awareness, and the risk that the whole set-up would be transformed into one of Arienti's art installations.

Rather than pause to analyse every part of the exhibition, let us skip ahead to the last room, a space that, in both a literal and conceptual sense, served to lead the visitor outside. By setting the reality of Italian collections centre stage, the exhibition had inhibited the urge to be projected directly into Africa, emphasizing the most immediate context that gave form to the gaze of the spectators, as well as the stratification of mediations through which we are reconnected with the continent.

Only in the last room were we brought 'to meet Africa', broadening the polyphonic approach of the exhibition to include a number of African voices that, although not representing any sort of totality, were certainly significant. This marked a departure in relation to the Italian voices that had thus far populated the exhibition, but it did not represent the abandonment of the collection in favour of the field, of the museum in favour of real life. The link was still to be found in the world of the collection.

Three videos projected onto the wall relayed accounts from three African 'collectors': in the first, traditional chief Wabo Tekam speaks (and does not speak) about the objects held in the 'house of skulls' (a building in which ancestors' skulls are conserved), and shows us a number of the statues that are collected there; in the second, the speaker is Nouaye Taboue Flaubert, the curator of the museum of the kingdom of Bandjoun, where the royal treasure and other community objects are held; in the third, by way of contrast, Professor Lazare Kaptué, cosmopolitan doctor and university lecturer, guides us through the objects and souvenirs he has collected over the years, which now decorate his home (see Figure 5.2). Different worlds, then, that nonetheless exist side by side in the same village, voices to be laid over Italian voices, interrupting their discourse, and creating the first, small cracks in their air of self-sufficiency and self-referentiality. With this comes a – possibly fatal – threat to their collections: the bringing into question of the canonical criteria by which the 'authenticity' of 'traditional African art' is established. Many of the objects shown by the African 'collectors' would not have found a place among the Italian collections; they would be considered mere 'copies', or at best 'reproductions'.

This situation raises the question of whether it may not be 'time to bring the canon into better alignment with the corpus, with what African artists actually make' (Kasfir

Figure 5.2 Professor Kaptué Lazare's villa entrance hall: collected objects and paintings, pictures, decor and architectural ornaments make up a scene to impress the guests. Bandjoun, Cameroon, 2008. Photo: Ivan Bargna.

1992: 53) and whether this revision of the borders ought also to include African collections in Africa.

Strange as it may seem, in fact, *African* collections have never played a part in the process of defining African art and have often been relegated to recent, belated collections of 'counterfeits', even when they comprise works of historical and cultural relevance. Yet in a world where the dynamics of establishing the identity of cultural heritage plays an increasingly important political role, African collectors and museums are starting to claim the right to hold sway over their own symbolic resources, making their collections into a tool for constructing citizenship. In particular, 'given the reluctance of Western museums to return important pieces of historical African art to Africa, it is increasingly obvious that the new [African] scholarship must emerge to validate Africa as viable site of African collecting' (Okwunodu Ogbechie 2011: 233). Now that it is under attack, the canon reveals its nature as a means of power and knowledge whose purpose is to establish a legitimate order by means of a set of discursive and non-discursive procedures, including the increasing rarity of the works and their authentication.

The canon does not just define a valued and authorized set of objects, but also creates a community vested with expert knowledge that subscribes to it and keeps it alive. We should therefore really interpret the generic term 'African art collecting' as including many kinds of collecting (alternative, subordinate and less rigidly regulated practices), although in practice we tend to focus mostly on a restricted, accredited, authoritative and authorized group.

We see, then, that it is possible to follow this central theme of the collection without setting the museum and the field in opposition to one another. Rather, we have decoupled the practices of collecting from the unique model of the museum in order to better understand them in all their cultural diversity. Which is exactly what I have been trying to do in my research in Cameroon since 2002.

Collecting and exhibition practices inside and outside the museum

In spite of a widespread stereotype that African societies do not preserve material culture, in the Grassfields, the West Cameroon highlands, we can identify several collecting practices animated by different interests, motivations and aims. In fact, the modern Western museum is only one among many different ways of collecting and 'making worlds' through the order given by the collection (Pomian 1978): collecting is not a Western prerogative, or the consequence of colonial domination, but a bundle of different, widespread, transcultural practices of shaping and representing reality. Collections are forms of concrete thinking operating through things, in ways that are always locally diversified. Proceeding in this way, I try to distance myself from the cultural stereotype of the 'museum collection' and consider the collection in terms of what Wittgenstein called a 'family resemblance': that is, a series of overlapping similarities, where no one feature is common to all. That said, we must also specify that resemblances are not in the things themselves; rather, they emerge from an act of comparison, which is always oriented and located somewhere, in an individual and collective collection experience, and in a theoretical and methodological background and goal. Therefore, in spite of all, the museum largely remains our starting point for two main reasons: first, because the 'museum' is also found in Bandjoun; and second, because we can use the museum stereotype as a conventional prototype for identifying the similarities and differences that compose the always open range of possibilities that we call 'collection'. To be clear, in considering the museum as a stereotypical prototype, I do not ignore the fact that the concept of the museum and its definition change over time and that every history written in terms of continuity is a retrospective illusion or an ideological projection. I shall proceed, therefore, from what is most similar to the concept of the museum, and then gradually turn towards other collecting practices, trying at the same time to expand the use of the collection as a heuristic paradigm of research (Bargna 2016).

In Bandjoun, we can distinguish at least three kinds of 'collection': the king's collection, sets of objects and sculptures connected to family cults of the ancestors, and other more individually oriented collections, which constitute what we could call cabinets of curiosities or private museums, set up by the nouveau riche people of Bandjoun. These three kinds of collections are interrelated to each other, presenting a network of differences and similarities that allow us, at least in part, to leave the kingdom museum, and see it as one of the possible local collecting practices. The kingdom museum itself is not entirely an import from abroad filling a local void, but rather it imposes itself upon a pre-existing form of king's collection known in French as *les choses du pays* ('things of the country'). It is contiguous to objects and sculptures gathered in the family houses (*dshang*) that preserve the skulls of the family ancestors.

All these sets of objects can be considered 'collections' to the extent that they have been assembled and preserved in a special place, establishing relationships between themselves that are not random, receiving special care, and handed down to successors. To say that collections existed in the past and continue to exist in Cameroon, and elsewhere in Africa, is not to deny the differences with the concept of the museum. For example, the high level of replaceability of the objects, the lack of importance attributed to their age, and the scant attention paid to their preservation, by Western standards at least, are significant deviations.

The kingdom museum is a 'collection', explicitly presented as a 'museum' by the legitimate possessor – the public figure of the *fo* (king) who inherits and holds the collection, but who is not the owner – and the 'curator' (a young man trained as a museograph by an Italian NGO and the Ecole du Patrimoine Africain) who is delegated to manage it. The royal treasury is the subject of special care. Many objects kept inside the museum have a sacred aura, because they are charged with *ke*, or 'force', a power that places them in the sacred (Maillard 1984: 131–71). They do not simply attest to the power in place in a symbolic way, but they make it effective (Warnier 2009): their possession legitimates usurpation, while their loss undermines the established power (Maillard 1984: 86).

In this context, the kingdom museum collection appears as a weapon, a power-knowledge device, playing a role in the political arena. The museum itself is a stratified construction in which the contributions brought from the inside and the outside are mixed and mutually determined. That is, the social and public identity of the collection emerges at the intersection point between the local and the global, generated by cultural heritage policies and the different attempts to take advantage of them.

The different exhibition settings that have taken place in recent years, show an intense dialectic of construction and destruction, dismantling and renewal, that has affected the kingdom museum, trying to combine planning and bricolage through its ability to react to circumstances and seize opportunities that arise in current events.

These events allow us to move our attention from the collection as a product to the collection as a process, setting out the framework of multiple and contrasting agencies that decide the fates of a collection, the roles played by chance, and the several antagonistic collecting paradigms present within a single collection.

The role of the curator is legitimized by the king, who retains the final word on what can be accepted into or must be rejected from the collection; but in practical terms, the discretionary power of the curator is very broad and goes beyond simple executive functions.

The curatorial desire to elevate the standard of the museum's collection and to conserve in a safe place objects that would otherwise be menaced by thefts and termites resulted in important political ramifications. Bringing power-charged objects to the centre meant that the local political equilibrium was altered between the *fo* and the subordinated chiefs, who are indeed very resolute about keeping their autonomy and prerogative. It is no wonder, then, that in fact very few objects were given to the museum. The majority of such objects continue to be kept in compound shrines, used in rituals and usually kept invisible.

In different parts of Bandjoun it is also possible to find nouveau riche people, bourgeois, who made their fortunes in the city or abroad, presenting themselves as collectors and their collections as private museums. In this case, the accurate exhibition of objects collected, either as an integral part of the house's furniture or in a building expressly built to mimic a museum's display, is an important aspect of the collection's display, increasing the 'symbolic capital' of the owner (Bourdieu 1979).

Through heterogeneous things collected during their lives, these people display their 'modernity' and social success (Rowland 1996), writing their autobiographies by means of exotic objects, often souvenirs, gifts and photographs, and through the appropriation of traditional symbols and ornaments long ago reserved for the king. These heterogeneous objects speak about the lives of their owners, witnessing their travels, jobs, or political careers and the important persons they have known. What connects them, the principle of the intelligibility of the collection, resides in the biography of the collector, in the connections with these objects and the experiences they evoke. This is probably also true for another kind of collection: the collection of contemporary art located in the new cultural centre of Bandjoun Station, created by Barthelemy Toguo, an artist of international renown based in Paris, but born in Cameroon (Bargna 2008). This centre, whose architecture makes reference to the local style but is also distinct from all the other surrounding buildings, is devoted to the production, collection and exhibition of contemporary art. It brings to Bandjoun another kind of collection and display, different from those already in place. It will be interesting to observe how this artistic milieu, this 'station' where travellers from all around the world will arrive, will affect all the other collections existing in Bandjoun.

Similarly, how will Bandjoun Station be affected by them? Significantly, in 2009 the *fo*, the ultimate authority of the kingdom museum, allowed the display of a work of contemporary art in the core of the museum, the prestigious hall located at the end of the exhibition. It was a potentially disruptive, monumental installation, consisting of a pyramid of mud and soccer balls, created by the Italian artistic collective Alterazioni Video, a very transgressive group of art activists that I brought to Bandjoun (Bargna 2012).

Proceeding in this way means not only looking at a collection as an empirical object but also trying to expand the use of the collection as a heuristic paradigm of research.

This is the case in particular of my interpretation of the *nemo* (The House of the People), an architectural artefact with sculpted poles outside, in terms of a 'collection' of images. The *nemo* is presented as a house built by the people and for the people. Nobody is to be excluded from the *nemo*'s construction and everyone is expected to take part in it, either through work or by giving money.

The *nemo*, of course, is a building, and it may seem arbitrary to describe it in terms of collection. At most, it appears to be a container for possibly housing a collection. In reality, there is nothing inside the *nemo* at all. The sanctuary is empty. I propose nevertheless to regard the sculpted posts on the outside of the *nemo* as a sort of 'permanent collection', hosted in the exterior of the sanctuary, instead of treating them as part of an architectural artefact provided with an intrinsic unity. As a collection, the images sculpted on the posts compose an ensemble put together by one or more discourses or narratives. They are located in a strategic order of discourse, and they are used in individual and collective tactics aimed at enforcing or eluding the dominant narratives. They are, at one and the same time, both the expression of the established order and an accidental accumulation of 'objects', heterogeneous in their content and origin, because of the initiative of sculptors who are difficult to keep under control, yet whose contributions remain necessary.

In the iconography of the *nemo* we can find a collection of images that continually surpass both the plan of the curator and of its political patronage, that is, the king and the elites surrounding him. Post hoc interpretations of this iconography are often aimed at reducing dissonances and contradictions between the official political stances and the divergent visions of individuals and groups pursuing their particular interests and aims.

The *nemo* is involved in a larger dialectic of creation and destruction, which finds in iconoclasm a quite extreme possibility offered to opponents to manifest their dissent in an anonymous but clearly visible way. In this perspective, for example, the burning of the *nemo* does not appear as a mere accident, but rather as a recurring event motivated by political aims and personal interests. These motivations find a way to express themselves by contesting and renewing the criteria and content inspiring the *nemo*'s image collection.

The posts do not constitute *a* collection, but rather *several different* kinds of collections, marked by conflict. The materiality of the carved poles, the apparent architectural unity of the artefact, and its 'monumentality', allow the 'public transcript' to assert itself as the dominant discourse but, at the same time, the indeterminacy of the image lets several 'hidden transcripts' (Scott 1990) survive and express themselves in a subordinate and marginal way. All of these transcripts are on display but not equally visible.

Now the 'collection' begins to refer explicitly to the art world, as it originated in the West and then spread all around the globe, by making reference to global issues concerning world heritage, cultural identity displayed by the museums, and the international art market. In this context the canon is provided by Western catalogues, which arrive in Bandjoun as photocopies, and by photographs often downloaded from the internet or drawn from magazines. What is really happening is that through this *quotation* of themselves by means of the 'Other', the past takes an objective and detached form, increasing the gap between the past and the present. In this way the *nemo* tends to become part of a heritage to be enjoyed in terms of 'culture'.

The *nemo* seems to have become more and more like a sort of museum, which expresses in a material way the supposed union between the *fo* and his subjects, and offers an image of Bandjoun's cosmology to the world. The *nemo* is planned as a sort of catalogue, and it is intended to end in a published catalogue destined to accomplish the task, in glossing the speech that the architectonic text has begun.

Contemporary art practice and curatorship as remediation work

In my research on collecting practices in Cameroon, as well as in the Genoa exhibition, the focus was on the roles of images, texts, objects and museums, in mediating the relationships between cultures, groups and people. Now I would like to take up this theme from another angle, briefly referring to another exhibition that I curated: *Biografia Plurale: Virginia Ryan 2000–2016*, held in 2016, at Palazzo Lucarini Contemporary, in the Umbrian town of Trevi (Bargna and Coccia 2018). It was centred on one artist, Virginia Ryan, and her nomadic life: she is an Australian artist of Irish origin who arrived in Italy via Scotland, Egypt, ex-Yugoslavia, Brazil and, notably, Ghana and the Ivory Coast, where she spent fifteen years. The exhibition was dedicated to this last period of her life and work.

Biografia Plurale was the result of the joint curatorship between art historian Maurizio Coccia and me. The connection between contemporary art and anthropological curatorship was central to the project, highlighting the many levels, the many entries and exits, that are evoked and focused through Virginia Ryan's life and works. However, this meeting of art and anthropology was not limited to the exhibition: it does not arrive at an end, but it is an integral part of the creative and reflexive processes of the artist, who in Ghana worked together with the anthropologist and musician, Steven Feld, co-author of some Virginia Ryan artworks (Feld and Ryan 2016).

In many ways, Virginia's story is unique, but it can also be seen as a cultural biography condensing in her works dynamics that go beyond her person, and in which we can recognize parts of ourselves; it reflects the diasporic character of contemporary existence that consigns us to permanent movement, imposing upon us the relentless and patient toil of mending the frayed strands of our lives as best we can. Mobility is a condition of our age that, on the one hand, unites us and, on the other, divides us: there are those who travel in business class and those who find themselves on a boat heading for Lampedusa, those who set off on a journey out of choice and those who do so out of necessity. Mobility as an expression of individual freedom must be set alongside the mobility of expulsions, deportations and forced transfers. Here the question is not one of cultural diversity but of social inequality.

Virginia Ryan's life, then, is plural: it is one and many and intersects with the lives of others. Retracing it allows us to reflect on the ways through which people, navigating by sight, draw the canvasses and the sets of their lives, but it also allows us to ask ourselves about the relationship between artistic practice and cultural diversity in a world increasingly marked by deep social inequalities. This is an inescapable question for a 'white artist' in Africa, but also one that guides every contemporary act of expression, representation and performance. It is exactly for this reason that Virginia Ryan's work does not originate from an independent and sovereign perspective that acts upon a reality that is immediately available; it passes, instead, through the laborious remediation of the images and artefacts made by others, whether they be works of other artists, photographs of everyday people, films, advertising or the urban landscape; things she has collected over the years.

Virginia Ryan's work operates in that place of dialogue and disagreement that lies between Western rhetoric, fuelled by literature, cinema and the many and varied representations that African people give of themselves. It is a vast archive of memory and of visions, both unique and shared, in which individuals represent themselves in relation to others. For this reason her work, and no less her story, is plural. What emerges from the work is an image of Africa that is post-exotic and post-nostalgic. It is contemporary and urban; it does not wait to be discovered, to be represented (the colonial imagination of conquest); it has always provided self-representation. Ryan creates images of images, just as anthropologists construct interpretations of the interpretations of others. In her work, then, she adopts a strategy founded upon the combination and modification of existing images. The works are dense and stratified, and they consistently provide multiple options for interpretation. Virginia Ryan does not only provide a new context for the images but chooses to work on a collective imagery. She adopts by recreating.

The curatorial project, designed and built with the artist, does not simply show, it participates in this work of constant remediation (Bolter and Grusin 2000), seeking to make visible the intermedial construction of reality by creating a distancing effect that curbs our desire for immediacy. The process involved does not proceed from reality to the medium that represents it and puts it into images, but from medium to medium, on the principle that reality has always only ever been mediated (Mazzarella 2004).

The aim of the curators was that of stimulating visitors so that they look *through* the works of Virginia Ryan, to glimpse at the web of mediations in which they have taken shape. The exhibited photographs, negatives, film posters, film records, publications (the collected artefacts upon which the artist works) appeared both as integral parts of Virginia Ryan's and the curators' work and, autonomously, as fragments of other irreducible life histories.

It was not, then, a case of providing an ethnographic context (a background) to artworks placed in the foreground, but rather of placing different artefacts in relation to each other. Each of them, in their materiality, holds traces of contexts, lives, meetings, exchanges, retellings. While many of these artefacts (images, objects) have been incorporated in Virginia Ryan's work – while conserving some autonomy – others were presented in a way that evoked an uncertain status: they were enigmatic 'things', fluctuating without rest between *objet trouvé*, ethnographic document and artwork, showing a mediated and re-mediated composite character. This way of presenting artefacts allowed us to bring out the chiasmus, the partially shared ground, that made the joint curatorship possible, and, at the same time, it revealed the point from which the different approaches of the anthropologist and art curator arose: the first one insisting on relationships (looking *through* the images), and the other on the semantic and syntactic integration of artworks (looking *at* the images).

Conclusions

While anthropologists have historically devised their own academic remits – stepping away from the museum into the field, from the object towards the person – today this contradistinction has been set aside: the museum is itself increasingly present in the world and makes its mark on a wide range of cultural dynamics. For the anthropologist, then, the exhibition space is not simply the place in which research conducted elsewhere is reconstructed and communicated, but rather a zone of contact and friction, in which anthropological knowledge is performed, by working collaboratively with words and with things.

Of course, this can also be said for contemporary art curatorship but, beyond the consonances, the proximity and the mutual exchanges that link curatorial practices of contemporary art and anthropology, the differences must be traced in their respective positions in the broader social and cultural scenarios: with all the limits of a generalization, I believe that we can say that while the anthropologist, centring his practice on ethnography, tends to bring the exhibition space into the world, the curator, on the contrary, more focused on the care and management of works that respond to the entrepreneurial logic of the system of art, tends to reabsorb the world in the 'museum', however it is intended. In this frame, a 'rhetorical rejection of the market is often a precondition for the successful marketing of artworks' (Graw 2010: 9) and, as it appears in the practices of the New Institutionalism that emerged at the end of the 1990s, public engagement, participation and interaction have turned criticism of the institution into a tool of self-legitimization at the service of the institution itself (Doherty 2006; Voorhies 2017).

Whereas the curator, in his or her maieutic, managerial role, tends towards a celebratory representation of the artist, glossing over unresolved issues and failures (Glicenstein 2015: 74–5), and privileging a 'curatable art' (Balzer 2015: 58) that conforms to the requirements of curatorial practice, the anthropologist finds the greatest profit, heuristically speaking, in obstacles and contradictions.

94   *The Anthropologist as Curator*

Even if the academic anthropologist, as we know, is subject to increasing institutional pressure towards more efficient and more effective performance that limits and remodels the times, places and ways of research, the intensity of the constraints does not seem comparable yet: the binding link with the field and the 'point of view of the native', even if not intended as an external referent to which to correspond in terms of an *adequatio rei et intellectus*, remains in place. Our desire for coevalness should not make us forget the 'virtue of patience', despite our 'anxiety of belatedness' (Marcus 2015): the time pressure we are increasingly subject to should not let us neglect the necessary distance from the mainstream, which is the condition of our critical gaze.

When Clémentine Deliss (2012: 68), director of the Weltkulturen Museum in Frankfurt, Germany, asserts that: 'fieldwork has to take place within the museum itself and no longer on journeys to distant lands. Today expeditions take place within the [museum] stores', we may agree that there are no longer any 'distant lands', so to speak. However, the need to step outside the museum stores has not changed.

References

Amselle, J. L. (2016), *Le musée exposé*, Paris: Editions Ligne.
Appadurai, A., ed. (1986), *The Social Life of Things: Commodities in Cultural Perspective*, Cambridge: Cambridge University Press.
Augé, M. (1988), *Le dieu objet*, Paris: Flammarion.
Balzer, David (2015), *Curationism: How Curating Took Over the Art World – And Everything Else*, London: Pluto Press.
Bargna, I. (2008), 'Bandjoun Station dove sta? Sull'incerto confine dell'esporre arte qui e altrove', *Africa e Mediterraneo*, 62: 50–4.
Bargna, I. (2012), 'Between Hollywood and Bandjoun: Art Activism and Anthropological Ethnography into the Mediascape', *Journal des anthropologues*, 3–4 (130–131): 101–30.
Bargna, I. (2013), 'Traditional African Art in Biography, Collections and Archives', in L.-P. Nicoletti (ed.), *The Primitive Avant-Garde: The Alessandro Passaré Collection*, Milan: Scalpendi Editore.
Bargna, I. (2014), 'Filming Food Cultural Practices in Cameroon: An Artistic and Ethnographic Work', *Archivio di Etnografia*, 1–2: 113–33.
Bargna, I. (2016), 'Collecting Practices in Bandjoun, Cameroon: Thinking about Collecting as a Research Paradigm', *African Arts*, 49 (2): 20–37.
Bargna, I. (2018), 'La cena dei desideri: antropologi, artisti e persone senza fissa dimora, davanti al futuro', in T. India (ed.), *La definizione culturale del tempo*, Palermo: Edizioni Fondazione Ignazio Buttitta.
Bargna, I. and Coccia, M., eds. (2018), *Plural Biographies. Virginia Ryan: Art, Africa and Elsewhere*, Milan: Fabbri.
Bargna, I. and Parodi da Passano M.G., eds. (2010), *L'africa delle meraviglie. Arti africane nelle collezioni italiane / Wonders of Africa. African Arts in Italian Collections*, Cinisello Balsamo: Scalpendi.
Basu, P. and Macdonald, S. (2007), *Exhibition Experiments*, Malden, Oxford, Victoria, Wiley-Blackwell.
Baudrillard, J. (1972), *Pour une critique de l'économie politique du signe*, Paris: Gallimard.

Facing the 'Curatorial Turn' 95

Belting, H. and Buddensieg A. (2009), *The Global Art World: Audiences, Markets, and Museums*, Ostfildern: Hatje Cantz Verlag.

Belting, H., A. Buddensieg and P. Weibel, eds. (2011), *Global Studies: Mapping Contemporary Art and Culture*, Ostfildern: Hatje Cantz Verlag.

Böhme, G. (2017), *Critique of Aesthetic Capitalism*, Milan: Mimesis.

Boltanski, L. and Esquerre, A. (2017), *Enrichissement. Une critique de la marchandise*, Gallimard, Paris.

Bolter, J. D. and Grusin, R., (2000), *Remediation: Understanding New Media*, Cambridge MA, MIT Press.

Bourdieu, P. (1979), *La distinction*, Paris: Plon.

Conn, S. (2010), *Do Museums Still Need Objects?* Philadelphia: University of Pennsylvania Press.

Deliss, C. (2012), 'Performing the Curatorial in a Post-Ethnographic Museum', in M. Lind (ed.) (2012), *Performing the Curatorial Within and Beyond the Art*, Berlin: Sternberg Press.

Derlon, B. and Jeudy-Ballini, M. (2008), *La passion de l'art primitif. Enquête sur les collectionneurs*, Paris: Gallimard.

Descola, P. (2005), *Par-delà nature et culture*, Paris: Gallimard.

Doherty, C. (2006), 'New Institutionalism and the Exhibition as Situation', in A. Budak and P. Pakesch (eds), *Protections: This Is Not an Exhibition*, 172–8, Kunsthaus Graz and steirischer herbst, Graz, Austria.

Enwezor, O., ed. (2012), *Intense Proximity: An Anthology of the Near and the Far*, Paris: Artlys.

Feld, S. and Ryan, V. (2016), 'Collaborative Migrations. Contemporary Art as/in Anthropology', in R. Cox, A. Irving and C. Wright (eds), *Beyond Text? Critical Practices and Sensory Anthropology*, Manchester: Manchester University Press.

Geczy, A. and Karaminas, V. (2013), *Fashion and Art*. London: Bloomsbury.

Gell, A. (1998), *Art and Agency. An Anthropological Theory*, Oxford: Clarendon Press.

Gioni, M. (2013), *Il Palazzo Enciclopedico (The Encyclopedic Palace)*, *Biennale Arte 2013*, Venezia: Marsilio.

Glicenstein, J. (2015), *L'invention du curateur. Mutations dans l'art contemporain*, Paris: PUF.

Graw, I. (2010), *High Price: Art Between the Market and Celebrity Culture*, Berlin: Sternberg Press.

Greenblatt, S. (1991), 'Resonance and Wonder', in I. Karp and S. D. Lavine (eds), *Exhibiting Cultures: The Poetics and Politics of Museum Display*, 42–56, Washington, DC: Smithsonian Institution.

Kasfir, S. (1992), 'African art and Authenticity: A Text Without a Shadow', *African Arts*, 2.

Kirshenblatt-Gimblett, B. (2006), 'World Heritage and Cultural Economics', in I. Karp, C. A. Kratz, L. Szwaja and T. Ybarra-Frausto (eds), *Museum Frictions: Public Cultures/ Global Transformations*, Durham and London: Duke University Press.

Landry, C. (2006), *The Art of City-Making*, London: Earthscan.

Latour, B. (1996), *Petite réflexion sur le culte moderne des dieux faitiches*, Paris: Synthelabo Group/Les empecheurs de penser en rond.

Lind, M., ed. (2012), *Performing the Curatorial Within and Beyond the Art*, Berlin: Sternberg Press.

Lipovetsky, G. and Serroy, J. (2013), *L'esthétisation du monde. Vivre à l'âge du capitalisme artiste*, Paris: Gallimard.

Maillard, B. (1984), *Pouvoir et religion. Les structure socioreligieuses de la chefferie de Bandjoun (Cameroun)*, Berne: Peterland.

Marcus, G. E., ed. (2000), *Para-Sites: A Casebook against Cynical Reason*, Vol. 7, Chicago: University of Chicago Press.

Marcus, G. E. (2015), 'Ethnography between the Virtue of Patience and the Anxiety of Belatedness Once Coevalness is Embraced', in S. Dalsgaard and M. Nielsen (eds), *Time and Field*, Oxford: Berghahn.

Mazzarella, W. (2004), 'Culture, Globalization, Mediation', *Annual Review of Anthropology*, 33: 345–67.

Miller, D., ed. (2005), *Materiality*, Durham, NC; and London: Duke University Press.

Okwunodu Ogbechie, S. (2011), *Making History: African Collectors and the Canon of African Art. The Femi Akinsanya African Art Collection*, Milan: 5 Continents Editions.

O'Neill, P. (2012), *The Culture of the Curating, and the Curating of Culture(s)*, Cambridge, MA: MIT Press.

Pietz, W. (1985, 1987), 'The Problem of the Fetish', *Res*, 9: 13.

Pine, B. J. and Gilmore, J. H. (1999), *The Experience Economy. Work Is a Theater and Every Business a Stage*, Boston: Harvard Business Publishing.

Pomian, K. (1978), 'Collezione', *Enciclopedia Einaudi*, Turin: Einaudi.

Price, S. (2010), 'Museums and Their Collaborators: Anthropologists, Art Historians and Collectors', in I. Bargna and G. Parodi da Passano (eds), *L'africa delle meraviglie. Arti africane nelle collezioni italiane / Wonders of Africa. African Arts in Italian Collections*, Cinisello Balsamo: Scalpendi.

Rifkin, J. (2000), *The Age of Access: The New Culture of Hypercapitalism*, New York: Penguin.

Rowland, M. (1996), 'The Consumption of an African Modernity', in M. J. Arnoldi, C. M. Geary and K. L. Hardin (eds), *African Material Culture*, 188–213, Indianapolis and Bloomington: Indiana University Press.

Scott J. (1990), *Domination and the Arts of Resistance. Hidden Transcripts*, New Haven: Yale University Press.

Voorhies, J. (2017), *Beyond Objecthood: The Exhibition as Critical Form since 1968*, Cambridge, MA: MIT Press.

Warnier, J.-P. (2009), *Regner au Cameroun, Le Roi-Pot*, Paris: Karthala.

6

Ethnographic Terminalia: co-curation and the role of the anecdote in practice

The Ethnographic Terminalia Collective
(Members of the collective and authors of this
chapter in reverse alphabetical order)

Stephanie Takaragawa, Trudi Lynn Smith, Fiona P. McDonald,
Kate Hennessy and Craig Campbell

In any collaborative relation there is a fear of deep checking in. What do we do in the event of the force of clashing taste? It might turn out that we were falling through ice after all, not making tracks in the same-enough way. Some collaborators seek a secure job as the referent. [...] Some collaborators demand that everything confirms the circuits of their enjoyment. We are interested in the elaborate strange logic of the world. Being in the scene that is pulsating, not separating what's out there or in us.

Lauren Berlant and Kathleen Stewart. 2019.
The Hundreds. Durham: Duke University Press

Introduction

Anecdotes are brief, unofficial accounts of events that have become an unexpected yet critical tactic for our curatorial collective. The Ethnographic Terminalia Collective functions as a leaderless cooperative. While we each maintain individual research, art and curatorial programmes, in the Ethnographic Terminalia project we aim to operate with a collective voice. As we capture in this chapter, we curate, write and make things together and make decisions on a consensual basis with the intention of sharing duties and obligations equally. We are held together by a mutual interest in the intersections of ethnographic epistemologies, creative practices, artistic expression and exhibitions. In these intersections, anecdotes have been central to finding our collective voice in order to either fill a gap or clarify a misunderstanding within the larger story of what we have worked on together. They are significant and useful accounts because of the way they reduce and reconstitute shared experiences, lessons we have put into practice and problems we still seek to solve that may otherwise be forgotten and written out of our history. While anecdotes are typically considered unofficial accounts with a tenuous authoritative claim, they are also valued for their affective force in ethnographic and qualitative research. We have come to understand the anecdote as a critical component of our curatorial practice. Treating it as such helps us to focus on maintenance work (Zárate 2018) rather than merely the product or exhibition. By maintenance work we mean the shared social connections and affective assemblages that allow for exhibitions to happen, rather than simply focusing on the exhibitions themselves.

Ethnographic Terminalia has worked in a collaborative curatorial mode aimed at developing and fostering space for anthropology and art interactions since 2009. The anecdote has been critical for enabling and sustaining our collaborative labour. When we tell anecdotes we honour, mark and respect the invisible labour that is so fleeting, hard to register and even more difficult to remember. Anecdotes can help to recall the energies invested in producing the projects, the publications and the ephemeral by-products of Ethnographic Terminalia's work. In this chapter we show how sharing anecdotes among ourselves, what we sometimes call anecdote-ing, is generative of co-action and care. It participates in the reconstitution of shared memories laced with the sustained practices of observing and listening. We have also come to value conflict and dissent as mechanisms to help us move outside of our individuated worlds and the networks we occupy towards more integral forms of collaboration, more honest forms of learning and new ways of being *with* each other. In this chapter we unpack the sociality and complexity of anecdotes within the collective action of the anecdote-ing practices of the Ethnographic Terminalia Collective that draw from curatorial opportunities for shared remembering, and at other times the reality of collective forgetting (Connerton 1989; Brockmeir 2002).

Co-action

For ten years, the Ethnographic Terminalia Collective has worked to curate projects with individuals and groups inside and outside of the academy with the goal of constructing capacious places that can support an array of social formations (including reflection, creation and contention) in contemporary anthropology. Our collective has worked with more than 150 artists (visual artists, musicians, poets, photographers, etc.) and anthropologists to date in an ongoing, creative collaboration between anthropological researchers and practising artists. We create and curate artworks, anthropological research and performances in gallery spaces. We have installed works and created workshops within academic and public realms across North America (www.ethnographicterminalia.org). These events have often been produced in tandem with the annual meetings of the American Anthropological Association (AAA); in this context they have functioned as a kind of para-site to these academic meetings (Marcus 2000). Additionally, we have curated and organized projects alongside events such as the Margaret Mead Festival at the American Museum of Natural History (AMNH), New York, and the International Symposium of Electronic Arts (ISEA). Over the years, the Ethnographic Terminalia Collective has configured an audience that actively participates in exploring the creative liminal space between disciplinary boundaries.

Our approach to curation is negotiated and fostered between Stephanie Takaragawa, Trudi Lynn Smith, Fiona P. McDonald, Kate Hennessy and Craig Campbell – the five core members – creating unique physical and intellectual spaces. One thread of our work is an interest in the generative spaces that are provided by theories and practices of art and anthropology, including the ethnographic turn and sensory ethnography (Pink and Howes 2010; Howes 2006). We find that such spaces of disciplinary upheaval can agitate elements as they mix with our projects and provide unexpected possibilities. These turns have provided a nexus for re-examining anthropology as a discipline – its boundaries and its own epistemologies – as well as to think through the ways that multimodal and intermedial forms can help expand conventional sites of publication and exhibition (Collins et al. 2017).

As a collective, we struggle to come up with a term or words to describe what it is that we do. What are these social formations, exactly? While exhibition is often the term we use for our projects, it is sometimes inaccurate in relation to our work together, in that the objective is not necessarily exhibition, but is perhaps more precisely explained as a concept driven through a project. Through the process of collaborative work, we are working towards a paradigm that treats exhibitions as prototypes (Boyer 2011), which might act as a form and space for potential exploratory ethnographic epistemologies. We appreciate Dominic Boyer's observation that we 'operate [...] in a prototypical mode, as experimental assemblages of form, function, and effect, designed to provide new insights and ways of understanding' (Boyer 2011: 95). The role that anecdotes play in this prototyping/curatorial process is central.

Since forming as a collective, we have (at the time of writing this in early 2019) organized, installed and prepared an annual workshop or exhibition (sometimes two) for a total of eleven projects. In addition to this, we have published catalogues and 'rapid prototype' publications as well as other co-authored articles and chapters. The only exception to this record of creative production in public spaces was in 2017 when we turned our labour to developing an open-access archival project that we circle back to at the end of this chapter. Our curatorial projects range in scale, scope and audience from year to year. As anthropologists who curate, each year we experiment with a new exhibition or workshop format that takes our curatorial efforts (and the field of anthropology) in new directions and that is responsive to the unique locations and networks of people involved.

For example, in 2010, we presented a film by the late artist/anthropologist Susan Hiller (1940–2019) along with works by emerging and well-known artists and anthropologists in a small-scale commercial gallery in the Freret District, New Orleans, Louisiana (see Figure 6.1). Then in 2011, we moved on to experiment with thematically focused exhibitions. To do this, we undertook exhibiting a main work that required a year of planning and negotiation to present the work of Panamanian artist Humberto Vélez. This piece was installed alongside twenty-seven other experiments in and between art and anthropology that thematically occupied spaces within field-sites, studios and laboratories – which we presented in a centre for new media in Montréal, Québec. In 2013, during the Margaret Mead Film Festival at the American Museum of Natural History, New York, Ethnographic Terminalia was invited to create an installation that pushed the festival beyond the screen. To do this, we collaborated

Figure 6.1 Ethnographic Terminalia, New Orleans, Louisiana, 2011. Installation view. Photo: Craig Campbell). Floor plan preparation. Photo: Fiona P. McDonald.

with artist/anthropologist Zoe Bray who demonstrated her unique ethnographic techniques of 'thick description' by painting portraits of well-known anthropologists before hundreds of viewers coming and going from the museum (see Figure 6.2). We invited New York-based anthropologists Fred Myers and Audra Simpson to participate. During the performance and installation, we documented the scene and engaged with bystanders who asked us to explain what was happening as they sought out a sense of how this event might be connected to a museum of natural history. From our role in negotiating the space for this live performance through to representing it on our website (where all of our projects have a digital afterlife, as well as the catalogues we publish through the AAA) was an undertaking involving constant interactions with a myriad of parties. These interactions were (and continue to be) facilitated through anecdotes.

Figure 6.2 'Seeing ethnography', 2013. Installation view. American Museum of Natural History, New York. Photos: Fiona P. McDonald.

Our effort to think through and describe anecdote-ing as a collective draws on a body of interdisciplinary literature that theorizes the anecdote. Without a doubt, the anecdote has played a unique role in the curatorial work we have done over a decade. The fragmentariness of anecdotes as they are performed has the capacity to disrupt the neat structuring processes of collective memory work. Yet this same term is applied in very different conditions. When the anecdote is written down and incorporated into a narrative it is domesticated. It serves a new function. What we are after in this chapter is to capture the performance of the anecdote, not the recollection of the anecdote. Thus, any of the anecdotes we relate here do not secure a particular historical account (though they may do so inadvertently) but rather they highlight processes of negotiation in our curatorial projects. Anecdotes for us are not just an opportunity to see shared memory in formation but to see curatorial processes in action. Anecdotes under the conditions of curation allow us to tell each other what we think will work and what concerns us; what doings or makings seem (in different contexts anyway) to have failed or succeeded in the past. For example, one of us may say: '*I was at this show in March and saw an arrangement of photographs that worked really well, maybe we can try something like this when we show …*' or '*Wait … wait … We tried using this adhesive a few years ago and destroyed the wall, we need to find a different solution before we get there.*' It is here that the anecdote also becomes central to the articulation of skills and expertise in installation tactics.

The span of these years of working together has provided us with insights about what it means to work collectively. Our work from inception, to production, to reception, to reflection generates opportunities to revisit spaces of collaboration/collectivity towards the end goal of informing possibilities for ethnographic praxis. Continually in a process of revision, the collective sees its work as process-based when formulating questions. This process draws on an eclectic array of models from cabinets of curiosities, sensory technologies, phantasmagoria, histories of exhibitions from museums and galleries, to world fairs, always engaging with site-specificity to draw the viewer and ourselves out of the traditional exhibition space, and outwards towards multiple audiences. In this process, the anecdote has emerged in our creative and collective process as a critical concept.

The realization that anecdotes feature as a central curatorial tactic for us as a collective came to light in May 2016 during a residency at Microsoft Research (MSR) in Cambridge, Massachusetts. Fellow anthropologist Mary Gray invited us to be part of MSR's residency programme where we spent time unpacking work we had done in previous years and discussing possible future projects. Up until this point in the history of our collective we had never had a dedicated opportunity to focus exclusively on exploring and reflecting upon *what* our curatorial practice *is*. The process of reflecting on each project has somehow become embedded in our practice of anecdote-ing, which emerged due to the nature of our globally dispersed group that meets predominantly via Skype. There have been times when we were able to intentionally create time to discuss how a show went immediately after the opening reception in order to reflect on highs and lows while it was fresh in our minds. But these have been infrequent, though fortuitous, opportunities, given that none of us have never lived in the same city while being part of the collective and meeting primarily online. We work collaboratively through Google Drive, Dropbox, email, failed attempts at various online project management tools (such as Asana and Basecamp), and SMS text messaging. Using these digital tools and platforms heightened the value of being together in-person to anecdote, without time differences, dropped internet connections or the pressures to run to other meetings or happenings in each of our lives. In that space at Microsoft Research, we made extensive use of the whiteboard (Figure 6.3) as a technology that allowed us to intensively and transparently compose our ideas and reflections. Visualizing the anecdote allowed the curatorial and anthropological knowledge embedded deep within them to be visible to us. In that process we realized that we had been bearing witness to each other's unique actions in the collective in the various ways we remembered, shared nuances of events and collectively anecdoted the curatorial lessons of Ethnographic Terminalia. Were it not for the week at Microsoft where we had the opportunity for intense, in-person

Figure 6.3 Anecdote-ing at Microsoft Research, Cambridge, Massachusetts, 2016. Photos: Fiona P. McDonald.

reflection on what it is *we* do, how *we* do it and what comes next, this chapter may not exist.

Anecdotes in practice

Over the ten years of working together, anecdote-ing has figured prominently in the ways that we have presented curatorial and artist statements. In 2009, the first Ethnographic Terminalia project took place in Philadelphia. At that point we were globally distributed as a team from Canada, the USA and the UK (today we are situated between Canada and the USA, and at times from our respective fieldwork sites). As such, the finer details were worked out during the three-day installation timeframe in Philadelphia, Pennsylvania. In this exhibition, we were not only working against an internal goal of breaking away from the conference mode that required anthropological knowledge to be reduced to 15-minute paper presentations, but also trying to subvert traditional ways that exhibitions were installed. In retrospect, this first project was a series of individual projects with widely divergent aims installed in proximity to one another. While the works were not necessarily prototypes, the exhibition itself was. Not all that dissimilar to a performance, curating this project had the same stumbling blocks and some of the same challenges of performance because it evolved to respond to multiple genres. Performance art and Happenings still have an experimental spirit attached to them and are often events that are challenging to audiences. It is hard to do these well. It is hard to make them comprehensive, and we wanted our curatorial performance to push against the traditional forms of academic knowledge dissemination in order to be agitational as well as accessible.

Every time we engage in a project, what emerges are anecdotes that shape not only how we remember the exhibition but how we curate future exhibitions, all the while asking ourselves: how are we to innovate within useful and expected conventions? In this process of curating in a new city each year, coming to understand new locations and new institutions is just a small part of the learning curve, but a critical one. When we have curated projects that are more understandable and comprehensible to the space (again, relating to our commitment to site-specificity), to the community and to the historical moment, people have tended to respond better to it; however, in this situation the project does not do what we want it to do, which is challenging normative ways of knowing. For example, in our first exhibition (Philadelphia, 2009) we laid out a 'grid' (Figure 6.4) of didactic text. Fiona P. McDonald and Craig Campbell had worked to design the text as a gallery guide. When it came to installing 'the grid',

Figure 6.4 Ethnographic Terminalia, Philadelphia, Pennsylvania, 2009. Installation view of wall text. Photo: Craig Campbell.

we wanted to challenge those institutional ideas of using visible text to anchor visual works. We did not remove the text from direct proximity to the individual projects, it was available in a flipchart-like format next to the work for those who wished to read more about the piece. Our decision to focus on the visual and material aspects of each project was aimed at encouraging people to engage with the pieces in more substantial

Figure 6.5 Ethnographic Terminalia, Denver, Colorado, *Aeolian Politics*, 2015. Installation view of wall text. Photos: Trudi Lynn Smith (top) and Fiona P. McDonald (bottom).

and significant ways by compelling them to *learn from the objects* rather than from whatever was in the text. We opted to use a grid display of didactic materials at the entrance, putting all the text together and away from the installed pieces. However, as this was not well received (anecdotal feedback we each received from colleagues after the exhibition in our own networks), we retreated from this model in subsequent years, choosing to conform to more conventional uses of artist statements mounted in visible proximity to the works themselves. We have had to decide which aesthetic and ideological battles to fight within each iteration of our projects, and we have been constantly hoping to explore new ways to engage audiences, all the while negotiating with exhibitors. Each year we came back to the reality that it is hard to be challenging and unconventional when we run the risk of alienating our audiences; the tension between innovation and convention has propelled our own exploration of the spaces between art and anthropology.

Finally, by 2015 we made a choice through negotiation among ourselves (negotiation that was built on years of anecdotes not only about the labour, materials, and techniques of installation, but also about the curatorial effects of the didactic wall texts) to go all out on the wall text and conform to convention, given that we were in a space with the legibility of a traditional art gallery. To do this, we conformed to use the more traditional decal wall text, logo and sponsors acknowledgement (Figure 6.5).

The goal of writing collaboratively about the anecdotes that push our curatorial practice, as exemplified in the example above, is to explore the workings of collective labour in the performance of curation and the defining of the liminal space between art and anthropology. This reveals the processes by which knowledge is produced in curatorial praxis. Elsewhere we have written about the role of collaboration in our work as a collective (Ethnographic Terminalia Collective 2019), but in this chapter we focus specifically on one social behaviour of anecdote-ing that binds our creative efforts.

Anecdotal theory

In Erin Peters' article 'Curatorial Studies: Towards Co-creation and Multiple Agencies' (2016), she introduces the need to incorporate an expanded consideration not only of the agency of curators but that enacted by both audiences and objects/things. As we have demonstrated in our reading of the 'grid' from Philadelphia and other didactic texts used by our collective, curatorial statements (and their emplacement) have a clear agency. Such a consideration of multiple agencies is also helpful when thinking about the specific agency of the anecdote in our practice. We had a 'hunch' about the role of anecdotes in our collaborative curatorial practice, and during our time at MSR it became manifest. As Fiona P. McDonald (in a co-authored article with Keith Murphy and Luke Cantarella) writes:

> Traditional ethnographic research tends to start with some sort of intuition that, if followed, constitutes a good risk out of which the work can grow. Along the way, such intuitions pile up, coalescing into a long process of what could be called

Ethnographic Terminalia

107

hunchwork, an ongoing attempt to tether hypotheticals to the actuality of present circumstances. The first step in hunchwork is often that intuition that the project itself is feasible and worthy of study. Other steps include a hunch that the project is timely, that the methods employed are the proper ones, and that the chosen interlocutors are the right people to talk to. And, as we write, we follow a hunch that the texts we produce are adequate and accurate representations of the worlds we explore in our fieldwork. It's hunches all the way down. (Murphy, McDonald and Cantarella 2017)

Such hunchwork for us was by no means a fixed or even planned practice but rather processual, tentative, and improvisatory. Anecdotes go hand-in-hand with hunchwork, and so we might say it is anecdotes all the way down, too. Anecdotes work across the range of situations we find ourselves in, from planning and executing to recalling and narrativizing. In this vein, it was the work of Jane Gallop (2002) in *Anecdotal Theory* that resonated with us in relation to our own curatorial practice, delivering an additional register for validating the anecdote. Gallop demonstrates a method of theorizing based on anecdotes; essentially, she composes an anecdote from her life experience and then performs a reading of it. This work of telling and analysing the telling marks both an ethical and a critical commitment in the tradition of 'weak theory' that focuses on encounters and entangled modes of emergence.

What happens, then, when the anecdote is the result of collective knowing and retelling? The unique quality of anecdotes for the Ethnographic Terminalia Collective also means addressing the inherent bias and subjectivity that comes with anecdotes. We each carry our own distinct perspectives, and yet when we anecdote together it creates a sort of consensus by way of inter-rater reliability that allows us to fact-check a multi-perspectival and emergent narrative of either a curatorial moment, or lesson or memory. In this effort, contesting notions about what art and anthropology really are produces a space for productive friction. The reality is that we may really not share consensus of what art does or where it belongs. We may not even really share consensus of what anthropology is exactly. To function as a collective, we have had critical conversations and produced discourses that allow us to generate a space that probably does not fit easily for any of us. Yet there is adequacy, there are moments where the accounts provide a good-enough ground on which to proceed. We are drawing each other into a collective and dynamic process for art and anthropology that de-privileges individual practice; it is in this process that anecdote-ing helps us to foster our collective sociality in the terrain of curatorial praxis.

Our intent as the Ethnographic Terminalia Collective has been to consistently respond to and critique the intersections, interstices, and interactions that inform the disciplinary boundaries between contemporary art and anthropology through the co-action of curating. We continue to consider disciplinary horizons and boundaries as a way to explore generative and emergent possibilities in and of multimodal ethnography, while interrogating ideological formations and positions. Over ten years of curating collaborative exhibitions, installations, publications, and workshops, the anecdote has become an emergent form of sociality that stands in as a critical and improvisatory device in our collaborative curatorial work. The provisionality of the anecdote as it is conventionally understood is produced through an array of informal interactions. It seems to be the raw material of narrative, of memory becoming collective memory. This provisionality of the anecdote is a probing of shared experience and recollection of that experience. An anecdote is a brief recomposition of reality. Anecdotes condense a variety of rhetorical gestures as they are entertaining, they position the speaker within our team and yet their informality invites a more casual, yet accurate, set of expectations that joyfully contain bits of wisdom produced from the shared creative labour of curating and creating large-scale projects and publications.

For us, anecdotes often start with a verbal prompt ('*Oh wait do you remember …*', or '*It is like that time when …*', or '*How are we going to do this?*', or '*Let's not forget when* ██████ *said we should* ██████ *and we knew then we had to* ██████ '), or a physical trigger in a location we are standing or walking through ('*Wait that wall looks a lot like the paint will peel if we use those* ██████ ', or '*Yikes! Is this place even ADA approved?*'). Given the intimacy of working together in a creative and professional capacity for a decade, it can be as slight as a raised eyebrow at a certain topic (such as budgets, spreadsheets, fundraising, etc.), to a smirk (indicating '*I do not remember it that way at all, oh wait that is because I had run out to get something at* ██████ *!*'), to a hand resting on the shoulder in a moment of reflection (suggesting '*We will not make that mistake again!*'). This is the unique linguistic and physical vocabulary that we co-created as curatorial peers together through nuance and presence and care in order to communicate in the spaces between projects. In the same way that Roland Barthes never shows the reader the photograph of his mother in the book *Camera Lucida*, we feel laying out extant textual anecdotes cannot ever capture the infinite scenarios that transpire over donuts, in DIY stores, electronic stores, galleries, taxis, up ladders, on public transit, during Skype calls, at conferences and in bars (Barthes 1981). Therefore, we have used this chapter to unpack the relevance of the process of anecdote-ing, without exposing the intimacy of the content that has signification only to us. Anecdotes, when done collectively, draw the subject (the problem we are solving) back into the object (the lessons we have learned), thus slowing down and complicating the route to any kind of results in a process that inspires and brings forth a formal informality into our collaborative knowledge-work and curatorial labour.

The anecdote also allows for the recounting of the witnessed actions of others in and an acknowledgement of the value of everyone's actions and skills within the collective. Therefore, it is the layering of activities, actions and interactions over time and space that sediment the objects and expressions of Ethnographic Terminalia's work. No single anecdote could possibly capture this process. For us, one anecdote springboards to another. From shared Google docs to phone calls, Skype sessions, and late-night text messages, we worked to elicit anecdotes from each other in the preparation of this chapter. What became apparent is that anecdotes emerge in the contexts *between* the curatorial projects we install or the publications we write. Like our exhibitions as prototypes, the anecdote occupies a potential liminal space between action and knowledge in curation. Again, it circles back to our prioritization of process before product in the works included in our projects, and an acknowledgement that our curation stands as a kind of performance. These mini-stories can be precious, tedious, humorous, dead serious or dull, and it is difficult when we attempt to translate them into textual form. Exploring multimodal moves across disciplines, crafts, methods, practices, and histories within the larger field of contemporary art and anthropology might be similar to what Irit Rogoff calls 'unframed knowledge' – the power of such unframed knowledge provides the opportunity to remake categories. 'When knowledge is unframed it is less grounded genealogically and can navigate forwards rather than backwards' (Rogoff 2010: 41). Our curatorial practice is one of collectively working forwards towards something ill-defined or ungrounded, something we might even imagine as a shared structure of feeling, but one that draws upon looking backwards to what we have done together. More specifically, we used the telling and retelling of our shared history/experience of each show (down to minor stories of installing specific works, dealing with particular vendors, etc.) to generate the next project. A set of common attractions bring about the coordination of ideas and people in settings that demand modes of engagement that differ radically from textual knowledge, but rather are a balanced coordination constituted as an effort to alter discourses surrounding the production of anthropological knowledge. In this sense, Ethnographic Terminalia is a project oriented towards the aesthetics of anthropological knowledge, and beyond to intellectual commitments, reconfiguring the ways in which we know about and talk about the world. In this instance – through anecdotes.

Building on Gallop's experiment with anecdotal theory, Holly Pester argues for an appreciation of the 'critical potential of the anecdote as part of the formation of critical theory, wherein the anecdotal puts the relationship between lived experience and critical theory into play. [...] We can take from this that anecdote as research method, where body and affect are not divorced from the narrative formations that take place in the archive, creates a scene and event of knowledge production that again involves material conditions and social entanglements' (Pester 2017: 120). In the context of Ethnographic Terminalia, we might substitute curatorial tactic for research method and shift from the archive to the site-specificity of gallery and exhibition spaces. Anecdotes tether labours – component to lived experience – to critical questions of identity, representation, and agency. Over the years our project has ranged broadly and our theory has been performed most consistently through critical curatorial practice.

In *Identity Anecdotes: Translation and Media Culture*, Meaghan Morris presents a typology of anecdotes by describing two diverging definitions of the anecdote within textual environments. One being a 'narrative of *detached* incident' and the other being a 'short narrative of a *particular* incident' (2006). The latter 'suggests that an incident has been separated, like a stray button or a lost tooth, from a prior and larger whole' (2006: 8). The idea of a narrative being detached from a particular incident is somewhat less interesting for our curatorial project. All historical narratives are of course detached. As Randolph Starn notes in the context of historiography: 'Mainstream history's default position is that anecdotes are a guilty indulgence unless severely disciplined. Contrariwise the jarring anecdote has its uses precisely in disrupting the detached pose and forced coherence of history-as-usual and, for history-struck literary critics, literary-criticism-as-usual' (Starn 2008: 140). The work of the anecdote is not only to the cohesion of the event it either creates or represents, but also in the *communis opinio* (the generally accepted view) it generates. Furthermore, in the telling of anecdotes, body, labour and affect are inserted back into the curatorial flow.

Contrary to Starn's position on the disruptive power of the anecdote we can also see how our anecdotes surreptitiously construct the whole. Surreptitiously because our labour, and the labour of the anecdote, tends to be underestimated and disruptive. Consider how Jean Bessette, a scholar of English literature whose work bridges archival and historiographic theory as well as digital and multimedia studies, has used Starn's definition of the anecdote. She writes: 'If, as Randolph Starn asserts, "the jarring anecdote has its uses precisely in disrupting the detached pose and forced coherence of history-as-usual" (140), then collections of anecdotes [...] can amplify the single anecdote's unruly potential to disrupt cohesive accounts [...]' (Bessette 2013: 23–4). For Bessette, the archival anecdote maintains a disruptive capacity that is welcome in her historiographic ethos. But what becomes of these anecdotes when they have performed their disruptive task and have become incorporated into another story? The anecdote, though it retains the name, does not always retain the disruptive effect. Indeed, we could argue that the anecdote is only temporarily appropriated as an affective vessel. Affect moves on, it slips out from under our fingers and dissolves before our gaze, as we move on to new actions within the performance of curation.

Within ethnographic practice anecdotes and the quoted, translated, interpreted and paraphrased words of others are used extensively (if not paradigmatically). This use of anecdotes builds the foundation of ethnographic knowledge, it is a component part of ethnographic knowledge production. Yet there has always been a distrust by some of such ethnographic knowledge:

> The anecdote is a slippery knowledge maker, its politics suspect. On the one hand, it claims the authority of the first person, of presence. But this 'I was there' aspect of anecdotal knowledge brings with it the force of an authority and the undoing of that authority in equal measure. While anecdote traffics in the authority of the personal witness, its undoing emerges in its lack of verification – the *singularity* of that witness. [...] Anecdote is fundamentally unverifiable; if it were verified, vetted, it would cease to be anecdotal. (Loveless 2011: 24, emphasis in original)

So why invite such slipperiness into our practice? Perhaps, in alignment again with what has been called 'weak theory', we can imagine a curatorial practice founded on provisionality, tentativity, and care. The nervousness of the anecdote delivers situation and affect within a frame that allows others points of entry, rather than being repelled by certitudes and closures. It is, what we might call a convivial technique.

Care

Whereas José Esteban Muñoz and others (like Bessette 2013) argue for recognition of the anecdote as a valid form of knowledge in marginalized and subaltern communities, we seek also to mobilize more mundane functions of the anecdote in our curatorial practice. We have found, on reflection, that the anecdote is a critical component to our curatorial work and to the functioning of the collective. In this sense, our group work is oriented around problem-solving and what we call *creative thinking in time with care* to collectively remember and forget. While 'anecdote' is the shorthand we use, we foreground the generative dimension of care as a way to describe our creative and curatorial process as a whole. The anecdotes we allude to in this chapter are built on care and they function for us as an adhesive that binds, bridges, builds, and facilitates through the provisionality of care in the development of projects, social relations and changing the field of anthropology. At the same time, as we aim to illustrate, anecdotes assist with disassembling and disarticulating curatorial lessons in unusually productive ways.

The anecdote in the context of the Ethnographic Terminalia Collective is told for a variety of reasons. It is to exemplify and to entertain (as stated by Loveless), and it is also to interpolate and to reify care and trust created through co-action in curatorial projects. In the continuous work of care and maintenance that goes into collective curation, moments of interpellation help to generate group solidarity because they also work to generate collective memories and tactics. The internal and uncommunicated narratives of individuals with a shared experience require moments of reconstruction, representation and reflection. As anecdotes get told over and over again they start to take on new meanings but they also coalesce disparate memories of what happened, how it happened and why it happened. At certain moments it seems we are all telling similar versions of the same story. The breadth of collective anecdotes spans from shared realities of learning about time management for planning and installation, exhibition space selection, floor plan negotiations, technology installation, jerry-rigging cables, designing secure display devices, applicable art/anthropological theory being referenced in a work we are curating, virtual collaborations and poor internet connections, exhibition displays, adhesive materials, public programming, fundraising, contractual agreements, performance spaces and, most importantly, care.

Conclusion

As a collective effort that has reached ten years of working together, we draw upon our archive of anecdotes to look to the future, knowing that together we have helped to open up a critical curatorial space for art and anthropology. And while the Ethnographic Terminalia project will inevitably come to a close at some point, we also see anecdotes as functioning as ends unto themselves. Individually, an anecdote can hold valuable data, but networked together, in the same way our collective is, when organized under the logic of curation, anecdotes become bonded through entangled forms of sociality and through mundane social acts: conversations and gossip amid planning sessions, workshops, installations, de-installations, and collaborative writing. Anecdotes – one among many sociable acts – have become our focus because we have a hunch that it is doing something interesting (Murphy, McDonald and Cantarella 2017). Specifically, attending to the work of anecdotes might advance a space for anthropologists to work productively as curators in unconventional ways.

In this chapter, we have outlined how the anecdote, and the co-action of anecdoteing, has functioned in our collaborative curatorial processes. In the practice of collaboratively writing this chapter we realized that the anecdote was an accidental curatorial tactic for us – not an intentional curatorial method. Insofar as we can call it a tactic, we recognize that it was an entirely inadvertent one. In attempting to contribute to the ongoing discourse that theorizes anecdotal behaviour in curatorial landscapes, anecdotes have become a central way of social formation rather than a specific mode of curatorial research (McFadden 2015). They are the fodder that creates a new space for art and anthropology.

In 2017, we turned our collective efforts away from an exhibition form to reflect on the Ethnographic Terminalia project as a whole and build out an open-access, pedagogical archive. At this moment, we find that anecdotes trouble our archive in productive ways, and help us to remember the finer lessons learned over ten years. In this project, the collective is producing a 'research archive' of past exhibitions. How can we disrupt the narratives we have constructed? Through anecdote-ing? By foregrounding discontinuity and difference? Valuing serendipitous connections that emerge? In our effort to build a virtual archive that is a repository of both our work (the publications, spreadsheets, budgets, emails and boxes of ephemera in each of our offices, etc.) and the work of those we have exhibited, we find this effort extends a narrative of 'what happened', 'how it happened' and 'why it happened'. Queer theorists of the archive (from Muñoz (1996) and Cvetkovich (2003) to Bessette (2013) and others) have insisted on the importance of the ephemeral and the an-archival. The archive, we learn through experience, is a disciplining machine. Its operations are founded upon choice and selection. Ann Stoler specifically teaches us how reading along the archival grain (something akin to 'studying up') allows us to understand the implicit closures embedded within archives (Stoler 2010). It could be said that this is part of the critique against the archival grain, but the point is that our attention to the anecdote is not simply how Ethnographic Terminalia produces collective histories and histories of the collective, but that we welcome the anecdote as a force that destabilizes normative narratives within our own archive of experience. Someone may ask: Is the anecdote about the archive at all? Yes. It may not be about the formal archive we are building but it most certainly is about the collective's archive of feelings, ideas, orientations, memories, stories, and so on, and the fact that each work was selected during moments of critical reflection and engagement that become the foundation of anecdote-ing in our curatorial practice.

References

Barthes, Roland (1981), *Camera Lucida: Reflections on Photography*, New York: Hill and Wang.

Berlant, Lauren and Kathleen Stewart (2019), *The Hundreds*, Durham, NC: Duke University Press.

Bessette, Jean (2013), 'An Archive of Anecdotes: Raising Lesbian Consciousness after the Daughters of Bilitis', *Rhetoric Society Quarterly*, 43 (1): 22–45.

Boyer, Dominic (2011), 'A Gallery of Prototypes: Ethnographic Terminalia 2010, Curated by Craig Campbell, Fiona P. McDonald, Maria Brodine, Kate Hennessy, Trudi Lynn Smith, Stephanie Takaragawa', *Visual Anthropology Review*, 27 (1): 94–6.

Ethnographic Terminalia

Brockmeir, Jens (2002), 'Remembering and Forgetting: Narrative as Cultural Memory', *Culture & Psychology*, 8 (1): 15–42.

Collins, Samuel, Matthew Durington and Harjant Gill (2017), 'Multimodal: An Invitation', *American Anthropologist*, 19 (1): 142–6.

Connerton, Paul (1989), 'Chapter 1: Social Memory', in *How Societies Remember*. Cambridge: Cambridge University Press.

Cvetkovich, Ann (2003), *An Archive of Feelings Trauma, Sexuality, and Lesbian Public Culture*, Durham, NC: Duke University Press.

Ethnographic Terminalia Collective (2019), 'Function and Form: The Ethnographic Terminalia Collective Between Art and Anthropology', in Dominic Boyer and George Marcus (eds), *Collaboration in Anthropology Today*. Ithaca: Cornell University Press.

Ethnographic Terminalia Collective website: www.ethnographicterminalia.org (accessed 15 April 2018).

Gallop, Jane (2002), *Anecdotal Theory*. Durham, NC: Duke University Press.

Howes, David (2006), 'Charting the Sensorial Revolution', *Senses and Society*, 1 (1): 113–28.

Loveless, Natalie S. (2011), 'Reading with Knots: On Jane Gallop's Anecdotal Theory', *S: Journal of the Circle for Lacanian Ideology Critique*, 4: 24–36.

Marcus, George, ed. (2000), *Para-Sites: A Casebook against Cynical Reason*, Chicago: University of Chicago Press.

McFadden, Kegan (2015), 'Anecdotes as Research and Letting Things Die', curator talk given 12 February 2015, Plug In Institute of Contemporary Art, Winnipeg.

Morris, Meaghan (2006), *Identity Anecdotes: Translation and Media Culture*, Thousand Oaks: Sage.

Muñoz, José Esteban (1996), 'Ephemera as Evidence: Introductory Notes to Queer Acts', *Women & Performance*, 8 (2): 5–16.

Murphy, Keith M., Fiona P. McDonald and Luke Cantarella (June 2017), 'Collective Hunchwork', in the *Theorizing the Contemporary series, Cultural Anthropology*, https://culanth.org/fieldsights/1177-collective-hunchwork (accessed 11 June 2018).

Pester, Holly (2017), 'Archive Fanfiction: Experimental Archive Research Methodologies and Feminist Epistemological Tactics', *Feminist Review*, 115 (1): 114–29.

Peters, E. A. (2016), 'Curator—Curatorial Studies towards Co-creation and Multiple Agencies', *Contemporaneity: Historical Presence in Visual Culture*, 5 (1): 122–8.

Pink, Sarah and David Howes (2010), 'The Future of Sensory Anthropology/The Anthropology of the Senses', *Social Anthropology/Anthropologie Sociale*, 18 (3): 331–40.

Rogoff, Irit (2010), 'Practicing Research: Singularising Knowledge', *MaHKUzine #9: Summer 2010, Doing Dissemination*, 9: 37–42.

Starn, Randolph (2008), 'Historicizing Representation: A Formal Exercise', *Representations*, 104 (1): 137–43.

Stoler, Ann (2010), *Along the Archival Grain: Epistemic Anxieties and Colonial Common Sense*. Princeton: Princeton University Press.

Zárate, Salvador (2018) 'Maintenance', in the *Theorizing the Contemporary series, Cultural Anthropology*, https://culanth.org/fieldsights/1359-maintenance (accessed 17 November 2018).

7

Coming together differently: art, anthropology and the curatorial space

Judith Winter

What we mean when we use the term 'curator' obviously encompasses a broad spectrum of practices. Like all disciplines the activity of curating is continually being redefined. This is a process that is pushed, challenged and accelerated in correspondence with artists and various sites both within and beyond the gallery. In my own circumstances, this way of working was simply a continuation of art school experiences. Suffice to say that in the late 1980s critical discussion concerning 'the curatorial' came largely through practice and courses in departments of art history or those primarily concerned with the museum sector. There were a few notable exceptions for postgraduate students, including the 'Independent Study Programme', affiliated with The Whitney Museum of American Art, New York, which brought together those pursuing studio practice, exhibition-making and critical writing, and Michael Asher's 'post-studio art' course at the California Institute of the Arts, Santa Clarita. These experimental programmes explored the historical, social and intellectual conditions of artistic production. They were exemplary artist-led models. However, to my knowledge, the first courses dedicated to critical curation began with 'The Center for Curatorial Studies' at Bard College, New York (1990) followed by the Royal College of Art, London (1992) and De Appel Curatorial Programme, Amsterdam (1994).

In thinking about the professionalization of curating and the more recent expanded use of the term 'curate' beyond the museum and gallery, it may be helpful to return to the roots of the term, which means deeply nurturing, from the medieval Latin *curatus* (to cure) and equivalent in Latin *cūrātum* – to take care of, to take trouble, to be solicitous or attentive. Traditionally, those charged with the role of 'curator' were custodians or 'keepers', who gathered all manner of artefacts and curios from across the fields of natural history, geology and archaeology as well as different cultures. From historical finds, to everyday items, initially these materials were held in wunderkammer or cabinets of curiosity. Over time they grew, becoming idiosyncratic collections that later were to be ordered into encyclopaedic resources, which form the basis for connoisseurship and academic studies. The history of collecting, conservation and museology leads off from these traditions, while contemporary approaches to 'the curatorial' emerged out of questions concerning the politics of representation and mediation of lived experience. For the curator and anthropologist, or for that matter any interlocutor, this is the basis of critical study that explores the social, historical and ideological forces that underpin a discipline. For those working in experimental ways with artists and participants, 'the curatorial space' remains an ambiguous location, one that is integral to the creative process and emerges through response to practice, described most insightfully by the curator Maria Lind,[1] as 'a way of linking objects, images, processes, people, locations, histories, and discourses in physical space' (Lind 2009).

Around 1997, I recall being drawn into discussions about the location of the curator, artist and diverse publics. I am ambivalent about defining this moment as an 'anthropological turn' in contemporary art. It seems almost too obvious to state that art and anthropology continue to share a discursive space and a common concern with human existence, creativity and social organization. What remains interesting is how the conversation is heightened at times when we need to come together to reimagine alternative futures or answer significant ethical questions – whether social, environmental or technological. However, when I listen to recent discourse among academics and arts professionals, what I hear are counter-attempts to define new territory, or defend our 'professionalized' world.

Recently I was introduced to Roy Wagner, who describes the discipline of anthropology as a form of digressive practice, one that opens up our relationship between experience, thinking and writing. Wagner is best known in anthropology circles for *The Invention of Culture,* published in 1975, which proposes that imagination and creativity lie at the heart of anthropology. As such we invent our cultures, and this takes place through a dialogue between people and the social world; and it is in this unfamiliar and unpredictable space that art and anthropology converge to imagine other ways of knowing and being. This perspective will not resonate with everyone, but what I propose is that this ambiguous space shifts attention away from academic strictures or institutional conventions and opens up a location to speculate rather than contain or contextualize life.

Keeping things alive: resisting containment

In following these thoughts, I am reminded of the writing of the artist Robert Smithson (1938–73) who described the invention of the art institution as one where the 'lived world' is displaced. The artist challenged the curator and audience to question the impulse to re-present or objectify life. He speaks of the museum as 'asylums and jails' and how art 'placed in a gallery... loses its charge, and becomes a portable object or surface disengaged from the outside world' (Smithson 1972: 39). The artwork in these terms is in convalescence – looked on as inanimate, waiting for critics to pronounce them curable or incurable. One understanding of the curator stems from the impulse to mediate or contextualize the lived world, while another quite different understanding is related to the act of curing, as a way to allow things to transform, grow or take on a new life.

Coming Together Differently   117

A series of ephemeral site works, which highlight these ideas, involved Smithson pouring large amounts of construction materials – asphalt, glue, concrete – over a ravine and embankment where industrial waste products were usually discarded. As the materials were released, they were unbounded, finding their own way into the world without undue control. For the artist, these 'material flows' speak of life as unpredictable, an exploration of decay and renewal. Narrated over a film documenting these works, Smithson describes in great detail how he is 'prone to mine regions, volcanic conditions and wastelands. He uses the example of approaching hurricanes, the sense of anticipation, followed by the violent experience of trees being torn and uprooted from the ground, and how this moment then gives way to a sense of calm equilibrium. As such, these works contradict our impulse to fix conditions. Or for Smithson, they disrupt the usual mechanistic world view, they are 'entropy made visible', spotlighting 'the way natural forces interact in a kind of anthropic way.' (Smithson and Cummings, 1972). For those attempting to keep the practices of Smithson and his artistic collaborator, Nancy Holt,[2] such works also challenge intermediaries to find ways beyond the objectification of the world and the impulse to canalize or petrify human life.

I was reminded of these kinds of material experiments while compiling photographic documentation for the exhibition *Out of Sight, Out of Mind* at Lisson Gallery, London (1993). The gallery was returning to its foundational ethos and considering ways to present to a new generation those practices that pushed the boundaries of exhibition-making in the late 1960s. It was here that I was introduced to many individuals who were working *with* artists in undefined territory – not curator – not gatekeeper – not translator, but as 'critical others' whose role was to find the right conditions to bring works into being. It occurs to me that these kinds of 'facilitators' had often been practitioners and studio assistants and were closely related to both the artist and the site. This way of working emerged out of what the historian Rosalind Krauss described as the expanded field of sculpture. This space and approach was anthropological at core, concerned with lived experience, material processes, environmental conditions and temporality. For the discipline of sculpture this described a locus of practitioners who were exploring 'the juncture between stillness and motion, time arrested and time passing' (Krauss 1977: 5). This move beyond a static, idealized medium to a material that was continually in-forming made palpable the world as one that was unpredictable and unstable. A place where both viewer and artist stand 'before the work, and the world, in an attitude of primary humility in order to encounter deep reciprocity' (Krauss 1977: 283)

In the photographic documentation of *Glue Pour*, 1969 (see Figure 7.1), I am drawn to Lucy Lippard, who appears on the right of the image. Lippard is a writer and activist who became a significant role model for many emergent artists, writers and curators working in the 1990s. Lippard invited Smithson to participate in the exhibition *955,000*[3] for the gallery at the Vancouver Art Gallery, 13 January to 8 February 1970. What most interested me, then and now, about this kind of practice is how relevant these projects are to current debates concerning collaboration, and in particular the relationship between art, anthropology and material studies. Participants were drawn together in the process of making, including writers, filmmakers, social theorists and

Figure 7.1 Robert Smithson, *Glue Pour*, Vancouver, British Columbia, December 1969. Smithson with Dennis Wheeler, Ilya Pegonis and Lucy Lippard Photo: Christos Dikeakos. Copyright © Holt/Smithson Foundation/licensed by VAGA, New York.

a broad range of students, as well as suppliers of materials, technicians and 'incidental others' connected with a specific location. *Glue Pour*, for example, involved support of UBC students Ilyas Pagonis and Duane Lunden and Smithson's collaborator, Dikeakos, describes the event in his own résumé as '*Glue Pour and the Viscosity of Fluvial Flows as Evidenced in Bottle-Gum*'. The bright orange drum of liquid adhesive, literally binding itself with the landscape, was donated by the National Starch and Chemical Company – at the time, this was Canada's largest manufacturer of consumer glues, a subsidiary of UK giant Imperial Chemical Industries (ICI). The work was documented by Vancouver-born artist/filmmaker Dennis Wheeler,[4] who struck up an important friendship with Smithson, sharing many interests in cosmology, anthropology, philosophy and geology.

It may be helpful for those working in fields outside the arts, to understand more about the possibilities of working in these responsive ways. I became aware of this approach through Lippard's publication *Six Years: The Dematerialization of the Art Object*,[5] which gathered together a diverse array of practices, the inclusions and exclusions of which were idiosyncratic and personal, devised to expose the chaotic range of ideas that were 'in the air'. While the book's content and title would provoke questions around materiality – authenticity, permanence and aesthetic experience – Lippard was also concerned to avoid the continual issue of being defined. The front cover of the publication transgresses its own labelling by speaking directly to the issue – it includes various terms being thrown around in the art world – the 'so-called' conceptual or information art with vaguely designated areas as minimal, anti-form,

Coming Together Differently   119

systems, earth or process art. In the preface for the second publication Lippard comments:

> since I first wrote on the subject in 1967, it has often been pointed out to me that dematerialization is an inaccurate term, that a piece of paper or a photograph is as much an object, or a 'material' as a ton of lead. Granted. But for lack of a better term I have continued to refer to a process of dematerialization, or a de-emphasis on material aspects (uniqueness, permanence, decorative attractiveness). 'Eccentric Abstraction', 'Anti-form', 'Process Art', Anti-Illusionism' or whatever … (Lippard 1973: 5)

As someone searching for new ways to work with artists, this book was a revelation to me and, together with essays published in 1971 entitled *Changing,* proposed a different way of working *with* artists that explored life as a process and art as a living force. Other exemplars that I discovered at this time included, in Europe, Konrad Fischer and Hans Strelow's *Prospect 68* and the *Skulptur Projekte Münster*, co-founded by Kasper König and Klaus Bußmann in 1977; and, in the US, ephemeral, performative and activist practices that were given visibility through niche publishing initiatives, such as printed matter[6] that in turn created a locus for many transatlantic connections between artists and facilitators (curators, writers, arts professionals) beyond the art institution.

These projects were ephemeral and as such made tangible through documentation. They resonated with those interested in the overlooked, abandoned or less visible spaces beyond the art institution. For instance, Smithson's *Asphalt Rundown*, Rome 1969, is an experiment that takes place in a gravel quarry, and follows from ideas that had been percolating from around 1967, when the artist began exploring industrial areas around New Jersey and became fascinated by watching dumper trucks excavating tons of earth and rock. He writes about these anonymous industrial processes as the equivalents of *The Monuments of Antiquity* and these experiences also informed the first series of *Nonsites*, in which earth and rocks collected in one location were then installed in a gallery as sculptures.

Growing up and working in northeast England, in a region synonymous with process industries – iron, steel and chemicals – I was particularly drawn to Smithson's practice, which explored the symbiosis between environment, materials and production. In 2005, while working as inaugural curator at mima (Middlesbrough Institute of Modern Art) I was able to visit the artists' retrospective organized by Eugenie Teal and Cornelia Butler at the Whitney Museum, New York. The *Nonsite*, took on new relevance once understood as drawings, or cartographic models – 'abstracted, three-dimensional maps that point to a specific location, leading somewhere' (Roth 2004: 92–3) or, more accurately, 'elsewhere'. By making visible the parameters of what was meaningful, undermining the assumptions concerning where art was to be found, artists such as Smithson countered the prevalent voice of the art world. For Smithson, the 'ready-made' of Marcel Duchamp or the pseudo-factory system set up by Andy Warhol had both elevated everyday objects into works of art through relocation or reworking for the commercial art world. Duchamp and Warhol thus emphasized the role of the artist and their ideas and removed attention from production to consumption. Returning to Middlesbrough, the works also highlighted the politics of representation, with questions concerning centre and peripheries and with debates that ensued about the separation of the gallery from the economic realities and conditions of the region. Reading the catalogue for the exhibition on the return flight, I turned again to the interview Smithson had with the art historian Moira Roth in March 1973, who set the scene:

> It was a period when art-world figures were not only fine-tuning their various readings of Duchamp – who had died in 1968 – but also when people were both puzzling over and wanting to define the many shifts that had occurred in art-making during the late 1960s and early 1970s. (Roth 2004: 81)

This resonated with many of my contemporaries, who were inspired by the legacy of Duchamp, whose readymades removed the preoccupation with traditional or artisanal skills and turned their attention to the changing meaning of making art it was reconfigured to take into account post-industrial production and DIY culture. In accord with Smithson, many artists were questioning the isolation of objects from their means of production, transcending the lived and natural world in a kind of pseudo-practice that Smithson described in the interview as a 'Voltairean sarcasm' (Roth 2004) by which I understand him to mean relevant to the art world itself (an inside joke).

Artists working in the 1960s and 1970s offered future generations an alternative way of working beyond the institution. Superficially there are similarities in the documentation of such projects with those working in visual anthropology. Such practices are understood through the ephemera that now exists in archives and museum collections and includes notes, postcards, film, photographs and drawings made during road trips and site visits (alone and with others). However, the material gathered and collected is not a result of 'research'. For Smithson and other land artists the world is a studio, a field of practice, where understanding grows through relationship, intuition and encounter. By extending beyond the boundaries of the studio or limits of the canvas, such artists perceive the world as 'an arena in which to act' (Rosenberg 1959: 22). There is no overarching research question or predetermined methodology, the approach is always relative to the principles of the artist and unfolding conditions.

In these terms, the work is always an invention that corresponds to specific conditions and therefore unpredictable, unknown and always incomplete. *Asphalt Rundown*, for example, came about following a conversation with the gallerist Fabio Sargentini at L'Attico. The role that he played is integral to the work, as a site for discourse and negotiation; locating the suppliers of 1,000 tons of asphalt, securing the open-mine quarry and a team of anonymous production workers. L'Attico emerged from a small private gallery, opened by Bruno Sargentini (Fabio's father) in 1957 and devoted to Art Informel[7] in Italy, and this relationship to chance is also relevant to the kinds of artists invited to work in the space. Through the early 1960s Fabio started to make exhibitions alongside peers and contemporaries who were pushing at the walls of the gallery space and challenging the norms of a previous generation. Many of the works reflect wider social and political concerns. The gallerist plays host to peers, artists, curators and writers visiting Italy from the US, creating ephemeral, time-based events and performances.[8] This inheritance affords the possibility of retaining the ethos of independence, funded through freelance projects, art sales and niche publishing. By taking this approach L'Attico expanded the parameters of the space by creating off-site events and actions and, later, in the 1970s, the gallery became increasingly nomadic.[**]

By way of contrast, Smithson's *Concrete Pour* was a response to the exhibition *Art by Telephone* at the Museum of Contemporary Art, Chicago, Illinois. Curated by the temporary director, David H. Katzive, who drew on the work of Chicago émigré, artist and educator László Moholy-Nagy's 'telephone pictures' of 1923[9] as a inspiration for the exhibition and off-site projects. Invited artists were asked to communicate new work using the protocol of telephone communication and avoiding all blueprints or technical plans. The work was then carried forwards by a technical crew under the guidance of Katzive. In common with the abstract paintings of Moholy-Nagy the exhibition created a space for discussion concerning authenticity, or what Walter Benjamin described as forms of mechanical reproduction that dissolve the 'aura' or ritualistic function of art, 'its presence in time and space, its unique existence at the place where it happens to be' (Benjamin 1973: 214). The continuum of these questions – the exploration of how technology, industrial production and high-speed travel have changed our experience of the world, both spatially and temporally, is also clearly linked to a growing understanding of the part artists, architects and designers have played in shaping the modern world. It is no accident that Katzive used the work of Moholy-Nagy (1895–1946) as a trigger. Moholy-Nagy was a seminal figure in the Chicago art scene, having emigrated to America in 1937 and set up the New Bauhaus. His American struggles to create a modern art school were highly respected by the creative community, with Moholy-Nagy continuing to implore the industry (and whoever would listen) to think 'not only aesthetically, but morally' stating that 'we must control the application of our materials, technique, science and art in creating for human needs' (Moholy-Nagy 1936). In turn Smithson's *Concrete Pour* corresponds with these ideas and with Chicago as a city synonymous with a modern spirit and concrete as the leitmotif of aggressive modernism.

Reimagining these ways of working, I am interested to know what they might tell us in the present time. Pouring concrete into a ravine interrupts the material's association with construction, returning the material to its volcanic origins as liquid rock. As the anthropologist Michael Taussig described after Vitruvius, 'You start with stone. You make a powder. And then in the process of building, you add water and end up with a new form of "stone" in accord with the shape desired. It sounds like magic but we call it technology' (Harkness, Simonetti and Winter 2015). There is an interesting relationship here between concrete production and ways of curating. Concrete that is forming is said to be 'curing', which is an almost imperceptible state. Although at first glance the material may appear to be solid, it still requires attention; asking to be kept liquid by being misted with water. What can be discovered is that the longer the concrete remains in this formative state, the longer its crystals continue to grow and meld with other materials. The strength of the material comes through its relationship with iron, aggregates and atmospheric conditions. Smithson's archives for this work suggest that it is the way materials cure that really matters – the care and attention to specific conditions that are relevant rather than the way they are objectified. For

122   *The Anthropologist as Curator*

the curator David Katzive these experiences 'fresh out of University of Chicago', were ones that allowed works to remain free from institutional demands, and it was through these ephemeral projects that there were 'amazing things happening out of this notion of impermanence'.[10] (Katzive and Firmin 2009)

Un-learning in correspondence with artists and sites

The interview with Katzive echoes with my own formative experiences. In 1989/1990, immediately out of art school, I worked at Riverside Studios, London, with the curator Zoe Shearman.[11] At this time Riverside was an experimental public gallery that supported both emergent artists and those who had played a significant role in challenging institutional frameworks. It was a modest space, whose ethos was both critical and artist-led. In 1990, I continued this journey through postgraduate study, with the idea of deepening my knowledge as part of the first cohort of 'sculpture studies' students at the University of Leeds, under the leadership of the art historian, Benedict Read (1945–2016).[12] The course combined history, theory and criticism, but, more significantly, it emphasized understanding through conversation. All studies were augmented through studio visits with artists, curators, conservators, technicians, archivists, and so on. These ideas were intensified through its association with the Henry Moore Institute, that drew on the vibrant site-specific exhibitions, talks and events developed by Robert Hopper (1946–1999) at Dean Clough, Halifax, that linked students to contemporary artists, curators and writers and opened a door into working in the arts.

What I recognize from these practices is how differently they were played out in a pre-digital age. They required a working rhythm that was orchestrated through material handling, direct working relationships, analogue systems such as archiving and written correspondence; and, as such, daily routines were often unpredictable, requiring different forms of response and judgement. Communications were rarely instantaneous and photographic documentation for publishing demanded slow and careful negotiations, and, often, physical travel between the studios of artists, photographers, designers and printers. Strong and lasting associations were forged through patterns of working life and social relations that were implicit in each and every project. It is worth remembering that the internet didn't enter common use in the UK until the mid-1990s when Microsoft announced internet mail and a few fledgling companies started to offer free use-anywhere internet. It is hard to imagine, in an age of digital communications, how much this altered correspondence and ways of being and knowing. In the gallery, research remained relatively active, involving discussions with artists, pouring through vast amounts of original printed matter or hours tracking down material in libraries and archives. First and foremost, gallery assistants, curators and writers were expected to engage with artwork directly. It was through these daily routines that one followed histories, theories and critical others.

It was through these practical experiences that emergent artists, curators and writers were exposed to critical discourse. In 1996, for instance, I recall listening to Catherine David describe a way of working for documenta X,[13] Kassel. As the first woman to be appointed as artistic director for perhaps the most significant barometer of contemporary art, what she voiced was received as a provocation that was able to reach the conscience of the art world, offering a critical assessment of the political, social, economic and cultural issues that informed artists and curators. Five years later, returning to Kassel, I recognized that these events marked the end and beginning of new centuries and they brought into stark view the skewed perspective of institutional authority. This experience then fuelled my return to documenta 11, which was led by artistic director Okwui Enwezor and co-curated with a team of six – Sarat Maharaj, Octavio Zaya, Carlos Basualdo, Ute Meta Bauer, Susanne Ghez and Mark Nash – who explored the location of culture and how this was changing through the global knowledge systems. The simultaneous presentations were formed through a series of preceding events: 'transdisciplinary platforms' entitled: *Democracy Unrealized* took place in Vienna and Berlin; *Experiments with Truth: Transitional Justice and the Process of Reconciliation* in New Delhi; *Créolité and Creolization* in St Lucia; and *Under Siege: Four African Cities* emerged through dialogue in Freetown, Johannesburg, Kinshasa and Lagos. When looking at the way that these exhibitions were curated and presented one can clearly see the lines of communication and the opportunities to create rich and meaningful debate across disciplinary fields.

Experience drawn from working with artists and visiting exhibitions and events with arts professionals, was invaluable to my own curatorial approach and informed my ways of working as I moved from small-scale, artist-led initiatives to public spaces: from mima to Dundee Contemporary Arts (DCA). For example, at documenta 11, I recall the sculpture park created by the artist Dominique Gonzalez-Foerster, *A Plan for Escape*, that consisted of objects with their own stories. The work made tangible the imaginary, historic and invented meanings that merge with our immediate experiences. The artist was not documenting the harsh and complex realities created through the failure of modern architecture, nor was he drawn to upholding the modernist or superficial aesthetic style – instead the work revealed the nascent potential of modernity, charged as it is with dreams and promises for future reimagining.

Directly related to my curatorial programme at DCA, was Thomas Hirschhorn's ephemeral and accumulative Bataille Monument, built in a social housing estate in a mainly Turkish neighbourhood in the Nordstadt area of Kassel. This was a walk-in container that hosted a visual archive of the writer, philosopher and essayist Georges Bataille (1897–1962). I was aware that the artist had previously made similar kinds of anti-heroic artworks, homages to philosophers Spinoza (Amsterdam, 1999) and Deleuze (Avignon, 2002). These projects were situated in spaces not dedicated to art, in overlooked and forgotten localities, and produced using readily available cheap or discarded materials (cardboard, brown tape, plastic, etc.). These hypersaturated environments overwhelm those implicated in the work, through a sense of data and knowledge overload. The material grows during the lifetime of the temporary monument, it is constantly in-forming through a correspondence between artist and residents. Given the situation of Kassel, this created a deeply uncomfortable experience for those who ventured beyond the centre of the town – professional art world, critics and scholars alike – it made palpable the unfamiliar, uncertain or 'other'. Forgoing the traditional terms of knowledge production, the work kicked back the gallery's ritualistic role of displaying, collecting and consuming social realities. Later, visiting The Gramsci Monument in Biljmer[14] (2009), I was able to ask the artist about the relationship with residents, how the work comes into being? 'the process is very straightforward – a call to residents who want a temporary job, each [is] ... paid a wage to produce the monument, it requires a commitment ...' (Hirschhorn 2009). Occupying the monument over a few hours one started to understand more about the relationship between aesthetics and politics – transgression, imagination, creative freedom, and so on. The link here to anthropology no doubt will be familiar, Bataille had been influenced by Marcel Mauss's publication *The Gift,* an anthropological study of reciprocity. His analysis of the *Potlatch* ceremony inspired Bataille to write *The Accursed Share* and, in turn, this led to a conversation with the artwork. What seems relevant here is the notion of art as something that implicated others, underpinned by obligations – the obligation to give, the obligation to accept and the obligation to reciprocate. It struck me that this temporary monument was also working as a curatorial space, a 'total social phenomenon – one whose transactions are at once economic, juridical, moral, aesthetic, religious, and mythological' (Hyde 1983: xvii), and its meaning, therefore, cannot be adequately described from a singular perspective. As such the work triggered a field of references that led back to various avant-garde tendencies in the early twentieth century, that tell of the unspoken hierarchies of attention in Western institutions, the search for ways of coming together to explore authentic and immediate experience.

Countering research methodology

In 2012, I returned to Kassel for documenta 13. I was particularly interested in the curatorial framework devised by Carolyn Christov-Bakargiev, dedicated to 'forms of imagination that explore commitment, matter, things, embodiment, and active living in connection with, yet not subordinated to theory'. Organized from four simultaneous positions or states (stage, siege, hope and retreat), described as 'phenomenal spatialities' that mirrored the conditions that artists and critical others find themselves navigating. A key concern was how to move beyond the art world, to acknowledge the way creative practices help recalibrate and shift our ways of working. I was particularly drawn to a series of small publications produced under the collective title: *100 Notes – 100 Thoughts* and the contribution made by Michael Taussig, which I read on a train journey between Kassel and Berlin. Between its pages, I recognized this imaginative travel; weaving in the thoughts of artists and critical thinkers (including Benjamin, Didion, Genet and Burroughs, among others). Far more than a mere 'thing', Taussig proposed the site of the notebook, that created a life of its own, as he states, 'chance determines (what an odd phrase!) what goes into the collection, and chance determines how it is used' (Taussig 2012: 5). I took this as a provocation to his own field of anthropology, to 'Imagine a social science that not only admits to this principle but runs with it!'. This is a space that 'retains loyalty to feelings and experience' (Taussig 2012: 6). Here, intuition plays a key role; not as some spurious gut feeling, based entirely on chance, but a way of working that is described by Deleuze in his reading of Henri Bergson (1966). For Bergson and Deleuze, intuition is a legitimate approach, not just a 'disorderly sympathy'. It is a decisive turn in a given duration or state of responding with things. That provides us with precise ways of knowing and differentiating lived experiences and reality itself (Deleuze 2011: 13–14). Writing at completely different moments in time, these philosophers recognize that intuition is deeply problematic phenomenon for twentieth- and twenty-first-century organizations. In our present world where human judgement is being circumnavigated through automation and institutional frameworks the discussion seems prescient. It also may provide some suggestions to why the present order and representation of the world is deeply unsettling, particularly for those who lived and worked in different ways in a pre-digital epoch. In accord with Bergson, intuition accompanies a plurality of meanings and irreducible multiplicities. These multiplicities require participants to ask questions: What is the problem or challenge? How do we differentiate what might be a problem from what seems a given or is conventional? How do I consider the issues that present themselves as a continuum in the unfolding of time? It is here, in the borderlands of art and humanities, that there is created a space to explore the changing world and speculate about our collective futures.

This more ambiguous space is not one that is associated with current debates concerning art and anthropology, which focus on a 'critical' understanding around many complex issues of representation. Although, in our present time, this has offered an alternative to the superficial and unmediated knowledge that circulates through popular media (social, state-owned or commercial) and has enabled artists to move beyond historicism by focusing attention on present conditions, it might also be argued that 'anthropology' is in danger of being prized as the social science of 'alterity'. As art critic and historian Hal Foster was to foresee, this resonated with artists who were working beyond the gallery and led to the appropriation of methods and strategies outside the frame of the art world, including social systems and the conflation of anthropology with ethnography. My understanding is that Foster's key concern is that many emergent curators and artists are not critically questioning or acknowledging the location of intermediaries and thus are in danger of turning the materials associated with specific communities into 'cultural proxies'. Such a critique is directed towards participatory or socially engaged models, where the artist is typically utilized as the 'outsider', or sanctioned to engage with 'the locals' in the production of 'their self-representation' (Foster 1995:171–204). In accord with Foster, it was these issues that Hirschhorn addressed, by revealing the paradox of such 'quasi-anthropological roles' and by making visible an alternative to ethnography that avoids the issue of hiding behind the voices of others or speaking on their behalf.

These discussions concerning the issues of representation and the relationship between theory and practice stretch back through the twentieth century and inevitably challenge participants to consider freedom, intellectual authority and social responsibility. While this may create a sense of déjà vu, conditions, of course, are never quite the same. This also echoes with the critical discourse in the mid-1980s where perspectives were deconstructed, pushed and provoked by a generation of visual theorists and art historians (Berger, T. J. Clark, Griselda Pollock, Rosalind Krauss, Fred Orton, etc.) whose writing found a platform in the academic journal October (founded in 1976), an influential vehicle for discussions around cultural production, making and interpreting art. Together with *Artforum* and early *Artscribe*, these publications became markers of 'criticality' and relevant touchstones for practices that were embracing an expanded field of art described by Krauss. By attempting to understand the phenomenon of modernist art, in its historical and theoretical context, a generation of art students were beginning to find common ground with critical others. In reality many artists of this period were also discovering their voices, through turning attention towards those avant-garde experiments that challenged institutional structures throughout the twentieth century, including Situationist International (SI), Asger Jorn's Imaginist Bauhaus, Process art, Fluxus and the Artist Placement Group, and so on. In common with these experimental critical theories, my own curatorial journey was allowing me to connect to those artists who were telling of the ambiguities of language, the inadequacy of representation and how histories were complex and contradictory.

Most recently I came across an interview with the academic and activist, Gayatri Chakravorty Spivak, around critical intimacy, that describes a way of un-learning, 'a sort of stream of learning how to unlearn and what to unlearn' (Paulson and Spivak 2016:24–50) Spivak reveals how our present conditions create a new challenge for academics and intellectual authority. By acknowledging that our positions are growing and changing, she states: 'I don't really work from within an expertise. I have to really be on my feet learning new things all the time, and as I learn these new things my positions change' (Op. cit.). These values past and present coalesce as a search for the 'possibility of imagining' that resonates with artists and anthropologists 'as a training for the ethical impulse'. This kind of un-learning somewhat surprisingly recalibrates our relationship to modernity, by echoing with early artist/educators, searching for ways to escape the political atmosphere of Nazi Germany and find ways to encourage a new generation to make their own critical judgements: 'One can suffocate with knowing but never with experiencing. We lose easily what we have heard or read or learned, but we do not lose what we have experienced' (Albers 1935).

The notion of un-learning accords with current thought about the relationship between art and anthropology, rooted in educational philosophy rather than ethnography. Un-learning also reminds me of my experiences working with the Berlin-based artist Manfred Pernice at DCA and curators Mike Stanley (1975–2012) at Modern Art Oxford and Frank Maes at the Municipal Museum of Contemporary Art (SMAK), Ghent. Pernice's work exists in an ambiguous space, a form of travel that explores the complex borderland between sculpture, architecture and human stories of time and place. This was a project that began as an incidental conversation about how to link three different locations while also challenging the convention of touring exhibitions. Elements from each iteration of the journey were to be incorporated into the work via text, autobiographical references and collated ephemera. Each journey was given a distinct title. At Oxford: 'baldt1', 'Brei' in Ghent, and 'déjàVu' at DCA,[15] referring to the repetition of exhibition-making, but it also connected the viewer to objects and artefacts that may seem familiar, even though clearly displaced and continually shifting their meaning. One of the works, entitled *Tutti*, was a large reel-shaped container that could be entered and climbed via a spiral staircase to give a view of the work within the space it occupied – an exhibition space within an exhibition space – neither sculpture nor architecture; the contents and display of each quadrant reconfigured. In Oxford, the curators worked with the anthropologist Dan Hicks, from the Pitt Rivers Museum, who created an evening bringing together twenty writers, artists, critics and musicians to respond to the work. From a vantage point, literally on top of the work, I read some pages from my own notebook that described the journey taken with the artist while co-curating the exhibition: a series of entangled thoughts threaded together from recollections of early visits to Berlin just after unification, through to experiences of visiting Pernice in his studio and living space in former East Germany, and finally my own position on the viewing platform of the structure inside the gallery space. In Scotland, we created a more low-key event with the anthropologist Tim Ingold. What struck me was how the structure *Tutti* facilitated such different conversations and questions. Its outer walls peeled open and, rather than containing objects, it occupied a space, clearly unfinished or incomplete, always waiting for those who wished to participate.

Art, anthropology and the curatorial space

What I have noted about this shared space, is that meaningful experiences are often formed like unsanctioned or unplanned travel (with the same sense of risk, tension and enjoyment). In this undefined location individuals are given licence to push against the confines and walls of a particular location. This places the artist and curator, as much as anyone else, in active tension between institution and self-identification. Michel De Certeau emphasized this idea in his observations around the devices, actions and procedures that individuals use on a daily basis to subvert disciplinary powers. These 'tactics' are not intended to be destructive, but are launched with the aim of retaining some sort of self-control. In this way, everyday life is made up of endless attempts to navigate that which we know will otherwise be closed down. This ambiguous and shared space beyond professional identity 'makes use of the cracks that particular conjunctions open in the surveillance of the proprietary powers. It poaches in them. It creates surprises in them. It can be where it is least expected' (De Certeau 1984: 25). This is a location where we are able to retain freedom, that allows us to reclaim or reimagine those things that are beyond our control. It is a locus that the artist Moholy-Nagy describes as inspiration, a moment when 'conventions and inhibitions of the daily routine are broken through' (Moholy-Nagy 1938: 15).

I am thus interested in the possibilities of this kind of unsanctioned space, which has been described by those who have a deep commitment to their respective disciplines, but I want to ensure that dialogue continues beyond academic confines and disciplinary boundaries. Here one can return to Roy Wagner's *Invention of Culture*, which begins by asking what happens if we think about the 'inversion of conventional identification' (Wagner 1975: 79). It is this space that echoes 'the curatorial space' described by Maria Lind, a way of working that is ambiguous, that allows for detours and, as such, is integral to the creative process.[16] These ideas resonate in practice rooted in anthropology – for example the research initiative Knowing from the Inside

(KFI). This was an experimental research project, funded by the European Research Council, that I was part of for the last five years, set up to explore the common threads that link *anthropology, art, architecture and design*. Its central premise was how to reconfigure the relation between practices of inquiry and the knowledge to which they give rise, by experimenting and trialling a range of procedures that allow knowledge to grow from direct, practical and observational engagements with people, places, materials and situations. Led by the anthropologist Professor Tim Ingold, this project involved researchers and associates from across the globe. It countered the general approach to academic research and specialism and instead revealed a way of working that challenged traditional ways of knowing, by establishing a space where different disciplines could correspond with each other. This location then was one that was clearly educational and speculative, that allows different ways of working and different voices to come together and challenge assumptions, or move beyond their own self-imposed limits. Of course, for anthropologists, artists and curators this kind of invention is subject to the traditions and ethical responsibilities, but for some it may offer a way to temporarily jettison convention. As Roy Wagner points out, many of the stories that have been passed down through generations (Herodotus, to traveller's tales of the Middle Ages, to anecdotes from participants) demonstrate that culture is always an imagining of sorts, and he reminds his peers that 'an "anthropology" which never leaves the boundaries of its own conventions, which disdains to invest its imagination in the world of experience is in danger of turning stories into an ideology' (Wagner 1975: 3). And as Ingold reminds us 'There can be no invention without convention, else it would be meaningless. And vice versa, there can be no convention without invention, for how else could it arise save from past improvisation? In life, conventions are never given but are the hard-won and always provisional outcomes of our incessant and never wholly successful attempts to make ourselves understood' (Ingold 2016).

Notes

1   See: Lind, M. (2010) *Maria Lind: Selected Writing*, Sternberg Press, London. Lind is a curator and writer based in Stockholm. She was the director of the graduate program at the Center for Curatorial Studies, Bard College, New York (2008–10); director of *Iaspis* in Stockholm (2005–7) and Kunstverein München (2002–4); curator at Moderna Museet in Stockholm (1997 to 2001); and co-curator of Manifesta 2, Luxembourg in 1998.
2   Smithson died in a plane crash in Amarillo, Texas, 20 July 1973, after photographing the site for *Amarillo Ramp*. His work continued through the support of the artist Nancy Holt (1938–2014), who he collaborated with and married in 1963. The two artists' work is intertwined, and further details can be found at the Holt-Smithson Foundation, an organization that exists to continue the creative and investigative spirit of the artists.
3   The exhibition followed on from *557,087*, at Seattle World's Fair Pavilion. This was a radical new approach to curation that consisted of sixty-nine artists and was sponsored by the Contemporary Art Council of the Seattle Art Museum. It was followed by *955,000* held in Vancouver. The titles refer to each city's population in

1969. The third number show took place in December of 1970 and featured artists that Lippard had previously never worked with. This exhibition, titled *2,972,453* took place in Buenos Aires at the Centro De Arte Y Comunicación.

4 Wheeler may be familiar to visual anthropologists. He made the film *Potlatch: A Strict law Bids Us Dance*, 1975, that was restored and distributed in 2007. The film was made in collaboration with the Kwakwaka'wakw First Nations of Alert Bay, British Columbia.

5 The front cover of the book serves as both a title and a descriptor of the book's contents. It reads 'Six Years: The dematerialization of the art object from 1966 to 1972: a cross-reference book of information on some esthetic boundaries: consisting of a bibliography into which are inserted a fragmented text, art works, documents, interviews, and symposia, arranged chronologically and focused on so-called conceptual or information or idea art with mentions of such vaguely designated areas as minimal, anti-form, systems, earth, or process art, occurring now in the Americas, Europe, England, Australia, and Asia (with occasional political overtones), edited and annotated by Lucy R. Lippard'.

6 Printed Matter is a non-profit organization dedicated to the dissemination, understanding and appreciation of artists' books. First established in Tribeca, New York, in 1976 by Sol Lewitt, Lucy Lippard, Carl Andre, Edit DeAk, Walter Robinson, Pat Steir, Mimi Wheeler, Robin White and Irena von Zahn. As an independent organization it presented forms of ephemeral, performative and distributed artwork and explored the possibilities of publishing as a curatorial site.

7 *Art Informel* is a French term, used to describe a wide range of responses to abstract painting across Europe through the 1940s and 1950s. The common thread being the use of informal procedures, improvisation and gestural movement. An important source of this kind of painting was the surrealist principle of automatism – creating art without conscious thought through the immediacy of experience.

8 'A decisive step towards a new conception of the exhibition space occurred in the meetings that Sargentini had in Rome with Italian-American dancer Simone Forti, who was a former pupil of Anna Halprin in the US and introduced Sargentini to the latest developments of the New York music and contemporary dance scene' (Cerizza 2014).

9 *Art by Telephone* paid homage to a work by László Moholy-Nagy who claimed to have ordered five paintings of porcelain enamel by telephone. Their production was dictated to the director of an enamel sign factory. 'I had the company's color scheme in front of me and I sketched my pictures on graph paper. On the other end of the line the director of the company had the same squared paper before him' (Moholy-Nagy and Gropius 1969). The transmitted artwork was executed in three different sizes to explore modifications and how the scale altered the space relationships. This was an experiment in art and mechanical reproduction that used ways of working that reflected the modern age (communications) and anonymity of production.

10 Interview with David Katzive, Oral History Transcript, Art Spaces Archive. Interviewer: Sandra Q. Firmin, Curator, UB Art Gallery, Buffalo, New York, Wednesday, 11 November 2009. For further information see David Katzive Papers: Smithsonian Archives of American Art.

11 Riverside Studios, Hammersmith, London was a pioneering art centre situated in the complex of the Film Studios. Zoe Shearman was curator of the gallery (1990–94). She curated or co-curated the first UK solo exhibitions in a public institution of Eric Bainbridge, Louise Bourgeois, Mat Collishaw, Peter Fend, Yoko Ono, Bethan Huws,

Tania Kovats and Simon Patterson, among others; 'off-site' projects by various artists including Judith Barry; and the seminar series Legitimate Practices in partnership with Artforum (with Thomas Crow, Isabella Graw, Hans Haacke, Chris Dercon and others). She introduced British audiences to various artists including Ida Applebroog, IRWIN, Ilya Kabakov and Tim Rollins + K.O.S (1987–90).

12 Ben Read, art historian and authoritative writer on British Victorian sculpture and son of the art historian Herbert Read. From1990 to 1997, he was director of the Sculpture Studies Programme under the auspices of the Henry Moore Foundation.

13 Documenta, Kassel, Germany. Founded in 1955 by Professor Arnold Bode with the express aim of bringing Germany back into dialogue with international trends in the arts following the Second World War. Bode's aim was to represent works that had been deemed by the Nazis to be degenerate, as well as present works that had never been seen in Germany, in the destroyed Museum Fridericianum. The first documenta was a retrospective of modern movements and individual artists that included: Kandinsky, Matisse, Klee, Picasso and Henry Moore. Over 130,000 visitors flocked to Kassel, which acted as a forum for contemporary art. A second exhibition was organized for 1959 and this then developed into the exhibition cycle: documenta. A new format for the exhibition was introduced in 1972 by Artistic Director Harald Szeemann. Each documenta is curated by a different artistic director and curatorial team. Much more than a survey of contemporary art, it sets out to create a dynamic discourse that is intended to provoke discussion around the role of art in contemporary society.

14 Conversation with Thomas Hirshhorn while planning the exhibition: *It's Burning Everywhere*, DCA (Dundee Contemporary Arts), Scotland, 19 September to 29 November 2009. Recreated in 2011 by Kunsthalle Mannheim, Germany. Supported by Creative Scotland, Pro Helvetia and Stephen Friedman Gallery, London.

15 Manfred Pernice: *Déjà Vu*, Dundee Contemporary Arts (DCA), Scotland, 5 March to 8 May 2011.

16 Many curators have proposed similar ways of working that emerged at the end of the 1990s and early 2000s. For further information see: M. Lind (ed,) 2011, *Performing the Curatorial*, Berlin: Sternberg Press. The anthology came out of a series of public seminars in 2010 and 2011, supported by the University of Gothenburg, Sweden.

References

Albers, J. (1935), *Abstract Art* [Manuscript], Josef and Anni Albers Foundation. Bethany, Connecticut. [online] Available at: http://www.albersfoundation.org/teaching/josef-alb ers/lectures/.

Benjamin, W. (1973), 'The Work of Art in the Age of Mechanical Reproduction', in *Walter Benjamin: Illuminations*, 211–44, London: Fontana Press.

Cerizza, L. (2014), *The Gallerist: Fabio Sargentini of L'Attico, Rome*. [online] Art-agenda. com. Available at: https://www.art-agenda.com/reviews/the-gallerist-fabio-sargentini -of-l'attico-rome/.

De Certeau, M. (1984), *The Practice of Everyday Life*, Berkeley: University of California Press.

Deleuze, G. (2011), *Bergsonism*, New York: Zone Books.

Foster, H. (1995), 'The Artist as Ethnographer', in G. Marcus and F. Myer (eds), *The Traffic in Culture: Reconfiguring Art and Anthropology*, Berkeley: University of California Press.

Hyde, L. (1983), *The Gift: How the Creative Spirit Transforms the World*, United States and Canada: Random House.

Ingold, T. (2016 [1975]), 'Foreword to the Second Edition', in R. Wagner (eds), *The Invention of Culture*, Chicago: University of Chicago Press.

Katzive, D. and S. Firmin (2009), Interview with David Katzive for Art Spaces Archive [Oral History Transcript], Washington, DC: Smithsonian Institution, Oral History Program.

Krauss, R. (1977), *Passages in Modern Sculpture*, New York: Viking Press.

Lind, M. (2010), *Maria Lind: Selected Writing*, London: Sternberg Press.

Lippard, L. (1973), *Six Years: The Dematerialization of the Art Object from 1966 to 1972*, New York: Praeger.

Moholy-Nagy, S. (1938), *The New Vision: fundamentals of Bauhaus Design, Painting, Sculpture and Architecture*, New York: Dover Press.

Moholy-Nagy, S. and W. Gropius (1969), *Experiment in Totality*, 2nd edn, 31–2, Cambridge, MA: MIT Press.

Paulson, S. and G. Spivak (2016), *Critical Intimacy: An Interview with Gayatri Chakravorty Spivak*, Los Angeles: LARB [online].

Rosenberg, H. (1959), *The Tradition of the New*, New York: Horizon Press.

Roth, M. (2004) 'An Interview with Robert Smithson (1973)', in E. Tsai and C. Butler (eds), *Robert Smithson*, 81–95, Los Angeles: The Museum of Contemporary Art , University of California Press.

Smithson, R. (1972), 'Cultural Confinement', *Artforum International*, October: 39.

Smithson, R. and P. Cummings (1972), *Interview with Robert Smithson for the Archives of American Art* [Oral History Transcript], Washington, DC: Smithsonian Institution, Oral History Program.

Taussig, M. (2012), *Fieldwork Notebooks. 100 Notes – 100 Thoughts, Documenta 13*. Kassel: Hatje Cantz.

Wagner, R. (1975), *The Invention of Culture*, Chicago: University of Chicago Press.

8

From Of, to With, to And? Anti-disciplinary exhibition making with art and anthropology

Jen Clarke

Much has been written about contemporary art's 'appropriation' of anthropological methods since Foster's influential critique 'The Artist as Ethnographer' (1996), however most discussions continue to focus on the nexus of art and ethnography, or artists' critical interventions in museums (e.g. Grimshaw and Ravetz 2015). Appropriation, from the Latin 'to make one's own', may be 'one of the most basic procedures of modern art production and education'(Verwoert 2007: 1). Nonetheless, perhaps because of increasing tensions between autonomy and heteronomy in art (Buckner 2013; Sansi 2015) the appropriation of art by other disciplines is felt as a 'colonization' or 'invasion', terms normally reserved for acts of cultural imperialism. While interdisciplinary collaborations *can* be clear-cut, such as *commissioning* an artist or designer to bring scholarly knowledge to wider publics, increasing 'impact', transdisciplinary (or anti-disciplinary) 'experimental' fieldwork methods have also become popular, even part of mainstream anthropology, which surely already employs inventive tools and technologies in exploring alternative formats for anthropological knowledge. Anthropologists now regularly draw on techniques and representational devices from art or design, 'border crossing' between anthropology and art (Schneider and Wright 2006, 2010; Schneider 2011), to create novel outcomes or facilitate discussion as the rise in 'labs' at international conferences attests. Relatedly, as lines between 'social practice' in art and social research blur (Sansi 2015), anthropologists are increasingly taking on curatorial roles in contemporary art settings and/or employing artistic methodologies in exhibition-making. This chapter explores some dynamics of anthropology and art practice in this broad context by discussing specific experiences of being 'curator' and being 'curated', looking at forms of identity, knowledge and, warily, aesthetics.

With the interchanging and muddling of roles between artist and curator, it is now common practice that artists work as curators (Filipovic 2017). And it is increasingly the case that anthropologists, without academic training in art but interested in horizontal practices, take on the mantle of curator or artist, and claim this work *as* art. However, using the term 'curation' can be problematic, since there are significant differences between *being* a curator and the act of curating; an opportunity now open to many 'dilettantes' is the 'product of a profound shift in the definition not only of

134 *The Anthropologist as Curator*

the curator but of the artist and the critic' (Kowalski 2010: n.p.). Border crossings prove difficult in practice, not least because one often begins full of assumption (by which I mean 'assumption' as not only the presuppositions involved, what is tacitly understood, and expected to happen, but also the assumption of responsibility). Such difficulties, as I shall describe, are, I think, central to what it means 'to curate' or 'be curated' in specific situations. Referring to the etymological origins of the verb, the Latin *curare*, to care for, has also become prevalent in curating as a critical practice (Obrist 2014; Krysa 2015). While these notions converge convincingly with the *ethics* of anthropological fieldwork (Clarke 2014), at the same time I am aware of the potential for naivety about the politics involved, and the risk of being patronizing. In what follows I reflect on a collaboration with professional artists, making exhibitions, doing exactly this: claiming work *as* art, and negotiating naivety. I consider two very different experiences, one that, for me, was instructive because it failed, and another that I see as relatively successful, and the questions thrown up about disciplinarity and knowledge, representation and aesthetics, questions that can be too easily discounted in inter- or anti-disciplinary undertakings. In describing the work I pay attention to two particular things: the presence and use of text or contextualization, and the use, understanding and interpretation of materials, which *arguably* distinguish art from anthropology (Krysa 2015: 427–8). I begin by introducing an anti-disciplinary project Knowing from the Inside (KFI) that I was fortunate to be part of, before recounting two experiences of exhibition-making I undertook as part of the project, with optimistic ambitions towards the 'refunctioning' of anthropology through collaboration (Marcus and Holmes 2008; cf. Korsby and Stavrianakis 2018). Although my collaborators gave permission for me to write about the exhibition, I have depersonalized details in order to work through and take ownership of my learning and how that informed subsequent practice. I also hope to avoid simple 'Capital-C' Criticism – my understanding of this is influenced by the curator Irit Rogoff's definitions: 'Capital-C' Criticism is about making value judgements and critique is about examining assumptions, but *criticality* aims further. Though 'a contingent and not entirely satisfactory term', criticality is about recognizing the limitations of one's thoughts and '"living things out" […] as opposed to pronouncing on them' (Rogoff 2006: 2). Three years later, for my final exhibition for the project, my work was curated by an artist, subjected to an art-school-like 'crit' as part of the 'show'. I share some of the conversation below, before reflecting on larger questions these experiences brought forth.

'Knowing from the Inside'

As a postdoctoral research fellow for the KFI project led by Tim Ingold, I worked with a multitude of artists, academics, designers and others who shared an interest in 'reconfiguring relations between practices'. Instead of treating artefacts as completed objects analysed retrospectively to determine meaning, our project explored generative currents of materials and the experience of practitioners together – thus, 'knowing from the inside'. We experimented with *forms* of knowledge, approaching knowledge as something that 'grows', as Ingold describes, from *practical* engagement, thinking *with*, *from* and *through* things (2013). Our project was anchored in anthropology but operated through collaborative sub-projects working with creative practices, without insisting on distinctions between theory and method. I see this approach as 'anti-disciplinary' and a form of 'research creation', working at the intersection of art practice and theory, attuned to *process* (in a Whiteheadian sense) rather than output (Manning 2016). A major theoretical concern for anthropology, practice provided us with a way to avoid intractable debates in philosophical aesthetics, though I have found myself caught up in them to some extent, as this chapter demonstrates. It was also a means of overcoming distinctions between acts and objects, and focusing on process, as well as allowing a broader reassessment of forms of representation and knowledge.

As Ingold (2018b) later argued, more than any other discipline in the social sciences, anthropology is about learning how to learn, and the basis of our collective experiments was playful exploration of thinking-through-making, learning by following along with what is going on with material(s) – where knowledge is produced through bodily practices such as dancing, weaving and drawing. While others worked with eco-building or laboratory theatre, to cite two examples, my work for KFI emphasized the incorporation of contemporary art practice[1] as a vehicle for research, working with media/methods including printmaking, performance and site-specific installations, through a series of international residencies and exhibitions. Occasionally my artworks were sold (half of the proceeds going to the gallery), their price determined by a curator, ostensibly crossing into professional practice.

Speculative Ground (2014): from curation to commission

Art practice and exhibition-making, including multiple if modest forms of curating, have always been part of my research, including 'durational' residencies and exhibitions in conventional art gallery settings as well as 'alternative' sites. The exhibition *Speculative Ground*, in 2014, was a fringe event for an anthropology conference, a project emerging from earlier collaborations with a fellow anthropologist who works with architecture and art, and an environmental artist with whom I had cooperated in a variety of ways. The exhibition included two forms of curation, though this was not a term we used at first. As academics with full-time salaries as well as generous budgets for fieldwork my colleague and I did not seek funding for our curatorial work as we had been privileged to do in other circumstances. We developed a proposal for funding, gaining additional funds to cover standard Scottish artist fees for the artist and her collaborator, a choreographer, as well as material costs. It is still too rare that artists receive standard artist's rates; ensuring they would be properly paid meant, we hoped, establishing a strong foundation for the project, acknowledging a common inequality that can sneak into interdisciplinary research projects that engage independent researchers and artists: money.

The exhibition consisted of two elements. First, a curated display of 'proposals on paper' or visual 'provocations' – critical and creative engagements with the Scottish

136 *The Anthropologist as Curator*

government's recently published Land-Use Strategy. Involving clear-cut curatorial responsibilities, we lightly curated the work; in the publication we wrote that we were not driven to judge works by artistic merit but hoped to find common ground between the submissions and how they illuminated our understanding of the issues, acknowledging different value-systems and visual languages. For the second part we intended to develop a collaborative approach, *combining* methods across art and anthropology, but in practice it operated as a *commission,* the language the artists employed in subsequent descriptions. It began on the banks of a river in the countryside. During our first meeting the choreographer (whose first degree, notably, was anthropology) presumed the anthropologists would act as 'expert commentators', inviting us to observe the artists' improvisatory practices and write an account of it. Perhaps I did not do a good job of explaining myself or my methods but after making clear this was not how we would approach things, we were left in a space of uncertainty. We intended a 'shared-investigation' but the presumptions about what anthropologists do, and what artists do, revealed some profound difference in expectation (a predicament aggravated when later using the term 'curation' to describe our role).

'Sticks and stones …' (materials)

Inspired by the riverbank ecology, we had hit upon the idea of attending to interruptions and obstructions as a way of approaching entangled interactions between living and non-living elements, and their more-than-human timeframes. Environmental art is about making work in and for other contexts, balancing concept and media through an informed understanding and use of *language in materials/media* as well as ideas, so the artist, trained in environmental art, was especially sensitive to this.[2] As we explored the exhibition space, responding to the context, the building interior (one wall covered in smooth, grey stones, presumably manufactured) as well as the riverbank, my anthropologist-colleague made a suggestion about producing stone-*like* weightless objects from synthetic materials: though a mere suggestion, with interesting connotations, this was anathema to the others, who implied it was amateur. It is not that artificial materials are dismissed or not used in contemporary art, far from it, but rather that, for them, the work was not *about* the question of materiality, in that sense. In their final work the artists displayed 'real' stones alongside audiovisual documentation of dancers performing with them, shaping their bodily practices. Their work, though in line with British traditions of environmental art, and even the phenomenological spirit of the KFI project, nevertheless exposed a schism in our 'ways of seeing' in relation to materials. As Grimshaw and Ravetz point out: 'If anthropologists have long been alert to interlopers of one kind or another, artists are equally sensitive to work that appears to resemble their own practice but fails, in their judgment, to be the real thing' (2015: 427–8).

Ultimately we developed entirely disconnected works for the exhibition. The artists made work *about* the specific ecology of the riverbank, bringing it into the exhibition space through the materials and work they (re)presented. Having failed to find a way in to working together with the riverbank, we chose to respond to the space (an academic building) as well as the conference theme – the Scottish Enlightenment – in conversation with our own emerging research practices. Having just returned from fieldwork in Japan, responding to the aftermath of the 3.11 disaster, I was working through feelings about complex gender politics (see Clarke 2019). Enlightenment thinking is arguably marred by anti-feminist discourse of philosophers such as David Hume, so I wanted to produce experimental 'interventions' to the specific site responding to this. I drew on poetry by William Blake, characters and lines from his poem *The Daughters of Albion*, which was inspired by Mary Wollstonecraft's *A Vindication of the Rights of Woman*. I used copper wire, beeswax, silk thread and Japanese paper combined with objects found on site, responding to the light – and the stains on the walls. I made a woodcut print, based on my drawing of a dense entanglement of power lines (that in Japan cross every street overhead) on almost transparent Japanese paper made from *abaca*, that at several metres long wrapped the walls. Next to the works I displayed detailed interpretative texts, including botanical descriptions and the properties of *abaca* (the preferred material for dielectric materials, used in diverse products from power-transmission ropes to teabags, hats or vellum); a deliberate overabundance of material and material *detail*. On reflection, I was responding to our discussions about materials and materiality, in a complicated manner; an effort I will analyse in more detail later on.

Palimpsests and Remnants (2017)

Three years later my final KFI exhibition, *Palimpsests and Remnants* (2017) explored relationships between process and objects in art and anthropology. This was my sixth in a series of exhibitions and residencies in Japan, Taiwan and Scotland in that period. By then my work had been curated in a number of different ways, including in a commercial gallery. I had performed and exhibited collaboratively with artists and others. For this exhibition I invited Alana Jelinek, a London-based artist and theorist whose participatory projects I had been involved with for a number of years, to act as curator as we are both interested in facilitating diverse forms of audience engagement and participation. This exhibition was also site-specific in a limited sense – the work responded to the idea of a museum-turned-gallery as a metaphor as well as the 'aesthetic' of the space. (The Anatomy Rooms where the exhibition was held was previously a university anatomy department, and was now an artist-led studio; the space I was using still furnished as the Museum Room.) As Alana described in her curator's statement, the exhibition was 'a dialogue' between the artworks, artefacts and detritus of my practice for the past three years and Alana's artistic practice, here as curator, 'paying attention toftrans the space, its formal and spatial qualities, working with its histories of use, allowing nails, electric cables and other remnants to be present'.

The exhibition had two related parts: *Remnants*, a display of selected 'detritus' from my workshops, alongside collaboratively produced Japanese calligraphy, and *Palimpsests*, an installation addressing processes including cyanotype, *ikebana* and mixed-media printmaking. *Ikebana*, a Japanese tradition of flower arrangement with roots in Zen Buddhism, is an act of consolation and remembrance, its principles expressed through relationships between materials, space and time. Creating 'portraits' of four female friends who made it possible for me to live and work in Tohoku, I also wanted to emphasize the hybrid nature of *ikebana* – as an object, considering the vessels and materials, and as a practice. *Ikebana* is inherently temporal – the material's plant life subject to decay and decomposition, but also given the emphasis on the gestural, embodied experience of making. For *Remnants* I wanted to examine the weak materiality of the quasi-objects produced during workshops, then archived or abandoned. I was interested in considering through *the language of materials* the sense of neglect, or lack of care, in the way stuff was discarded ('archived', or not) in a context where the 'care' of *curare* was often cited. Where was the value of 'the work' located? How did this relate to how things are given value in ethnographic or art collections? My idea was to produce an exhibit that dealt lightly with this interesting problem, exploring different *hybrid* forms (Jones 2015), without heavy use of explanatory narrative or interpretation.

The 'crit'

In my view, anthropological exhibitions rely on contextualizing devices more than art, though art's interpretation strategies are complex in other ways. Our aim instead was to let the work 'speak for itself', allowing visitors to 'listen' to the work through the way it was displayed and how space was used. We did not use language to present an interpretation of the work beyond short artist and curator statements. Instead, we held a 'crit', a group investigation where a range of interpretations about what the work signified or evoked was discussed. A 'crit', or critique, is a crucial part of fine art education in the disciplining of the person as an artist. The audience, a group of about twenty artists and academics, were led in discussion by Alana while I remained silent. The two interweaving sections were recognized as process and 'archive'. As one audience member said, the trick is 'within the *fuzziness* of such a rich process that feels like years of work' how to 'guide us to precise moments'. Alana drew out what these might be for different people: the intensity of the cyan blue [cyanotypes] with celestial references 'pulled back into now' by the use of natural materials; the plant matter, 'still alive, these things are alive' that gave a sense of 'the becomings after life' as well as of waiting, and, in the tension between natural and non-natural, questions of temporality. For others this feeling was echoed in the use of the chairs, where the *ikebana* 'portraits' literally sat, reminding one artist of the representation of domestic Dutch interior still lives, with flowers becoming memento mori, reminders of (our) death. For others, the placing of the chairs created a polite distance, incongruous against the rest, so much 'out of order'.

The work raised the question of how to *restitute* 'process'. There was, literally, as an anthropologist remarked, no map, no contextualizing text. While everyone noted the tactility of making, against this, in *Remnants* we chose to include the injunction 'do not touch' for objects on display; someone said this 'does something' to the engagement, turning the materials into museum pieces – or evoking their desire to be. The audience speculated on the material and the lack of framing, sensing desire from fraying, soft edges of paper, but also a lack of control, a sense of destruction, veiled within multiple layers of images, images of disaster and regrowth. For some the exhibition conveyed 'authoriality' along with the strong sense of being 'in progress'. For others, the same work conveyed a *lack* of authority, even randomness; for them the message was 'things happen to us' – just as the disaster did in Japan. Signs saying 'fragile' and displays including packaging materials gave a sense of things travelling, of distance and the need to protect, though for others this felt 'like a conceptual joke'. It all clearly conjured Japan, via paper, *ikebana*, ceramics, calligraphy, but 'not a pristine' Japan. An anthropologist (who knows me and my writing but not my visual work) commented that the work was clearly also *about* the artist: 'it all leads to her, what *constitutes* Jen'. Such thoughtful, verbalized interpretations raised questions about art, knowledge and authorship. These interpretations are also potentially wider than those we could have encouraged through tighter interpretation; and yet for me the experience of making, the exhibition *and the crit* produced knowledge irreducible to language. 'We know more than we can tell' as Polanyi insisted (1983). Working with Alana, and with the principle of waiting for the work to 'speak', allowed that. It was a way of 'provoking' the field, rather than representing what was already given, what I already 'knew'; and thus a means for me to rethink my own practice(s) and position from a different point of view – which returns me to the work of anthropology.

Self-creation and professional identities

Working between art and anthropology, easy to claim in theory, is difficult in practice. The first exhibition was successful by some measures, but for me it was a failed *project*. Whether the *work* failed is not necessarily for me to say (in hindsight, it worked as a kind of provocation, though it was complicated rather than complex, in terms of materials and their interpretive and poetic framings, as well as in execution). I can say I did not properly account for the audience (thus it would fail as art, according to certain definitions; Zangwill 1999). Collaborations with anthropology should begin by questioning existing relations. I think we failed by not questioning ourselves, working from assumptions, asserting expertise. Part of the language of such projects is the use of the word 'curator', which, for the artists, implied an imbalance in authority; a detail, but, as Roger Sansi has suggested, 'In the end, border hunting often appears as the nervous reaction of those not quite sure of the grounds of their territory' (Sansi 2015: 137). Was this failure the result of 'nervous reaction', sheer defensiveness? What happens to a collaboration when it becomes a 'commission'? The problem relates to the politicization of professional identities. As Mouffe argues, these are not pre-given but discursively constructed 'the result of processes of identification [...] the question that arises is the type of identity that critical artistic practices should aim at fostering (Mouffe 2007: 4). What type of identities might we foster? Nowadays artists are sometimes referred to as 'artworkers', recalling the post-Fordist worker, unable to

140 *The Anthropologist as Curator*

separate work and life, identity and job. This blurring of art and 'life' might be the utopian ideal for contemporary art (Jelinek 2013), but what is at stake is our 'capacity to define ourselves' (Sansi 2015: 151)? The art historian and feminist Angela Dimitrikaki has identified how being an artist or curator:

> means having a professional identity, associated with remuneration for labor [...] this predicament is not only relevant to women. Yet having been excluded from it for too long, women in art tend to be more attached to this professional identity. For many women, being recognized as a professional artist (or indeed a professional anything) is a hard-won gain. (Dimitrakaki 2018, n.p.)

In this light, it makes sense that the artists insisted on their professional role (especially these women artists, seeking to further establish themselves in an academic setting in which they said they felt unable to speak). It is also the case for Alana Jelinek (2013), who argues that artists should 'police the boundaries' of art, following Rancière's definition. As Sansi points out (2015) professional hurdles are associated with being an anthropologist/academic too: advanced academic production, a Ph.D. and so on, which interestingly is at odds with ideas about deskilling and amateurism that are often promoted by academic and artistic approaches to practice. Reflecting on these issues I came to wonder whether identity, self-creation through *dissensus,* could be a positive thing. Might this lead to a level of self-reflexivity, generative of … something else?

I am driven by a desire to develop myself as well as my skills, alongside those I work with, and learning enables me to share with others. Anthropology as learning (and learning to learn), a form of self-development, can be aligned with art; both promise *self-creation*. Making art can be a way of making oneself, a 'subjective intervention' that 'recreate[s] the self in the same movement by which it objectifies something beyond that self' (Leach 2007: 108). More than this, in the art world, art-making is considered desirable *self-fulfilling* work (Dimitrakaki 2018, n.p.), one excuse when artists are expected to work without pay! Nevertheless, both disciplines are dubious about research intersecting with *self*-expression, which, while evident in art education, is disparaged. This recalls debates in anthropology about auto-ethnography, should the researcher 'loom' too largely in the work (Venkatesan 2010).

All the artists referred to here define their identity by asserting a particular way of seeing, ways of working with material, an 'aesthetic' and the value of art as a skilled way of generating knowledge. In one sense, differences in terms of *aesthetic* decision-making (formally, as well as in terms of content), may have betrayed a lack of training, even at times an 'amateur' approach to art-making. To be amateur suggests sheer enthusiasm, doing something for pleasure, but it can also mean something unprofessional, substandard. As Sansi advises: 'if we accuse someone of being an amateur, we make a number of assumptions on *what is valued as work*. So we probably need to get back to these assumptions' (Sansi 2018, n.p., my emphasis). So, what is valued as work, or, indeed, as knowledge?

A problem of knowledge *forms*?

It is clear that anthropologists do not value 'methods' and media *in the same way* artists do. This is not to impose a hierarchy, *ideally* there is no hierarchy of knowledge that depends on the media used, whether for anthropological representations or other forms, as Sarah Pink argues (2012): knowledge produced through one medium can be related to, but cannot replace or be replaced by, knowledge produced through another; art practice then offers a unique mode of forming knowledge. An image I return to when trying to describe what art does and what anthropology does has to do with folds and folding: for me anthropology seeks to unfold: to set out, open up, explain, each unfolding unique to those who encounter it; artworks, conversely, are folded in complex forms, like gifts, wrapped, they demand something else of the viewer.

Anthropologists working with art tend to fall into two categories – borrowing artistic methods and *methodologies* (as in 'ethnographic conceptualism') or making art/artists the subject of investigation using established anthropological methods (Jelinek 2016); what I call anthropology *with* art versus anthropologies *of* art. An important difference between these is practice, clearly. In my experience it is risky to employ artistic methods and to try to call the work 'art' without understanding values and politics in art. Whether 'borrowings' result in work that can legitimately either be called anthropological or presented as 'real' artwork has been the subject of lively debate in visual anthropology for decades (Grimshaw and Ravetz 2015). Jelinek (2016) suggests most 'multivalent' efforts of exhibition-making fail, *as art.* It is true that contemporary art is less and less defined by media, and that while many trained artists have technical expertise, artists often 'work with' media they have not trained in, as Sansi points out (2015). But, as Jelinek argues in *This Is Not Art* (2013), what *disciplines* artists is not technical expertise but training that is a form of self-development within the particular 'habitus' of practice (usually the art school), including scenarios such as the 'crit'. What I have learned from being curated by and working with Alana is the value of forbearance, or a 'moral aesthetic' (Carrithers 2005): a capacity to hold one's own view while seeking to understand another's, being informed by but not *determined by* another; a disciplined way of being.

So, while not defined by technical expertise, having the skills to 'treat a material so that it becomes a medium of expression' as well as a theoretical or conceptual basis for work matters (Eisner 2008: 9–10). Art education thus is not only about technical skill (something that the long-running debate about what constitutes art versus craft also picks up on) but also *tacit* knowledge. This focus on knowledge, albeit the sorts that are difficult to declare, might be problematic for those who work with the concepts of amateurism, 'un-learning' or anti-disciplinarity (central tenets of the KFI project) in their border crossings. However, un-learning can be seen as learning *without explanation,* as we sought to do with the 'crit' – echoing Rancière's *Ignorant Schoolmaster;* not the opposite of knowledge, but an approach. It is certainly an important concept for rethinking standardized notions of work as well as knowledge, central to movements in higher education resisting the corporatization of universities, and art practices that seek to 'un-learn privilege' (as the Casco Art Institute, Utrecht, does, to give a different curatorial example, by drawing on postcolonial theory and feminist art practice). Interestingly, for Grimshaw and Ravetz (2015), art is predicated on a state of 'not knowing', and it is this challenge to knowledge that makes the use of art 'disruptive' to anthropology, always focused on generating 'new knowledge'. Directly opposing 'knowledge' and 'art' is, I think, problematic, as I have suggested. Indeed, the question of whether one gains knowledge through art is a long-standing one in the philosophy of art, certainly since Plato (Gaut 2003). But if we understand not knowing as a *way in* to knowing, art *as* knowledge (or knowledge 'forming' as Alana Jelinek argues), things open up.

Aesthetics? (Content and form)

It is precisely the fact that anthropology is constituted by knowledge that is responsible for its 'underdeveloped aesthetic'. And, if anthropology 'with' art is predicated on art and anthropology's analogous ways of engaging with the world (Ingold 2013), this is only possible because it also 'followed a break with certain key assumptions about art and artists – specifically, the centrality of form, originality, the imagination, innovation and individuality' (Grimshaw and Ravetz 2015: 424). Aesthetics, identified as a key problem for 'ethnographically inflected artistic work', is overlooked, these authors contend, in favour of 'ethics', seen as 'a vehicle for content rather than an outcome actively shaped by an emergent play of content and form' (ibid.: 430). It would be an oversimplification to generalize that anthropology prioritizes content over form while art prioritizes form over content. While many argue art cleaved away from aesthetics long ago (Arthur Danto posits that this happened following the 'anaesthetic' 'ready-mades' of Marcel Duchamp a century ago), within contemporary art there remain manifold references to 'aesthetics' in practice and theory. But, as I experienced in the first exhibition, a lack of attention to *matters of form* 'bewilders artists, for whom it is the aesthetic that holds the key to art's transformative potential' (ibid.). Thus, (re)introducing aesthetic issues into anthropological practices is not only 'deeply unsettling' but also 'potentially transformative'. That said, as a category of thought, aesthetics has been roundly rejected by anthropologists interested in art *practice* (e.g. Ingold 2013), perhaps partly due to the weight and complexity of philosophical debate regarding theories of beauty and experience (Bunn 2018). Important criticism (often from anthropology) has pointed to the limitations of classic European aesthetic theories, for example how the Kantian idea of disinterestedness limits understandings of non-Western art and aesthetics (Marcus and Myers 1995). Basically, if aesthetics is reduced to the question of beauty or ugliness (as it can be, crudely, via Kant's notion of subjective judgement), then anthropology's approach to aesthetics differs, tending towards an understanding drawn from its Greek roots 'aesthesis', meaning 'perception'. I hold that subsuming aesthetic experience to perceptual experience (as Ingold arguably does) circumvents much of the politics of art.

For contemporary artists who use material as metaphor, aesthetics in practice is about relationships between content and material or form, finding a satisfactory way of 'resolving' a problem. (If we accept that art is about practice, not principles (Buckner 2013)).

Attempting to understand how aesthetics is *used* does not necessitate a reduction to formalism (there are both moderate and extreme approaches), indeed as theorist Johanna Drucker describes there has been a resurgence of 'formal voluptuousness' and 'material intelligence', which has revitalized conceptualism since the 1990s (2005: 77). The rising fascination for 'new' materialism is also impacting. While it is inappropriate to generalize, since there are as many differences between artists' ideas about aesthetics as there probably are between art and anthropology;, it is important to highlight that the debate is occurring within art worlds, and that anthropology does recognize how contested aesthetics is, already, in theory (Marcus and Myers 1995: 14). And theory informs practice (informing theory …). This does not mean that all artists work or see in the same way. Perhaps the 'problem' is not aesthetics but the politics of representation: viewed conservatively both art and anthropology might be seen as *representing* the world, out there, giving form to pre-existing 'content'. Contemporary art does not aim to represent but to perform, to make the world happen; *joining in* with this speculative attitude was both the premise and the finding of the KFI project (see also Sansi 2018).

Convergences or conjunctions

Convergences in art and anthropology can be seen in terms of inter- or transdisciplinarity. There are many definitions related to integrating or exchanging knowledge across subject boundaries (see Toomey et al. 2015). For me, the term *inter-* implies between-ness, open to points of contact, though disciplinary distinctions remain. Developing clearer understandings of 'resistances' *as well as* the convergences would help establish the ground for such 'hybrid' work (Grimshaw and Ravetz 2015). *Trans-* suggests a traversing of distinctions and a different kind of relation within a single practice (e.g. Laine 2018). Either might produce art that is 'anthropological', which Ingold defines via four principles (2018): generosity, open-endedness, comparativeness (asking: why this direction, rather than another?) and being critical, which is meant not in the sense of making judgements about things as they are, but rather a speculative criticality.

Perhaps the reification of 'pure' art or anthropology is the mistake; hasn't appropriation taught us that everything is hybrid, somehow? (Schneider 2003). Or thought of in another way, could anthropology *and* art function as a *conjunction,* and do something *other than* the hybrid convergences of inter- or anti-, disciplinarity? What outcomes are possible, when taking an approach that acknowledges debate, in both disciplines? What matters to me, crucially, is producing work that 'speaks for itself', and that legitimately satisfies conditions for *both* disciplines. What I learned from these experiences curating and being curated was learning to recognize limitations, in myself as well, and so developing *criticality* in specific encounters, instead of seeking to resolve tensions theoretically, since any outcome, proposition or project is always dependent on the specific encounter. I learned to think of art anthropology and curation as 'an 'ecology of *practices*', a 'mode of questioning' that situates the relevance and limits of one practice in relation to others by considering how knowledge gleaned from one field might be brought to bear on others (Stengers 2005). From this perspective, divergent practices '*impinge upon*' one another, a relational approach not unlike Rabinow and Marcus's (2008) notion of the contemporary; this does not preclude an understanding of roles, or professions, defined in disciplinary terms. I felt the first failure keenly, because valued relationships effectively ended. But it forced me to ask questions about how I want to work. Eventually I came to appreciate, as much as possible from an artist's point of view, why it matters that art might be considered as 'knowledge forming', tackling relationships between content and form, addressing materials and process, and what learning with these (with-or-and art), might bring to anthropology, as well as being reminded of what anthropology brings me.

Notes

1   Contemporary art is a very loose term. The art historian Terry Smith identifies three 'types': the spectacles of massive museums and art markets; postcolonial art 'of transnational transitionality'; and 'new modes of visual imagining'. The last is perhaps the most pertinent, if enigmatic (Smith 2016: 395). It is not my goal to further define the term, except to point to the idea that contemporary artworks can operate as *acts of thought* as Smith also suggests (2009).
2   As it is described in the course materials of the Glasgow School of Art, Scotland.

References

Buckner, C. (2013), 'Autonomy, Pluralism, Play: Danto, Greenberg, Kant, and the Philosophy of Art History', *Journal of Aesthetics & Culture*, 5.

Bunn, S., ed. (2018), *Anthropology and Beauty: From Aesthetics to Creativity*, Abingdon: Routledge.

Carrithers, M. (2005), 'Anthropology as a Moral Science of Possibilities', *Current Anthropology*, 46 (3): 433–56.

Clarke, J. (2014), 'Disciplinary Boundaries Between Art and Anthropology', *Journal of Visual Art Practice*, 13 (3): 178–91, Available online: https://knowingfromtheinside.o rg/files/koryu.pdf.

Clarke, J. (2019/forthcoming), 'Apocalyptic Sublimes and the Recalibration of Distance: Doing Art-Anthropology in Post Disaster Japan', in Philipp Schorch, Martin Saxer and Marlen Elders (eds), *Researching Materiality and Connectivity in Anthropology and Beyond*, London: UCL Press.

Dimitrakaki, A. (2018), Feminism, Art, Contradictions, *e-flux journal*, #92 June, Available online: https://www.e-flux.com/journal/92/205536/feminism-art-contradictions/ (accessed 1 February 2019).

Drucker, J. (2005), *Sweet Dreams: Contemporary Art and Complicity*, Chicago: University of Chicago Press.

Eisner, E. (2008), 'Art and Knowledge', in J. Gary Knowles and Ardra L. Cole (eds), *Handbook of the Arts in Qualitative Research: Perspectives, Methodologies, Examples, and Issues*, London: Sage.

Filipovic, E., ed. (2017), *The Artist as Curator: An Anthology*, Berlin: Verlag der Buchhandlung Walther Konig.

Foster, H. (1996), 'The Artist as Ethnographer?' in H. Foster (ed.), *The Return of the Real: The Avant-garde at the End of the Century*, 171–203, Cambridge, MA: MIT Press.

Gaut, B. (2003), 'Art and Knowledge', in Jerrold Levinson (ed.), *The Oxford Handbook of Aesthetics*, 436–50, Oxford: Oxford University Press.

Grimshaw, A. and Ravetz, A. (2015), 'The Ethnographic Turn – And After: A Critical Approach towards the Realignment of Art and Anthropology', *Social Anthropology*, 23 (4): 418–34.

Hamburg, C. H. (1952), 'Art as Knowledge', *College Art Journal*, 12 (1): 2–11.

Herrington, J. (2014), 'Can Knowledge Be Found in Works of Art?' *Runway, Australian Experimental Art*, Issue 26.

Ingold, T. (2013), *Making: Anthropology, Archaeology, Art and Architecture*, London: Routledge.

Jelinek, A. (2013), *This Is Not Art*, London: I.B. Taurus.

Jelinek, A. (2016), 'Response: An Artist's Response to an Anthropological Perspective', *Social Anthropology/Anthropologie Sociale*, 24 (4): 503–9.

Jones, A. (2015), 'Material Traces: Performativity, Artistic "Work", and New Concepts of Agency', *TDR/The Drama Review*, 59 (4): 18–35.

Korsby, Trine Mygind and Anthony Stavrianakis (2018), 'Moments in Collaboration: Experiments in Concept Work', *Ethnos*, 83 (1): 39–57.

Kowalski, M. J. (2010), 'The Curatorial Muse', *Contemporary Aesthetics*, 8, Available online: https://contempaesthetics.org/newvolume/pages/article.php?articleID=585 (accessed 1 October 2018).

Krysa, J. (2015), 'The Politics of Contemporary Curating', in R. Martin (ed.), *The Routledge Companion to Art and Politics*, London: Routledge.

Laine, A. (2018), *Practicing Art and Anthropology, A Transdisciplinary Journey*, London: Bloomsbury.

Leach, J. (2007), 'Differentiation and Encompassment: A Critique of Alfred Gell's Theory of the Abduction of Creativity', in Amiria Henare, Martin Holbraad and Sari Wastell (eds), *Thinking Through Things, Theorising Artefacts Ethnographically*, London: Routledge.

Manning, E. (2016), 'Ten Propositions for Research-Creation', in N. Colin and S. Sachsenmaier (eds), *Collaboration in Performance Practice*, London: Palgrave Macmillan.

Marcus, G. and Myers, F. (1995), *The Traffic in Culture: Refiguring Art and Anthropology*, Berkeley: University of California Press.

Marcus, G. and Douglas Holmes (2008), 'Collaboration Today and the Re-Imagination of the Classic Scene of Fieldwork Encounter', *Collaborative Anthropologies*, 1: 81–101.

Mouffe. C. (2007), 'Artistic Activism and Agonistic Spaces', *Art & Research: A Journal of Ideas, Contexts and Methods*, 1 (2), Summer an Verwoert: Living with Ghosts: From Appropriation to Invocation in Contemporary Arthttp://www.artandresearch.org.uk/v1n2/verwoert.html.

Obrist, H. U. (2014), *Hans-Ulrich Obrist: The Art of Curation, Guardian*, Available online: https://www.theguardian.com/artanddesign/2014/mar/23/hans-ulrich-obrist-art-cura tor (accessed 1 October 2018).

Pink. S. (2012), 'Advances in Visual Methodology, an Introduction', in S. Pink (ed.), *Advances in Visual Methodology*, London: Sage.

Polanyi, M. (1983), *The Tacit Dimension*, Gloucester, MA: Peter Smith Publisher.

Rabinow, P. and Marcus, G. (2008), *Designs for an Anthropology of the Contemporary*, Durham, NC, and London : Duke University Press.

Sansi, R. (2015), *Art, Anthropology and the Gift*, London: Bloomsbury.

Sansi, R. (2018), 'Unlearning the Role Game: Artists, Amateurs, Historians and Neighbors in the Periphery of Barcelona', *Field*, 11, Available online: http://field-journal.com/issue-11/unlearning-the-role-game (accessed 9 February 2019).

Schneider, A. (2003), 'On "appropriation": A Critical Reappraisal of the Concept and Its Application in Global Art Practices', *Social Anthropology*, 11 (2): 215–29.

Schneider, A. and C. Wright, eds. (2006), *Contemporary Art and Anthropology*, Oxford: Berg.

Schneider, A. and C. Wright, eds. (2010), *Between Art and Anthropology: Contemporary Ethnographic Practice*, Oxford: Berg.

Schneider, Arnd (2011), 'Unfinished Dialogues: Notes toward an Alternative History of Art and Anthropology', in Marcus Banks and Jay Ruby (ed.), *Made to Be Seen: Perspectives on the History of Visual Anthropology*, 108–35, University of Chicago Press.

Smith, T. (2009), *What Is Contemporary Art?* Chicago: University of Chicago Press.

Smith, T. (2016), 'Art, Anthropology, and Anxiety', *HAU: Journal of Ethnographic Theory*, 6 (1): 371–402.

Stengers, I. (2005, March), 'Introductory Notes on an Ecology of Practices', *Cultural Studies Review*, 11 (1).

Toomey, A. H., Nils Markusson, Emily Adams and Beth Brockett (2015), *Inter- and Trans-Disciplinary Research: A Critical Perspective*, GSDR 2015 Brief, Lancaster Environment Centre: Lancaster University.

Venkatesan, S. (2010), 'Ontology Is Just Another Word for Culture', motion tabled at the 2008 Meeting of the Group for Debates in Anthropological Theory, University of Manchester, UK, in *Critique of Anthropology*, June, 30 (2): 152–200.

Verwoert, J. (2007), 'Living with Ghosts: From Appropriation to Invocation in Contemporary Art', *Art & Research: A Journal of Ideas, Contexts and Methods*, 1 (2), Available online: Arthttp://www.artandresearch.org.uk/v1n2/verwoert.html.

Zangwill, N. (1999), 'Art and Audience', *The Journal of Aesthetics and Art Criticism*, 57 (3) (Summer): 315–32.

Curating the intermural: graffiti in the museum 2008–18

Rafael Schacter

Introduction

Over the last ten years, curating has become, almost by accident, a key part of my anthropological practice. Falling into the role through my position as an ethnographer working within the visual arts – the initial relationship of one-sided knowledge acquisition I had with my artist interlocutors transforming into a more collaborative process of co-production as I slowly earned their faith – this practice of what I termed research-led curating was, for the most part, undertaken in a largely impromptu manner. While the training I had undertaken in anthropological and more general social–scientific methods was able to transplant itself, in a fairly elementary fashion, into this alternate presentational format – one broadly based on the short-term public display of commissioned artworks rather than the more conventional production of scholarly texts – my main concerns during this early period were on both how to stay true to my informants' life-worlds and how to reciprocate their generosity and goodwill. At the same time, however, experimenting with different techniques of making my research public, as much as the different modes of undertaking this research itself, soon came to act as an extension of these initial impulses towards fidelity and restitution alone: commitment to my informants seemed, in fact, to *necessitate* experimental techniques, fidelity to their practices demanding different modes of presentation, and my responsibility thus lay in how to balance these former and latter aspirations, how to ensure both were implicitly supported by each other. As such, while issues such as reflexivity and representation, engagement and participation, all played pivotal roles in the curatorial position I came to adopt, these sprang more from the post-writing culture milieu that I emerged from, from the intellectual richness of the material culture subsection at University College London (UCL) that I was lucky enough to have been housed within, rather than via any conscious enquiry into the theories and lineages of curating per se (in both its museological and art historical incarnations). I simply considered myself an anthropologist engaged in the active production, rather than theoretical

148   *The Anthropologist as Curator*

interrogation, of the wider exhibition format itself, an anthropologist utilizing the potentials of curating, not a curator per se.

Thanks, in no small part, to the initiative of this book's editor Roger Sansi, however, as well as to invaluable ongoing conversations with both anthropological colleagues (such as Jonas Tinius, Alex Flynn and Khadija Von Zinnenburg Carroll) and curatorial collaborators (such as Mara Kolmel and Silvana Lagos,[1] Merv Espina and Renan Laru-an[2]), I have more recently been able to begin consciously thinking through my past and present curation in a more cohesive manner: probing what insights I have gained from the different modes of exhibition-making I have undertaken; analysing what these strategies enabled in terms of their public reception; reviewing how the anthropological framing affected my overall practice as much, perhaps more importantly, as the practice affecting my way of understanding anthropology itself. In an essay written parallel to this (Schacter 2019)[3] I have thus moved to examine my current and forthcoming work, concentrating more closely on the concepts of the curatorial outlined by Sansi in this book's introductory chapter and exploring, in particular, my recent curation of the project *Motions of this Kind* (an exhibition focusing on contemporary art from the Philippines and a major output of my extended postdoctoral work in the region). In this chapter, however, I will be reflecting upon my past curatorial work within the arena of *graffiti* – the central topic of my studies over the last decade and a subject area I continue to engage within today.[4] Rather than attempting a broad conceptual sweep, then, a state-of-the-art examination of the relationship between the curatorial and anthropological itself, I want simply to look back at three key projects I have participated in over this last decade, to explore how they helped me to further understand, and share that understanding, of the practice of graffiti itself.

Starting with my MA dissertation in 2005 (latterly published in 2008 as *An Ethnography of Iconoclash*), my academic output has focused upon the area of *independent public art*, a term, coined by the theorist Javier Abarca, incorporating graffiti, street art, as well as a wide range of other autonomous urban aesthetic practices functioning outside of the institutionalized space of corporate or state-funded public art. Conducting the research for my doctorate in this field in Madrid, Spain, between 2007 and 2010 (although working in a multisited fashion throughout – studying the movement of both my artist interlocutors as much as the artefacts that they made), my earliest method of making myself in some way 'useful' for the collective[5] I was embedded with was via photography – trying, and initially wildly failing (which my informants were very quick to let me know) at least to offer something back to them, to atone for the extra baggage (the ever-increasing questions) that I brought to the table. Although my photography did slowly improve (to a level of acceptability at least), conversations with my fieldwork partners eventually led to curating: my position in the academe was one that my informants' found simultaneously amusing and validating – especially due to what was then the subcultural (and illegal) nature of their practice – and while each of them had their own relationships with particular artists, critics or academics involved in curatorial pursuits,[6] my day-to-day existence among them meant that this initially colloquial, latterly practical, movement, was an entirely natural, albeit unanticipated one: I was there (which made things easier), I was an academic (bestowing a level of legitimacy), and I was eager to assist (to find a functional 'role' within the group). While the artists I worked with spent the vast majority of their time making public work (I would suggest at least 80 per cent of their practice taking place within the context of the street), each of my interlocutors had a studio practice that they simultaneously pursued – especially as their public work most often happened at night, leaving their daytimes less encumbered. This was a practice generally set within an equally independent framing, however, working with artist-run spaces and small, self-supporting galleries rather than within the sanctioned, commercial gallery realm, yet, as time went on, it was one that was inevitably beginning to intersect with a more institutionalized context than they were accustomed to. Conducting my fieldwork during an era in which street art in particular was going through a process of rampant co-option, an appropriation meaning that commercial galleries and dealers were beginning to take on an increasing role – individuals, to be clear, who were emerging from outside the tight circle of like-minded adherents that had been present up to that point – the issues surrounding the act of curating, the movement from street to studio, were very much at the forefront of all my interlocutors' minds: How could one ever present an art that was, by its very essence, <u>public</u>, intrinsically *ornamental* – an adjunct to a secondary surface, an adornment of the city – within the interior space of a gallery? How could one ever present an art that was, in its very nature, <u>impermanent</u>, innately *ephemeral* – an artefact that lived and died and drew its very power from that – within the milieu of fine art in which conservation was key? How could one ever present an art that was, in a fundamental sense, <u>performative</u>, deeply *corporeal* – an art that was about the act as much as the artefact – within the dispassionate realm of the white cube? And how, even more to the point, could one ever present a practice that was, by principle, <u>uncollectable</u>, entirely *inalienable* – a form that was produced to display one's commitment and ability and neither meant nor capable of being sold – within the institutional, acquisitive frame of the corporate market?

While much of the knowledge I gained through my fieldwork was transmitted to me tacitly rather than verbally, through what my informants did as much as what they said, these four key factors – the ornamental, the ephemeral, the corporeal and the inalienable – were issues that were entirely inescapable during this time, issues openly debated and discussed by my interlocutors on a regular basis. More to the point, however, they were issues that a curatorial practice in particular explicitly helped to think through and bring to the fore: the complex artefactual status of graffiti (its position as both attachment and embellishment of its surface), its complex temporal status (its position as innately transitory and fluid), its complex corporeal status (its position as action not simply image), as much as its complex ethical status (its position as act of commitment not simply commodity), were questions that curating could not help but bring to the surface, questions foregrounded through an implicitness impossible to deny. These issues were thus not only the key themes that continued to flow in and out of my curation over the following decade, matters at the heart of the three case studies that I will outline below, but were concerns that helped to reveal the paradoxes at the heart of this visual practice, the paradoxes emergent in the display of an aesthetic entirely resistant to this very fact.

Street Art at the Tate Modern, 2008

Alongside the Los Angeles Museum of Contemporary Art's ground-breaking show *Art in the Streets* in 2011, the Tate Modern's 2008 *Street Art* project stands as a high point – in terms of visitor numbers, critical attention and wider global media impact – within the history of graffiti and street art's curation since its first institutional appearance in the early 1970s.[7] The exhibition radically transformed the public comprehension of street art. Moving forwards, it was not only branded as something radically distinct from its graffiti ancestor but was given institutional validation at a level previously unimaginable. It was a moment in which the debate surrounding the validity, let alone legality of this illicit visual form, was opened up and challenged, yet so too a moment in which the plurality of the form became in many ways reductively singularized.

The project was formed of two key elements: the first, a series of six large-scale murals painted directly upon the north facade of the Tate Modern site – curated by artist and author Cedar Lewisohn, and featuring one of my key field informants, Sixe Paredes, alongside fellow artists Blu, Faile, JR, Nunca and Os Gemeos; the second, a 'walking tour' in the surrounding Southwark area incorporating fifteen artworks by a further five artists, which I myself curated (and will focus on mainly below), and which featured the artists 3TTMan, Eltono, Nuria Mora, Nano4814 and Spok, five of my closest interlocutors. The dual aspect of the exhibition focused both on the technical virtuosity housed within this reinvigorated form of contemporary muralism (as seen on the north facade), as much as the site-specific and multimedia diversity of street art, its status as a public, poetic, interrogative urban aesthetic (as seen in the work in the surrounding Southwark area). Yet although below I will go on to examine the specifics of these two factors, *Street Art* was, first and foremost, an exercise for me in research reciprocity and enablement: enabling me to continue my research while simultaneously providing platforms for my interlocutors' burgeoning outputs, facilitating the continuance of my research relationships while concurrently giving something back other than my presence, the project was a way for me both to deepen ties and to create more collaborative, horizontal connections with my research partners.[8] It was a way for me to participate in their practices in a deeper, more integral manner, to grasp, as Victor Turner said, their 'deepest knowledge' through speaking their 'Essential We-talk' (Turner in Tedlock 1991: 71). It was a way for me not to paint or sculpt or engage in their *visual* activities, but rather to re-present these activities collaboratively, to mediate their work both collectively and publicly. This was hence a means of proving my commitment to them and their wider practice in an embedded, physical, concrete manner, a way of showing that I was willing to push the way they were pushing, to work the way they were working. As such, from very early on, the project became about ensuring that their work was presented in a way that was consistent with their wider practice (seemingly obvious but entirely crucial), consistent with what I had learned through my fieldwork up to that point. (See Figure 9.1.)

Within the *Walking Tour*, then, the first key prerequisite was the work's *publicness*, its space (unlike, oxymoronically, at LA MOCA's *Art in the Streets*) within the dirt

Curating the Intermural   151

and noise of the city, within the dense medium of the urban realm. Street art and graffiti's status as ornament, as something that by its very nature was attached to a surface, affixed to the city (an argument central to my monograph *Ornament and Order*, 2008, and summarized in my essay *Graffiti and Street Art as Ornament* 2016), thus here remained pivotal. Its status as something that was not produced on a neutral surface but that lived and breathed within an already extant concrete materiality, that was steered, activated by its surrounding environment, was hence our basic starting point. Rather than simply presenting the artists with a series of objects or spaces to work upon, then, the project started with the artists' own input: going on a series of walks with the group within the wider Southwark area (during both day and night), exploring the streets in a manner to which they were accustomed (in which they would examine the city, in a way I was entirely unpractised in before I began my fieldwork – a way of focusing on the hidden spaces of the city that were habitually neglected by their everyday users), the sites were hence chosen in the same manner that these artists would select spaces when conducting work *independently*. The prime curatorial task was thus turning a wish list of spaces into a practical reality, to use the institutional power of the Tate brand to convince the local council, local businesses, local galleries, schools, NGOs and (the dreaded) Transport for London,[9] that we could legitimately (and, more importantly, legally) produce work on these properties. The sites of production hence remained entirely authentic to these artists' quotidian practice. They were the sites they would experiment upon with or without sanction, with or without the accredited documentation that I kept close to hand. They were sites where their work could be conducted in a truly site-specific manner, in which the reality of the city was never separate from the nature of the work itself. The installations and murals dotted around the Tate hence remained impervious, I argue, to the institutional authority that they were connected to. They aimed to engage the local community with aspects of the urban environment that would otherwise by ignored or disregarded – to push people to look at the city, to engage with their environment, in a more heightened, embodied, playful manner – irrespective of their official status. It was this potential, this belief in the beauty in the everyday that the artists wanted to activate – something revealed, in fact, through my own witnessing during the show of map-holding tour-goers uncertainly contemplating parts of the urban environment that were entirely disconnected with the project, questioning whether they were part of the tour or not, whether they were *art* or not. Yet alongside the curatorial outlook employed to underscore the ornamental, site-specific nature of street art and graffiti, the approach to ensure that their work was conducted in as independent a manner as habitually undertaken, one other aspect of the *Walking Tour* project remained crucial. This, the *Signs* project by Eltono and Nuria, aimed to reinforce the essentially inalienable aspect of this practice, graffiti and street art's status as artefacts participating within a gift, not a commodity, economy, their status as objects that could be given yet never sold (Weiner 1992). (See Figure 9.2.)

Signs (2008), which had previously been completed by the pair the year earlier in Gothenburg (at Galleri 54) and Berlin (at the Senatsreservenspeicher), was a participative project in which the public played a pivotal role. Experimenting with ideas of ownership and authenticity, value and context, public and private, it was a

Figure 9.1 Map of the *Walking Tour*, part of the exhibition *Street Art* at the Tate Modern, London, 2008. Copyright © Rafael Schacter.

Curating the Intermural

SPOK
Spok is closely associated with the New York tradition of Subway art, and, from his teens, was travelling around Europe and the United States with a spraycan. Already a renowned street-writer throughout Spain, he developed a remarkable photorealist style while studying for a fine-arts degree in his hometown of Madrid. Since then, his skills have been much in demand for decorating shopfront grilles across the city, or for commissions from advertising agencies and companies as diverse as Nike and L'Oreal. 'The work that we do just for ourselves... we're going to go and paint no matter what,' he says. 'People don't understand, they say it's vandalism or you're wasting your time or whatever. But for me, it's the only true art form.'

EL TONO AND NURIA
Since 1999, the French artist El Tono and the Spanish artist Nuria have often worked in partnership, though both are also well-known for their solo work. El Tono's name (which means 'The Tone') relates to his personal signature, an image of a tuning fork. Although he started making conventional street art, he now creates geometric shapes that, he feels, contribute positively to the urban landscape. 'The whole point is to intrigue people, to make people reflect in some distinctive way, to produce something for people to wonder at.' Nuria's street art combines forms reminiscent of hard-edged modernist abstraction with softer colours. Her signature image is a key. The two artists usually collaborate for gallery commissions. Their joint work plays with undermining ideas of what is inside and what is outside the traditional gallery space, and often invites visitor participation. For Tate, they have made a number of street signs, which have been posted around the surrounding area. A note on the back of each sign invites you to bring the placard back to the gallery. In exchange, they will be signed by the artists and given back to you at the end of the exhibition.

NANO 4814
Born in Vigo, Nano 4814 has been living in Madrid for about four years. He originally came to street art from a skateboarding background, which gave him a strong relationship with the streets. 'Being there at the precise moment, being able to display on the wall what's in my head, that's why I do it,' he has said of his work. Among his most striking projects are his *City-Lights*, made from disused light boxes in rundown neighbourhoods or by abandoned buildings. He transforms the boxes, originally used for advertising, to carry poetic messages, such as 'It shines and disappears' – a line that captures the ephemeral and transient nature of street art itself. His street images include a series of recurring icons, most notably *El Choquito*, a little squid squirting ink, that he sees as 'a perfect metaphor for the writer in the street'.

3TTMAN
3TTMan's spontaneous, painterly style has affinities with both Pop art and cartoons like Tom and Jerry or Bugs Bunny, combining bold compositions and often garish colours with sometimes brutal imagery. Originally from Lille, he started painting on canvas, and only later began working on the street. His name derives from the French *trois tête man*, or three headed man – a recurring figure in his work, which reflects a divided, often directly contradictory spirit. He talks about this three-way consciousness as 'three ways of expressing something in the same process, three ways of thinking in the same body'. In Madrid, he often targets billposters as a surface for his work, cutting away and painting over the original advertisement to transform commercial imagery into art. 'We're playing with the city, playing with what we've got around us,' he says. 'We're playing with advertising for advertising something else, a thought, an idea.'

Figure 9.2 *Signs*, London, Eltono and Nuria, fifty hand-painted signboards, site-specific part of the *Walking Tour*, for the exhibition *Street Art* at the Tate Modern, London, 2008, curated by Rafael Schacter.

work that aimed to highlight the tension within the binaries intrinsic to their practice, between street and gallery, commodity and art. Eltono & Nuria first spent a week producing fifty hand-painted signboards – utilising the pair's key stylistic motifs – before working over a morning to place these works throughout the local area. Setting them in front gardens and backstreet bushes, on busy roundabouts and in local parks, the public were then invited (through a text screen-printed on the back of each placard, as well as information on the Tate website and exhibition pamphlet), to claim the signs and return them to Eltono and Nuria within the museum itself. 'Dear Visitor', the signs read (in both Spanish and English),

> This signboard is part of Eltono and Nuria's artwork presented with the Tate Modern. If you want to actively participate in the installation and keep the placard, please bring it to the Tate Modern during 'The Long Weekend' on the 24th, 25th and 26th of May between 14.00 and 18.00. It will be signed and numbered by the artists and given back to you with its certificate at the end of the weekend. We kindly ask you to leave the signboard in its place in case you are not interested in this project, allowing someone else the possibility to participate. Thank you, Eltono and Nuria.[10]

As a project then, *Signs* perfectly expressed the complexity of placing street art and graffiti within the gallery context. Not only did this movement to the interior, to the institutional, turn a gift into a commodity, it turned it from ornament into pure decoration, an ornament without attachment, an ornament wrested from its surface. The independent works my informants produced within the regular practice were not made for instrumental purposes, not for financial gain or mainstream fame.[11] They were made through an act of commitment to the city, through a gift, a presentation, a contribution to the life of their locale. Simply transforming these practices into products, transfiguring their work into a gallery space and offering it for sale (as numerous artists who came under the street art label did), made no conceptual sense to Eltono and Nuria, made no conceptual sense to many artists who were making this transition from the independent to institutional domain during this time. To be clear, these artists understood that to practice their work full-time, to live as artists, they had to create methods of survival, methods of navigating the institutional realm. But this didn't mean selling public works, selling what were meant as gifts. That would simply invalidate their very practice itself. *Signs* thus sought to address these issues, to play on the importance of public art as, by its nature, something public; to play on the power of its ephemerality, its appearance and dissipation from the street as something that, in fact, kept it alive; to play on the taught relationship of inside and outside, street and institution; and to play on its gratuitousness – done without request, done for free, done for the city. Highlighting the fact of inalienability, the boundary between in and out, the transfiguration of value that the museum enabled, the project disturbed the way that the street and institution interacted, disrupted the concepts of value, scarcity, ownership, that the institution innately relied upon. It restated the fact that works in a public space were produced quite explicitly *for* the street. And it thus began, along with the other elements of the *Walking Tour*, to further complexify the concept of curating within the realm of graffiti and street.

Yet while the above discussion outlines some of the key curatorial ideas that the *Walking Tour* project attempted to unpack, as a space, in and of itself, from which to *conduct* my fieldwork (rather than present it), a space from which to be physically and professionally embedded, the *Street Art* exhibition was an incredible research experience at a point pivotal to the genre's transformation.[12] In particular, the prominence, perhaps unsurprisingly, of the mural element of the project, as something that held the entirety of the media's attention and that was, by the Tate's marketing team at the least, strongly pushed as a unique global event, began to steer the wider perception of street art in a quite particular and singular direction. It began to steer the perception of street art solely as big, graphic, public paintings, as a singular form of neo-muralism rather than the range of complex and plural aesthetic practices it had previously been understodo as. Moreover, it set street art, I argue, on the road towards recuperation, not simply due to its institutionalization or artistic appropriation, but through its relationship with the then exponentially expanding discourse of the creative city promoted by Richard Florida et al. (discussed at length in Schacter 2015). Functioning through what are today the thousands of Street Art Festivals that have spread across the globe – and that are, I argue, a direct result of the media success of the *Street Art* exhibition[13] – these projects, produced at the behest of cultural managers and urban planners rather than of artists or curators, have not only today become the dominant mode whereby street art is encountered (in particular through its digital distribution), but have turned the practice into one in which financial rather than cultural value is at the fore, a practice not simply selling itself, but (perhaps more perniciously) *selling a false notion of place*.[14] Although the Tate exhibition was not strictly a street art festival, then, it became implicitly linked to a festival-like context through acting as the launch event for the Tate's (short-lived) *Long Weekend* project (a 'four-day festival of art and performance'), cementing the link between street art and the festival mechanism. More to the point, while one would imagine that the artists featuring in the exhibition would have been insulated from any aspect of this co-optation through working with such a grand, respected institution, the warning signs of this imminent appropriation were very much in place. Not only were both the *Long Weekend* and the *Street Art* exhibition sponsored by Nissan Qashqai – a fact that the artists were *not made aware* of prior to their arrival in London – but the murals ended up functioning as a backdrop for a BMX competition photographically documented by the sponsor for their own brand 'content', a usage of the murals as mere corporate wallpaper, as edgy background for their vision of cool. This led to a near revolt by the artists (marshalled by the strongly politically engaged muralist Blu,[15] and visibly recorded in the message 'please don't feed the sponsors' within his work), who were dismayed by the seemingly purposeful lack of communication regarding this sponsorship from the Tate hierarchy. Along with other similar incidents – the facts, for example, that the company employed to remove the murals from the Tate walls were paid more than the artists themselves, the fact that the Tate refused to arrange an opening launch for the artists (something that I then personally organized) – it was a moment of recognition that all was not quite as it seemed. The conspicuous absence of any street art or graffiti-related projects at the Tate in the ten years since the show opened (not even a whisper of such), has only reinforced the feeling that the museum had utilized this project for the pure cultural capital it could accrue – placing the institution at the forefront of a new global culture while keeping its artistic value at arms' length. As such, even as two of the artists involved in the mural project, JR and Os Gemeos, have today fully crossed over into the mainstream art world, the hierarchies of value that the Tate stands as a key global mediator of, were kept firmly in place. And while both elements of the project were instituted with bold intentions, and they enabled many of the issues related to the genre to emerge, the institution itself overawed and dominated these intentions, appropriating them and the artists for its own particular gain.

Mapping the City at Somerset House, 2015

Exhibited at London's Somerset House, a prominent arts and cultural hub in the capital and the fifth most visited cultural institution in the UK, *Mapping the City* took place in the then dilapidated, formerly palatial, rooms of the 'New Wing'. The second of three exhibitions I curated at Somerset House as part of the cultural organization Approved by Pablo (the third of which, *Venturing Beyond*, will be discussed below), *Mapping the City* had a key contention at its heart, one central to my doctoral thesis: graffiti was not simply a form of image-making but a performative, participatory act, one in which the city appeared not simply as a medium but as a collaborative partner, as the entire frame of reference, in fact, for the practice itself. Mapping space through their artistic production, each inscription charting a bodily presence within the city, I argued that the individuals involved in this aesthetic practice formed a very particular, embedded, sensual relationship to the city, a relationship not simply of transfer and travel but of exploration and creation, an active intermixing of self and landscape: through producing their work on this living canvas, through inhabiting its streets, navigating its topography, evading its authorities, these individuals gained a conception of our urban world that few other people had access to, an alternative vision bound through a deep investment within the politics of space. As the French artist Honet emblematically said,

> It seemed to me that you start liking your city differently when you look at it in a new way, when you get to know spots that nobody else knows. You realize that a city is not only about the obvious. There are just so many strange things in our environments connected to the past, connected to each place's culture and history. Yet most people don't perceive these details, not because they are hidden, but because they are out of our regular focus – usually somewhere on top or in a corner, somewhere hiding in plain sight.

Wanting to find a way of visually unlocking this hidden knowledge, these stories left out-of-focus, these secrets in plain sight, for *Mapping the City* we thus commissioned forty artists – each of whose work has been deeply influenced by their relationship to the street – to produce maps of their cities, cartographic representations that could reveal personal understandings of the urban environments in which they were immersed. Seeing maps simply as graphical depictions of spatial and navigational dynamics, these artefacts were here understood as symbolic representations dependent as much on their *users* as their *uses*: they were not only seen as volatile, as artefacts subject to inevitable change and historically and culturally specific, but as objects that could tell us as much about those who made them as the location in question itself. The artists in *Mapping the City* were hence tasked with one directive: *represent your space*. All we asked was that they produce works that could help *us* understand how their surroundings appear to *them* – to craft images that presented distance through a bodily rather than mathematical mode, through subjective surveyance rather than objective ordinance. Each map thus sought to provide the ultimate 'insider' view of the city, a counter-cartography of the clandestine and concealed, the subjective terrain and intuitive landscape of the city as lived. Yet, crucially, by revealing these topographies, the project aimed to help engender a new way of understanding of the city for our viewers themselves. Challenging normative conceptions of the structure of urban space, it aimed to expose the contested layers and substructures of the urban realm – the critical geographies of the city – and thus stimulate our visitors to view their own spaces in the self-same manner themselves.

Mapping the City hence sought to make an argument that was similar, in many ways, to that made at the *Street Art* exhibition at the Tate. Exploring the corporeal performativity of graffiti, its status as an act integrally located in the city, inherently in and of urban space, what was key was to narrate its status, not simply as image but as action, not just as form but as practice. While style is of course critical to graffiti, it remains one part of a larger whole; the production of the image is, within the subculture, as equally important an aspect of the image, something rarely mentioned outside graffiti circles and something which acts as a huge impediment to its wider comprehension. One of the key themes that the project aimed to explore was thus the link to the situationist movement of the 1960s, in particular, to Guy Debord's famous notion of *psychogeography*: as an act rejecting the functional, scientific understanding of our environment and instead focusing upon a space's rhythms and atmospheres, psychogeography meant to explore the intimacy between physical environment and human emotion, the intertwined relationship between body and space. It meant to think about the city in a way stretching beyond the habitual, in a manner that could see past its traditional, literally top-down depiction. In this way, the mechanism of the map not only enabled us to work around the basic dilemma of graffiti in the institutions – how to display it within an internal space when this was something, as previously suggested, that was logically impossible – but also to deconstruct the power traditionally invested in maps themselves: it enabled us to critique the 'google map'-centred understanding of the city, the dehumanizing, supposedly 'neutral' representation that this form of surveillance comes to create, while finding a way to present graffiti *knowledge* rather than graffiti itself within the institution.

Eltono's sculptural map, for example, entitled *Promenades* (2015), rested upon a project produced between 2013 and 2014 while living in Beijing, China. *Promenades* was about 'walking, observation and spontaneity', about 'moving crosscurrent in the city with time for contemplation to be able to observe details that most people don't notice'. It was about wandering in the urban environment with 'total freedom of time and space', 'to walk in one direction with no goal', to engage in the city through experiment and play: to *drift*. Based upon a key understanding emergent from Eltono's graffiti practice – that the knowledge and understanding gained from the experience of being in the street was in many ways as important as that which was created through the practice of producing graffiti in itself – *Promenades* thus distilled these ideas into one in which the graffiti image was now tangential, the act of being in the street itself the goal. After working in this location for more than twenty years, walking in the city evolved from a necessary activity into a pleasurable one, one providing unlimited inspiration, providing potential and possibility with every step. Each of the different ten sculptural forms visible in Eltono's sculpture thus mapped the exact route he took on each of his ten *Promenades* – each of which were available for view, in great detail, on his website "(which we of course provided our visitors with links to – see http://www.eltono.com/en/projects/promenades/promenade-no1/ for an apposite example). The piece thus mapped out both time and space, the hours he took on each journey as much as his exact spatial movements. It mapped out his relationship to the city, his need to embed himself within this space. Yet, like all his work, the final piece was an abstraction of his original performance. It was a method of taking what Eltono had achieved, what he had experienced in the city, and moving it into the gallery space without simply replicating or debasing it. Moreover, it was a tool that, for him, acted as an example (for himself, for our viewers) of the possibilities that the city contained when one restored a childlike curiosity to one's actions, when one engaged in the unlimited creativity of the uninhibited.

Figure 9.3 *Paris Verticale, Series 3*, Honet Giclée on cotton paper 118.9 cm by 84.1 cm. Exhibited at Somerset House, London, 2015, for *Mapping the City*, curated by Rafael Schacter.

In Honet's poetical, mythological map of Paris, however, *Paris Verticale* (2015) (see Figure 9.3 above), he attempted to form a vision of his city from a contemplative rather than a scientifically rational perspective. This was one that not only reinforced his understanding of the practice of graffiti, but that also portrayed his deep knowledge of Paris's ancient catacombs. Rejecting the static nature of the two-dimensional maps that we so often see, this was a map that expressed the nature of lived space through the image of the staircase, an artefact often understood both as a depiction of the assent (or descent) from hell to heaven and as a vertical reconfiguration of a labyrinth. In Honet's design, however, the journey he depicts is from the 'deepest places of Paris, such as the catacombs, to the highest bell-towers, monuments, or rooftops'. The names on the side of each stair thus represent a 'tour from the *Abbesses* metro station to the Eiffel Tower, from the nadir to the pinnacle of the capital'. As with all the icons and symbols housed within the work, the three crests have particular significance: the far left image is the Parisian coat of arms (within which Honet has incorporated an ouroboros, an important mythological symbol often representing eternal return); the central emblem depicting a 'lantern for the underworld, a coq on top of a church-bell, and two hammers for breaking the walls in between' (a perfect visual condensation of Honet's exploration through the city); while the final crest, at the far right-hand side, bears his personal insignia and famous motto, *Aventures Extraordinaires*. Masking is also key to Honet's map (and his work more generally).

160   *The Anthropologist as Curator*

The three hooded figures on the stairs symbolize the idea of a 'secret society', the mysterious, the secret, the ritual, while the central, suspended figure – the Hang Man (the twelfth card of the Tarot) – symbolizes a new point of view, 'life in suspension between the Divine and the Universe'. Honet thus attempts to move away from the concrete, one-dimensional, non-symbolic understanding of our environment and to recentre the mythological, folkloric and poetical elements of our built environment. His cartographic representation thus not only reorients us to think through the city via a perpendicular rather than traditional top-down lens, to literally look at it from a contrary position, but enjoins us to go beyond the everyday and into the world both above and beneath our feet. It is a map of the city as imagined and understood, as felt and explored by Honet, a map of the extraordinary adventures he has enacted in the city he loves.

Also depicting the city of Paris, Ken Sortais' installation, *It is in nature, always, that one should seek advice* (2014), stretches the very idea of the map even further, perhaps to its very limits. (See Figure 9.4.) Made up of two elements, the first a large latex wall hanging referencing Hector Guimard's ornamental subway entrances, the second a sculptural effigy of a cat taken from the Montmartre Cemetery, the installation attempted to bring these two famous spaces directly into the viewers' realm. With Sortais seeing the Paris metro as 'a mirror of an underground universe, plunged in the twilight and the artificial light, a dark reflection of our unconsciousness', and the cat similarly acting 'as a testimony to the city of the dead, a ghost town constructed by the living', the work can be seen to allude to the Gothic history of the French capital, layering literary, cinematic and mythological references with fragments of his own personal experience. Yet it is through Sortais' particular *process* (rather than his metaphorical analysis), his unique method of 'stealth molding', that the work truly comes to life: creating sculptural imprints of the city's architectural forms via a series of night-time, furtive acts of clandestine casting (that can, of course, be understood in clear relation to his graffiti practice), Sortais then returns the freshly made castes to his studio where he juxtaposes the distant historical eras and intimate geographical locations they materially hold within the mutant tableaux he creates. His works thus come to explore the past that is enveloped within the present, the radical pluralism of the archaeological landscapes we inhabit. His map, what he terms a 'phantasmagoric universe' of fantasy and reality not only brings his personal vision of Paris to life but acts as a true method of artefactual reintegration: incorporating the nuances and idiosyncrasies of the city's forms back into the gallery context, it acts as a map of a space physically related to it, re-presenting and transforming it. It acts as a map directly tracing the disregarded topography of the city, its magical materiality.

Through these various works (alongside the thirty-seven others exhibited), maps thus became the channel to reconstitute that which had been learned in the street, not simply that learned though *my* own research, but through my informants' decades-long relationships with their own locales. The maps became instruments through which one could present the concepts that graffiti holds rather than graffiti itself, through which one would not simply falsify the ornament (the decoration without structure) but rather create a radically new structure in itself. Ranging from the literal to the highly metaphoric, from the figurative to the abstract, each map became a

Figure 9.4 *C'est à la nature toujours qu'il faut demander conseil* (It is in nature, always, that one should seek advice). Ken Sortais, latex wall hanging and latex, acrylic, foam and wood sculpture, 285 cm by 220 cm (wall hanging), 96 cm by 41 cm by 23 cm (sculpture). Exhibited at Somerset House, London, 2015, for *Mapping the City*, curated by Rafael Schacter.

distillation of these artists' understanding of both space and practice, physical locales and mental concepts alike; each map striving to extract the knowledge that their maker had formulated through their practice in the city, and to capture this in material form. At the same time, through working in a set of rooms that had, until that time, never been open to the public, we were able to find a further, more tangible method of focusing on our key exhibition theme. Enabling our visitors themselves to enter into a new, previously hidden space (as similarly undertaken in my 2017 exhibition *Silver Sehnsucht* in London's Silvertown district), to explore a site normally concealed from their presence, further reinforced the theme of encounter and engagement integral to the project itself, our audience mapping out a new part of the city, engaging with space through senses beyond vision alone. Moreover, keeping the set of rooms in their original condition, choosing not to turn it into a white cube but to embrace its integrity, further underscored this. The overwhelming public response to the exhibition, not

The Anthropologist as Curator

only the 20,000-plus visitors we welcomed during its one-month run but the huge media pickup of the event, served to reinforce our belief that the public, if not the conventional art world, were deeply interested in the intricacies of this image world. Going beyond the one-dimensional understanding of graffiti as an exoticized image rather than an everyday act, the project thus functioned not only as output, a way of circulating arguments from my research in a much wider sphere than the traditional academic milieu, but as further substantiation of the argument in itself. It provided me with another way of supporting the thesis set forth, the reasoning borne out by my interlocutors, through their material, cartographic remediation of their practice in the street.

Venturing Beyond at Somerset House, 2016

In *Venturing Beyond*, however, a project exhibited in 2016 in Somerset House's grand Terrace Rooms, the task set out was to explore the relationship between graffiti and utopia as part of a wider celebration of the 500th anniversary of Thomas More's famous book. A connection rarely, if ever, made (one more commonly associated to its dystopian opposite in fact), our project leaned upon a conceptualization of utopia emerging not from More, but from the German philosopher Ernst Bloch: his maxim, '*Thinking means venturing beyond*', was here taken as one that could connect graffiti practice to a particular understanding of utopia, as an act that, as Bloch said, did not work through 'visualizing abstractions' of the future, but rather through concretely striving towards it, a practice not simply creating images of a perfect time to come but pushing forwards towards that reality itself. This, for Bloch, was a position in which people must 'throw themselves actively into what is becoming', not to reflect passively but to explore, to become 'truly present', truly active within 'the lived moment' (Bloch 1986: 3, 4, 8). To venture '*beyond the limits*' could hence be something understood in both actual and figurative terms; an attempt to physically breach a space as much as a desire to form a new way of thinking about and acting in the world. As such, 'venturing beyond' could be understood not only as an intrinsically utopian act in Blochian terms, but, we suggested, a perfect commentary on graffiti itself. Graffiti ventures beyond not only in a literal sense, compelling its practitioners to encounter new places and transcend architectural and legal boundaries, but also metaphorically, provoking its adherents to go beyond conceptual frontiers, to form new ways of thinking, acting and being in the world. It literally and metaphorically breaks new ground; it literally and metaphorically forges new paths. In this manner, *Venturing Beyond* set out to explore graffiti not as the dystopia it is traditionally believed to be, the anti-social, disruptive, amoral act, but as something inherently pro-social, inherently idealistic and affirmative. It aimed to explore it as something acting as an alternative voice in our cities (whether loud and brazen or more subtle and difficult to decipher), a voice striving to challenge the normative regulations of contemporary society. The fourteen artists in *Venturing Beyond* were thus commissioned to explore these connections, to explore the participative and performative foundations of graffiti, the foundations of community and liberty at its heart. They were asked to explore the ways in which this practice forges new possibilities, challenges social and aesthetic conventions, to explore the ways it strives to recreate utopia not as a future ideal but as an act set within the concrete, everyday realm of the street. Yet although, as in *Mapping the City*, many of the works produced here were on paper or canvas, the pieces I want to highlight in this section are the more performative, participatory, or site-specific projects that were exhibited for *Venturing Beyond*. Attempting to generate and commission ephemeral artworks was, in fact, part of our own curatorial desire to venture beyond the normative way of presenting graffiti practice itself.

In Brad Downey's work *(Untitled) Dreamcatchers* (2016), for example, we presented a structurally site-specific work that, although scattered throughout the exhibition space, remained almost entirely invisible for the majority of its two-month existence. (See Figure 9.5.) Producing a range of designs and patterns using the most mundane of objects, the commonplace wall-plug (of a variety of colours and sizes that he had collected from all over the world however), Downey's works were installed directly *behind* other artists' pieces, all the time using the same medium as that which was used to hang the frontispiece works themselves. Existing both on and *in* the walls of the gallery space, both inside and outside, visible and invisible, *(Untitled) Dreamcatchers* thus revealed – albeit only once a week, for 30 minutes, when their anterior works were briefly removed – what was *other* to the gallery space. It revealed the space we never see but that is always already there. It moved beyond the restrictions of the gallery, violating and trespassing the restrictions of its physical architecture. It moved beyond the restrictions of form, transfiguring a nondescript, utilitarian object into a sublime, aesthetic one. Just as Downey's public practice of interventionism, his practice of reappropriation and reuse, of critique and questioning, comes to explore (and overturn) the customs and conventions of the street, here he instituted the same process within the

Figure 9.5 *Cache*, Brad Downey, wall plugs, screws, size variable. Exhibited at Somerset House, London, 2016, for *Venturing Beyond*, curated by Rafael Schacter. The frontispiece work, by the artist Saeio, has here been removed.

164   *The Anthropologist as Curator*

museum. He ruptured the rules (both social and spatial) that have become embedded so deeply that they are perceived as the norm. He broke the boundaries between the private and the public. He refused, as with all his work, to abide by correct modes of practice; interrogating his surroundings, probing their restrictions and possibilities alike. Downey's installation can thus be understood to have been venturing beyond in the truest sense, to have both exceeded the physical restrictions of the gallery while attempting to provoke the viewers' imaginations: to compel us to venture beyond thought, to imagine the object that exists outside the spectrum of visibility.

In the series of works exhibited by Parisian artist Saeio,[16] however, a group of paintings on paper and canvas (each self-titled by their medium) as well as a video piece, *Nolens Volence* (2015), produced with his partner in the PAL[17] collective, Rizote, the artists sought to reveal the clash set up between two disputative scopic regimes – that of the graffiti artist and that of the graffiti eraser. Exploring what graffiti artists call 'the buff', the organized, systematic erasure of graffiti images by institutional forces, his series of works sought to expose not merely the fact of the encounter in itself, but rather the entirely new aesthetic form that emerged out of this confrontation: the never-ending cycle of production and destruction that these two parties produced came to form an interactive visuality created by artist and eraser, an aesthetic amalgamation marking out two distinctly confrontational ways of seeing. Emphasizing the utopian ideals held by both artist and eraser, however, each party striving for the perfect city – devoid of graffiti on the one hand, overflowing with it on the other – for Saeio it was the beauty of this battle itself that he found inspiring, the agonistic clash of ideals that he embraced. In the video work in particular,[18] however, we find the two artists exploring the interaction between eraser and erased not just visually but performatively. Filming themselves openly (and illegally) painting graffiti in the street, Saeio and Rizote here produce a series of images following the naive aesthetic of the erasers themselves: painting a range of flat, block shapes in both the rigid style and (inevitably) off-colour hues (always perfectly clashing with their surround, always just one tone off their background surface) employed by the vandals of graffiti, by the graffiti *iconoclasts*, they subtly subvert the image through their free-form, spontaneous style, through their technique of using the language and grammar of the eraser with the liberty and insight of the artist. The Latin title of the piece then, *Nolens Volence* (meaning 'whether willing or not'), outlines the fact that these municipal employees are forming a particular visual aesthetic through the act of overpainting, a series of (accidental) minimalist masterpieces (seen in cities all across the globe) whether conscious of this fact or not. Moreover, it outlines the fact that each erasure is simply one part of the process outlined in Bruno Latour's (2000) famous *iconoclash*, the sign of the passionate image war that inevitably leads to the rise of yet more images, the passionate cycle of defacement and re-facement at the heart of many utopian practices. Questioning the visual forms we are surrounded by, the regimes of acceptability as much as the regimes of desire, Saeio thus playfully turns the tables on the city, producing a vision of graffiti that too closely resembles that which it rejects: a vision of graffiti in which the utopian vision of artist and eraser are disconcertingly allied.

In a similar way, for Filippo Minelli, an artist whose smoke performance from *Venturing Beyond* features on the cover of this book, it was the contrast between dystopia and utopia that he aimed to confront, here not that formed between graffiti artist and graffiti remover, however, but within the wider contemporary moment in which we live. Entitling his works *The Only Emergency is the Absence of Emergency*, an appropriation of Hedieggerian phrase, Minelli saw this expression as one integrally related to our current political moment; towards a time in which the constant, heightened state of crisis we live within in fact occludes the true emergencies existing *behind* that which we are compelled to witness; towards a time in which the truest of dangers are situated far from our force-fed news cycle, the dangers marginalized, occluded, by the (self-generated) noise of the political demagogues we are now, once again, surrounded by. As such, for Minelli, the smoke bomb performances he produced for *Venturing Beyond* functioned not only as a visual representation of silence, as a performative, independent, ephemeral act emergent from and referencing the artist's graffiti background, but as acts compelling us to confront the constructed notion of the media emergency. The formal, spectacular beauty of the intervention enabled Minelli to create a moment in which we could be rescued not 'from emergencies', as Santiago Zabala has perspicuously described it (2018), but rather rescued 'into' them, Minelli thrusting us into the emergency and hence 'saving us by revealing what has been hidden in plain sight'. This can not only be seen to follow the Blochian imperative to push forwards the status of reality, to actively throw oneself into what is becoming, but utilizes the aesthetic of protest and war to go beyond the constructed conflict that in fact often faces us. As an apposite example, then, the 'crisis' surrounding graffiti could, in fact, be seen to point to the real emergency behind the conflict: the increasing privatization and sequestering of public space. The predictable media war fought against these images, the near fifty-year battle waged against the application of paint on surface, can hence be seen to conceal the increasing patterns of surveillance, the increasing corporatization and museumification of the public sphere, let alone the perfect temporal symmetry between the rise of contemporary graffiti and the increasing privatization of public space. Not only underscoring the vitality of the ephemeral, of the chance act, Minelli's performances push towards a way of seeing beyond the realities that have been constructed for us, a way of venturing beyond our increasingly mediated age.

The focus on an increasing amount of ephemeral, active performances within *Venturing Beyond* was thus a choice from which a focus beyond the image, beyond fixity, could be initiated. The curatorial aim was hence not merely to show graffiti but to think through it, to explore its equally conceptual and material bases. Experimenting with ephemerality (in Minelli's work), with performance (in Saeio's), let alone the very boundaries of the gallery (in Downey's), the exhibition attempted to move beyond the tropes that graffiti is so often likened to – that of urban decay and broken windows, of gangs and anti-social behaviour – and instead explore the ways in which it forced us to think, move, act and venture beyond the everyday. The very idea, for example, that graffiti could be about flow and immediacy rather than wanton vandalism, that it could be a space for formal and conceptual experimentation rather than brute anarchy, is rarely, if ever, invoked. The idea that it could be about an embodied citizenship – a participatory engagement with, rather than passive estrangement from, the city – is seemingly forever silenced by the figure of the violent, disaffected, graffiti-spraying youth: a caricature, an interminably summoned spectre, repelling any critical thought. *Venturing Beyond* thus attempted to focus on the way that being physically present and active in the city, being sensitive to the possibilities that it offers, can come, in fact, to change how its practitioners look at their environment, to change the way in which they react to the entire world that surrounds them, the way that they imagine the future, respond to the present, visualize the past. It explored the way it enhances its producers' critical skills, heightens their productive powers, extends their empathetic capacities. The way that being so committed, so singularly dedicated to a practice, can focus the mind beyond the limits of what can be accomplished, beyond the edge of the possible.

Conclusion / intermural art

The *Walking Tour*, *Mapping the City* and *Venturing Beyond* each helped me not only to re-present my research but to rethink it, to refocus upon what these public art practices were truly attempting to achieve, to re-examine the beliefs and propositions of my interlocutors themselves. They helped to address the question of graffiti's implicitly ornamental status , the oxymoronic chaos of graffiti-in-the-gallery, underscoring the basic impossibility of this fact at a time when this was becoming ever more present, ever more normalized. They helped to address the basic question of ephemerality, the impermanence of this practice brought to light both through our focus on performances in which conservation and fixity was extraneous, and through highlighting the practice, rather than the image, of graffiti. They helped to address the basic inalienability of the practice, its status as a gift not a commodity, as a presentation to the city not a product for the market. As such, the exhibitions in which I participated aimed to highlight the basic impossibility, in truth, of *ever* curating graffiti: they aimed not to show graffiti but to *not* show it. To think through it rather than display it, to keep the inherent paradox of its exhibition at the forefront of our minds. Yet, in the same moment, they helped to augment and develop my own understanding of the practice itself. They not only presented the theories and research I had already gathered, but provided new spaces from which to see this practice in action, to understand my informants' relationships to the street and the institution, to see how they dealt with the increasingly anxious relationship between the two. Moreover, it provided a platform from which my interlocutors could themselves express their beliefs and actions within a zone directly intended for this – a space of possibility and openness in which their judgements and sentiments could be directly explored. It thus not only provided a totally new site for the public to understand this complex, coded visual practice, but also enabled me to steer the conversation away from the popular, irrepressible binaries that I believed impeded a more astute understanding of graffiti; to move away from the restrictive discourse of 'art versus vandalism', wherein a highly diluted, parochial notion of beauty is habitually employed; to bypass the media misrepresentations in which graffiti is either prized for its commercial value or used as a visual shorthand for disrepair and decay. My ethnographic research thus not only enabled an approach that could move away from these black-and-white dichotomies, but the collaborative curatorial approach functioned to not overdetermine my own results but leave them more open to my informants' direct questioning. My anthropological research was thus hugely improved, solidified, stretched by my curatorial practice, while my understanding of anthropology itself, as something that could be truly cooperative, participatory, plural, was, I believe, developed via practice itself. Rather than multiplicity leading to enforced simplification, to a reduction of intelligibility through the babel of voices, here plurality ensured that my theses were re-presented to, and represented by, my research partners, that findings were both revealed and created through the process of exhibition-making.

Yet alongside the focus on the four key themes outlined above, what I latterly came to realize was that the space these artists were creating within these collaborations was in fact beginning to create a radically new mode of practice in and of itself. From the very beginning of my research, this relationship between out and in had been crucial. As told in a key ethnographic vignette in my monograph (Schacter 2014), in which my informant 3TTMan tore a huge sea of bill posters from their position in the city before hauling them through the streets and into a local gallery space (where he proceeded to install, collage and overpaint them), this movement was a critical way of dealing with the ornamental, ephemeral, corporeal, inalienable nature of their public practice while working within an interior domain. Of course, modern graffiti had appeared in galleries and museums for many years – since almost its very genesis, in fact. Yet much of this earlier output had simply come to replicate what occurred in the street within the studio context rather than approaching the studio as a space of site-specific relevance itself, rather than attempting to push outside the frame of the public sphere. Much of what was formed was thus as attenuated as the work produced by these practitioners' land art predecessors – predecessors (and perhaps closest art historical relatives) who likewise struggled to integrate their innately situated, al fresco art into the sterility and purity of the white cube. Although there have naturally been exceptions to this rule – artists who have, for example, attempted to replicate the feeling and energy rather than simply the visuality of graffiti, to develop the formal rather than the situational quality of the practice – many of these past transitions remained firmly within the structure of the exterior discourse rather than attempting to unite out and in, to develop out into in. During my research, however, what became clear was that a critical mass of artists emerging from this image world had begun moving beyond this quandary, utilizing graffiti as a base to work from rather than a structure to work within, as an outlook and a premise rather than a prescribed mode of action. They were each embracing, I came to realize, the space of the *intermural*, the space between the street and the studio. As outlined in more depth within my most recent book, *Street to Studio* (Schacter 2018), this was a movement, I argue, in which artists had begun to use graffiti in four broad ways:

i) as a *formal foundation* – using the visual sensibilities and aesthetic insights garnered from graffiti practice, yet redirecting (rather than replicating) them within the studio context;

ii) as a *conceptual palette* – using graffiti as idea not image, as a visual and social environment that can in itself be artistically investigated, dissected and reconstructed;

iii) as a *methodological tool* – using the procedural techniques and methods of graffiti yet subverting and reimagining its traditional regulations and codes; and

iv) as an *ethical imperative* – using the independent ethic rather than the aesthetic of graffiti, in particular for its innately critical rather than its material or visual disposition.

These were artists who were thus not slavishly reproducing their exterior practice within an interior realm but who were, rather, taking the essence of graffiti – its visual principles, its spatial structures, its technical methods, its entrenched ethics – and reinterpreting them within the studio domain. These were artists utilizing the institution as a space of potential in itself (rather than a space for mere presentation), a space in which they could translate and dissect many of the key ideas discovered within their graffiti practice, where they can not only re-present them but further develop them within the milieu of the fine arts. These were artists who had come to merge their illicit education with a knowledge of more established artistic movements (from *arte povera* to Dada, pop art to performance art, new media to de Stijl), forming a creative amalgam influenced as much by graffiti as by contemporary art: an amalgam, in fact, of classical and subcultural aesthetics. Journeying from the infused heat of the street to the calm introspection of the studio, from the former's extremity to the latter's reflectivity, they had begun to develop a radically new practice at the juncture of graffiti and contemporary art, a compound form that is both a departure from graffiti and implicitly, irrevocably, tied to it – that is both a part of contemporary art and yet occluded by that very term.

Seeing how categories and classifications come to determine much of the way in which the resulting artefacts are received, however, seeing how names and genres help us to read a work's content rather than just its form (as we can so clearly see with the term 'graffiti' itself, of course), I came to believe that it was crucial to develop a new term for the work here being described – the work undertaken in all the three projects outlined above – in order to help bring these diverse, disparate practices into some form of cohesion. The expression I have thus adopted, *intermural art*, literally means 'art in between the walls'. It is, a term meant to denote work not simply emerging from inside the walls (the *intra*mural space of the studio, gallery or institution) or from outside them (the *extra*mural locale of the street, the spaces unprotected by the 'weight' of the city walls), but rather work that is situated at the very boundary *between* these two spaces. What is key to intermural art is thus its liminal position between inside and out. Highlighting the fact that the work within this setting has developed *from* out to in (while often meandering back again), as well as the fact that the outside acts as the *foundational premise* for all latter production, this inherent status of in-between-ness also serves to underscore the ways in which this practice can critique and extend these relative sites, the way it can play with and on the very notion of the border. Yet intermural art is not simply a term to be ascribed to all

Curating the Intermural

contemporary art that has emerged from artists who have previously practised graffiti (this would be *too* much of a catch-all). Rather it must be clearly manifest in one (or more) of the four ways outlined above: to display a particular *formal* sensibility (a certain way of handling line and colour, born through producing images in the most testing and diverse of working environments), a particular *situational* sensitivity (a certain mode of site-specificity emerging from the years spent inhabiting the concrete physicality of the city), a *conceptual* perceptivity (a certain manner of treating notions such as authenticity, originality, ephemerality and decay) or an *ethical* positionality (a certain approach to the ideas of publicness and community, independence and criticality) – all of which can be seen to have emerged due to, because of, in view of, this ancestral form.

The notion of the intermural is thus, for me, something that emerged directly out of this curatorial activity, through the co-production and collaboration undertaken with my informants over this last decade. Moreover, it is something that I believe can help to tie these various practices and exhibitions together, that can help us to see the common root, the common ancestor, the common position, no matter how formally and conceptually diverse they may be. As such, and to be very clear, the formation of this neologism has not been undertaken simply to create more noise – another term to flood the many already existent, another genre to carve out yet another niche – but rather in order to give greater insight into these artists and their practices, to show where their work has come from and where it is going. It has not only emerged directly out of both an ethnographic and curatorial engagement, but remains entirely contingent on the paradoxes at the heart of the practice itself. I thus hope that, as a term, intermural art can provide new insight into these various artists' work, showing the joint inheritance so crucial to their contemporary output – yet can also come to shine a clearer light on the aesthetic of graffiti itself. I hope it can start to enable an understanding that sees graffiti not simply as mindless destruction, but as a complex, multifaceted aesthetic; as an implicitly pro-, not anti-social act; as an act of commitment to the city, a practice deeply intertwined with the past, present and future of the urban realm itself.

Notes

1 With whom I curated *Silver Sehnsucht* at London's Silver Building in 2017.
2 With whom I am curated *Motions of this Kind* at the School of Oriental and African Studies' Brunei Gallery, London, in 2019.
3 Entitled *A Curatorial Methodology for Anthropology*, this paper will be part of the UCL Material Culture subsection's latest edited volume on new methods in anthropology.
4 Moreover, I felt that rather than going over ground already discussed in this volume (in particular by Sansi in the introduction), my contribution to this current book would be more valuable through discussing my graffiti-related practice.
5 The collective, a studio of artists called *Nov Nueve*, were a group who incorporated the entire range of possible graffiti practices, from the most consensual to the most agonistic of modes. This is explored at length in my monograph, based on my doctoral thesis, *Ornament and Order* (Schacter 2014).

6 To be clear, graffiti has been present in the gallery since its very earliest days (United Graffiti Artists exhibition at Artists Space in 1975 being a commonly used example of this), and has consistently moved in and out of this space since that time. I often feel as if there is a wilful ignorance of this fact.

7 *Art in the Streets* gained the highest audience figures, 201,352, of any show in the history of the institution. While numbers are difficult to judge for the Tate exhibition, conservative estimates also put it at around the same 200,000 mark.

8 One of my collaborators at the Tate found my position highly entertaining however. As both researcher and enabler, I was accused, light-heartedly but repeatedly, of "feeding the chimpanzees" that I was supposed to be studying. I was, however, very comfortable being imbricated within my interlocutors / chimpanzee's lives, as explained more above.

9 Most commonly attempting to prosecute rather than enable graffiti or street art.

10 Forty-seven of the fifty signs placed in the area were returned to the Tate, signed, and gifted to their new keepers.

11 Much debate has focused on whether early street art works were simply a form of subcultural advertising, a way of selling the brand of the artist themselves – something that could then move from cultural capital to financial capital via a savvy form of entrepreneurial activity. While in many cases this did of course occur, it contravened some of the key principles that street art took from its graffiti roots. As discussed more in Schacter 2017, street art's crucially non-instrumental status, its ability to sell nothing but itself, emerged from the aneconomic position formed within graffiti, a key part of the understanding of street art as genre.

12 For more on street art as an artistic period, see Schacter 2017.

13 While there were other large-scale Street Art events preceding the Tate exhibition of course, such as Melbourne's Stencil Festival (active since 2004), and NuArt in Norway (active since 2005), the worldwide press attention the *Street Art* exhibition received, as well as institutional validation it gave to the genre, did I believe act as the point where Street Art began moving into new potentially awkward territory. It began to change the very nature of what Street Art was.

14 This is a complicated story that, as said above, is discussed in more depth in Schacter 2015. It is not, however, that I think that large-scale muralism is itself negative. I am a huge admirer and supporter of this practice both historically and contemporaneously. I believe that muralism can have a huge effect on a local environment, serving to reinvigorate communities and open up ideas that are otherwise hard to address. Yet the way that Street Art has been utilized, as a form of entirely un-site-specific practice, as a practice that uses the city as canvas rather than as living space, has been genuinely disheartening. More to the point, it has led to the active displacement of marginalized communities, actively participating in developer led gentrification, a tragic development for what was once a progressively engaged, political aesthetic.

15 Blu is perhaps the most politically active of artists working within this contemporary muralism frame. He has since entirely stopped painting at such festivals, continuing to work in a purely self-funded fashion.

16 Tragically Saeio died in a car crash in 2017, at the peak of his creative powers.

17 The PAL crew (Peace and Love) are one of the world's foremost contemporary graffiti collectives. Including the artists Horfee, Gorey, Tomek, Mosa, Esso, Skub and Saeio.

18 See https://vimeo.com/113796229 for the video.

References

Bloch, Ernst (1986), *The Principles of Hope*, Cambridge, MA: MIT Press.

Latour, Bruno (2000), 'What Is Iconoclash? Or Is There a World beyond the Image Wars?' *Iconoclash: Beyond the Image Wars in Science, Religion and Art*, Cambridge, MA; London: MIT Press.

Schacter, Rafael (2008), 'An Ethnography of Iconoclash: An Investigation into the Production, Consumption and Destruction of Street-Art in London', *Journal of Material Culture*, 13 (1): 35–61.

Schacter, Rafael (2014), *Ornament and Order: Graffiti, Street Art, and the Parergon*, Farnham; Burlington, VT: Ashgate/Routledge.

Schacter, Rafael (2015), 'The Ugly Truth: Street Art, Graffiti and the Creative City', *Journal of Art & The Public Sphere*, 3 (2): 161–76.

Schacter, Rafael (2016), 'Graffiti and Street Art as Ornament', in Jeffrey Ross (ed.), *Routledge Handbook of Graffiti and Street Art*, Abingdon; New York: Routledge.

Schacter, Rafael (2017), 'Street Art Is a Period. Period!' in Konstantinos Avramidis and Myrto Tsilimpounidi (eds), *Graffiti and Street Art: Reading, Writing and Representing the City*, Farnham; Burlington, VT: Ashgate.

Schacter, Rafael (2018), *Street to Studio*, London: Lund Humprhies.

Schacter, Rafael (2019, forthcoming), *A Curatorial Methodology for Anthropology*, UCL Press.

Tedlock, Barbara (1991), 'From Participant Observation to the Observation of Participation: The Emergence of Narrative Ethnography', *Journal of Anthropological Research*, 47 (1) (Spring): 69–94.

Weiner, Annette (1992), *Inalienable Possessions: The Paradox of Keeping-While-Giving*, Berkeley, University of California Press.

Zabala, Santiago and Leonardo Franceschini (2018), 'Why Only Art Can Save Us: An Interview with Santiago Zabala', Available online: https://arcade.stanford.edu/blogs/why-only-art-can-save-us-interview-santiago-zabala (accessed 9 August 2018).

10

The curator, the anthropologist: 'presentialism' and open-ended enquiry in process

Alex Flynn

The arts seek a connection with anthropology, we are told. The introduction to this volume describes how Hal Foster coined the term 'the ethnographic turn', pointing to the growing interest of artists and arts practitioners in issues of identity and its representation in the 1990s. Foster identified a kind of mirroring, in which practitioners from historically very different fields, gazed at each other projecting an ideal type, encompassing all that they would like to see in themselves. This gaze was identified as a type of 'envy', and, bearing in mind Foster's fondness for Freud, it was perhaps a gaze associated with that which the other once possessed (Freud 2008: 57): the anthropologist lamenting how before committing to 'rigorous discipline' s/he was once 'open to chance' (Foster 1995: 304), the artist envious of the 'self-critique' implicit to anthropological practice (ibid.: 305) and his/her own lack of critical rigour.

Foster's critique of what he saw as an obliteration of the field of the other through a specious and mildly fraudulent encounter, dates from the mid-1990s, but in trying to understand why some arts practitioners became interested in anthropology, a few of these observations still have resonance today. In Brazil, the context in which this chapter is written, but also arguably more globally, art practitioners see potential in a one-to-one scale of dialogue, a concrete site-specificity that is methodologically inherent to the anthropological project. As Foster identified, the anthropological project is, at least when viewed from the outside, imbued with a reflexivity of practice that brings ethical questions to the fore in a way that is useful for some contemporary arts practitioners. Particularly for curators working in museums that house ethnographic objects, anthropology has increasingly been mobilized to respond to the ethics and practicalities of presenting non-Western art in Western contexts.

At the 2018 Royal Anthropological Institute's conference 'Art, Materiality and Representation', Emily Pringle, Head of Learning Practice and Research at Tate Modern and Tate Britain, convened a panel entitled 'Curating with an Anthropological Approach'. In her presentation, she argued for the necessity of an anthropological focus in the conception of contemporary curatorial strategies and museum practices. The panel put forward pressing questions: To what extent should non-Western objects be framed according to aesthetic criteria and how could they be 'appropriately' contextualized?

174   *The Anthropologist as Curator*

How could contemporary art practices disrupt and contribute to understandings of ethnographic objects? In what ways could an anthropological approach inform, both negatively and positively, the way museums represented people and art? Tate is just one of a number of large institutions to rethink the display, contextualization, signification and even potential restitution of their collections, many of which came about through colonial projects and expeditions. Berlin's Humboldt Forum, a hugely expensive cultural undertaking that will house ethnographic objects in a reconstructed Prussian palace, has also sought to foreground its willingness to engage with an ethics premised on horizontality. Restitution has begun even before the opening of the museum and such events make for good public relations, here, for example, in an article appearing on the museum's site entitled 'Return to Alaska':

> Suddenly, an almost reverential silence spread around the room for a good ninety seconds – interrupted only by the clicks of countless cameras: Hermann Parzinger, president of the Stiftung Preußischer Kulturbesitz (SPK) handed John F. C. Johnson, vice president of the Chugach Alaska Corporation, an object from the collection of the Ethnologisches Museum, part of the Staatliche Museen zu Berlin.[1]

Cases such as those of the Tate and the Humboldt Forum point to a growing critique and, indeed, hostility, from perspectives that have long been kept at the margins: a British Museum curator was recently obliged to defend their institution by declaring that 'a lot of our collections are not from a colonial context; not everything here was acquired by Europeans by looting'.[2] Faced with mounting doubts as to the ethical provenance of the museum collections, these curators' interest in anthropological approaches can be placed into Foster's first and fifth categories of why artists are interested in anthropology: anthropology as the science of alterity, and the self-critical dimension of the anthropological discipline premised on reflexivity.

Curatorial strategies informed by anthropological perspectives are not limited to the display and contextualization of ethnographic objects however. The important Afro-Atlantic Histories exhibition organized by the Museum of Modern Art of São Paulo (MASP) puts forward Brazil as a central location in the transit and diversity of Afro-Atlantic histories, with the exhibition serving to anchor a full year's programming of talks, courses, workshops, publications and screenings. Displaying 450 artworks from the sixteenth to the twenty-first centuries, the exhibition seeks to articulate a re-evaluation of what blackness means in Brazil, a question that one of the curators, the anthropologist Lilia Schwarcz, has made central to her scholarly research. Professor in the Anthropology Department at the University of São Paulo, Schwarcz has been a curator at MASP since 2015, and this dual role places an anthropological perspective at the heart of MASP's programming; a hybrid anthropological and curatorial tone that is latent to the exhibition's stated aim 'to encourage new debates and questions so that our Afro-Atlantic histories can be themselves reconsidered, revised and rewritten'.[3]

Ethical concerns and the mobilization of anthropological perspectives to respond emerge from the first two examples of the Tate and the Humboldt Forum, but what emerges from the third example of MASP is more the anthropological preoccupation with positionality, power and sedimentation of knowledge, or rather, a recognition of knowledge systems as inherently skewed by those who control the site and means of knowledge production. This reflexivity shifts the focus away from the universal and towards the specific, in this case, to question canons and positionalities of speech. How can MASP acknowledge its position as an elite cultural institution? Founded through a partnership between leading São Paulo industrialists and Nelson Rockefeller, as part of wider North American Cold War cultural policy (Mantoan 2016 Faria and Costa 2006), how can MASP reconfigure its origins to serve wider publics? What kind of expographic work, or work that is specifically configured through the design of exhibits both within and without the museum, particularly on issues of Brazilian identity, can be put forward to move away from the museum's original purpose, to 'foster partial modernizing practices disguised as national culture [for] an upper and middle-class' (Lima 2010)?

Each of these locations is of course radically different, and the questions that curators at institutions like the Tate, the Humboldt Forum or MASP face surrounding institutional identity, exhibition of works, reception of publics and degrees of accessibility, to name but a few concerns, are intrinsically linked to the contexts in which they are based. Anthropological perspectives offer useful tools for curators in this sense to reflexively understand the positionalities that such institutions occupy, while also suggesting pathways forward to respond to such demands. Echoing the practice of creating unmediated dialogue with the other in a framework of one-to-one discussion, and engaging with site-specific responses to particular critiques, institutional curators have mobilized anthropological approaches to unfurl a double rejoinder to those who question the museum's role.

The potential of such an approach is its portability and sensitivity to unique and particular contexts, that is, its very anthropological-ness. In contrast, a noticeable weakness of Foster's critique is that it fails to fully take account of how artistic practice in Brazil is subject to different contexts, potentials and limitations to, for example, practice in Mexico, North America or Europe. What lies behind this omission is the question of Foster's own positionality, which can be better glimpsed in a short passage from the original version of his essay (1995), one that was not included in the version for the subsequent monograph *The Return of the Real* (1996):

> This turn to the ethnographic, it is important to see, is not only an external seduction; it is also driven by forces immanent to *advanced art*, at least in *Anglo-American* metropoles, forces which I can only sketch here. (1995: 305 my emphasis)

Foster's use of the term 'advanced art', and the notion of 'Anglo-American metropoles' articulates a type of disclaimer, suggesting that the author's knowledge of what is driving the ethnographic turn from within is limited to the larger cities of the United Kingdom and the United States. It also, deliberately or otherwise, creates a connotation in suspension, a suggestion that, first, art can be separated between that which is 'advanced' and that which is not, and, second, that this separation might be premised along geographic lines. We will return to a consequence of this seeming Eurocentrism later in the chapter, particularly with regard to how artists who identify as indigenous challenge Foster's characterization of artists engaging with alterity. For now, having

176   *The Anthropologist as Curator*

briefly sketched some current spaces of encounter, we can begin to construct a speculative nexus of interconnection, intervention and sheer mutual incomprehension that characterizes the engagement between anthropological and curatorial practice.

Meeting points

A growing number of anthropologists have an interest in and have written about both contemporary art practice and anthropology's relationship with art more widely (Flynn 2018; Foster 1995; Ingold 2013; Gell 1998; Grimshaw and Ravetz 2015; Marcus 2010; Sansi 2015; Schneider and Wright 2006, 2010, 2013; Ssorin-Chaikov 2013; Strohm 2012; Fillitz and Van der Grijp 2018). Some of these authors, a number of whom appear in this volume, have sought to extend their conceptual discussions of contemporary art practice and anthropological research by engaging in a complementary curatorial practice. Rafael Schacter and Nikolai Ssorin-Chaikov in particular have organized large, complex and multifaceted exhibitions, and Ssorin-Chaikov has put forward 'ethnographic conceptualism' (2013) as a result of this process. My own curatorial practice has developed over the last four years, first working within the curatorial team of a year-long residency programme based within an occupied building in the centre of São Paulo, the *Residência Artística Cambridge*, (Flynn 2018, 2019 forthcoming) and latterly co-curating an exhibition on the phenomenon of *editoras cartoneras*, which opened in São Paulo in November 2018, before travelling to London.

While there exists a recognition of what Arnd Schneider and Chris Wright term 'border crossings' (2006: 1) or, more particularly, the porous frontier that anthropological practitioners traverse when confounding codes of expectation as to how their work is presented or developed, this porosity is not acknowledged by all. Eduardo Viveiros de Castro's photographic practice, dating from his early career as a graduate student in the social sciences, and later from early periods working in the field, was recently the subject of an exhibition at the Sesc Ipiranga cultural centre in São Paulo. Perhaps mindful of confusion that could be caused by an anthropologist exhibiting visual media in an exhibition space often used for the display of contemporary art, the title of the exhibition pointedly reads, 'Variações do Corpo Selvagem: Eduardo Viveiros de Castro, fotógrafo', thus making plain a symbolic switching (and delineation) of roles. This is not the forum for an art history-style critical reading of the potential or otherwise of exhibitions that are constructed by anthropologists acting as curators. More pertinent is to construct an index of potential commonalities that stimulate such encounters.

Perhaps the first point of commonality could be conceived of through the practice of 'accompanying', or better, perhaps, 'presentialism'. In curatorial and anthropological work there may arise the possibility to 'accompany', respectively, the artists with whom the curator is working, or the interlocutors who are part of any anthropological research process. This process of accompanying can be thought of as deeply presential in both cases: anthropologists often commit to following their interlocutors' daily routines and practices and some curators work in a similar way, visiting artists in their studio, attending openings of the artist's exhibitions and being present at a variety of events in which the artist will participate. This embodied and affective construction of a field of work facilitates the creation of bonds of trust between various actors over a substantial period of time, another important intersection of practice: curatorial work, like anthropological work, may be conducted over an extended period that creates opportunities for a deepening of initial connections or relations. One curator friend of mine, perhaps a little tired at the end of the day, commented that as a curator accompanying an artist, one might be expected to be present at the majority of the artist's events, open studios and the like, provide a sounding board for their ideas, arrange coffees to chat, catch up and gossip, discuss possible funding opportunities and offer to proofread their texts. For curators who work in this manner, the act of accompanying an artist becomes deeply processual, which suggests an intersection with how anthropology understands and conceives of long-term ethnographic field research.

The construction of a field is suggestive of a multiplicity of actors and, in mediating between different worlds, occupying an interstitial position and potentially acting to try to stitch disparate realities together, there is the hint of another sphere of practice that the anthropologist and curator may traverse, if not together, then at least on intersecting paths. A curator might be simultaneously understood as a potential gatekeeper of resources, a project manager of logistical processes, a mediating presence between different professionals and an intellectual and conceptual interlocutor for the artist. This notion of the curator as a type of open social interstice derives from the idea that putting together an exhibition often entails working in a team of people with many different roles.

Thinking about my recent exhibition *Cartoneras: Releituras Latino-Americanas*, for example, the immediate project team consisted of two curators, of whom I was one, and a head of production with an assistant. From this starting point, the expographic (the technical design of the exhibition displays and furniture) and visual identity team was four strong, installation and construction another three, and there were a further five key actors at the Casa do Povo, where the exhibition was held, ranging from the director, to the head of programming, to production and external relations. The exhibition displayed the work of two filmmakers, whose films were translated and subtitled by a specialist in this field, the educational team counted on a director and a further two pedagogues, all exhibition texts were revised and translated by a team of two and a further person was responsible for social media content and feed. Beyond this operational sphere, the research team was composed of myself, Lucy Bell and Patrick O'Hare, colleagues on an AHRC research project, and there were of course the artists whose work the exhibition put on display. Included in the programming was a symposium, which twenty-five of the artists attended. The exhibition also counted on a publication, which brought together four texts in *cartonera* form, that is, bound with a hand-painted cardboard cover, and this book was put together by an external graphic designer.

In total therefore, this medium-size exhibition placed the curators within a field of fifty-two different actors, each with a unique positionality and set of responsibilities, and this is counting solely the people with whom the curators maintained an almost daily contact. Anthropological work adapts to each circumstance in which it is conducted and won't necessarily involve work with so many people, but being essentially relational, the research process places the researcher amid many different positionalities and often requires a certain amount of mediation. This multiplicity of actors, and the pressures that traversing often deeply stratified social contours can exert, are a point of connection between two very different practices, and therefore a productive point to consider.

Within this diverse field of actors and narratives, both the anthropologist and curator face a certain expectation to synthesize, create a discernible thread, articulate and mobilize a conceptual vocabulary, and thus compile a coherent line of thought for a wider sphere. Synthesis is common to many fields, but the expectation of a certain production of knowledge from a diverse set of starting points perhaps signals a third meeting space of practice. While the construction of knowing goes right back to the colonial roots of anthropology, on the curatorial side, this demand has certainly accelerated since the 1990s as Victoria Walsh notes: The development of formal research practices in the art museums now effectively parallels those of the university: initiating and leading research projects funded by the public and private sectors, running doctoral programs, supporting fellowships, developing research centres, hosting seminars, and organizing conferences for specialist audiences (2016: 1).

Walsh here refers to curators with an institutional position, curators who can easily traverse between the art school and the art museum, but these expectations are also pertinent to the independent curators based in São Paulo with whom I work. I have written in more detail about curatorial practice as a form of knowledge production elsewhere (Flynn 2018) and although knowledge production is a broad field, there is a productive detail about curatorial and anthropological practice that offers the possibility of encounter. The processuality to which I refer above connects with a notion of *longitudinal* knowledge production, and curators, like anthropologists, may develop their thinking and practice across a series of exhibitions, papers and talks, much in the same way that anthropologists may approach their work through departmental research seminars, conference papers, journal articles and monographs. For both practitioners, these outputs register as indexes on a trajectory, each instance connecting to another in the manner that Alfred Gell (1998: 250) argued characterizes the production of artworks. For certain curators and anthropologists, Gell's analysis of how an artist's œuvre consists of individual pieces, each an index of agency distributed through time with four differing temporal relations between each instance of the wider body of work, is useful to think through a space of mutual encounter:

Prospective orientation

1. Strong: Preparatory Sketch → Finished Work
2. Weak: Precursory (not planned as the start of a series) → Further works in a series

Retrospective orientation

1. Strong: (Past) Original ← Subsequent copy
2. Weak: Original work ← Subsequent work that is recapitulated and developed through a process of stylistic evolution

The emphasis on the mid to long term in certain anthropological and curatorial careers creates a possibility for the elaboration of this 'œuvre' and Irit Rogoff gestures towards this in her attempt to distinguish curating – the operational everyday business of exhibition-making – from 'the curatorial':

> The curatorial is an ongoing process; it doesn't think it's over when the event of knowledge has taken on some sort of tangible form and is materially sitting there. It recognizes that its existence is a way station in a process; a milestone in a process. (Rogoff 2012: 27 cited in Walsh 2016: 2)

Knowledge production for both practices can therefore, in at least certain, perhaps more institutionalized, contexts, be conceived of as being elaborated within a particular timeline; a temporality that goes beyond short-term urgency and the need to respond, instead putting forward an incremental accumulation of reflexive output, a tendency that some might interpret as a riposte to the power-laden regime of 'facticity' (Lash 2007).[4]

At this point it might be productive to summarize the interconnections discussed so far. First, the presential, processual nature of work that invites one actor to accompany the other in their day-to-day practice and the manner in which this may lead to the development of affective and embodied relations. Second, the realization of a field of work in which there are multiple actors, each with unique spheres of practice, to whom the curator or anthropologist has diverse responsibilities, while also perhaps being called upon to mediate what are diverse positionalities. And third, the emphasis of synthesizing a conceptual narrative from within (although not necessarily about) these positionalities and multiple actors, the construction of a body of work, and the temporality in which this may occur, premised upon the idea of an indexical relationship between talks, exhibitions, books, and so on, and the inherent possibility of reflection that this suggests.

At this point it is important to note the limitations to such a summary, even within a speculative framework, given the lack of a concise definition as to what a curatorial role might presuppose. Unlike the discipline of anthropology, where it is almost unquestioned that one cannot lay claim to being an anthropologist without (1) having undertaken long-term immersive field work that (2) led to the subsequent award of a doctoral degree at (3) an accredited higher institution of study, curating has fewer and less established standardized norms with which to discern those who are from those who aren't. Harald Szeemann, considered by both Jens Hoffmann and Hans-Ulrich Obrist as the father of modern curatorial practice, was an independent curator, having resigned from the Kunsthalle Bern in 1969 to found the Agentur für geistige gastarbeit, an autonomous network of collaborators who developed exhibitions for multiple institutions. Essentially freelance, Szeemann shifts rather tellingly between uneasy typologies of curatorial practice, including Graham and Cook's (2010) classification of 'freelance curators' like Szeemann, 'embedded curators', those in a permanent, fixed institutional role and thus constrained to a certain extent by that institution's logic, and 'adjunct curators', those who are more autonomous, albeit with access to institutional connections and networks, and seek to enable artists via a processual approach (2010:

150–3). Such categorizations struggle to capture more nuanced portrayals, but, with limited space, this chapter can only put forward an apology as opposed to a defence regarding the type of curatorial practice that is being set alongside anthropological practice, and move forwards to a further space of encounter, albeit one that is constructed from without as opposed to within.

Critiques

These spaces of encounter can be complemented by specific critiques that are levelled at curators and anthropologists alike, suggesting that curatorial and anthropological practice may act in similar spaces and with similar motives, thus prompting similar friction and unease. Within the wider decolonial turn presently occurring in anthropology, Ramon Grosfoguel (2016) has articulated the notion of *extractivismo epistemológico*, epistemological extractivism. Grosfoguel starts by acknowledging the important work of Leanne Betasamosake Simpson, a Michi Saagiig Nishnaabeg scholar, and her critique of how, beyond their mineral resources, indigenous knowledge systems are being extracted and assimilated by an ongoing colonial system of power. This perspective finds a powerful echo in the work of Linda Tuhiwai Smith (2012), who identifies the need to decolonize academic research on indigenous communities by making a more meaningful attempt to deconstruct categories of otherness, particularly bearing in mind anthropology's traditional overdetermination of such dichotomies as the observer and observed, and the anthropologist and indigenous other. As Macarena Gómez-Barris notes, 'Smith's work reminds us that extraction operates through material and immaterial forms of converting indigeneity into exchange value, where intellectual and spiritual resources are taken to produce new forms of colonial currency' (2017: 10). A recent example of this process can be found in the recent controversy (among many others pertaining to the publication) surrounding the name of the anthropology journal known as *HAU*, a Maori word, but entirely decontextualized and presented purely as an anthropological concept.

Anthropologists have long commented on problematic instances of curatorial work, for example in exhibitions like *Magiciens de la Terre* (Paris, Centre Georges Pompidou, 1989, curated by Jean-Hubert Martin), *Primitivism in 20th Century Art: Affinity of the Modern and the Tribal* (New York, Museum of Modern Art (MoMA), 1984, curated by William Rubin) or *Art and Artifact* (New York, Buffalo Museum of Science, 1989, curated by Susan Vogel). These critiques stem from the idea that works, objects and, indeed, the everyday objects of life have been removed from indigenous communities, taking them out of the contexts in which they were produced to depoliticize them and re-signify them for the consumption of an occidental gaze. What has begun to occur in recent years, however, is the extension of this critique from the curators of such exhibitions, to the very anthropologists within Eurocentric academe, who formerly made such critiques of the curators. Grosfoguel notes: The extractivist mentality seeks the appropriation of traditional knowledge [...] so that academics from Western universities pretend to have produced 'original' ideas as if they had the 'copyrights' of the idea (2016: 133).

The work of Bolivian social scientist Silvia Rivera Cusicanqui is significant in this regard, beginning with a critique of the curatorial process of the Reina Sofía museum in Madrid, via her co-curated exhibition *The Potosí Principle. How Can We Sing the Song of the Lord in an Alien Land?* to her linked criticisms (2010) of the work of decoloniality scholar Walter Mignolo for having 'built a small empire within the empire, strategically recovering the contributions of the Indian school of subaltern studies and many Latin American instances of critical reflection on colonization and decolonization' (2010: 58). Clearly, the notion of accompanying work in fields where intellectual property is so important, but at the same time, there exists so little protection of such property beyond informal relations of trust, places both the curator and the anthropologist in a similar space. Having encountered a faint echo of Hal Foster's critique of artists seeking to articulate otherness, from his own positionality within an 'Anglo-American' metropole, we will return to the broader point implicit here in the conclusion.

The hierarchies in which the anthropologist and the curator operate also create a shared sense of friction. Not all curators work from institutions with the financial security this may or may not bring, but lines of hierarchy between artists and curators, although increasingly challenged, are still entrenched in schemes of verticality that characterize many other working environments, including the anthropological field. As Martha Rosler notes, 'artists may channel mysterious energies, but others get to make the choices. Choice trumps creation and choice is linked to all rewards, including an enlarged audience for the chosen artists' work' (2003: 1). This sense of an unequal relationship between actors, working in many cases on projects of mutual interest, finds a partial resonance with Arnd Schneider's comment on the relationship between anthropologists and their interlocutors in this field, in this case arts practitioners, when he notes that such exchanges necessarily occur within an uneven hermeneutic field (2015: 25-6).

Points of processual difference

What then might be the difference between the agencies and intentions of a curator and those of an anthropologist? What are the different questions both reflexively, and at stake, for these two practices? There may be certain similarities and potential points of encounter between the anthologist and the curator, but, following a recent provocation from curator Simon Njami regarding the articulation of identity, shouldn't the question be rather 'how' as opposed to 'what'? Is it perhaps in the how that a perception develops that, for all their similarities, these practices may in fact present differences that place them beyond any kind of equivalence?

What follows are reflections based on my own curatorial practice that point towards what emerges from a processual standpoint. As such, there can be no pretension to provide a more rigorous deconstruction: these are merely observations that relate to a particular experience within a particular context. If we start from the presupposition that both curatorial and anthropological practice overlap to a certain extent in their production of knowledge, the very notion of 'expography', or exhibition design, foregrounds an important difference in conception, planning and execution. Exhibitions, even if exclusively textual, work with a logic of the visual. Anthropology,

182   *The Anthropologist as Curator*

however, has a well-established difficulty engaging with this register, as Lucian Castaing-Tayor commented in 1995, remarking on anthropology's 'iconophobia'. Anna Grimshaw (2001) traces a history from Alfred Haddon's Torres Strait expedition, the first anthropological field-site, that seeks to understand how although the visual formed part of the expedition's data, the emphasis that the research team placed on the development of 'sophisticated scientific methods' (2001: 22) meant that the photographs became ancillary to a more powerful legitimizing mechanism: the rigour of a new discipline. Despite Haddon's own enthusiasm for the inclusion of a *cinematographe* among the expedition's kit (other items included a Galton's whistle, eye tester, *ohrmesser* and some marbles), the visual became a way to describe and illustrate the primary narrative, rather than something that could have been considered as research method in and of itself.

What Castaing-Taylor and Grimshaw point towards is the static relationship that anthropology presupposes between the viewer and the viewed. With reference to exhibition-making, James Elkins has long argued that 'seeing is metamorphosis, not mechanism' (1996: 12), calling attention to the complex intersubjectivity that is at play when one is engaged on a visual plane, and the transformative element that is implicit to this relationship. What powerful arts figures, such as Chris Dercon, speaking here in 2013, understand is the unlimited potential this transformative element possesses when it occurs within a space populated by many other people:

> The museum of the future is going to be like a university, like a campus, where the art is one thing, but the fact that you have so many different encounters and that you can test your ideas out, that you can throw your questions out about gender, identity, about the world [...] This is the museum of the future.[5]

What particularly is at stake here is aesthetics, not merely as object of study, but, potentially, as tangible research practice. In an exhibition, knowledge may be constructed through not merely the aesthetics of the visual, but also through the inherent spatiality of the context. Working with a three-dimensional and inherently sculptural presentation, the curator has an opportunity to engage with the polyvalence afforded by different uses of space. What might be the significance inherent in opting to exhibit a certain object on a table, or floor, or wall? How might an exhibition seek to work within long-established traditions of research on the importance of the line? Being physically installed into a given space, how will the curator come to terms with the multiple axes of orientation that any exhibition demands, dimensions of verticality, horizontality, questions of scale, and how these modifiers act upon the relationships between a multiplicity of objects, the visitor to the exhibition and the path that the visitor might take? Each of these considerations calls into question the notion of a neutral presentation of knowledge in a textual format and the supposed divorce of form from content that is an unquestioned assumption about anthropological text. As Kiven Strohm states:

> What aesthetic experience activates, particularly in those moments of collaboration between anthropology and art, is a disruption and redistribution of roles and

The Curator, the Anthropologist   183

places of anthropologist and the other and, in turn, of what can be seen, heard, thought, said and done in the anthropological episteme. (2012: 117)

Exhibition-making foregrounds the inherent interdependence of content and form and also, as Lucy Bell and I argue (forthcoming 2019), the indivisibility of social and aesthetic forms more widely. Both of these factors impact on the type of knowledge that can be produced and how that knowledge is articulated in conjunction with a visitor/ reader who is not static, but can view the 'text' from a variety of angles, move around it, begin at the end, and end at the beginning. Another point here is the specificity of each space in which an exhibition is created, in contrast to the supposedly neutral 'blank page | white cube' aesthetic of scholarly publishing outlets. A curator organizing a set of ethnographic images for exhibition, for example, must take into account the space in which this will occur and the connotations that this space already confers. The same exhibition within a public library, a corporate bank's private collection, a university exhibition space or a museum like São Paulo's Estação Pinacoteca, a space that was used for the torture and imprisonment of political prisoners during the Brazilian military dictatorship (1964–1985), will acquire different meanings. This is a question of affordances: how will these spaces inflect upon the works, how will the dialogues between the works be intervened by silenced histories, pre-existing discussions, relations and imbalances of power?

This polyvalence of spatiality argues for the recognition of a multiplicity of publics. Impossible as it is to generalize about curatorial practice and, indeed, for this very reason, Szeeman declined to term himself a curator, but rather an *Ausstellungsmacher*, or exhibition-maker. Many curators with whom I work will envisage a professional public for their show, but also be highly aware of their obligation to a broad, undefined and unknown public. The element of a work placed tangibly into space is important here: for all the pertinent critique of museums and biennales as restricted in terms of access, it is worth noting how, especially in non-commercial spaces in which art is exhibited, people can enter; and educational programmes, although many times underinvested, are specifically tasked with creating a broader and more diverse visiting public. The 2018 São Paulo biennial, which like many biennials is accused of being an elitist institution, received 190,000 free admission visitors in the first three weeks after its official opening. Such transit, when placed into comparison with the circulation of the majority of anthropological textual output, provides a stark contrast. Anthropology's knowledge production mechanisms, far from being open (the Brazilian Scielo system is a notable exception) are captured within a cooperate model of what might be coarsely termed 'pay-to-play': individuals without a university affiliation, that is, a huge percentage of the general population, must pay a fee ranging from $20 to $50 to merely access a single article.

Not only is access hugely limited, therefore, but such limitations can mean that the publics that anthropologists address are much more homogenous than those that might casually wander into the São Paulo biennial pavilion, located as it is in the largest park of the city, a green space that tens of thousands of people visit every weekend. First, the vast majority of those who access anthropological writing will be other scholars because of the paywall. Our language of writing, our aesthetic rendering of 'rigour' is commonly and anecdotally accused of being impenetrable to non-experts and thus articulated only in the safe space of academia (see, for example, blog posts on Anthro{dendum}[6] or University College London's (UCL's) Global Social Media Impact Study blog[7]). While efforts to create a 'popular' or more 'accessible' anthropology are under way, the basic tension between legitimacy, rigour and the specificity of language remains.

This comparative homogeneity of the anthropological public perhaps suggests one of the sharpest contours of difference that exists between the two fields of practice. The curator imagines the reception of their work with a diverse variety of publics in mind and, particularly, institutional curators explicitly work to broaden these spheres. In the case of MASP's *Afro-Atlantic Histories*, for example, creating a public was underpinned by diverse resources including an online summary of the exhibition's content, programmes, aims and theoretical ambit, in both English and Portuguese, visual representations of the works on display in the space, five short-form professionally produced videos with participating artists describing the exhibition's relationship to questions of racism in Brazil (all subtitled in Portuguese), plus other links to further online sources of content via Facebook and Instagram. Engaging audiences and seeking to create circulation between the institution of the museum and the city in which it is based is not above being subject to critique, for example, of overdetermination of meaning, or a certain patronizing attitude to the cultivation of a public. However there at least exists a commitment to open a knowledge production process outwards; to communicate with those who helped create it, in a language that has a degree of accessibility.

Releituras (rereadings)

Having discussed how anthropologists and curators imagine different publics based upon a polyvalence of spatiality, I would now like to draw on an ethnographic example regarding how these differences manifested themselves in the exhibition *Cartoneras: Releituras Latino-Americanas* I co-curated with Beatriz Lemos. (See Figure 10.1.) The exhibition, which took place in the Casa do Povo cultural centre from 1 November 2018 to 9 February 2019, featured over 350 *cartonera* books from 35 different collectives. Drawing on works from Brazil, Mexico, Paraguay, Argentina, Chile, Peru, Bolivia, Colombia, Germany and France, we (the Grupo Inteiro, composed of Carol Tonetti, Cláudio Bueno, Ligia Nobre and Vitor Cesar and the coordination of the Casa do Povo, in discussion with the curatorial team) agreed on four different display modules: first, a staircase module with integrated seating area and storage space installed in the entrance hall of the building; second, a set of two parallel lines of shelving that echoed the staircase module; third, three iron-framed units on which to hang the curatorial texts, display three video units and foreground a collection of artists' books; and fourth, a small set of parallel shelving for a rotating special collection. The design was driven by the concept that all books on display should be fully accessible to visitors as opposed to being protected by display cases as is more common: we thought of the books as points of potential interaction, making possible a space of relations and exchanges,

Figure 10.1 The exhibition *Cartoneras: Releituras Latino-Americanas*, São Paulo, Brazil, 2018. Photos: Filipe Berndt.

a space in which other events could take place. While the design included a certain didactic content – tutorial videos showing different methods of how *cartonera* books are created and a documentary film explaining how *cartonera* had originated – it was our intention that the space should essentially function to welcome visitors to come in and sit down, pick up a book and come to their own understanding of the *cartonera* phenomenon. We also thought of the books as enacting a type of proto-*cartonera* library, as we were creating a concentration of *cartonera* literature never before experienced in a public space. It seemed to us that just as a university library could be a starting point for many research processes, a *cartonera* library could function in the same way, although importantly, with different basic rules of access, copyright and interaction.

In this sense, a fundamental component of the exhibition was a workstation where the public programme team members were based. This was equipped with cardboard from a nearby recycling cooperative, paints, paintbrushes, box cutters, and so on – in short, a typical *cartonera* workspace – so that visitors, seeking to take home the exhibition catalogue could bind and decorate it with cardboard, thus creating their own *cartonera* book. (See Figure 10.2.) The workstation also provided a free printing facility so that visitors could bind whichever PDF text they had chosen in *cartonera* form. Over the duration of the exhibition, over 300 catalogues were created in this manner and roughly 30 scholarly and activist texts were bound, allowing us to work alongside people integrating *cartonera*, both literally and affectively, into their research

Figure 10.2 The workstation of the public programme team, *Cartoneras: Releituras Latino-Americanas*, São Paulo, Brazil, 2018. Photo: Filipe Berndt.

process, making plain the transition of a literary work into the processual and visual sphere.

Such processes were contextualized by the affordances of the Casa do Povo itself, created in the aftermath of the Holocaust by São Paulo's Jewish diaspora as a living monument. At the time we were conceiving *Releituras*, the Casa do Povo was seeking to create a library of its own extensive archive. On many occasions, after an exhibition, expensive furniture and fittings are destroyed. *Cartonera*, however, among many other things, symbolizes and exemplifies a repurposing of so-called waste material to make multiple social interventions. In this manner therefore, it was natural that in our planning discussions we agreed that the exhibition displays should be reused for the Casa do Povo's forthcoming library, a proposal that was entirely coherent with the ethos of what was being exhibited. The localization of the Casa do Povo was also important. Located in Bom Retiro, the Casa do Povo is a focal point in a neighbourhood that has long welcomed immigrants, starting with Jewish refugees in the 1930s and 1940s, Greek, Syrian and Lebanese communities in the 1960s, the Korean community in the 1980s and, more recently, Guarani speakers from Paraguay and Chinese immigrants. *Cartonera* is a pan-Latin American phenomenon: the exhibition included texts in Portuguese, Spanish, Guarani and Portunhol Selvagem among others in English, French and German. The Casa do Povo's connection to the street and community, its open door without security, welcoming people into a shared space, were at the forefront of our minds in designing the exhibition's public programme: a series of events and a *cartonera* symposium, with the intention to reach a broad and diverse public, sparking unexpected connections.

The Curator, the Anthropologist

I would like to highlight three particular events here. First, the *cartonera* collective Dulcinéia Catadora led three workshops in the exhibition space exploring immigrant women's perspectives of São Paulo. The participating group, comprising representatives of different feminist and lesbian, bisexual, transgender (LBT) collectives, worked together to create a series of texts that spoke to their experience of living in Brazil's largest city. Over the three sessions, the participants created a *cartonera* book of these short texts, which through a complex series of folds, became an A2 placard of protest to be used in a protest march following the third session. Second, in the process of working throughout the exhibition, two members of the public programme team created their own *cartonera* publisher, Sin Fronteira Cartonera, echoing how Dulcinéia Catadora came into being during Eloísa's workshops at the 2006 São Paulo biennale. Over a series of sessions, they produced six books, including *Dialogos, reflexiones y desafios en Colombia: Hacia un feminismo popular,* a text organized by the Colombian feminist collective Red de Mujeres de La Sabana. And finally, to close the exhibition, we organized the event 'Iy mūn ku māk pax', designed to bring into focus languages spoken in Brazil beyond those of the colonizers, Portuguese and Spanish. This event took place over two days and, inspired by the bilingual texts of the *cartonera* collective Yiyi Jambo that create a deft interplay between Portunhol Selvagem, Portuguese and Guarani, the event sought to work with themes of how colonial structures have systemically silenced indigenous languages and literature. Juanito Cusicanki and Beatriz Morales of Aymara and Quechua ethnicity respectively, were invited to present their indigenous alphabets, based on their oral knowledge. In the second workshop, representatives of Guarani, Pankararu and Baniwa peoples spoke about their experiences of state kidnapping and the following imposition of Portuguese on their communities. Contextualized by these moving accounts, the title of the event came to hold a particular significance: from the shamanic chant maxakali / tikmū'ūn, Iy mūn ku māk pax, meaning 'my beautiful voice'.

The notion of welcoming people into the exhibition space and allowing the different uses of space to spark interventions also informed the *encontro cartonero*, a two-day event to which we invited *cartonera* practitioners from various cities across Mexico and Brazil as well as Buenos Aires, New York and London. The *encontro* occurred within the exhibition space and sought to create an opportunity for practitioners to catch up, exchange and sell books, make connections and discuss new projects. We organized a series of roundtable discussions to stimulate conversation on *cartonera*, and the *encontro* generated an important co-edition that was subsequently integrated with the exhibition: a collection of political texts, entitled *BR*, responding directly to the recent victory of Jair Bolsonaro in Brazil's 2018 presidential elections.

This forum was also an important opportunity for the wider *cartonera* community to question us as a research team and seek clarification on our motives for becoming involved with *cartonera*. At the *encontro,* a representative from Pensaré, a collective based in Chiapas, Mexico, pressed us directly on how relations between *cartonera* publishers and academics could have unwelcome consequences as they reinforced the hierarchical system of oppression already in play. These critiques were important for us as a project team to reflect on the hierarchical relations that indeed structured our interactions and the limitations that acted upon our attempts at horizontality, as

The Anthropologist as Curator

European, white researchers, with contracts at powerful British institutions of higher education. Perhaps, more than anything else, the form of the *encontro* allowed us to better appreciate the complex inequalities and hierarchical knowledge production relations that exist in the interface between *cartonera* publishing and a wider world.

My final point pertains to open-endedness and can be best illustrated through the exhibition team's reworking of my *texto de parede*, the curatorial text *displayed* within the exhibition, as opposed to the longer text *printed* in the catalogue. The careful process of constructing these differing formats revealed how, although anthropological and artistic practice might be on what James Clifford described as 'speaking terms' (1988) in their intentions, there exist important contours of difference. If the curator potentially thinks about various different languages – not just linguistic but also spatial – there is at once, perhaps, a concomitant resistance to a language characterized by overdetermination. Although the term curatorship has, in a sense, become generic (Balzer 2015), I would suggest that among the curators with whom I work, while there is a commitment to accompany, mediate, negotiate and, ultimately, synthesize, there is an equally powerful, unnamed and deep-seated commitment to leaving an exhibition open to interpretation, respecting the agency of the artist and allowing the visitor to come to their own understanding of what is being presented. My curatorial text was extensively edited and revised by members of the exhibition team. The alterations revealed to me the contested sense of how to write a text, and how I was obliged to adopt an open-endedness that I suggest may characterize curatorial practice in distinction to the golden thread model of narrative that can often be sought within anthropology, for various practical reasons. In the revisions, there was a central preoccupation that stemmed from an unease with the authorial voice: the exhibition team felt my original text sought to impose itself, that it was controlling, that it sought to direct the reader towards a narrower range of interpretation.

In one example, the team redacted my specific question, 'How did an underfunded and overlooked marginal activity practiced by three young cultural actors come to spread so far?' and its rejoinder, 'there is no simple answer to this question' and replaced this 'hook' (the result no doubt of multiple funding proposals and book synopses) with a more open-ended series of questions, ensuring that the visitor would be free to ask multiple questions of *cartonera* publishing:

> What kind of phenomenon is cartonera? What kind of 'social proposition' does it put forward? How does this gesture, which came about in a moment of crisis, appropriated in different contexts, transform itself into a tool to grasp such particular worlds?

Further edits reinforced a commitment to open-endedness. Revisions removed an explanation I sought to impose, 'What perhaps more than anything else has driven *cartonera*'s rapid growth is …' and rejected a binary opposition that anthropological training has perhaps led me to adopt, in juxtaposing *cartonera* publishing with 'more traditional teleological movements'. This may be recognizable to anthropologists as a common writing strategy within the discipline, by which we deliberately create a contrast with another phenomenon to aid the position and determination of the subject under discussion. These details are small but significant and, contextualized by the three-dimensionality of the sociable space I have described above, create an entirely different pathway towards proposing an investigation of a given phenomenon. Indeed, I would suggest that fine-grained work in the encounter between anthropology and curatorial practice reveals practitioners with different positionalities and motivations, practising fundamentally different ways of creating and communicating knowledge.

Conclusion

What might we conclude from the similarities, critiques and differences outlined in a speculative manner above? What might be their implications for our practice as anthropologists? What does Kiven Strohm's suggestion (prediction?) that anthropology could be radically 'reordered' in a Rancière sense mean? Regarding differences, or points of mutual misapprehension, the notion of multiple publics stands as an important marker: we never know who will read our papers and, while anthropological work *does* travel in unexpected ways, transit and circulation is almost always a given for an exhibition; it is one of the central motives in conceiving of a display of works, to invite people in to see what has been created. This brings us to the spatiality at play, the accessibility of that space and the presence of a multiplicity of languages in the different formats in which artistic and anthropological work is presented. The visual plane of any exhibition, the expography that intervenes and complements displayed work, marks an important break with some, but not all, of anthropological output. It calls into question how anthropological work that derives from embedded and embodied relations can oftentimes be so efficiently emptied of the relational dimensions of affect from whence it came. Further, and perhaps most importantly, there is the concept of open-endedness. In practising a resistance to overdetermination, a refusal to didactically control how meaning can be imparted, curatorial practice exits from its conversation with much of anthropology, because it increasingly seeks to invoke affective relations to spark collaborative work.

Such a model for the production of knowledge has radical implications for anthropology. For Rancière, artistic practices are not privileged means of understanding 'reality', but '"ways of doing and making" that intervene in the general distribution of ways of doing and making as well as in the relationships they maintain to modes of being and forms of visibility' (2014: 8). By offering alternate ways of seeing, artistic practices are capable of 'intervening' in different arrangements and distributions and Kiven Strohm and I both suggest that a deep anthropological engagement with artistic practice will necessarily create a reordering of the distribution of roles in the discipline, particularly with regard to artists who identify as indigenous, a reconfiguration that will only gain greater force as time goes on.

This brings us back to the artist as ethnographer. I have already commented on a certain Eurocentric positionality that Foster assumes, and indeed Foster erases all difference between, for example, a Brazilian artist invoking the cultural alterity of the Huni Kuin in his or her practice, and an artist from the United States doing the same. He labels both as primitivist fantasy, premised upon the idea 'that the other has access to primal psychic and social processes from which the white (petit) bourgeois

190   *The Anthropologist as Curator*

subject is blocked' (1995: 303). In this reading, all artists in 'advanced art' occupy the same positionality, which perhaps provides a timely reminder of the particularity of the anthropological approach, and why indeed, artists and curators have sought to incorporate this one-to-one potential into their practice.

There can be a tendency for critics like Foster to assume privileged access when it comes to the understanding of forms – the ways they work, the possibilities they afford and their transformative potential (Flynn and Bell 2019 forthcoming). The post-critical turn of recent years has made clear that to 'render the thoughts and actions of ordinary social actors as insufficiently self-aware or critical' (Anker and Felski 2017: 14) is a practice rooted in subject–object dualities and colonial relations. However what Foster seems to reach for in his essay is much more than reading or ascribing meaning into work that the creator cannot. Rather, there seems to be an articulation of not just an authority over the work of the (perhaps indigenous) other, but in fact, a reading and ascribing of his/her very *identity*, all from his standpoint as a white, male scholar. For such artists, and here we can think of practitioners such as Jaider Esbell or Denilson Baniwa, of Makuxi and Baniwa ethnicity respectively, Foster reserves only two lines, redacted from the later 1996 version:

> There is the assumption that if the invoked artist […] *is* perceived as other, he or she has automatic access to it [transformative alterity]. (1995: 302)

How are we meant to interpret this? His comment seems to indicate that there may be artists who exist outside of the Anglo-American metropoles, but their otherness must always be held in doubt. First, this otherness cannot be asserted by the artists themselves, because only those from within the Anglo-American sphere have the right to 'perceive'. Second, if an indigenous artist, for example, is 'perceived' (and therefore ratified) as other, then his or her access to a 'transformative alterity' – that is, their unique recourse to their own embodiment, being and sense of self – can be held in doubt, as this artist *may or may not* have 'access' to that which they claim to be.

The introduction to this collection places Foster's essay as a key part of a wider contextual framing and, since its publication, it has clearly dated in a way that in a sense prefigured the kinds of critiques of Eurocentrism and white-man-explaining-non-white-histories that art practitioners would face in the 1990s. In this sense, the essay is still relevant, but not because of the concerns that it articulates on how anthropology and art will empty each other through amateur attempts at collaboration. Instead, it highlights through its Eurocentrism that, for artists and anthropologists alike, the question of *who* discusses representation and identity is not neutral. Who occupies these roles? Who selects these narratives?

The process of restitution, of reclaiming objects looted in colonial expeditions has gathered pace since the UNESCO convention framed in November 1970, which introduced a series of obligations regarding 'the means of prohibiting and preventing the illicit import, export and transfer of ownership of cultural property'.[8] Museums have been confronted with these questions for over a decade now, but for anthropologists restitution stemming from epistemological extractivism is still a relatively new phenomenon. However, a shift is occurring within the fields in which anthropologists work, and very noticeably so in Brazil, and this shift is being realized by contemporary art practitioners who identify as indigenous. In this engagement between anthropology and contemporary art, an example of a reordering in a Rancière sense is beginning to take place, one that requires further analysis and reflection. At present, restitution is being discussed and enacted by museums and cultural institutions. But it is perhaps university-based anthropological departments that may have to grapple with these tangible questions ever increasingly in the years to come.

Notes

1   https://www.humboldtforum.com/en/stories/return-to-alaska, accessed 10 November 2018.
2   https://www.theguardian.com/culture/2018/oct/12/collected-histories-not-everythi ng-was-looted-british-museum-defends-collections, accessed 10 November 2018.
3   https://masp.org.br/exposicoes/historias-afro-atlanticas, accessed 10 November 2018.
4   Both of these models have been subjected to critique of course. David Balzer points instead to a system of curatorial knowledge production that fetishizes the new to the point where the claim of originality is enough to sustain the acceptance of work (2015: 10); while Sandström and van den Besselaar (2016) have researched the concern that high volume output with regard to academic publishing comes with a doubt as to the quality of the work.
5   https://www.goethe.de/resources/files/pdf48/Dercon_Transkript.pdf, accessed 10 November 2018.
6   https://savageminds.org/2014/05/05/anthropologists-as-scholarly-hipsters-part-ii-crit iques-from-the-margins, accessed 10 November 2018.
7   http://blogs.ucl.ac.uk/global-social-media/2015/11/27/why-popular-anthropology/, accessed 10 November 2018.
8   http://portal.unesco.org/en/ev.php-URL_ID=13039&URL_DO=DO_TOPIC&U RL_SECTION=201.html, accessed 11 November 2018.

References

Anker, Elizabeth S. and Rita Felski (2017), *Critique and Postcritique*, Durham, NC: Duke University Press.
Balzer, D. (2015), *Curationism: How Curating Took over the Art World and Everything Else*, London: Pluto Press.
Clifford, James (1988), *The Predicament of Culture*, Cambridge, MA: Harvard University Press.
Elkins, J. (1996), *The Object Stares Back: On the Nature of Seeing*, New York: 4miscSimon & Schuster.
Faria, L. and M. C. da Costa (2006), 'Cooperação científica internacional: estilos de atuação da Fundação Rockefeller e da Fundação Ford', *DADOS-Revista de ciências sociais*, 49 (1): 159–91.
Fillitz, T. and P. van der Grijp, eds. (2018), *An Anthropology of Contemporary Art: Practices, Markets, and Collectors*, London: Bloomsbury Publishing.

Flynn, A. (2018), 'Contemporary Art in the Global South: Occupation // Participation // Knowledge', in T. Fillitz and P. Van der Grijp (eds), *An Anthropology of Contemporary Art: Practices, Markets, and Collectors*, London: Bloomsbury.

Flynn, A. and L. Bell (2019, forthcoming), 'Returning to Form: Emulation, Trans-Formalism and Experimental Methodologies between Anthropology and the Arts', in *Anthrovision*.

Foster, H. (1995), 'The Artist as Ethnographer?' in G. Marcus and F. Myers (eds), *The Traffic in Culture: Refiguring Art and Anthropology*, 302–9, Berkeley: University of California Press.

Foster, H. (1996), *The Return of the Real*, Cambridge, MA: MIT Press.

Freud, S. (2008), *General Psychological Theory: Papers on Metapsychology*, New York: Simon & Schuster.

Gell, A. (1998), *Art and Agency: An Anthropological Theory*, Oxford: Oxford University Press.

Gómez-Barris, M. 2017, *The Extractive Zone: Social Ecologies and Decolonial Perspectives*. Durham, NC: Duke University Press.

Graham, B. and S. Cook (2010), *Rethinking Curating: Art after New Media*, Cambridge, MA; London: MIT Press.

Grimshaw, A. (2001), *The Ethnographer's Eye: Ways of Seeing in Anthropology*, Cambridge: Cambridge University Press.

Grimshaw, A. and A. Ravetz (2015), 'The Ethnographic Turn–and after: A Critical Approach towards the Realignment of Art and Anthropology', *Social Anthropology*, 23 (4): 418–34.

Grosfoguel, R. (2016), 'Del "extractivismo económico" al "extractivismo epistémico" y "extractivismo ontológico": una forma destructiva de conocer, ser y estar en el mundo', *Tabula Rasa*, 24: 123–43.

Ingold, T. (2013), *Making: Anthropology, Archaeology, Art and Architecture*, London: Routledge.

Lash, S. (2007), 'Power after Hegemony: Cultural Studies in Mutation?' *Theory, Culture and Society*, 24 (3): 55–78.

Lima, Z. (2010), 'Nelson A. Rockefeller and Art Patronage in Brazil after World War II: Assis Chateaubriand, the Museu de Arte de São Paulo (MASP) and the Musee de Arte Moderna (MAM)', Working paper, Available online: http://rockarch.org/publications/resrep/lima.pdf.

Mantoan, M. (2016), 'Uma aventura moderna na América do Sul: arte e cultura no contexto da Guerra Fria', Anais do II Simpósio Internacional Pensar e Repensar a América Latina. PROLAM: Universidade de São Paulo, Available online: https://sites.usp.br/prolam/wp-content/uploads/sites/35/2016/12/Marcos_Mantoan_II-Simposio -Internacional-Pensar-e-Repensar-a-America-Latina.pdf.

Marcus, G. E. (2010), 'Contemporary Fieldwork Aesthetics in Art and Anthropology: Experiments in Collaboration and Intervention', *Visual Anthropology*, 23 (4): 263–77.

Rancière, J. (2004), *The Politics of Aesthetics*, trans. Gabriel Rockhill. London and New York: Continuum.

Rivera Cusicanqui, S. (2010). *Ch'ixinakak utxiwa: una reflexión sobre prácticas y discursos descolonizadores*, Buenos Aires: Tinta Limón Ediciones.

Rogoff, I. (2012), 'A Conversation between Irit Rogoff and Beatrice von Bismarck', *Cultures of the Curatorial*, Berlin: Sternberg Press.

Rosler, M. (2003), 'Someone Says …', in J. Hoffmann (ed.), *The Next Documenta Should Be Curated by an Artist*, Available online: http://projects.e-flux.com/next_doc/martha_ro sler_printable.html.

Sandström, U. and P. van den Besselaar (2016), 'Quantity and/or Quality? The Importance of Publishing Many Papers', *PLoS ONE*, 11 (11), Available online: https://doi.org/10.1 371/journal.pone.0166149.

Sansi, R. (2015), *Art, Anthropology and the Gift*, London: Bloomsbury Publishing.

Schneider, A. (2015), 'Towards a New Hermeneutics of Art and Anthropology Collaborations, *Ethnoscripts*' 17 (1): 23–30.

Schneider, A. and C. Wright, eds. (2006), *Contemporary Art and Anthropology*, Oxford: Berg.

Ssorin-Chaikov, N. (2013), 'Ethnographic Conceptualism: An Introduction', *Laboratorium*, 5: 5–18.

Strohm, K. 2012, 'When Anthropology Meets Contemporary Art: Notes for a Politics of Collaboration', *Collaborative Anthropologies*, 5: 98–124.

Tuhiwai Smith, L. (2012), *Decolonizing Methodologies: Research and Indigenous Peoples*, Dunedin, New Zealand: Otago University Press.

Walsh, V. (2016), 'Redistributing Knowledge and Practice in the Art Museum', *Stedelijk Studies (Between the Discursive and Immersive)*, 4 (4): 1–16.

11

Between automation and agency: curatorial challenges in new terrains of digital/visual research

Eva Theunissen and Paolo S. H. Favero

Introduction

Today, more than ever before, we are confronted with research participants who are as familiar (if not even more familiar) with using means of visual representation as we, researchers, are. Digital technologies have surely played a central role in this process, as they permeate the lives of an ever-growing number of individuals (indeed especially those living in 'wired' societies). Ethnographic field-sites are no exception to this. Impacting the ways in which (visual) ethnographers 'record, process, analyse and communicate their findings' (Tratner and Sanjek 2015: ix) these technologies become crucial mediators in the relationship between researchers and their interlocutors and also, at a later stage, their readers/viewers.

In response to these infrastructural changes, there has been an outpouring of scholarship on online ethnography, virtual ethnography and digital ethnography (see, for instance, Boellstorff et al. 2012; Hine 2000, 2015; Hjorth et al. 2017; Horst and Miller 2012; Pink et al. 2015; Turkle 1997). As Hine (2015) points out, 'ethnographers can go online and find field sites there' (Hine 2015: 23), indicating that the specific locales that qualify for 'field site' have shifted quite dramatically over the past approximately twenty years. Haverinen (2015) further indicates that 'online' in 'online ethnography' often applies equally to '*what* is being researched, *how* the research is being conducted and especially *where* it is located in terms of ethnography' (Haverinen 2015: 83, original emphasis). This argument runs in parallel with what is conventionally claimed with regard to visual anthropology, which simultaneously stands for an object of study, the research methodologies adopted, and the selected representational formats (see Banks and Murphy 1997; Wright 1998). In this chapter, we would like to capitalize upon this overlap and the inherent ambiguity contained in visual *and* digital ethnography as involving, to differing degrees, all three domains. In such a scenario we would like to examine the role of archival and curatorial practices.

Archival metaphors are abundant in scholarship on visual and digital culture, such as YouTube studies (see for instance Prelinger 2009; Gehl 2009). In his study of the political economy of YouTube, Gehl (2009) argues that 'YouTube is an archive awaiting curators' (Gehl 2009: 45). Fossati (2009) inquires whether 'YouTube – and similar participatory online repositories – makes the role of the curator obsolete' (Fossati 2009: 459). In his explorations of iDocs as a research tool, Favero (2013) suggests that the passage towards curation is unavoidable. Elaborating further on his previous observations, in this chapter we will look in detail at the challenges that occur when entering the terrain of visual ethnography from the perspective of curation and archiving. We will address the implications of this perspective for what concerns both the *production* and the *communication* of research insights.

Background

Before entering our discussion with the help of concrete examples, let us share a few reflections on the use of digital technologies as research methodologies in fieldwork contexts. Anthropologists have indeed long relied on a varied range of analogue recording technologies and tools in the field. As is well known (but also often forgotten), the discipline was really born with a camera in its hand (cf. Grimshaw 2001). And in the present day, digital technologies are increasingly integrated into the standard '"method toolbox" of ethnographic fieldwork' (Favero and Theunissen 2018: 164; see also Collins et al. 2017b). Whereas acts of organizing and interpreting fieldnotes have always been particularly messy and laborious, as we have argued elsewhere, the inclusion of digital tools in fieldwork may relieve some of these issues (Favero and Theunissen 2018). This was the incentive behind the creation of *EthnoAlly*[1] a research tool designed to function as a field assistant for ethnographers and social researchers in general. This tool offers us, we believe, an interesting entry into the debate, as it was in fact created with the purpose of facilitating acts of producing, archiving, managing and communicating visual and multimodal ethnographic material. The tool consists of a smartphone application that the ethnographer may use to create fieldnotes such as still and moving images, sounds and text notes. In addition, the smartphone app provides these notes with geolocative and temporal metadata. The tool may further assist researchers in conducting participatory fieldwork, for instance by asking research participants to create visual diaries of their everyday lives. The multimodal fieldnotes created with *EthnoAlly*'s smartphone application are automatically synchronized with, stored and visualized on a web platform (a cloud located within the premises of an academic environment). The researcher may utilize the sum of this material in an interview setting, and conduct what we have referred to as 'multimodal elicitation' interviews. And indeed, the platform could also be used for sharing the materials and research insights with broader audiences leading to a format that we could classify as an iDoc (see below).

Part of the appeal of implementing digital research tools such as *EthnoAlly* into ethnographic field practices is the ease with which the different media units and modalities are archived and ordered. The automation involved in these processes indeed takes a portion of the field labour out of the researcher's hands. Yet, how much are we actually in control of this process? One of the challenges we have dealt with during the design and testing phase of *EthnoAlly* concerns the open-ended dilemma of representational formats. How can the diverse multimodal fieldnotes be linked with one another in a manner that is both anthropologically relevant *and* formally/aesthetically appealing (Wright 1998: 17)? How to combine the use of partly automated digital data with established qualitative and in-depth methodologies? What are the epistemological implications of choosing (as we did) an online video interface for joining up the multimodal fieldnotes? Are there alternative representational formats and interfaces that provoke different interview questions, and that, in addition, yield alternative research insights? While debates on representational formats are by all accounts decades old (see for instance Clifford and Marcus 1986; Collier and Collier 1986; MacDougall 2005, Favero 2015), today they are certainly reinvigorated by the growing spread of digital media and technologies.

In what follows, we will further expand on these questions and examine the shifting roles, responsibilities and position(s) of the researcher resulting from and responding to 'new' digitized contexts. The remainder of this chapter is divided into two sections and will take the form of a dialogue between the two authors of this piece.

Building on Favero's teaching experiences in the domain, we will introduce the use of participatory iDocs as a research technique. iDocs merge the practice of documentary film with possibilities offered by the internet; and interactivity is a main component of these digital/visual forms. Producing digital/visual material in such a scenario, the researcher becomes as a *curator* rather than a director of ethnographic content (Favero 2017a: 284) and authorship materializes as 'a collaborative endeavour generated in a dialectic between image-makers and what we must consider [...] an "emancipated" spectator' (Favero 2017b: 10, citing Rancière 2009). We will critically examine what this altered position of the researcher encompasses in practice, and which possible curatorial challenges may arise. We will then take a closer look at some of these challenges. The obstacles that we dealt with in the process of developing and testing *EthnoAlly* will function as a framework for raising a set of methodological and epistemological questions that need to be addressed when integrating digital/visual formats such as iDocs in ethnographic research. It may be tempting to merely look at the participatory labour of research participant and researchers, and hence to commend the democratization of knowledge production in this milieu. However, the researcher also needs to account for what we could call the 'invisible' curator, that is, the algorithmic infrastructures that sustain and also increasingly direct, manage and thus *participate* in present-day processes of cultural knowledge production. Taking a portion of the labour out of the researchers' hands, it could be argued that these algorithmic apparatuses threaten the authority or the representational agency of the researcher. In the discussion that concludes this chapter, we will reflect on these issues in greater depth. In order to temper this polarizing and even deterministic debate, we propose to reconsider our conception of (human) *agency*. This involves broadening the horizon of participation, collaboration and curation in order to account for the non-human agents that increasingly define the stage of digital/visual research.

Part 1 The curatorial affordance of iDocs

As we have anticipated above, iDocs can be looked upon as containers of a broad array of digital/visual practices and forms that can be incorporated in ethnography. Before we go any further in describing its research potential, let us briefly define what we mean by this term.

Presenting the iDoc

The term 'iDoc' conventionally refers to documentaries that use interactivity as a delivery mechanism and that therefore merge the practice of documentary film with possibilities offered by the internet. This definition is however far from unproblematic, as it carries a tension between two terms ('interactive' and 'documentary') that hardly seem to be coherent with each other, and around which there is also, individually, very little agreement. In fact, if documentary film's core ambition is to adhere to what is conventionally referred to as pre- or pro-filmic reality and hence to cling to the 'myth of photographic truth' (Sturken and Cartwright 2001); and if interactivity is about a 'two-way flow of information' (Meadows 2003), hence building upon the eventual modification of content by the viewer, how can these two share a space without conflict? As a consequence of these doubts, the world of iDocs today is consolidating the idea that this emerging form must be defined away from possible reductions to consolidated labels and categories. iDocs can be seen as an independent visual form where the 'i' may take on a multiplicity of significations. Rather than standing for 'interactivity', 'i' could also stand for the personal pronoun 'I' in capitals (hence foregrounding the personalization that is part of the world of iDocs and digital media at large); or for 'intelligent'; or for 'eye', thereby foregrounding the visual and sensory stimulation embedded in these practices. Despite being increasingly used by news platforms, iDocs can still be considered, however, as an avant-garde territory. Lacking an established market, they live in the cracks of more established visual forms. They are hosted at documentary festivals, in the context of internet design competitions and in the world of contemporary art. We personally believe that iDocs still have a long way to go before they can win the hearts of passionate image-makers and image-viewers. Yet, in the context of visual research, they carry the potential of stimulating us to explore further what can be done with visual data today.

In recent years scholars have given birth to typologies for defining this terrain. Nash (2012) divides the field into three formats: the 'narrative', the 'categorical' and the 'collaborative'. The first allows the viewer to connect events in a time-based sequence (similar to linear documentaries); the categorical does something similar yet on the basis of particular topics that exist simultaneously for the viewer; and the third directly engages the viewer as a producer of content to be inserted into the work. Aston and Gaudenzi (2012) distinguish, instead, between 'conversational' films (which trigger a dialogue between the viewer and the machine used for viewing the doc); 'experiential' films (which, with the support of specific interfaces, bring digital content in touch with physical reality); 'hypertext' (the explorable database); and 'participative' films (which actually ask viewers to take on an active role in the making of the documentary by adding their own materials). Pushing these categorizations a little further and merging them with established genre distinctions in documentary film (see Nichols 2001), we can probably also create another typology based on the triad 'active', 'participatory' and 'immersive'. Before we describe this typology any further, let us warn the reader that we do not consider these categories to be self-contained, stable and clear-cut. The space of iDocs is better understood as a continuum where each product may contain more or less of each of these tendencies and ambitions.

With the first of these terms, 'active' we refer to those documentaries that offer viewers a variety of angles from which to explore the materials that make up the documentary itself. Conventionally using different media (such as video clips, photographs, sound files, maps, etc.), these iDocs constitute a creative archive that does not, however, allow viewers to actively change or expand the materials on display (unless minimally, by inserting comments, etc.). Making up the vast majority of iDocs present in the market, these products can be exemplified by projects such as *Prison Valley* (a doc that focuses on Fremont County, a valley whose economy is almost exclusively centred on the 'prison business') and *Choose your own Documentary*, a live performance where spectators have to choose the narrative path by voting. Typically, such documentaries allow viewers to choose their own path while jumping between different media (photos, videos, texts, maps and sounds).

'Participatory' iDocs instead seem to focus primarily on the creation of new materials. Sharing the very process of editing and production with the viewers, they are exemplified by Al-Jazeera's *Palestine Remix*. Viewers are here asked to actively re-edit snippets of materials on Palestine directly from the company's media archives. The new crowd-edited short videos will then be directly incorporated into the archive, hence becoming available for the next viewers. Another example of this type of iDocs is *A Journal of Insomnia*, where the materials uploaded can only be visited upon a nightly appointment and where the visitors are also interviewed on the basis of their experiences of this particular condition. In a similar way to *Palestine Remix*, this iDoc also offers a concrete opportunity for generating materials that future viewers are able to explore and reflect upon.

Finally 'immersive' iDocs are, in our view, the ones that aim more explicitly to close the gap between the image and the everyday lived experiences of the viewer. Potentially experiential, haptic and/or emphatic, such iDocs move along a continuum that goes from expanded emplaced participation (bordering on augmented reality) to Virtual Reality (VR) documentaries. Examples of this type can be found in *Karen*, a smartphone application bringing a therapist into the life of the user. Building upon the principle of provocation and nuisance, therapist Karen sends out SMS-looking messages, requesting users to connect with her. The algorithm grabs information about the users' views and habits and progressively pushes them, by means of increasingly refined questions, to rethink their own views upon themselves.

iDocs as research technique

Favero's first experiment in teaching ethnography though iDocs took place in 2011 at the Lisbon University Institute (ISCTE-IUL). Serving a wide range of anthropology students as well as teachers, journalists and artists, this summer course was aimed at combining the principles of ethnographic research and filmmaking with the possibilities for non-linear image-based communication. To do this, Favero adopted an open source program called Korsakow, which builds on the principle that the construction of the narrative of the 'film' depends upon the choices of the viewer. Korsakow therefore forces the filmmakers to lose control of their material. Filmmakers must in fact learn to archive the material in short snippets, called small narrative units (SNUs), and code each snippet with specific 'in' and 'out' words. The generative algorithm will do the rest, sticking SNUs together on the basis of the coding (tags).

In this context, authors are hence, as Favero suggested earlier, no longer directors but curators (Favero 2013). They coordinate a generative archive of multimodal data (photographs, videos, sounds, texts, etc.) leaving the actual construction of the narrative open to the viewers. For most students, and especially those coming from an anthropological or journalistic background, this was a nearly impossible task. They resented losing the opportunity to offer an explanation and constantly attempted to subjugate the software to their needs of linearity. This moment was an eye-opener and led Favero to abandon the engagement with this as a tool for communicating research results and to focus instead on its potential for generating new research material. iDocs could help stimulating new insights in the act of editing and sharing images with the viewers, rather than help to communicate pre-produced and ready-made interpretations.

In his following courses and workshops, Favero pushed the insights gathered from the Lisbon experiment further. In Antwerp, Delhi and Mumbai he tested the validity of iDocs as tools for coordinating group-based ethnographic work with a larger team of researchers, progressively also testing the incorporation of a variety of new tools and techniques. We incorporated the use of emerging technologies (geolocative smartphone applications, wearable cameras, etc.) but also increasingly explored different forms of participation.

The Antwerp workshop, that was conducted on behalf of the 2015 International Visual Methods Seminar (IVMS), started up with the selection of a suitable place for conducting research. The participants selected multicultural De Coninckplein as venue for the study, which is a square located in the centre of the city. The task was to grasp the core cultural, social and political characteristics of this place while alternating between moments of individual work and group work. During daily brainstorming group sessions, we started progressively pinning down topics, forms, insights, technologies, and so on addressed by the participants on their return from the square. We wrote such notes down on paper and eventually started drawing them on a blackboard.

During these ongoing exchanges, that lasted for five days, form and content were progressively brought to bear upon each other. The group developed choices of topic alongside choices of medium and visual form. They ended up collecting a variety of different materials: interviews with and photographs of the people encountered on the square; video explorations of the movements of people and vehicles in various corners of the square (we called these videos the 'rhythms' of the square); found historical material (grabbed online) that represented this space in earlier epochs and that was then reproduced by the participants by means of repeat photography; drawings representing the various symbols found on the walls of the square, which we eventually presented as an interactive card game (aimed at helping viewers to learn more about the politics of the square), and so on. The variety of audiovisual technologies deployed (ranging from GoPro cameras, to smartphones, DSLR cameras and drawings) combined with the just-mentioned techniques associated to them, helped us to generate a multilayered representation of the square. Thanks to the presence in the group of a participant with coding skills, we ended up opting to design a 360-degree space into which the viewers could enter, and in which they could find the various media that the group had collected.

The final design also incorporated the presence of a side menu allowing the viewer to choose whether to explore the content by moving within the 3D environment, or by searching for specific media and topics. In the menu we also added a brief introduction to the history of the square, as well as a lengthy reflection on the methodology and on the ethical issues we encountered during the research. Finally, we also envisioned, similarly to most iDocs, a space where viewers could upload their own images or stories about the square or comment on what they had found within this platform. Entitled 'Your Square', this area would allow users to link multimodal material through conventional social media platforms, hence converting this space into a productive matrix of participatory ethnographic data.

Different degrees of participation

The IVMS workshop highlighted different dimensions of participation. The first one has to do with the production of materials by the hands of the research *team*. In fact we ignited a set of stimulating discussions regarding the nature of collaborative knowledge production. While producing the materials, the participants ventured out on a series of individual missions, by a common intent. Each individual would focus on one particular slice or aspect of the square. This material would then be negotiated with that found by the other participants (and ideally, through the web page, also with the inhabitants of the square). Together they explored, on the basis of the exposure to each other's material, possible new ways of addressing the topic under scrutiny. This collective way of working liberated the individuals making up the team from dependency on one specific medium or visual form. This was not a space to make a film, or a photographic exhibition, or a sound installation. Rather, all the various materials could communicate with each other and prompt each other for further multisensory, multimodal and multi-perspectival enquiries. This multiplicity of voices, allowing for the creation of an in-depth understanding of the place or community under study, cannot but remind us of the first historical anthropological missions (such as Torres Straits or Griaule's Dakar–Djibouti mission). It hence mitigated the Malinowskian myth of fieldwork as a solitary endeavour (1961[1922]).

The second level of participation (which feeds back to the category of 'active' iDocs discussed above) is located at the level of narrative construction. Just as in the intensive course in Lisbon, here too the participants of all these other workshops had to find a way to let go of the control of the material by allowing the viewers to stitch together the bits and pieces making up the platform. In such contexts, viewers are active in the construction of a novel non-linear and archival narrative, hence giving birth to new interpretations. The acknowledgement of this shift entailed for the participants of these workshops an entry into the world of curation, and hence a move away from more conventional ideas of direction and authorship. Rather than guiding the viewer into their personal narration, this work has taught them to carefully reflect on how to assemble the materials online and then to progressively let go of the control over the narrative in a gesture that highlights the nature of knowledge as a matter of 'assemblage' (Latour 2005) and as a 'processual aspect of human social relations' (Banks 2001: 112) rather than a static thing 'out there' waiting to be discovered and 'documented'.

And, finally, the third level is indeed made up with viewers being able to engage with the platform by commenting upon, adding and removing materials. A proper form of participatory iDoc, this platform hence allows for the progressive production of new research materials through the very platform on which they are shared. Through these passages, the boundaries between the communication and the production of research materials are increasingly blurred.

Now that we have pointed out some of the affordances of incorporating iDocs into visual/ethnographic fieldwork, we will navigate a number of the critical issues and potential drawbacks of integrating iDocs and similar formats into (visual) ethnographic research. As we will show, these hiccups may occur at different stages, and will depend upon whether the researcher chooses to use such formats to *produce* or to *communicate* research materials and insights (and indeed, these research stages increasingly merge). Depending on these choices, the researcher needs to critically examine a number of methodological, epistemological and ethical questions that we will structure on the basis of two overarching questions.

Part 2 Critical questions

In this section we will, with the help of two core questions, address the possible limitations and drawbacks of incorporating iDocs into ethnographic research at different stages. Doing this, we will raise a set of issues that, as we contend, the researcher needs to take into consideration when using this digital/visual format.

Is this still ethnography? On multimodal formats, participatory media production and methodologies

A first crucial question that emerges when adopting iDocs in the context of research, is that their adoption as tools for communicating research results immediately opens up a number of implications *beyond* the terrain of representation and visual form. The use of iDocs in the context of visual ethnography is a response to (and also a reflection of) the changes in media ecologies that anthropologists engage with. These changes affect not only the 'life worlds' of our research participants, but also the researchers' own fieldwork practices. They have, as Collins, Durington and Gill (2017a) suggest, 'broadened our perspective to include other forms of media practice' (p. 142). Whereas

Between Automation and Agency

visual ethnography and – more recently – sensory ethnography have already raised critical questions about the 'centrality of text within contemporary anthropology' (Wright 1998: 19), the adoption of multimodal technologies seems to push this even further. Indeed we consider the turn towards 'multimodal anthropologies' (Collins, Durington and Gill 2017a) to be an opportunity to engage reflexively and ethically upon these broader infrastructural and communicational changes. As anticipated above, there are several challenges to be considered when engaging in such a milieu.

A first crucial challenge involves the implications of dealing with research participants who are 'digital natives', and hence fluent in creating and distributing 'user-generated content' (we are thinking of the nebula of SNS, user-generated video blogs on YouTube, etc.). What does it mean to operate in a milieu in which our representational authority and skilful expertise are questioned? After all, there is a relatively strong risk that we are merely reproducing the same mundane digital content and forms that our research participants *already* create on their own. In other words, can we still take seriously the task and effort of producing multimodal research formats, taking into account the relative ease with which our research participants also create such materials? As our interlocutors are getting more skilled in interpreting our ways of operating, the ethnographer's authority is constantly being monitored. How can this circle be interrupted without breaching the principles that underpin the world of 'participation culture'? What formal freedom can we exercise in a scenario defined by digital trends? Are iDocs and similar digital/visual forms, given their proximity to many other forms of popular digital communication, perhaps to be written off as sheer commercial gimmicks, as entertaining toys in the hands of a few curious and overenthusiastic fieldworkers? Indeed these questions cut right to the heart of a large number of contemporary scholarly debates on digital/visual practices, such as the blurring of the amateur/professional (see for instance Burgess and Green 2009; Jenkins 2006). In this context one can also be reminded of the debates (by now nearly three decades' old) about the impact of digital technologies and networks on our engagement with images at large (see, for instance, Crary 1990; Lister 2013 Manovich 1995; Mitchell 1994).

A second important aspect relates to the fact that the use of iDocs in the context of ethnographic fieldwork blurs the boundary between *communicating* and *generating* insights, hence creating a ripple effect. Producing multimodal material in the context of iDocs means engaging in truly open-ended, collaborative, participatory and crowd-sourced practices. Yet, given that viewers can continue adding new content, when and where does the production of ethnographic material end? In such a scenario, can fieldwork end at all? And, furthermore, does each and every individual fieldnote (in this case media unit) deserve a platform for display? Are there still selection criteria to differentiate between what goes in and what stays out of public view? These reflections trigger off a parallel with what Stiegler (n.d.) argues. According to him, 'information has value only as a result of hierarchisation in "'what happens'" (Stiegler n.d.). He observes that 'this is a plight of memory in general, that it [must be] a selection in the present, and that its passing, its becoming past, is its diminution' (Stiegler n.d.). What are the epistemological implications of working in a milieu where potentially each and every 'event' is equally worthy of being recorded, memorized and displayed? How can we demarcate which parts of this mass of data are ethnographically relevant? As we will show in more detail below, this dilemma is curatorial in nature.

While designing and testing *EthnoAlly*, we dealt extensively with such questions. We had to envision a way to accommodate the researcher's needs for small-scale, in-depth and qualitative material in a scenario characterized by large amounts of (relatively quickly produced) research data. How to combine large amounts of fieldnotes, part of which also hold metadata, without falling into the trap of big data ideologies (Favero and Theunissen 2018)? Our response to this dilemma has been to argue for a careful combination of big data with small and 'slow data' (Banks 2014). The continuing challenge for digital anthropology, as Broadbent (2012) shows, is 'to push the limits of traditional ethnographic investigation to incorporate the quantitative data [...] and traffic data (which tend to flatten out differences and highlight the generic) and enrich and augment it with the minutiae of the particular' (Broadbent 2012: 140–1).

So far we have argued that the adoption of iDocs in the context of fieldwork requires researchers to engage reflexively with the epistemological and methodological implications of such a choice. Perhaps one of the classic cases of conducting anthropological fieldwork, that is, the anxiety of never having gathered *enough* data to start 'writing up', is radically reversed today. Instead, we are presented with a possibly overwhelming multitude of digital data. On top of it, we are made acutely aware of the variety of means and strategies (technologies, tools and platforms, formats, templates and interfaces) that are available to compress and package these materials easily, quickly and elegantly. This brings us straight to address the digital infrastructures enabling all of these conditions. This is undoubtedly one of the key players of this entire set of negotiations, and in fact also a key *participant* that we have so far wilfully neglected to address. In other words, it is the proverbial elephant in the room.

The elephant in the room: on infrastructures and algorithmic curators

Let us imagine iDocs as a kind of *living archive*. Archives, as Parikka (2013) points out, were traditionally surrounded by 'an interesting aura' (Parikka 2013: 1). Partly inaccessible and 'not always understandable', they tended to appear as 'slightly obsolete and abandoned places where usually the archivist or the caretaker is someone swallowed up in the dusty corridors of bureaucracy, information management, and organizational logic that make the archive a system' (Parikka 2013). Archives were originally guided by principles of 'commandment', by laws of logic, authority, agency and order. As Derrida and Prenowitz (1995) suggested, archives are '*there* where authority, social order are exercised, *in this place* from which *order* is given' (Derrida 1995: 9, original emphases). Those in charge of creating and maintaining them are hence invested with the task of gatekeeping knowledge that is deemed to have a unique and memorable status.

Following this logic, we contend that it is appropriate to address iDocs and similar digital/visual forms, given their dynamic and open-ended structure, as *living* archives. In a way, they seem to take further the growing attention for matters of archiving and curating that has characterized the world of anthropology too. In 2008, for instance,

Fabian suggested that 'ethnographic texts can now be consigned to a virtual archive where they are accessible to the writer of ethnographies as well as to his or her readers' (2008: 4). He further argues that 'texts in a virtual archive take on a kind of presence that even the most skilled ethnographer could not achieve [...] prior to the Internet' (2008). This insight is, of course, particularly true in the context of digital anthropology, where the notion of the 'archive' appears to be a key concept. Yet, this notion is often used in such a way that it is not always clear whether the above-mentioned view of it as top-down and static (see the quote by Derrida and Prenowitz above) is still in place. As Pink et al. (2018) note, 'data archives' are instead 'dynamic, potentially "real-time", moving and changing (mis)representations of everyday realities' (Pink et al. 2018: 10, citing Kitchin 2014). In their view, they are dynamic not only because 'all individual files or data or other digital objects are continually modified by their users', but also because 'the *bodies of data* to which they belong or with which they are archived are incrementally being modified' (Pink et al. 2018: 10, our emphasis).

Transforming a space of display into a space of dynamic production of ethnographic evidence, iDocs carry the opportunity of offering an ongoing form of participatory and crowd-sourced data production. While posing a threat to the epistemological authority of the ethnographer, these practices make room for a progressive incorporation of a multiplicity (or a 'polyphony', see Aston and Odorico 2018) of voices and for ongoing dialogues (between researcher and researcher, researcher and material, researcher and viewer). iDocs, therefore, seem to offer the possible means for rethinking some of the critiques of anthropology's deep-seated authorial representational habits (with their evident colonial bias, see for instance Clifford and Marcus 1986). They respond to calls for anthropological texts (and visuals) that further involve research participants in their very making. Furthermore Web 2.0-driven digital/visual forms such as iDocs relieve some of the discipline's textual authority by enabling a wide range of representational media and modalities to co-exist and communicate in one converging platform.

So far, so good. Yet, when addressing these passages, the feeling is that we may have avoided addressing the elephant in the room. What stitches together the above-mentioned possibilities for active narrative construction and participation is the presence of 'mediators' made up by an algorithmic infrastructure. This infrastructure underpins the very platform on which the material can be viewed and interacted with. Both in the case of Korsakow and in that of HTML sites (and their links to social media platforms), these possibilities are made available (or unavailable) on the basis of (invisible) algorithmic principles that sustain the space in which the very content is uploaded. We are today only at the very beginning of our acknowledgement of the role played by the algorithmic principles guiding the digital infrastructures on which we rely. This is exactly the case for Korsakow, for instance, the free software system used to produce iDocs. Within this space, researchers are able to tag their video snippets (SNUs) according to their own logic; and in the same way viewers have the liberty to choose their own path of exploration of the material. The software responsible for this, however, enacts *automated* choices of selection that, in fact, influence the very acts of viewing, and hence also of meaning-making. After all it is the machine that, faced with multiple viewing choices (for instance, in the case of different video clips with the same 'in'-word), selects which clip to show at any given time.

In the present day a great deal of the curatorial 'labour' is automated and algorithm-driven. Taking this into account, is it still accurate to conceive of the researcher as a curator? Following Fossati (2009), we could ask ourselves: 'In a participatory culture, what is the role of a curator?' (Fossati 2009: 459). Perhaps, rather than reflecting exclusively on the above-mentioned issue of the never-ending character of an archive, we should question the extent to which the digital infrastructures on which we rely do in fact also 'participate' in, and even co-create the material that we, as researchers, collect and exhibit. As Uricchio (2017) argues, 'developments in machine learning have enabled algorithms to self-optimize and generate their own improvements', thereby complicating 'notions of authorship, agency and even algorithms' status as *tools*' (Uricchio 2017: 127, own emphasis). In a world in which 'data, the structure of data sets, models, software systems and interfaces all play determining roles in cultural production' (Uricchio 2017: 128) we find our very 'notions of culture and cultural production' fundamentally challenged (Uricchio 2017). In fact, this triggers off a set of critical questions regarding 'algorithmic black boxes' (Paßman and Boersma 2017: 139) that we hint at in this chapter. In the concluding section, we will address the epistemological assumptions that inform the view on algorithmic infrastructures as a challenge to the researcher's representational authority.

Discussion and conclusion

With this chapter we have attempted to offer a pointer in the direction of a series of challenges that emerge when entering the terrain of contemporary digital/visual practices. We have argued that the adoption of iDocs and similar digital/visual forms in ethnographic research offers the researcher the means for enabling more participatory and collaborative forms of knowledge production. The growing and often celebratory accounts of the emerging curatorial character of such spaces are blind to what we have called the 'elephant in the room'. With this term, we mean the algorithmically driven automations that underpin the various modalities through which researchers, research participants, readers and viewers are brought to interact with one another. Indeed when approaching the anthropologist as a curator we need to account for the ways in which the various technologies the researcher adopts also, in a way, define the stage of their activities. We have to be careful, however, not to polarize this discussion. The practices enacted in and through the dialectics between human and machine must be located along a continuum that goes from automation to agency. As a consequence of this, we need to rethink curatorial practices beyond human agency alone and also critically question the very meaning of the terms that compose this notion (i.e. 'human' and 'agency'). There is an obvious parallel here with what scholars in the field of STS, cybernetics and new materialism have argued for decades. Think for instance of the actor-network theory of Latour (2005), of Barad's account of agential realism (2003), of Hayles' writing on the post-human (1999) and Haraway's construction of the cyborg (1991). Scholars in the fields of postcolonial, feminist and queer studies have, too, in a similar vein, highlighted the intrinsically white male bias of conventional approaches to the notion of the human. What all these scholars may be seen to have in common is indeed a commitment to decentring the human as the agent par excellence and to revise our understanding of what it actually means to be human. We are therefore faced with the need for a grounded critique of the modern Western philosophical take on human subjectivity as propagated by liberal humanism. This view on human subjectivity and agency is characterized by Cartesian dualisms of subject/object, self/other, body/mind, culture/nature and inside/outside. In such a world view, agency is conventionally regarded as the sole outcome of human action and intervention. In this context, technologies appear as mere objects or instruments that are external to ourselves. We believe that it is time to overcome the understanding of agency as 'ex nihilo' (Rammert 2017: 91). As Rammert (2017) argues, this view on agency in fact goes hand-in-hand with what he calls 'the two grand illusions that have accompanied Western societies since the rise of Enlightenment and the rise of modernity: the idea of autonomous human action and the project of autonomous technology' (Rammert 2017: 89). Indeed this means also accounting for the entire web of symbiotic relationships with agents we tend to consider as non-human or post-human, and to reconsider agency as *distributed*. As Van Doorn (2011) points out, a perspective on agency as distributed 'does not imply an anti-human perspective' (Van Doorn 2011: 536). Instead, it is an acknowledgement of 'the ways in which the ever-increasing amount of technological mediators that surround us have radically expanded our experience of what it means to be "human"' (Van Doorn 2011: 536 referring to Haraway 1997; Hayles 1999; Thrift 2007; Verbeek 2005). Benjamin (1972), McLuhan and Fiore (1967), Kittler (2010) and other scholars have, over the years, pointed out that this is really why technologies have been developed, that is, to function as extensions of ourselves and moreover to increasingly *merge* with human capabilities. In this sense, technology has always been simultaneously human and non-human. With regard to photography, Zylinska (2015) has argued that this practice has always been characterized by a degree of automation. Building upon a historical integration of automated procedures at the level of chemistry (first) and electronics (later), as well as a number of automatic or instinctive reactions to the world surrounding the photographer, photography has from its very inception been at the same time human and non-human. In her view 'it is precisely through focusing on its non-human aspect that *we can find life in photography*' (Zylinska 2015: 132, original italics).

In the field of digital/visual research practices, Zylinska's (2015) argument could be applied to addressing the curatorial challenges researchers are confronted with. Rather than devising strategies for resisting the influence of algorithmic infrastructures on acts of curating and co-constructing representational formats and research output, we should try to broaden the horizon of participation, collaboration and curation. As we have suggested, this implies revising the modern Western ideal of human agency that informs the assumptions underlying today's *'participation culture'*. It furthermore implies adopting a change of perspective regarding what participation, collaboration and curation are made up of. By addressing these research practices in terms of a dialectic between the various agents, actors or actants involved (hence both human and non-human), we are offered an opportunity to rethink the manifold ways in which the key participants involved in this process increasingly inform, form and shape one another. From such a change of perspective, and once acknowledged, the proverbial elephant in the room may not be such a haunting presence after all.

Note

1   *EthnoAlly* was conceived by Favero and designed in collaboration with Alfonso Bahillo Martinez (University of Deusto, Bilbao, Spain), who also handled its technical realization/development. The tool has been designed in collaboration with Theunissen (who curated its UX and conducted the first ethnographic experiments on the field) and Ali Zaidi (who curated its UX and aesthetic features). *EthnoAlly* was made possible by a grant awarded by the Research Foundation Flanders (FWO).

References

Aston, J. and S. Gaudenzi (2012), 'Interactive Documentary: Setting the Field', *Studies in Documentary Film*, 6 (2): 125–13.

Aston, J. and S. Odorico (2018), 'The Poetics and Politics of Polyphony: Towards a Research Method for Interactive Documentary', *Alphaville*, 15: 63–93.

Banks, M. (2001), *Visual Methods in Social Research*, London: Sage Publications.

Banks, M. (2014), 'Slow Research: Exploring One's Own Visual Archive', *Cadernos de Arte e Antropologia*, 3 (2): 57–67.

Banks, M. and H. Murphy (1997), *Rethinking Visual Anthropology*, London: Yale University Press.

Barad, K. (2003), 'Posthumanist Performativity: Toward an Understanding of How Matter Comes to Matter', *Signs: Journal of Women in Culture and Society*, 28 (3): 801–31.

Benjamin, W. (1972), 'A Short History of Photography', *Screen* 13 (1): 5–26.

Boellstorff, T., B. Nardi, C. Pearce and T. L. Taylor (2012), *Ethnography and Virtual Worlds: A Handbook of Method*, Princeton: Princeton University Press.

Broadbent, S. (2012), 'Approaches to Personal Communication', in H. A. Horst and D. Miller (eds), *Digital Anthropology*, 127–45, London: Berg.

Burgess, J. and J. Green (2009), 'The Entrepreneurial Vlogger: Participatory Culture Beyond the Professional–Amateur Divide', in J. Snickars and P. Vonderau (eds), *The YouTube Reader*, 89–107, Stockholm: National Library of Sweden.

Clifford, J. and Marcus, G., eds. (1986), *Writing Culture. The Poetics and Politics of Ethnography*, Berkeley; Los Angeles; London: University of California Press.

Collier, J. and M. Collier (1986), *Visual Anthropology: Photography as a Research Method. Revised and Expanded Edition*, Albuquerque: University of New Mexico Press.

Collins, S. G., M. Durington and H. Gill (2017a), 'Multimodality: An Invitation', *American Anthropologist*, 119 (1): 142–6.

Collins, S. G., M. Durington, P. Favero, K. Harper, A. Kenner and C. O'Donnell (2017b), 'Ethnographic Apps/Apps as Ethnography', *Anthropology Now*, 9 (1): 102–18.

Crary, J. (1990), *Techniques of the Observer: On Vision and Modernity in the Nineteenth Century*, London: MIT Press.

Derrida, J. and E. Prenowitz (1995), 'Archive Fever: A Freudian Impression', *Diacritics*, 25: 9–63.

Fabian, J. (2008), *Ethnography as Commentary: Writing from the Virtual Archive*, Durham, NC; London: Duke University Press.

Favero, P. (2013), 'Getting Our Hands Dirty (Again): Interactive Documentaries and the Meaning of Images in the Digital Age', *Journal of Material Culture*, 18 (3): 259–77.

Favero, P. (2015), 'For a Creative Anthropological Image-Making: Reflections on Aesthetics, Relationality, Spectatorship and Knowledge in the Context of Visual Ethnographic Work in New Delhi, India', in S. Abraham and S. Pink (eds), *Media Anthropology and Public Engagement*, 67–91, Oxford: Berghahn.

Favero, P. (2017a), 'Curating and Exhibiting Ethnographic Images in a Digital Habitat', in L. Hjorth, H. Horst, A. Galloway and G. Bell (eds), *The Routledge Companion to Digital Ethnography*, 275–87, London: Routledge.

Favero, P. (2017b), '"The Transparent Photograph": Reflections on the Ontology of Photographs in a Changing Digital Landscape', *RAI Journal: Photography and Anthropology*, 7: 1–17.

Favero, P. S. H. and E. Theunissen (2018), 'With the Smartphone as Field Assistant: Designing, Making, and Testing *EthnoAlly*, a Multimodal Tool for Conducting Serendipitous Ethnography in a Multisensory World', *American Anthropologist*, 120 (1): 163–7.

Fossati, G. (2009), 'YouTube as a Mirror Maze', in P. Snickars and P. Vonderau (eds), *The YouTube Reader*, 458–64, Stockholm: National Library of Sweden.

Gehl, R. (2009), 'YouTube as Archive: Who Will Curate This Digital *Wunderkammer?'* *International Journal of Cultural Studies*, 12: 43–60.

Grimshaw, A. (2001), *The Ethnographer's Eye: Ways of Seeing in Anthropology*, Cambridge: Cambridge University Press.

Haraway, D. (1991), *Simians, Cyborgs and Women: The Reinvention of Nature*, New York: Routledge.

Haverinen, A. (2015), 'Internet Ethnography: The Past, the Present and the Future', *Ethnologia Fennia*, 42: 79–90. Retrieved from https://journal.fi/ethnolfenn/article/view/59290.

Hayles, N. K. (1999), *How We Became Posthuman: Virtual Bodies in Cybernetics, Literature and Informatics*, Chicago; London: The University of Chicago Press.

Hine, C. (2000), *Virtual Ethnography*, London; Thousand Oaks; New Delhi: Sage Publications.

Hine, C. (2015), *Ethnography for the Internet: Embedded, Embodied and Everyday*, London; New York: Bloomsbury Academic.

Hjorth, L., H. Horst, A. Galloway and G. Bell (2017), *The Routledge Companion to Digital Ethnography*, New York; Oxford: Routledge.

Horst, H. A. and D. Miller, eds. (2012), *Digital Anthropology*, London: Berg.

Jenkins, H. (2006), *Convergence Culture: Where Old and New Media Collide*, New York: New York University Press.

Kittler, F. (2010), *Optical Media*, Cambridge: Polity Press.

Latour, B. (2005), *Reassembling the Social: An Introduction to Actor-Network-Theory*, New York: Oxford University Press.

Lister, M. (2013), *The Photographic Image in Digital Culture*, London; New York: Routledge.

MacDougall, D. (2005), *The Corporeal Image: Film, Ethnography and the Senses*, Princeton: Princeton University Press.

Malinowski, B. (1961 [1922]), *Argonauts of the Western Pacific*, New York: E. P. Dutton.

Manovich, L. (1995), 'The Paradoxes of Digital Photography', in *Photography after Photography*, exhibition catalogue, Available at http://manovich.net/content/04-projects/004-paradoxes-of-digital-photography/02_article_1994.pdf.

Meadows, M. S. (2003), *The Art of Interactive Narrative*, Indianapolis: New Riders.

McLuhan, M. and Fiore, Q. (1967), *The Medium Is the Massage*, London: Penguin Books.

Mitchell, W. J. (1994), *The Reconfigured Eye: Visual Truth in the Post-Photographic Era*, London: MIT Press.

Nash, K. (2012), 'Modes of Interactivity: Analysing the Webdoc', *Media Culture Society*, 34 (2): 195–210.

Nichols, B. (2001), *Introduction to Documentary*, Indianapolis: Indiana University Press.

Paßman, J. and A. Boersma (2017), 'Unknowing Algorithms: On Transparency and Unopenable Black Boxes', in M. T. Schäfer and K. van Es (eds), *The Datafied Society: Studying Culture through Data*, 139–47, Amsterdam: Amsterdam University Press.

Parikka, J. (2013), 'Archival Media Theory: An Introduction to Wolfgang Ernst's Media Archeology', in J. Parikka (ed.), *Digital Memory and the Archive*, 1–22, Minneapolis; London: University of Minnesota Press.

Pink, S., H. Horst, J. Postill, L. Hjorth, T. Lewis and J. Tacchi (2015), *Digital Ethnography: Principles and Practice*, Los Angeles: Sage Publications.

Pink, S., D. Lanzeni and H. Horst (2018), 'Data Anxieties: Finding Trust in Everyday Digital Mess', *Big Data & Society*, 5 (1): 1–14.

Prelinger, R. (2009), 'The Appearance of Archives', in P. Snickars and P. Vonderau (eds), *The YouTube Reader*, 268–74, Stockholm: National Library of Sweden.

Rammert, W. (2012), 'Distributed Agency and Advanced Technology. Or: How to Analyze Constellations of Collective Inter-Agency', in J. Passoth, B. Peuker and M. Schillmeier (eds), *Agency Without Actors? New Approaches to Collective Action*, 89–112, London; New York: Routledge.

Rancière (2009), *The Emancipated Spectator*, London: Verso.

Stiegler, B. (n.d.), *Anamnesis and Hypomnesis: Plato as the First Thinker of Proletarianisation*, Available online: http://arsindustrialis.org/anamnesis-and-hypo mnesis.

Sturken, M. and L. Cartwright (2001), *Practices of Looking: An Introduction to Visual Culture*, Oxford: Oxford University Press.

Tratner, S. W. and R. Sanjek (2015), 'Preface', in R. Sanjek and S. W. Tratner (eds), *Fieldnotes: The Making of Anthropology in the Digital World*, ix–x, Philadelphia: University of Pennsylvania Press.

Turkle, S. (1997), 'Multiple Subjectivity and Virtual Community at the End of the Freudian Century', *Sociological Inquiry*, 67 (1): 72–84.

Uricchio, W. (2017), 'Data, Culture and the Ambivalence of Algorithms', in M. T. Schäfer and K. van Es (eds), *The Datafied Society. Studying Culture through Data*, 125–37, Amsterdam: Amsterdam University Press.

Van Doorn, N. (2011), 'Digital Spaces, Material Traces: How Matter Comes to Matter in Online Performances of Gender, Sexuality and Embodiment', *Media, Culture & Society*, 33: 531–47.

Wright, C. (1998), 'The Third Subject: Perspectives on Visual Anthropology', *Anthropology Today*, 14 (4): 16–22.

Zylinska, J. (2015), 'The Creative Power of Nonhuman Photography', in M. Elo, M. Karo and M. Goodwin (eds), *Photographic Powers*, 132–54, Helsinki: Aalto University, Available online: http://helsinkiphotomedia.aalto.fi/files/Photographic_Powers_Hels inki_Photomedia2014.pdf.

12

Anthropological sound curation: from listening to curating

Noel Lobley

Listening through online fragments to the scorched overtones and the soaring roars of the rasping *lesiba* mouth bow played by shepherds in Lesotho, I knew that the sounds had been recorded by an Englishman who, I would come to learn, operated in the vein of an Alan Lomax in sub-Saharan Africa. I was captivated. The richly shredded sounds were electrifying and physically coruscating in their complexity, more vital than anything I had been able to produce as a DJ and sound artist, textured like squelched acid house bass lines but conceived decades before acid house music existed. I would come to learn that *lesiba* sounds imitate and soothe animals, travel into vast valleys and feature on national radio in Lesotho. In an instrument-building workshop I would later try to build a *lesiba* to learn more about its principles, and I practically hyperventilated. I struggled with the elusive demands of the circular breathing required to animate a flattened vulture quill secured against a wire strung along a broom handle. It would require a move to South Africa to learn more about what might be behind the creation of such stunning sonics, and the discovery of unfurling pathways linking ethnography, sound art, curation and heritage activism.

The emerging intersections between anthropology, sound and curation are often loose, sometimes contradictory and usually experimental. Sound studies, perhaps more a constellation of ideas and practices than a field or discipline, have begun to take root in many other disciplines ranging from literary studies to ecology, and practitioners and theorists are always listening for new ways to perceive, conceptualize, document, design, control and experience sound. Such a diversity of approaches often emerges from a genuine diversity of training and influences. Drawing on her formative physical experiences in 1990s club culture while immersed in the oscillating patterns of low and high frequencies, Shelley Trower explores the links between sound, pleasure and pain through instrumental technologies such as the aeolian harp, sub-bass and vibrators. Trower reminds us that sound is often multiply sensed as 'the vibratory quality of sound can be experienced as palpable and audible and visible. We can feel, hear and see a subwoofer vibrate, and see its effects on other bodies or matter' (2012: 2).

The study of sound is also moving into areas previously unimagined, unseen and unheard. Anthropologist Stefan Helmreich, dedicated to the idea of the transduction or the translation of energy from one medium into another, listens within and through deep-water submarine cyborgs to experience how the energy fields of listening change through different technological bodies. He argues that sound, constantly elusive and operating at the limits of life, is 'often materialized as ghostly, inhuman, noisy'. It is quite possibly 'alive' (2016: xviii). If sound is multiply sensed, it is also often illusory, and Helmreich searches for the definition of a shape that keeps moving: 'sound has many apparitions, and it is shot through with definitional uncertainty. Is sound an acoustic wave, a phenomenological event, an object?' (2016: xviii). When anthropologists listen, act and produce, how does an elusive and illusory wave, a vibrating phenomenon, respond to curatorial impulses?

Curating sound?

What does curation even mean, or do, given its now near total ubiquity? Whereas it has been argued that ubiquitous listening might be enabling newer and more active distributed sensory habits (Kassabian 2013), the expanding literature on ubiquitous curating often questions the extreme dilution of a practice that has historically been precisely controlled. If, as David Balzer argues, we are living in a curationist moment – a period since the mid-1990s whereby everything is curated to the point where curation itself becomes the subject of artistic critical satire – this can also enable exploration of the wider relationships between taste, labour and the avant-garde of art. Balzer also points to development where 'artist-curators have also emerged as a new phenomenon in the curationist era' (2014: 85). Amid the rise of corporate curating and the emergence of celebrity curators, many of whom are often not trained to curate, the rush for visibility seems paramount. 'Which exhibition would you like from Bank of America?' asks Balzer (2014: 90). He identifies anxiety as 'one of the key drivers of the curatorial impulse in capitalist society and culture – an anxiety to ensure things are valuable and in turn to define them as somehow productive or useful' (2014: 121).

Media and technology author Michael Bhaskar has a complementary take, arguing that the buzzword of curation appeals to the personal in an age of information overload. Bhaskar presents curation as almost organic and vital, 'the necessary intermediary, for the modern consumer economy; a kind of membrane or purposeful filter that balances our needs and wants against great accumulations of stuff. At its broadest curation is a way of managing abundance' (2016: 85). But does such analysis foreground a uniquely first-world problem, one of being allowed access to everything all of the time? Valued as being of extraordinary use within an overloaded world, on the one hand curation often becomes a selective tool to construct personalized narratives and pathways through infinite choice. On the other hand, when everything is curated, the practice and term can also seemingly be rendered meaningless. According to Bhaskar, 'curation can be hard to grasp because its borders are diffuse and shifting. What is or isn't curation, or curated is never quite clear' (2016: 143). Bhaskar believes curation should bring measurable benefit as a litmus test that distinguishes good from bad curation: 'whether curation is explicit or implicit, thick or thin', Bhaskar argues, 'is less important than

Anthropological Sound Curation 213

whether it's useful' (2016: 306). The basic function of curating – 'where acts of selecting and arranging add value' (2016: 85) – clearly applies in both first- and developing-world contexts.

How can sound be usefully curated? The links between sound and curation are often not clearly delineated, given the ephemeral, invasive and immaterial properties of vibrating waveforms. Indeed, some sound curators even argue against the idea of curating sound, wary of curatorial impulses becoming oppositional to the instability and freedom required to respond to sound waves. Author and artist Salomé Voegelin proposes 'uncurating sound' as part of her argument for the need to consider sonic projects of long duration. Uncurating, she argues, 'seeks the audible and the inaudible anew all the time, embracing its passing ephemerality it embraces its own essence in disappearance, and accepts this fleeting property not as a structural necessity but as a generative designation'.[1] Artist, composer and writer David Toop, curator of Sonic Boom at the Hayward Gallery – the first major exhibition in London dedicated to sound – is also reluctant to embrace the need to link sound and curation.[2] Galleries can promote intimately focused listening, but can also contain, resist and constrain the properties that allow sound to work. To illustrate this principle, Toop the artist constantly plays with different modes of sonic engagement, exemplified when delivering a keynote at a conference on curating sound art without uttering a single word, choosing instead to silently generate a live visual text within layers of sound effects produced by selected audience members.[3] Toop was asking us all to listen differently to a familiar space and format.

Anthropologists and artists curating sound?

Anthropologists are now listening in to increasingly esoteric and elusive areas that help expand the discipline's approaches and subject matter. They descend underwater, attempt to understand post-human contexts where forests do the thinking, and try to reveal some of the ways sounds transmit social, political and economic values. Radio, for example, has become a fertile site for ethnography that may help us understand the future of communication alongside some of the standard anthropological concerns of old. In an afterword to the volume *Radio Fields*, media anthropologist Faye Ginsburg reminds us that 'understanding radio requires attention not only to the sonic – but also to the ways that radio is embedded in and sometimes constitutive of "inaudible" social practices such as kinship, religion, technology, personhood, and social movements' (2012: 269).

Where are the places and what are the methods for ethnography and sound to combine productively? In a recent keywords volume, Novak and Sakakeeny locate sound somewhere between the material and the metaphoric, sharply defining sound as 'vibration that is perceived and becomes known through its materiality' (2015: 1). They argue that 'metaphors for sound construct perceptual conditions of hearing and shape the territories and boundaries of sound in social life', concluding that 'sound resides in this feedback loop of materiality and metaphor' (2015: 1). As methods to study sound continue to develop within anthropology, for Novak and Sakakeeny, 'anthropology's signal contribution is the application of ethnographic methodologies and theories in everyday experiences of sound and listening'. Ethnography, they argue, 'offers sound studies an ear into the expressive, embodied, and participatory relationships with sound as it unfolds into powerful articulations of particular selves, publics, and transcultural identities' (2015: 7)

Ethnographic sound recording has never been a practice that was analysed as extensively as the broader process of fieldwork, but ethnographies of and about sound are increasing. Field recordings and sound archives have been central to the development of ethnomusicology, and its precursor comparative musicology, since the invention of sound recording. Indeed, pioneering anthropologists such as Jesse Walter Fewkes made some of the earliest field recordings on wax cylinders in the 1890s to record Passamaquoddy First Nations people. Phonograph recordings were also an important research tool during the interdisciplinary Cambridge Anthropological Expedition to the Torres Straits in 1898. However, for much of the twentieth century, sound recordings were preserved as documents, as frozen snapshots rather than being considered as more active objects. Nowadays ethnomusicologists are expected to be alert to the pros and cons of recorded sound, especially when considering what technology does not capture or even displaces. Philip Bohlman argues that 'as modernism modulated to postmodernism in the closing decades of the twentieth century the question of technologies' capacity to connect object to subject shifted to the growing possibility of an even greater alienation and displacement' (2017: 11). He identifies here a grand schizophonic era when sound is split from its source and interpretations and representations often rush in to fill the void. Kay Kaufman Shelemay also acknowledges that 'although archives have been part of the ethnomusicological heritage for more than a century, concerns have emerged that the materials they house can both canonize certain practices as "authentic", and can even be deployed as potential tools for political control (2017: 791).

Sound curators can work to supply context, interpretation and to enable the sharing of alternate narratives. Ethnomusicologists are increasingly interested in sound repatriation – tracing the ongoing links and possibility of shared benefits between static collections and the living communities whose sound is documented. It is also clear that the line between ethnographic and commercial sound recordings is becoming increasingly blurred, generating ripe listening conditions to explore the ethics of representation, hybridity and ownership. Sublime Frequencies, a label that connects rare and often raw global sounds with underground audiences in North America and Europe, might ostensibly appear to share in the lineage of curated ethnographic labels such as Smithsonian Folkways and Ocora, but the label's owners and artists often seek to challenge the authority of the ethnomusicological curator as the cultural gatekeeper. Sublime Frequencies is a record label with an ethnographic aesthetic governed by punk, 'a do-it-yourself, take-what-you-want ethos; a reaction against homogeneity, insularity and centralized narratives; and, most important ... a flair for the deliberately outrageous gesture and embrace of contradiction' (Veal and Kim 2016: 9). Who listens to such recordings? Mainly Western metropolitans it seems, an audience that 'has grown up in a confusing world of "posts" in which historical metanarratives are to be passed by, viewed with suspicion, or transcended' (Veal and Kim 2016: 16). In such circumstances of easy manipulation and reconfiguration of cultural materials, 'translation is a tricky undertaking' (Veal and Kim 2016).

Anthropological Sound Curation

Anthropologists, folklorists and curators can attempt this translation, while academic and artistic work engaging with oscillating sound objects – the social reanimation of archived sound – develops as a practice. In *The Beautiful Music All Around Us,* folklorist Stephen Wade starts with thirteen iconic field recordings from the Library of Congress documented between 1934 and 1942 in the southern states of the US. He then travels widely to seek out the performers, their families and others in the community whose memories and oral histories animate and personalize the human transactions that took place within the original recording sessions. Wade spends significant time with the singers and players who 'bring together lore and life, drawing from mother wit and the mood of the moment to create in their corners of America their own varieties of street joy' (2012: xiv).

Aaron Fox is a self-styled 'accidental archivist', an ethnomusicologist collaborating with cultural geographer Chie Sakakibara for Alaskan sound repatriation. Fox remembers how the Laura Boulton collection of Iñupiat recordings acquired in 1962 by Columbia University, New York, were initially a 'useless mess', and yet active outreach engagement with the Iñupiat community in Alaska over time led to his realization that 'nearly every member of the community can assert a familial stake in these recordings' (2017: 529). Catalysed from the outside by personal and institutional initiatives that enabled the return of archival recordings, many Iñupiat community members formed new groups and revived the songs and performed the dances that Laura Boulton did not get to see. Fox claims that the community successfully recovered, through disciplined re-creation, the heart of the music Boulton recorded with her eyes closed, 'by reconnecting it forcefully to the moral and aesthetic history of Iñupiat dance' (2017: 547). Fox admires these Iñupiat actors, realizing that through their regenerated performances 'they have also restored the archive itself' (2017: 547).

How does a sound curator enable the activist intervention of artists, allowing archives and collections to be reimagined, remixed, repurposed and differently owned and known? Curators already recognize the potential moment for the expressive and at times unknown interventions. In *Uncertain Curature,* Carolyn Hamilton and Pippa Skotnes focus on a range of expressive modes in archives in postcolonial South Africa, including, for example, photos and artworks that show the corpse of South African Black consciousness hero Steve Biko. They ask 'what conceptual work might be enabled that lies outside language; what might be made visible that otherwise might be only vaguely seen or occluded; and how alternative political readings are enabled through a range of lateral approaches?' (2014: 11). In exploring a range of experimental curatorial modes, they are really asking how artists curate futures.

Similarly, in *African Futures, a* series of interdisciplinary festivals initiated by the Goethe Institute in 2015 and held in Johannesburg, South Africa, Lagos, Nigeria, and Nairobi, Kenya, scholars and artists were invited to speculate and imagine the various futures for Africa.[4] Emergent themes included the uneven and often chaotic nature of archives, both in terms of access and location, and the importance of informal networks among people for sharing information. Author Adéwálé Ajàdí argues that proper documentation of both historical and contemporary African knowledge is essential in imagining an African future. He claims that, in Africa, 'we currently lack a disciplined approach to African knowledge systems and their documentation', and that 'worse still, the great many people who are embedded in informal cultural systems have few platforms, methods and tools to propagate what they know', leading to exclusion from knowledge systems of those who are not certified by formal systems (2016: 292).

The publication accompanying *African Futures* also features contributions from Kapwani Kiwanga, an artist and anthropologist who builds installations working with sound, archives, spoken word, organic materials and flowers and actively performs the role of anthropologist from the United States of Africa circa 2100 for her Afrogalactica trilogy of lecture performances.[5] In her speculative Sun Ra Repatriation Project, Kiyanga tries to contact Sun Ra in space, engaging with his own mythical practice as a contemporary ritual through radio astronomy.[6] Anthropologists, artists and curators working together can collect these creative interpretations and responses, linking futuristic imagination that can also be rooted within institutional archives.

In the sections that follow I trace and discuss the genesis and trajectory of some of my collaborative ethnographic sound curation, illustrating the ways in which the creative design and delivery of archival sound within different live and performance settings enables the imagination of alternative narrative pathways through colonial ethnographic collections.

Sound elicitation in Xhosa townships

When I first moved to Grahamstown in South Africa's Eastern Cape in 2007 to research the history and contemporary resonance of the Hugh Tracey collections at the International Library of African Music (ILAM),[7] I was initially drawn by ethnographic sound fragments, professionally recorded snapshots of local music made in villages, on mining compounds and in local performance settings across much of sub-Saharan Africa. The DJ and sound artist in me listened repeatedly on headphones at a library desk in ILAM to the sounds of massed Zulu choirs and Xhosa friction bows, talking drums, beautiful lullabies and the scorched *lesiba* overtones. However, the anthropologist in me was most animated by what these sounds might mean to the communities whose ancestors had been recorded. As I came to spend most of my time in the local townships – or Grahamstown East as the more marginalized parts of town were known to locals – I found myself moving through a vibrantly mixed soundscape, partly rural and partly urban in influence. During daily travels I would hear South African and American hip-hop and house, gospel and ceremonial Xhosa music all in close proximity to each other, often simultaneously. I began to wonder how it might be possible to curate a sonic pathway from archive to township and back.

However, most of the local producers, hip-hop artists and other musicians, community artists and activists who I came to know lived in the townships rather than in town, and very few identified with – or had even heard of – an archive that was tucked away in town behind the fisheries department towards the outer edge of Rhodes University's campus. The more I became part of the realities of everyday music-making – which would take place in *shebeens*, at hip-hop cyphers and street fora, inside taxis and makeshift studios in township bedrooms, and during ceremonies – the more I was asked about the purpose and history of Hugh Tracey and ILAM. My role as an

Anthropological Sound Curation

anthropologist soon came to be one of translation and mediation, of listening to the vastly different worlds of township streets and institutional archives and looking for the reasons for points of connection and disconnection.

The strongest connections nearly always flow through committed artists and activists. One spring afternoon in 2008, I arrived at a local community hall in one of the townships for a community event to hear a friend's band play gospel and other genres. It was there that I met with Nyakonzima ('Nyaki') Tsana, a dancer, who was on stage working with a group of young dancers – the Bionic Breakers – teaching them breakdancing and other hip-hop-influenced moves that drew from his own experience as an artist trained in ballet, physical theatre and contemporary and traditional dance. Afterwards, we walked back to town and began to spend more time together. I invited Nyaki to ILAM to listen to some recordings, in particular the 185 plus items of Xhosa music and language recorded by Hugh Tracey, mostly during the late 1950s. A few of the recordings were even collected in townships and villages close to Grahamstown.

Listening in the archive together with Nyaki instantly changed my awareness of the potential importance of these recordings. Nyaki recognized most of the songs we listened to – which mainly included ceremonial songs and Xhosa instruments such as the *uhadi* and *umrhubhe* bows. He could also translate most of the words in the songs, and was also able to assess from personal experience whether the songs were still currently known and used. Together we listened to 'Somagwaza', a song recorded in 1957 by Tracey among a group of Mpondo men in the Lusikisiki District in Cape Province.[8] Nyaki laughed with delight and affirmed, 'Yo – this is our Xhosa anthem. We always still sing this one'. As Nyaki began to explain how and where and when the song was still sung, I asked whether people would want to hear these recordings and, if so, how we could make this possible. Nyaki didn't think that most people would choose to come to the archive for headphone listening appointments, which seemed to be the preserve of students and researchers.

The best way to broadcast the archive, Nyaki predicted with certainty, would be to hire a donkey cart. First, we would need to make copies of the songs onto tapes and to share them with as many local artists as possible who would willingly learn them. Nyaki then decided that we should travel the townships with a donkey cart playing recordings and singing, before setting up a PA system outside the public library in Joza township. Bra Pet would let us have electricity and people would come. Nyaki knew that one of the most effective networks for sharing sounds and ideas was via the public performance spaces and art forms that people had already chosen to create for themselves: cyphers, DJ sessions and street theatre. In these spaces there was usually a sense of something happening, a reason to announce things and, importantly, a buzz.

After a few days preparing with a network of artists, we spent an entire afternoon as a collective, mobile, living archive curated by local artists as Xhosa recordings were mixed within a blur of poetry, story-telling, hip-hop and house DJ-ing. Archival and contemporary sounds could be heard across the street in the yard of a local old people's home, children came out of the public library to participate, elders arrived and were surprised to hear young artists DJ-ing Xhosa field recordings alongside other forms of electronic music. Some of the gathered audience publicly shared stories and memories of growing up hearing the sounds of the archival songs, others asked whose music this was, where it came from and how they could hear more. An audience grew reaching triple figures. People stood and asked questions about the unexpected archival sounds broadcasting from an increasingly scratched and dusty MacBook Pro resting on the street outside Bra Pet's mechanic store in Joza.

As we developed this method of sound elicitation, or finding ways to design and deliver sound within local social mechanisms, it became apparent that playing archival recordings in public was entirely unexpected to most people given the absence of any prior awareness of the existence of the archival record. These collaborative interventions mostly seemed to serve as catalysts, field recordings acting like shards or objects for inspection that brought varied responses ranging from vibrant nostalgia to distant memory, bemusement and occasional dismissal, but more commonly a strong appetite to hear again, to sample and use within teaching, electronic production and theatrical plays, and to own personally.

We watched the ways that artists and community members themselves chose to use the recordings. One afternoon while playing sounds in the house of Nyaki's aunt and uncle in Hlalani township, a Xhosa elder and neighbour walked confidently through the door as we were all listening, announcing that 'those kids don't know these songs any more'. He then led us all in a highly animated conversation, demonstrated dances that accompanied specific songs, and insisted on leading more listening sessions in his own house for which he rounded up more elders and younger children for them to teach. Nyaki and I spent many hours with groups of young artists sharing the archival Xhosa recordings from ILAM and listened to them debate the morals and messages in the songs. Some groups responded to messages about respectful ways for men and women to court by writing a play on the same theme, aimed at the contemporary realities of township life. We shared in workshops with young hip-hop beat-makers who chose to take these archival recordings and explore how the gorgeously scraped and whistled sounds of the Xhosa *umrhubhe* friction could be built into new electronic productions.

More than a decade later, the DJ, anthropologist and curator in me still listens to these ideas for different ways to activate and change the experience of archival recordings. For a long time, Tracey's unique recordings of Xhosa music had seemed destined to remain reduced as flattened items for preservation, separate from the lived humanity and values that animated the original performances. Collaborative curation that translated between local artistic practice and institutional archival processes offered the possibility for more animated sound stories to be told and performed, grown around the mined archival seed, creating new performances that could also be collected as part of the archive. As the archival record expands to include contemporary responses and new performances and narratives, the sound curator will continue to ask how archiving can benefit the communities whose expressive culture is documented.

Sound Galleries

I returned from the Eastern Cape to Oxford in 2008 with the aim of designing ethnographic sound experiences that could communicate cross-culturally in and beyond institutional gallery spaces. I knew about Louis Sarno's story and his recording

Anthropological Sound Curation

work before I arrived at the Pitt Rivers Museum (PRM), the University of Oxford's museum of anthropology and world archaeology.[9] Sarno was the man from New Jersey who experienced a musical epiphany when he fell in love with other recordings of BaAka music. He travelled to the Central African Republic in the mid-1980s to hear the music in context, and ended up staying with a BaAka community for most of the rest of his life. By the time of his death in 2017,[10] he had amassed an unprecedented and unrepeatable archive, comprising thousands of hours of BaAka music and soundscapes, mapping the entire range of music-making of a single community of hunter-gatherers across more than a generation. No field recordist had ever even attempted this before. Sarno recorded song ceremonies that called forest spirits and could last for days, the sounds of children learning and then mastering stringed instruments across decades, alongside earth bows, water drums and musicians playing in time to the pulse of sheets of insects, all documented from the close and subtle viewpoint of someone who lived permanently with a community.

When I first asked to hear Sarno's collection – which had been donated intermittently to the Pitt Rivers Museum as one of the few places where Sarno found support for his work – I was shown inside an old museum storeroom and presented with a battered suitcase. Inside were hundreds of hand-labelled C90 cassettes, many wrapped together inside an old brown jumper. Here was a major sound collection that could have been rendered almost entirely useless had the suitcase been dropped, given that many of the cassettes were – on the surface – indistinguishable from each other.

I spent several years organizing and curating this collection, the first priority being to digitize the sound and content labels, to enable their preservation and access, as there was a reluctance to play back original cassettes without professional equipment. Throughout this process I was training in both ethnomusicology and museum ethnography, learning how objects, images and other material culture is displayed, presented and framed, and how it is received by local and global audiences. Some ceremonial objects –such as Congolese nail fetishes and, indeed, many musical instruments – are considered active objects, their power animated by physical and ritual action, the very forces that are usually silenced behind glass cases in museums. I began to realize that the recordings could also be versions of active objects. As I listened closely to the thousands of hours of BaAka soundscapes recorded by Sarno, it seemed that much of the music was performed at night and a lot was performed by people moving – often women or spirits calling – and that the polyphonic and polyrhythmic structures and textures of the music offered participants multiple pathways through extremely complex collective webs of sound.

If there is a clear distance between ILAM and local African musicians, there looms an even larger geographical and cultural divide between the Pitt Rivers Museum in North Oxford and the villages and rainforests around Yandoumbé in the Central African Republic where Sarno had been based and made his recordings. Yandoumbé has few mechanisms for the circulation of recordings, and rather more means for the erasure of recordings, whether this be humidity, or military harassment of BaAka communities and the destruction of their resources. With collaborative fieldwork in the Central African Republic at the time inadvisable, I made the curatorial decision to enhance the sound collection drawing from sound studies and immersive sound composition, in order to broadcast through the gallery space and communicate some musical principles alongside broader historical and contemporary BaAka realities. Accordingly, together with composer Nathaniel Mann, we developed a series called 'Sound Galleries' during which we designed gallery spaces actively immersed in BaAka sound.[11] We curated, then mixed, live soundscapes that were broadcast in the dark to audiences who explored the collections in the PRM via torchlight. Thousands of hours of soundscapes were condensed into four curated hours, which included hunting songs and animal impersonations, the sounds of insects and animals, and the full range of BaAka instruments. Some of these events were streamed live with audio via webcams, and were even listened to and watched in the Central African Republic by a few of the BaAka who were featured in the recordings.

The anthropologist's role as sound curator was to enhance the awareness of the content of the collection and foreground the sound as an immersive and collectively experienced museum object. I worked closely with the collector Louis Sarno, hosting him for two different month-long residencies at the Pitt Rivers Museum in 2012 and 2013, during which time we listened together to many of his recordings while Sarno deepened the contexts and shared stories about his friends. We combined the different perspectives of the field recordist and the curator, while designing sound gallery experiences with the long-term aim of connecting the collections more closely with the contemporary needs of BaAka communities. 'Sound Galleries' initially remained almost entirely remote from the BaAka communities, but it also collected into one immersive performance space a collaborative team of allies, donors, philanthropists, anthropologists, health care providers and other support groups. Members of this network would come to mobilize support for Radio Ndjoku – a local station in the Central African Republic that was set up by Louis Sarno with Max Bale from RFI Planète Radio in France – to enable the weekly broadcasting of the Sarno collection directly for BaAka communities.[12] In October 2018 Max Bale travelled to the Central African Republic carrying a hard drive containing hundreds of sound files from the Sarno collection, and further collaborative museum projects are being designed around this initiative. Sound's invasive and illusive properties can be difficult to curate, but can also render it the ideal medium for curating in multiple spaces, whether offline on radio and on donkey carts, or online inside interactive sound installations.

Cape sound stories

When 'Sound Galleries' came to the attention of other festival programmers and venues, Nathaniel Mann and myself were invited to create a new sound work for Pop 16, a festival dedicated to the first hundred years of popular music, to be held at the Haus der Kulturen in Berlin.[13] The festival's central theme was the influence of 100 years of recording on popular music, curated to explore the styles, modes of interpretation and performance practices that the new technologies enabled. Taking as our own starting point South African recordings from the 1900s to the 1930s, we decided to collaborate with three other artists and write a live choreographed sound performance that animated five different ways of hearing the content of the selected recordings. We

Anthropological Sound Curation 221

worked with Andile Vellem, a professional South African dancer and artistic director of UnMute Dance Company,[14] together with Mpotseng Schuping, a South African artist and choreographer and company manager for UnMute, and also with Dom Coyote, a musical dramaturg experienced in the development of narrative in music performances.[15] We selected and gained permission to work with recordings from a variety of sources, including the South African Audio Archive Flat International[16] and the Historical Papers Research Archive at the William Cullen Library, University of the Witwatersrand.[17] We spent time researching the South African recordings in our respective countries before arriving in Berlin together for a week's residency, where we would compose a choreographed sound story to be performed in a black box-style theatre in the round.

The collaborative listening and composition process sparked many and often difficult conversations about the history and ownership of South African music. Among the recordings we all listened to – which also included colonial marching songs, children's songs and hymns in Afrikaans – was the first ever recording of Nkosi Sikile i'Africa, the song that would become the South African National Anthem. Recorded by Zonophone in London in 1923,[18] this particular performance features Sol Plaatje singing while Sylvia Colenso accompanied on piano. Plaatje – an indigenous rights activist and first secretary of the South African National Congress, the precursor to the African National Congress (ANC) – was at the time on a tour of Europe to raise international awareness of indigenous rights.

The five of us, inevitably, listened very differently to this recording. Nathaniel, Dom and I – three Englishmen – initially heard a slightly stiff and stilted anglicized version of a beautiful anthem. Andile and Mpotseng had not heard the recordings before we met in Berlin and they both responded with awe and some anger, both at not knowing that these recordings had been made and were available, and at the broader resonating issue of colonial oppression.

Andile decided he wanted to use dance to tell stories from his own background, growing up as a deaf artist in South Africa under apartheid. He chose to perform the story of his parents who were accomplished ballroom dancers but whose practice was cut short by apartheid. He also decided to choreograph a scene from when he first remembers he had lost his hearing as the result of mumps. While watching Michael Jackson performing on TV, Andile suddenly realized he could no longer hear, and he clearly recalls his sister taking his hand and pressing it up against the TV speaker so he could feel the vibrations. He would later dance this scene in multiple ways during our performance. Towards the beginning, Andile introduced an intimate dance cradling a hand-held Bluetooth speaker, which he then placed in the palms of audience members in the front row, so that they too could feel the gentle vibrations of archival recordings we were transmitting quietly through the speaker.

While composing together, we also learned to translate some of the frequencies in the recordings into sub-bass and transmit them to the stage by placing bass speakers underneath so that Andile could feel the vibrations. With Mpotseng also acting as sign language interpreter, we explored ways to immerse the venue in sound, recomposing some of the cadences in Plaatje's singing into electronic compositions, and amplifying Andile's choreographed moves and mixing his steps back into the live soundscape.

The Anthropologist as Curator

We designed multiple ways to deliver sound at different levels. When, in rehearsals, the colonial pomp of 'Marching on Pretoria' provoked discomfort in all of us,[19] we decided to play the recording through a crude car stereo-style speaker, which we attached to a long wire that Andile swung around him in circles at the head-level of the audience seated in the front row. At this point the intimacy of sound became physically threatening as the speaker swirled closer and closer to heads, requiring complete trust in the artistry of Andile Vellem who was performing his revulsion at the sound of colonial oppression.

During a thirty-minute live, choreographed sound story, sound was delivered in multiple overlapping ways through both cutting-edge and lo-fi technology. The moving soundscape was presented in darkness, punctuated by occasional spotlights, mixing national anthems, Afrikaans nationalism, hybrid jazz, children's games and live electronic composition. Through research, sound design and live composition we searched for the most effective and physical ways to present a soundscape for live choreography, performing personal stories and the moving body to animate archival recordings and histories that would always be heard differently by artists and audiences within and without South Africa.[20]

Xhosa arts archives

I now return to the Eastern Cape of South Africa, where the notion of sound curation has expanded from activating recordings via local social mechanisms to include creatively composed events, performances and installations that can enable stories of cultural transmission and identity to be told and owned differently.

I have been collaborating with Xhosa hip-hop artist and activist, Xolile 'X' Madinda since 2007, having first been introduced to him by Nyakonzima Tsana as part of the artistic network in Grahamstown. X spent many hours walking the streets with us in the town and the townships, playing archival recordings on tape players and introducing them at hip-hop cyphers and in recording sessions in Def Camp, his base and studio in Fingo Village township. During the last decade, I have witnessed X develop the Fingo Revolutionary Movement and the Fingo Festival, which blends cutting-edge South African DJs, rappers and poets with lectures and children's activities.[21] The Fingo Festival is now a fully established part of the National Arts Festival held annually in Grahamstown.[22] In 2016 X, a fiercely independent artist, started to develop his own arts space, Around Hip Hop Live Café, or 'The Black Power Station',[23] as a Pan-African space for local and other artists to generate, share and perform their own artworks.

A visionary artist from Fingo Village township in Grahamstown, X has been aware of ILAM and colonial collecting histories for decades, and, after intermittent collaborations with ILAM, he was inspired to develop his own community archive. Rather than simply request access to archival Xhosa recordings, X actively builds spaces that house performances using archival recordings and also creates new art and sound for today, drawing on input and advice from ILAM, anthropologists and curators to establish best practice.

As anthropologist–curator I embrace the value of creative co-curation with local communities and artists that can both generate different understandings of collected material, and also help create platforms for entirely new content-building. As X develops his new Pan-African arts centre, he and a team of young Xhosa artists and activists have already poured thousands of creative hours into the space, designing and building from mostly recycled and donated materials. Together they decided to renovate a derelict building – a former power station in Grahamstown – that has been leased to X by the Director of the National Arts Festival.[24]

Together we are exploring the possibilities for co-curation across the continent, building structures that increase the flow of people between the Eastern Cape and the US, addressing what it means to perform, own and curate people's own heritage. On 15 August 2018 we co-hosted an event entitled 'Graham's Legacy, Makhanda's Future' in The Black Power Station,[25] having spent nearly a month together with local artists preparing the space and content, which was all themed around the politically charged decision to rename Grahamstown as Makhanda, honouring a Xhosa warrior instead of a colonial oppressor. Our event brought together an audience of schoolchildren and artists from the township communities for a full programme of Xhosa hip-hop, *imbongi* praise poetry, physical theatre and contemporary dance, sound art, informal lectures, pantsula dancing and DJ-ing. The event was filmed, recorded and documented by multiple local artists as part of the emerging archive being produced by Around Hip Hop, X's company.

We also continue to co-curate events across continents, sharing and swapping content and curatorial ideas, exchanging video clips, WhatsApp images and recorded snapshots on a daily basis. The next major performance took place a month later, a restaging of Xhosa Chronicles, a play written and directed by Xhosa artist and public history performer Masxiole Heshu.[26] Masixole creates mobile performances that explore the erasure of Xhosa history and identity, often inspired by his curated walking heritage tours, which uncover the Xhosa histories that often lie buried in Grahamstown/Makhanda His earlier show *limfazwe* ('Battles') took the form of a curated taxi tour moving from town to township via significant monument heritage sites, and premiered at the National Arts Festival in 2017.[27] Actors performed and sang throughout the journey, and we disembarked several times to engage with live performances at heritage sites including Egazini ('the place of blood') in Fingo Village, where women performed and sang their memories of husbands and fathers who did not return from war. X chose to restage work such as these mobile performances within The Black Power Station, enabling directors and artists to work within a curated arts space, filming and documenting and archiving their own performances.

The challenges for the anthropological sound curator today seem to be, first, how archival sonic heritage can remain in contact with, accessible to and useful to contemporary communities, who can unlock and transform understandings of the knowledge recorded within, transforming archival processes that, to date, have largely focused on sound file preservation. Artists and community members will always find innovative ways to grow the sonic fragments into more active audible and visible presences, and the sound curator can help collect and share the artistic responses to archival collections and present different narratives on more equal platforms.

Second, and more future-oriented, the challenge would be to find ways to support or enable local artists and activists to generate their own instantly archivable material to form recognizable collections that reflect the issues engaged in contemporary performances. Institutional archives can support locally owned, autonomous creative spaces for the shaping and hosting of newly curated content. Much future energy is likely to be expended on expanding the relationships between curators and local artists, enabling creative collaborations both through archival and new collections. Curators can contribute to the growing awareness of the limitations of mined and extracted recordings, working with artists to explore ways to rebuild contexts within performance practices.

Conclusion: curating sound in the future

Locating anthropological meaning somewhere between cross-cultural insights and enlightened self-critique, Matthew Engelke reminds us that anthropology 'prompts us to reconsider not only what we think we know – what it means to be affluent, why blood matters, what constitutes reason – but also the terms by which we know it' (2018: 281). As we move towards an increasingly engaged anthropology, one that melds methods and outputs to more fluid realities beyond the production of texts, there still remains a real battle to establish the value of such applied anthropology. Exploring the categories of engaged, public and collaborative anthropology, Stuart Kirsch argues that an engaged anthropology is one that 'responds to questions about responsibilities to informants as well as the desire to address contemporary problems' (2018: 230), and that it differs from other anthropological projects in its willingness to seek solutions to problems by moving beyond the production of texts.

When Englishman Hugh Tracey began to tour sub-Saharan Africa with his microphones almost a century ago, he collected unique and often unrepeatable sonic moments from which he planned to extract and codify the logic of African music. The process of separating the recording from community happened almost immediately in most cases. When curators spend time working more extensively with local artists and communities, reasons are often revealed why recordings have typically prioritized a mapped way of archiving that reflects and repeats the ear and gaze of the outside inspector. Future curated collections could search for ways to represent the three-dimensional enacted and live performances that transmit values, experiences and personalities through bodies. Curators can develop collaborative practices that invite the institutional archives to respect and support local ways of owning, documenting and making accessible their performances. Locally managed spaces and resources that are embedded in community practices and resonate with the aesthetics of local people are already generating contemporary performances and productions that can transform institutional archival practice.

Anthropologists co-curating with local artists can continue to translate and mediate between the worlds of contemporary artistic production and institutional archiving structures, persuading the latter to bend towards often unexpected and original demands for access and support. In her exploration of the Pan-African engagements

Anthropological Sound Curation 225

with African American music, the poet and academic Tsitsi Ella Jaji argues that 'very few popular media (Western or otherwise) regularly present images of innovation, progress, technological advance, experiment, or invention emerging from Africa' (2014: 212). Anthropological curators listening closely to the visionary African artists developing their own street theatre, sound art, and Pan-African art spaces, can help document these very performances that activate and expand the notion of sound collections, while simultaneously transforming archives into more actively mobile collections and spaces for ideas that will increasingly be able to respond to live art.

Notes

1 http://salomevoegelin.net/public_html/salomevoegelin.net/uncurating_sound.html. Voegelin's ideas are also developed in this podcast: https://ora2013.wordpress.com/tag/uncurating/.
2 David Toop discusses Sonic Boom in the following video: https://www.afterall.org/online/exhibition-histories-talks-david-toop-video-online#.XYwcDCV7nGI.
3 http://soundstudies.org.uk/sound-art-curating-conference-goldsmiths-university-of-london-15th-16th-may-2014/.
4 http://africanfutures.tumblr.com/about.
5 https://www.contemporaryand.com/exhibition/the-institute-of-things-to-come-kapwani-kiwanga-afrogalactica/.
6 http://www.canadalandshow.com/podcast/waiting-for-sun-ra.
7 https://www.ru.ac.za/ilam/.
8 After the demise of apartheid, the Cape Province was broken up into the smaller provinces of Western Cape, Eastern Cape and Northern Cape.
9 http://web.prm.ox.ac.uk/reel2real/index.php/collections-sarno.html.
10 https://www.nytimes.com/2017/04/10/arts/music/louis-sarno-dead-studied-pygmies-music.html.
11 http://pittrivers-sound.blogspot.com/2014/05/curating-sound-galleries-at-pitt-rivers.html.
12 https://www.rfiplaneteradio.org/fr.
13 https://www.hkw.de/de/programm/projekte/2016/pop_16/pop_16_start.php.
14 http://unmutedance.blogspot.com/.
15 https://www.domcoyote.com/about/.
16 https://www.siemonallen.org/about.html
17 http://www.historicalpapers.wits.ac.za/.
18 http://www.historicalpapers.wits.ac.za/?inventory/U/collections&c=A1742/I/6027.
19 We worked with a 1902 recording of a marching song from the Second Boer War. It is sung with patriotic British pride, and is based on an American Civil War song.
20 A short news item about Cape Sound Stories featured on SABC news can be viewed here: https://vimeo.com/175221153.
21 https://www.facebook.com/FingoFestival/.
22 https://www.nationalartsfestival.co.za/.
23 https://www.pressreader.com/south-africa/mail-guardian/20180713/282157882016130.
24 A short video introducing X and The Black Power Station work can be viewed here: https://www.youtube.com/watch?v=vUKSX61qTno&index=2&t=0s&list=LL-kqqLFwRfYDhN9LOu5ZwLA.

25 https://www.facebook.com/events/290904318348810.
26 https://www.facebook.com/events/327878911108802/.
27 https://www.youtube.com/watch?v=KMoXevwlLn4.

References

Ajàdí, A. (2016), 'Wisdom and Its Effective Use', in L. Heidenrich-Seleme and S. O'Toole (eds), *African Futures: Thinking about the Future in World and Image*, 291–5, Bielefield: Kerber Culture.

Balzer, D. (2014), *Curationism: How Curating Took Over the Art World and Everything Else*, Toronto: Coach House Books.

Bhaskar, M. (2016), *Curation: The Power of Selection in a World of Excess*, London: Piatkus.

Bohlman, P., ed. (2017), *The Cambridge History of World Music*, Cambridge; New York: Cambridge University Press.

Engelke, M. (2018), *How to Think Like an Anthropologist*, Princeton; Oxford: Princeton University Press.

Fox, A. (2017), 'Repatriation as Reanimation through Reciprocity', in P. Bohlman (ed.), *The Cambridge History of World Music*, 522–54, Cambridge; New York: Cambridge University Press.

Ginsburg, F. (2012), 'Radio Fields: An Afterword', in L. Bessire and D. Fisher (eds), *Radio Fields: Anthropology and Wireless Sound in the 21st Century*, 268–78, New York; London: New York University Press.

Hamilton, C. and P. Skotnes, eds. (2014), *Uncertain Curature: In and Out of the Archive*, Johannesburg; Cape Town: Jacana.

Helmreich, S. (2016), *Sounding the Limits of Life: Essays in the Anthropology of Biology and Beyond*, Princeton; Oxford: Princeton University Press.

Jaji, T. (2014), *Africa in Stereo: Modernism, Music and Pan-African Solidarity*, Oxford; New York: Oxford University Press.

Kassabian, A. (2013), *Ubiquitous Listening: Affect, Intention and Distributed Listening*, Berkeley: University of California Press.

Kirsch, S. (2018), *Engaged Anthropology: Politics Beyond the Text*, Berkeley: University of California Press.

Novak, D. and M. Sakakeeny, eds. (2015), *Keywords in Sound*, Durham, NC; London: Duke University Press.

Shelemay, K. (2017), 'The Ethics of Ethnomusicology in a Cosmopolitan Age', in P. Bohlman (ed.), *The Cambridge History of World Music*, 786–806, Cambridge; New York: Cambridge University Press.

Trower, S. (2012), *Senses of Vibration: A History of the Pleasure and Pain of Sound*, New York; London: Continuum.

Veal, M. and T. Kim, eds. (2016), *Punk Ethnography: Artists and Scholars Listen to Sublime Frequencies*, Middletown: Wesleyan University Press.

Wade, S. (2012), *The Beautiful Music All Around Us: Field Recordings and the American Experience*, Urbana, Chicago and Springfield: University of Illinois Press.

Index

abaca 137
Abarca, Javier 148
abstract expressionism 27
abstraction 24–5, 30–1
abstract paintings 121
abstract shapes 28
academic humanities 21
Accursed Share, The (Bataille) 124
actor-network theory 19, 206
adjunct curators 179
Adler, Tal 54 n.9
advanced art 175, 190
advertising 92
aestheticization 78
aesthetics 10, 22, 28, 109, 133–4, 137,
    140, 142–3, 169, 182
  African 60
  appearance 81
  codes 82
  experience 82, 118
  forms 164, 183
  Mexicanist 23, 25
  and politics 124
  practice 148, 155, 157, 162
  qualities 82
  universalism 82
  value 7, 74, 79
Africa 77–8, 85, 87
  art 10, 73, 79–81
  artists 86, 221, 227
  collection 60, 86
  cultures 83
  and its diaspora 63–4, 66
  music 221, 224
  musicians 219
  objects 78–9, 82, 83–4
  people 61, 65, 92
  religions 84
  societies 68 n.5, 86
  'white artist' in 92
African-Canadian community 10–11, 61

African Futures (Ajàdí) 215–16
African Italians 77
African knowledge systems 215
African National Congress (ANC)
  221
Afro-Atlantic Histories 174, 184
Afrogalactica trilogy 216
agency 10, 14, 61, 84, 89, 106, 109, 178,
  181, 197, 206, 207
Agentur für geistige gastarbeit 179
AHRC research project 177
Ajàdí, Adéwálé 215
al fresco art 167
algorithmic curators 204–6
algorithmic infrastructures 207
algorithmic principles 205
Al-Jazeera 199
Alterazioni Video 90
alterity 2, 38, 43, 67, 125, 174–5,
  189
Amarillo Ramp 128 n.2
amateur 136, 190
amateurism 140, 141
American Anthropological Association
  (AAA) 11, 98
American Civil War song 227 n.20
American Museum of Natural History
  (AMNH) 98, 99
American Revolutionary War 65
Andre, Carl 129 n.6
anecdotal theory 106–10
Anecdotal Theory 107
anecdote-ing 98, 100, 102, 103, 106,
  108, 112
anecdotes 97–8, 99, 100–1, 102–6,
  111, 112
Anglo-American metropoles 175, 181,
  190
animism 84
'anthropological turn' 116
'Anthropologist as curator' workshop 8

228   *Index*

anthropology 5, 7–8, 19, 23, 26, 39, 59,
84, 93, 111, 124, 127, 128, 135,
140, 178. *See also* contemporary
anthropology; cultural
anthropology; ethnography;
German anthropology; multimodal
anthropology; sound curation
  aesthetic 27
  American 25
  approach 76, 174, 175
  of art 10–11, 13, 19–21, 23–4, 98,
106–7, 111–12, 125–6, 133, 136–7,
139, 141–3, 173, 176, 182
  and contemporary art 1, 11, 107–8
  convergences/conjunctions in 13,
127, 143–4, 183
  conversation on 48
  as critique 17–21, 31
  and curatorial practice 9–11, 36–40,
42–4, 47–53
  curators 227
  discourse 25
  engaged 224
  ethnographic practices in 73, 76, 125
  methods 3, 133
  as minor science 17
  modernist legacy 18
  of museums 1
  practice 8, 13, 18, 36–7, 39, 51, 99,
142, 147, 173, 176, 178, 180–4, 181,
188–9
  process 12
  research 61, 98, 167, 176
  theory 3, 36, 63, 111
  thinking 19–20, 30
Anthropology as Cultural Critique (*ACC*)
(Marcus and Fischer) 19
Anthropology Department 174
Anthropology of the Image Lab
(AIL) 26, 30
Anthropos Today (Rabinow) 20
anti-black violence 68 n.2
anti-disciplinary exhibition-
making 133–5, 143
anti-feminist discourse 137
anti-heroic artworks 123
Antwerp workshop 200
apology 10, 64, 68 n.5, 180
Applebroog, Ida 130 n.11

archaeological landscapes 160
architectural forms 23, 28
architecture 126–7
archives 8, 120, 138, 204
  anecdote 110
  collections 223
  material 27
  metaphors 196
  narrative 202
  practice 195
  recordings 222
  research 65
  sounds 216–18
Arienti, Stefano 11, 76, 80–1, 83, 85
Around Hip Hop 223
Around Hip Hop Live Café. *See* 'The Black
Power Station'
art 4, 18, 73. *See also* experimental art;
modern art
  vs. vandalism 166
  academies 35
  anthropology of 10–11, 13, 19–21,
23–4, 98, 106–8, 111–12, 125–6,
133, 136–7, 139, 141–3, 173, 176,
182
  appropriation 133
  biennials 3, 74
  commoditization 75
  convergences/conjunctions in 143–4
  discourse 1
  education 140, 141
  events 3, 7
  expanded mode of 6, 40, 126
  forms 217
  history 23, 26, 30, 115
  institution 116, 119
  interpreting 126
  making 31, 120, 126, 140
  markets 144 n.1
  museums 44, 178
  notion of 124
  politics in 141–3
  postcolonial 144 n.1
  practice 2, 3, 99, 135, 141, 142
  practitioners 173, 181
  professionals 123
  ritualistic function of 121
  role of curator 3
  school 115, 178

Index

theory 135
women in 140
works 24, 48, 60, 62, 65, 74, 78, 82, 93, 116, 137, 141, 178
world 3, 10, 17, 22, 91, 120, 125
writing 22, 24, 30
'Art, Materiality and Representation' 173
Art and Artifact (1989) 180
Art by Telephone 121, 129 n.9
artefacts 81–2, 90, 92–3, 126, 134, 137, 149, 157, 159, 163, 168
Artforum 126, 130 n.11
Artificial Hells (Bishop) 22
artificial materials 136
Art Informel 120, 129 n.7
Art in the Streets (2011) 150, 170 n.7
artist 2, 24–5, 75, 98, 116, 117, 119, 123, 125, 134, 135–6, 149, 167, 168, 173, 175
and anthropologist 2
as 'artworkers' 139
and identity 140
indigenous 187, 190
sound curation 213–16
work as curators 133, 212
'The Artist as Ethnographer' (Foster) 1, 133
artistic expression 97
artistic methods 141
artistic practices 11–12, 24, 52, 92, 137, 175, 188, 189
Artist Placement Group 126
Artscribe 126
Asher, Michael 115
Asphalt Rundown 119, 120
assemblage and design 9, 18
Aston, J. 198
audiovisual documentation 136
audiovisual technologies 201
Ausstellungsmacher 183
authentication 86
authenticity 86, 118, 121
authentic works 79
authority 10, 19, 21–2, 30, 46, 61–2, 67, 139, 151
autobiographies 89, 126
auto-ethnography 140
autonomy 9, 12–13, 82, 89, 93, 133

avant-garde 23, 25, 124, 126, 212
Aventures Extraordinaires 159
Averroes 27

BaAka community 219–20
Bainbridge, Eric 129 n.11
Bal, Mieke 41
'baldt1' 126
Bale, Max 220
Balzer, David 41, 191 n.4, 212
Bandjoun 85, 87, 89–91
Baniwa, Denilson 190
Barad, K. 206
Barber, Karin 41
Bard College 115
Bargna, Ivan 10–11
Barragan, Luis 27
Barry, Judith 130 n.11
Barthes, Roland 108
Bartra, Roger 21, 23
Basu, P. 4
Basualdo, Carlos 123
Bataille, Georges 123–4
Bataille Monument 123
Bauer, Ute Meta 123
Beautiful Music All Around Us, The (Wade) 215
Bell, Lucy 177, 183
Benjamin, Walter 121, 124, 207
Berger, John 125
Bergson, Henri 124–5
Berlant, Lauren 97
Berlin 44–50, 52, 127
Berliner Schloss 39
Berlin Exhibition 39, 44–5, 46, 51, 52
Berlin und die Welt. Konzept der Ausstellung des Landes Berlin im Humboldt Forum ('Berlin and the World. Concept of the Exhibition of the Berlin City-State in the Humboldt Forum') 46
Bessette, Jean 109
Bhaskar, Michael 212
Biennale d'architecture d'Orléans 23, 26
biennales 23, 183, 187
big data 204
Biko, Steve 215
Biografia Plurale: Virginia Ryan 2000-2016 (2016) 91

Bionic Breakers   217
Bishop, Claire   22
black box-style theatre   221
Black community   62–4, 67, 68 n.2
Black Lives Matter movement   68 n.2
Black Loyalists   65
Blackness   65, 174
'The Black Power Station'   222–3
Black Refugees   65
Blake, William   137
Bloch, Ernst   162
Blu   150, 156, 170 n.15
BMX competition   156
Boas, Franz   8, 18–19
Bode, Arnold   130 n.13
Bohlman, Philip   214
Bolsonaro, Jair   187
Boltanski, Luc, and Chiapello, Eve   7
'border crossings'   176
Boulton, Laura   215
Bourgeois, Louise   129 n.11
Boyer, Dominic   20, 51, 99
BR   187
Bray, Zoe   99
Brazil   173, 184, 187
'Brei'   126
Brewster, Sandra   65
Broadbent, S.   204
Buffalo Museum of Science   180
Bunzl, Matti   19
Bußmann, Klaus   119
Butler, Cornelia   119

California Institute of the Arts   115
Cambridge Anthropological
    Expedition   214
Camera Lucida (Barthes)   108
Cameroon   73, 76, 82, 86, 87, 89, 91
Campbell, Craig   98, 104
Canadian society   61, 62, 65
'Canine Wisdom for the Barking Dog/
    The Dog Done Gone Deaf'   48
Cannizzo, Jean   60–1
canon   81–2, 86, 91, 175
Cantarella, Luke   22
cape sound stories   220–2
'Capital-C' Criticism   134
capitalism   28
capitalist society   212
care   108, 110–11

cartographic models   119
cartographic representation   157, 160
cartonera   185–8
*Cartoneras: Releituras Latino-
    Americanas*   177, 184
Casa do Povo cultural centre   184, 186
Casco Art Institute   141
Castaing-Tayor, Lucian   182
Castello d'Albertis   79
catacombs   159
categorical format   198
celebrity curators   212
The Center for Curatorial Studies   115,
    128 n.1
Center for Experimental
    Ethnography   29
Central African Republic   219–20
Centre for Anthropological Research
    on Museums and Heritage
    (CARMAH)   38, 45, 54 n.9
Centre Georges Pompidou   180
Centro De Arte Y Comunicación
    129 n.3
ceremonial songs   217, 219
Certeau, Michel De   127
Changing   119
cheap/discarded materials   123
Choose your own Documentary   199
Christov-Bakargiev, Carolyn   7, 124
Chugach Alaska Corporation   174
cinematographe   182
Clark, T. J.   125
Clarke, Jennifer   11–12
Clarke, Michèle Pearson   65
Clifford, James   61, 188, 205
co-action   98–102, 107, 111
Coalition for the Truth about Africa
    (CFTA)   61, 64, 68 n.5
Coccia, Maurizio   91
co-creation   13, 46–7, 108, 206
co-curation   49, 80, 123, 127, 176, 181,
    184, 223–4
Colenso, Sylvia   221
collaboration   68 n.3
collaboration   5, 11, 13, 21, 27, 62–3, 98,
    102, 106, 117, 134–5, 139, 167, 169,
    182, 190, 207, 224
collaborative approach   136
collaborative curation   12, 98, 106–7,
    111, 167, 218

Index 231

collaborative exhibitions 107
collaborative practices 4, 224
collecting practice 59, 73–6, 79,
 86–91
collective experiments 4, 135
collective memory 101, 107, 111
Collins, S. G. 202
Collishaw, Mat 129 n.11
colonial domination 87
colonial expeditions 190
colonial history 60
colonialism 39, 46
colonial oppression 221–2
colonial system 180
commercial art 119
commercial gallery 99, 137, 149
commission 81, 133, 135–6, 163
commissioned artworks 147
commodity 19, 28, 154–5, 166
communication 39, 53, 67, 121, 122–3,
 200, 202–3, 213
community art 23, 24
community artists 216
community museums 3, 73
comparative musicology 214
'concepts' writing 50
conceptual art 118
conceptual artists 23, 51
conceptualisation 51
concept-work 26–7, 29, 30
concrete abstractions 25
concrete materiality 151
Concrete Pour 121
Congolese nail fetishes 219
connoisseurship 31, 115
Conrad, Joseph 60
construction materials 117
contemporary abstraction 24
contemporary anthropologists 18
contemporary anthropology 20–1, 30,
 98, 203
contemporary art 6, 8, 10, 12, 24–5, 30,
 31, 35, 36–7, 40, 76, 80–1, 89–90,
 93, 116, 123, 130 n.13, 133, 136,
 140–3, 144 n.1, 148, 168–9, 173–4,
 190–1, 198
 and anthropology 1, 3, 11,
 107–8
 in Berlin 39
 curation 3, 11, 21

curators 1, 8, 11–12, 73–5
 as ethnographic methods 5
 practice 3, 91–3, 135, 174, 176
Contemporary Art Council 128 n.3
contemporary artists 6, 7, 73, 122, 142,
 224
contemporary ethnography 14
contemporary sounds 217
Contentious Collections 54 n.9
conventional art gallery 135
conversation 48–9, 52, 64, 65, 107, 116,
 122, 124, 126, 137
'conversational' films 198
convivial technique 110
Cook, S. 179
co-production 49, 54 n.9, 147, 169
corporate curating 212
corporatization 165
corporeal 149, 157, 167
Corsín Jiménez, A. 5
Coyote, Dom 221
creative practices 97, 124, 135
creative process 110, 116
Créolité and Creolization 123
critical discourse 122, 125
criticality 126, 134, 143
critical theory 109, 126
critical writing 22, 115
critique 17–21, 31, 125, 134, 138–9,
 141, 168, 175, 180–1
Crooks, Julie 11, 63, 68 n.6
Crow, Thomas 130 n.11
culturalization 76
culture 61, 77, 91, 123, 128, 212
 anthropological notion of 74
 cannibalism 75
 capital 156
 diversity 73–6, 86, 92
 economy 74, 75
 forms 25
 identity 91
 imperialism 133
 practice 79
 production 3, 125, 206
 relativism 82
 transformation 74
curating 25, 35–8, 40–2, 44, 47, 49, 53,
 73, 104, 108, 115, 121, 133–5, 143,
 147–9, 155, 166, 179, 207, 213. *See
 also* sound galleries

Index

'Curating with an Anthropological
Approach' 173
curation 1, 6, 10, 14, 17–19, 29–30,
31, 35, 37, 44, 98, 101, 106, 108,
110–11, 133, 135–6, 148, 149, 150,
196, 202, 207
content and form 8–9, 12, 142–4,
183, 203
definition 21–7
participatory 3–4
sound and 211–15
curator 11, 23, 45–6, 82, 106, 122, 139,
177, 179, 184. *See also individual
entries*
artists work as 133
contemporary-art 73–5
as ethnographer 1–3, 5
fine art 13
managerial 13, 44, 93
as mediators 9, 36
as networking broker 36
sound 213–15, 218, 220, 223
curatorial 41–4, 50–3, 99, 101, 115, 169,
179, 191 n.4
discourse 46
expanded field of 6–8, 13, 36, 40
Curatorial, The (Rogoff and
Martinon) 40
curatorial approach 123, 167
curatorial design 19–20
curatorial laboratory 4–5
*Curatorial Methodology for Anthropology,
A* (Schacter) 169 n.3
curatorial practice 4, 9, 12–14, 17,
19–21, 30, 35–7, 39, 40–1, 43,
47–53, 59, 74, 93, 97, 102, 106–7,
109–10, 112, 149, 167, 176–8,
180–3, 183, 188–9, 195
curatorial space 111, 116, 124, 127
curatorial strategies 39, 173, 174
'Curatorial Studies: Towards
Co-creation and Multiple
Agencies' 106
curatorial turn 8, 17, 75
curatorship 52, 73–6, 81, 188
and ethnography 8
expanded field of 9
as remediation work 91–3
Cusicanki, Juanito 187

Cusicanqui, Silvia Rivera 181
cutting-edge technology 222

El-Dabh, Halim 48
Dakar Biennale 48
Danto, Arthur 142
data archives 205
data management 38
Daughters of Albion, The (Blake) 137
David, Catherine 122
Davis, Tracy C. 41
Dead Images 54 n.9
DeAk, Edit 129 n.6
Dean Clough 122
De Appel Curatorial Programme 115
Debord, Guy 158
decoloniality 181
decolonization 3, 10, 62–7
De Coninckplein 200
deconstructive approach 82
'déjàVu' 126
Deleuze, G. 123–4
Deliss, Clémentine 94
dematerialization 75, 119, 129 n.5
Democracy Unrealized 123
Democratic Republic of Congo 83
demonization 24, 28
demotic cosmopolitanism 67
Dercon, Chris 130 n.11, 182
Derrida, J. 204
*Designs for an Anthropology of the
Contemporary* (Rabinow and
Marcus) 29
deskilling 6, 140
detritus 137
dialogic approach 67
*Dialogos, reflexiones y desafios en
Colombia: Hacia un feminismo
popular* 187
dialogue 10, 49, 52, 63, 64, 65, 92, 137
diasporic character 91
didactic materials 105–6
digital anthropology 204, 205
digital communication 122, 203
digital ethnography 195
digital infrastructures 13, 14, 204–6
digital technologies 195, 196, 203
digital tools and platforms 102
Dikeakos, Christos 118

Dimitrikaki, Angela 140
Director of the City Museums
(*Stadtmuseen*) 39
disciplinary cannibalism 26
discourse 7, 14, 30–1, 38, 41, 44, 49, 52,
 62, 86, 90, 107, 109, 111, 116, 120,
 155, 166
discursive modality 5, 11, 22, 35, 38, 41,
 45–6, 48, 50, 51
discursivity 52–3, 79, 86, 110
display 6, 11, 36, 39, 40, 42, 44, 53, 60,
 62, 64–6, 82, 85, 89, 135, 147, 174,
 184–6, 189, 205
Documenta 130 n.13
documenta 11 123
documenta 13 124
documenta 14 47, 48
documentary films 185, 197–8, 199
documenta X 7, 122
'Do it' project (1992) 3–4
Downey, Brad 163–4
drawings 119–20, 135, 200
Dropbox 102
Drucker, Johanna 143
Duchamp, Marcel 3, 23, 119–20, 142
Dulcinéia Catadora 187
Dundee Contemporary Arts (DCA) 116,
 123, 130 n.14
durational approaches 4
Durington, M. 202
Durrans, Brian 61
dystopia 162, 165

ecology of practice 12–13, 143
editoras cartoneras 176
educational philosophy 126
Egazini ('the place of blood') 223
Eisenstein, Sergei 5, 24
electronic music 217
Elhaik, Tarek 5, 8–9, 13, 17–31
Elkins, James 182
Eloísa 187
Eltono 150–1, 154, 155, 158
embedded curators 179
embodied citizenship 165–6
encontro cartonero 187
encyclopaedic museum 59, 65
engagement 38, 47, 51, 59, 93, 109, 135,
 137–8, 147, 169, 224

Engelke, Matthew 224
Enlightenment 207
enquiry, practice of 20
enslaved Africans 65–6
enunciation 64, 65, 79
Enwezor, Okwui 1–2, 6, 37, 123
ephemera 120, 123, 126, 129 n.6, 149,
 167
 act 165
 exhibitions 75
 practice 119
 projects 122
 site works 117
ephemerality 155, 165–6, 213
epistemic xenophilia 43
epistemology 6–7, 66, 97, 99
Esbell, Jaider 190
Espacio Escultórico 27
Espina, Merv 148
'Essential We-talk' 150
Estação Pinacoteca 183
Estalella, A. 5
Eternal City 28
EthnoAlly 196–7, 204, 208 n.1
ethnographer 1–3, 5–7, 21–3, 38, 44–7,
 50, 147, 189, 195–6, 203, 205
Ethnographic Terminalia Collective 11,
 97–9, 102, 103, 107–9, 111–12
ethnographic turn 2, 10, 30, 37, 99, 173,
 175
ethnography 1, 5, 8, 14, 22, 25, 48,
 53, 62, 93, 125, 126, 205. *See also*
 anthropology
 collections 11, 13, 216
 conceptualism 5–6, 44, 176
 and curatorial practice 12
 and curatorship 8
 method 5, 9, 26, 30
 museums 1, 10–11, 59, 74
 practice 12, 14, 73, 110
 research 21, 40, 46, 47, 76, 106, 166,
 177, 197, 200, 202
 and scenography 27
 and sound 213–14, 216, 218
 writing 18–21
*Ethnography-by-Design: Scengraphic
 Collaborations in Fieldwork*
 (Hegel, Cantarella and
 Marcus) 22

234 *Index*

Ethnography of Iconoclash, An
  (Schacter) 148
ethnological collections 46
Ethnological Museum 39
ethnological museums 3, 39, 44
Ethnologisches Museum 174
ethnomusicologists 48, 214–15
ethnomusicology 214, 219
Eurocentrism 175, 190
European aesthetic theories 142
European anthropology 48
European Association of Social
  Anthropologists (EASA) 8
European Research Council 128
everyday objects 81, 115, 119, 180
exhibition 6, 8, 25, 35, 45–8, 50, 53, 59,
  60–2, 65, 73, 75, 97–9, 104, 123,
  136, 138, 155, 183, 186
  as ethnographic field 76–86
  experiments 4, 76
  practices 86–91
exhibition-making 9, 38, 44, 45, 50, 51,
  115, 126, 133, 135, 141, 148, 179,
  182, 183
'The Expanding Field' (Rogoff) 41
'experiential' films 198
experimental art 4
experimental methods 8
experimentation 4–7, 9–10, 18–19, 25,
  53, 60, 165
*Experiments with Truth: Transitional
  Justice and the Process of
  Reconciliation* 123
expography 12, 177, 181, 189
extractivismo epistemológico
  (epistemological
  extractivism) 180

Fabian, J. 205
Facebook 184
Faile 150
Fair Pavilion 128 n.3
Fanon, Frantz 64
Faubion, Jim 20
Favero, Paolo S. H. 12, 14, 196–7, 200,
  208 n.1
Feld, Steven 91
feminist art practice 142
feminist collectives 186

Fend, Peter 129 n.11
fetishes 83, 85
fetishism 83–4
Fewkes, Jesse Walter 214
field recordings 214–15, 217–19
fieldwork 4, 5, 8, 9, 14, 19–20, 21, 25, 26,
  28–31, 47, 48, 50, 52, 76, 103, 107,
  134, 137, 196, 202–4
filmmaking 30, 200
films 12, 92
fine arts 12, 138, 168
Fingo Festival 222
Fingo Revolutionary Movement 222
Fiore, Q. 207
Fischer, Konrad 119
Fischer, Michael 17–19
Flaubert, Nouaye Taboue 85
Florida, Richard 155
Fluxus 126
Flynn, Alex 10, 12, 14, 148
folkloristic archaism 74
Fontaine, Dominique 11, 63, 68 n.6
Forni, Silvia 10
Forti, Simone 129 n.8
Fossati, G. 196, 206
Foster, Hal 1, 2, 10, 125, 133, 173, 175,
  181, 189–90
Foucault, Michel 17, 19
Fox, Aaron 215
framing devices 42
Francis Bacon (Leiris) 27
Franklin, Sarah 38, 42
freelance curators 179
Freud, S. 28, 173
funding 38, 54, 135, 177, 188

gallery space 60, 98, 109, 120, 127, 158,
  163, 167, 218–20
Gallop, Jane 107, 109
Gaudenzi, S. 198
Geertz, Clifford 22
Gehl, R. 196
Gell, Alfred 24, 178
gender politics 137
Genoa 78, 83, 91
gentrification 74, 170 n.14
German anthropology 39
German bureaucracy 45
German identity 39

Index

Getty Initiative   26
Ghez , Susanne   123
Gibson, Chantal   65
Giclée, Honet   157, 159–60
Gift, The (Hyde)   124
Gifts to Soviet Leaders (2006)   5
Gill, H.   202
Gilroy, Paul   67
Ginsburg, Faye   213
Glasgow School of Art   144 n.2
global art   17, 74
globalization   3, 18, 36
Global Social Media Impact Study
    blog   184
'*Glue Pour and the Viscosity of Fluvial
    Flows as Evidenced in Bottle-
    Gum*'   117–18
Goeritz, Mathias   26, 27–9
Goethe Institute   215
Gómez-Barris, Macarena   180
Gonzalez-Foerster, Dominique   123
Google Drive   102
gospel   216–17
Gothic history   160
graffiti   12, 148–51, 154–69, 170 n.6
Graffiti and Street Art as Ornament
    (Schacter)   151
Graham, B.   179
'Graham's Legacy, Makhanda's
    Future'   223
The Gramsci Monument   124
Graw, Isabella   130 n.11
Gray, Mary   102
grid display   104–6
Grimshaw, Anna   136, 142, 182
Grosfoguel, Ramon   180
Guimard, Hector   160

Haacke, Hans   130 n.11
Haddon, Alfred   182
Halprin, Anna   129 n.8
Hamilton, Carolyn   215
Hamilton, Sylvia D.   65
hand-painted signboards   154
HAU   180
hauntology   66
Haverinen, A.   195
Hayles, N. K.   206
Hayward Gallery   213

healing   65–6
Heart of Africa, The (Schweinfurth)   60
Heart of Darkness (Conrad)   60
Hegel, Christine   22
Helmreich, Stefan   211–12
Hennessy, Kate   98
Henry Moore Foundation   130 n.12
*Here We Are Here: Black Canadian
    Contemporary Art* (2018)   64–5
heritage   36, 39–40, 74, 76, 82, 86, 89, 91
Her Majesty   156
Heshu, Masxiole   223
heteronomy   133
heterotopias   59
Hicks, Dan   127
hidden space   151, 161
hidden transcripts   90–1
Hiller, Susan   99
Hine, C.   195
hip-hop   216–18, 222, 223
Hirschhorn, Thomas   123, 125, 130 n.14
historical museums   44
Historical Papers Research Archive   221
historiography   109–10
Hoffmann, Jens   179
Holbraad, Martin   43
Holocaust   38, 186
Holt, Nancy   117
Holt-Smithson Foundation   128 n.2
Hopper, Robert   122
Horizon 2020 *Reflective Society*
    programme   54 n.9
hosting   46–7
house DJ-ing   217
human agency   197, 206–7
humanity   61, 125, 218
human science   17–18, 25, 30
human subjectivity   207
Humboldt Forum (HuFo)   39, 44, 46, 52,
    174–5
Humboldt -Universität zu Berlin   38
Hume, David   137
hunchwork   106–7
100 Notes – 100 Thoughts (Taussig)   124
Hundreds, The (Berlant and Stewart)   97
Huni Kuin   189
Hutcheon, Linda   62
hylomorphic model   17
'hypertext' films   198

236   *Index*

Iaspis 128 n.1
Iconoclash (Latour) 164
iconography 90
iconophobia 182
identity 2, 3, 86, 109, 133, 173, 175, 181, 223
Identity Anecdotes: Translation and Media Culture (Morris) 109
identity politics 3, 10
iDocs 196–7, 203, 204, 205, 206
  degrees of participation 201–2
  presenting 198–9
  as research technique 199–200
Ignorant Schoolmaster (Rancière) 141
ikebana 137–8, 139
image 14, 24, 30, 81, 90, 92, 139, 162, 164, 183
  based communication 200
  concepts 26
  making 156
  practice 167
  production 13
  work 24, 26, 27, 29–30
  worker 24–5, 30
imagination 23–4, 116, 124
Imaginist Bauhaus 126
'immersive' iDocs 199
Imperial Chemical Industries (ICI) 118
imperial history 60
inalienability 149, 155, 166, 167
incurable-image 26
Incurable Image: Curating Post-Mexican Film and Media Arts, The (Elhaik) 5, 8, 21, 25
independent curator 36–7
independent public art 148
Independent Study Programme 115
indigenous communities 180
indigenous languages 187
indigenous rights 221
industrial processes 119
information art. *See* conceptual art
Ingold, Tim 11, 127, 128, 134–5
innovation 35, 74–5, 106
inquiry, practices of 128
Instagram 184
installation 11, 22, 65, 79, 85, 90, 99–100, 102–3, 103–5, 107, 111, 135, 137, 154, 160, 164, 177, 201, 216, 220, 222

institutional archives 224
institutional imperialism 3
intellectual property 181
Intense Proximity: An Anthology of the Near and the Far (2012) 2
interactive visuality 164
interactivity 197–8
intercultural research 21
interlocutor 26, 44–5, 50, 107, 116, 147, 149, 166, 177, 181, 195, 203
intermural art 166–9
internal publics 22
international art
  market 91
  system 74
International Library of African Music (ILAM) 216–19, 222
International Symposium of Electronic Arts (ISEA) 98
International Visual Methods Seminar (IVMS) 200–1
Into the Heart of Africa (1989) 10–11, 60–2, 66, 68 nn.1, 2, 5
Into the Heart of Darkness. See Into the Heart of Africa (1989)
intuition 106–7, 125
Iñupiat community 215
Invention of Culture, The (Wagner) 116, 127
IRWIN 130 n.11
Islamic art 38
Italian collection 78–80, 84–6
It's Burning Everywhere 130 n.14
'Iy mũn ku mãk pax' 187

Jackson, Michael 221
Jaji, Tsitsi Ella 227
Japanese calligraphy 137, 139
Jelinek, Alana 137–41
Jewish diaspora 186
Johnson, John F. C. 174
Jorn, Asger 126
A Journal of Insomnia 199
JR 150, 156
Junaid, Bushra 65

Kabakov, Ilya 130 n.11
Kandinsky, Wassily 130 n.13
Kant, Immanuel 23, 29, 142
Kaptué, Lazare 86

Karen 199
Karp, Ivan 63
Katzive, David H. 121–2
Kester, Grant 22
kingdom museum 87–90
Kirsch, Stuart 224
Kittler, F. 207
Kiwanga, Kapwani 216
Klee, Paul 130 n.13
Knowing from the Inside: Anthropology,
  Art, Architecture and Design (KFI)
  (2013–2018) 11, 127–8, 134–7,
  143
knowledge 12, 41–3, 49, 61, 102–4,
  106, 109–10, 123, 128, 133–5, 139,
  141–2, 144, 147, 161, 175, 178–9,
  181–4, 188–9, 191 n.4, 197, 201, 206
Kolmel, Mara 148
König, Kasper 119
Korsakow 200, 205
Kovats, Tania 130 n.11
Krafthaus 39
Krauss, Rosalind 117, 125–6
Kremlin Museum of Moscow 5–6
Kulturprojekte 39
Kunsthalle Bern 179
Kunstverein München 128 n.1
Kwakwaka'wakw First Nations of Alert
  Bay 129 n.4

Laboratorium (Obrist and
  Vanderlinden) 4
laboratory curation 29–31
Lagos, Silvana 148
land art 23, 167
Land-Use Strategy 136
Laru-an, Renan 148
Late Editions project 29
Latour, Bruno 4, 19, 23, 164, 206
L'Attico 120–1
Le Corbusier 29
Legitimate Practices 130 n.11
Legoreta, Ricardo 27
Leiris, Michel 27
Lemos, Beatriz 184
Lemov, Rebecca 19
lesbian, bisexual, transgender (LBT)
  collectives 186
lesiba sounds 211, 216
letter 'a' concept 48

letter 'r' concept 47
Lévi-Strauss, Claude 24, 26, 30
Lewisohn, Cedar 150
Lewitt, Sol 129 n.6
liberal white privilege 10, 61
Library of Congress 215
Lidchi, Henrietta 60, 67
limfazwe ('Battles') 223
Lind, Maria 11, 116, 127, 128 n.1
Lippard, Lucy 117–19, 129 n.6
Lisbon University Institute (ISCTE-
  IUL) 199
Lisson Gallery 117
listening 212–13, 221
live art 227
live choreographed sound
  performance 220, 222
lived experience 11, 109, 116, 117, 125,
  199
live performance 100, 199, 224
live soundscape 220, 221
living archives 204
Lobley, Noel 13
lo-fi technology 222
Lomax, Alan 211
Long Weekend 154, 156
Los Angeles Museum of Contemporary
  Art (MOCA) 26, 150–6
Lunden, Duane 118
Lurch, Charmaine 65

McDonald, Fiona P. 98, 104, 106
Macdonald, Sharon 4, 9, 44–7, 50–1,
  54 nn.6, 9, 60, 67
McLuhan, M. 207
machinic capitalist culture 28
Madinda, Xolile 'X' 222
Maes, Frank 126
Magiciens de la Terre (1989) 180
Maharaj, Sarat 123
'Making Differences: Transforming
  Museums and Heritage'
  project 38, 46–8
Making Differences in Berlin: Museums
  and Heritage in the 21st Century 9
Malinowski, B. 9, 201
managerial curator 44
Manifesta 2 128 n.1
Mann, Nathaniel 220, 221
map 160–1

238 Index

Mapping the City (2015) 156–62, 163,
  166
maps 157
Maquet, Jacques 27
Marcel Duchamp (Paz) 27
'Marching on Pretoria' 222
Marcus, George 5, 8–9, 17–31, 144, 205
Margaret Mead Film Festival 98–9
Maria Lind: Selected Writing (Lind)
  128 n.1
marketing 77, 93, 155
Martin, Jean-Hubert 180
Martinez, Alfonso Bahillo 208 n.1
Martinon, Jean-Paul 40–1
mass consumerism 74
masterpieces 82, 164
material 12, 136–7, 142, 201–2
  culture 86
  experiments 117
  processes 117
  studies 117
materialism 84, 143
materiality 81, 93, 118, 136–7, 138, 213
Matisse, Henri 130 n.13
Mauss, Marcel 124
maxakali/tikmũ'ũn, Iy mũn ku mãk
  pax 187
mechanical reproduction 121
media 4, 7–8, 18, 21, 30, 77, 136, 141
media ecologies 202
media emergency 165
mediation 2, 6, 8, 29, 76, 85, 92, 116,
  178, 217
memento mori 138
memory 66, 75, 80, 92, 98, 101, 107
metaphor 137, 142, 213
Metwaly, Kamila 48
Mexican art 21
Mexican culture 25
Mexican society 26
Microsoft Research (MSR) 102, 106
Middlesbrough Institute of Modern Art
  (mima) 119
Mignolo, Walter 64, 181
military dictatorship 183
mimesis 13, 43
Minelli, Filippo 164–5
minimalism 27–8
modern aesthetics 24

Moderna Museet 128 n.1
modern art 3, 6, 23
Modern Art Oxford 126
modern art school 121
modern autonomous art 40
modernism 27, 28–9, 31
modernist aesthetics 23
modernist art 126
modernity 18, 23, 27–9, 89, 123, 126,
  207
Mohamoud, Esmaa 65
Moholy-Nagy, László 121, 127, 129 n.9
montage 2, 6, 9, 14, 18, 24–5, 28–9
Montmartre Cemetery 160
monumental sculpture 26–7
The Monuments of Antiquity 119
Moore, Henry 130 n.13
Moore Institute 122
Mora, Nuria 150–1, 154
Morales, Beatriz 187
Morris, Meaghan 109
Motions of this Kind 148
Mouffe. C. 139
multimodal anthropology 29, 203
multimodal ethnography 107, 196
multimodal formats 202–3
multisited ethnography 18–19
Municipal Museum of Contemporary Art
  (SMAK) 126
Muñoz, José Esteban 110
mural 150, 151, 155
muralism 150, 170 nn.14, 15
Museo de Arte Contemporáneo
  (MUAC) 27
Museo Experimental del Eco 28
museology 61, 63, 67, 115
museum 1, 4, 6, 31, 35–6, 38, 40, 53,
  66, 74, 77, 82, 85, 91, 93, 116, 133,
  144 n.1, 175, 182–3, 190–1. *See also*
  community museums; ethnological
  museums
  authoritative voice of 60–2
  collaboration 63
  collection 60, 75, 87, 89, 120, 174
  discourses 39
  ethnography 219
  institutions 44
  practice 64, 173
Museum Fridericianum 130 n.13

museumification   165
Museum of Asian Art   39
Museum of Contemporary Art   121
Museum of Culture   76
Museum of Cultures of Milan
   (MUDEC)   73
Museum of Modern Art (MoMA)   180
Museum of Modern Art of São Paulo
   (MASP)   174–5, 184
museum-turned-gallery   137
Myers, Fred   100

Nano4814   150
narratives   2, 7, 41, 62, 64–5, 90, 109,
   111–12, 178–9, 188, 200–2, 214,
   218, 221, 223
Nash, Mark   123, 198
National Arts Festival   222–3
National Starch and Chemical
   Company   118
natural history   100
natural materials   138
Nazi Germany   126
Ndikung, Bonaventure Soh Bejeng   9–10,
   47–50, 52–3
nemo   90–1
neo-muralism   155
New Bauhaus   121
New Institutionalism   93
'New Wing'   156
Njami, Simon   181
nkisi figures   83
Nkosi Sikile i'Africa   221
Nolens Volence (2015)   164
non-commercial spaces   183
non-human agents   197
Nonsites   119
non-Western art   142, 173
North American Cold War cultural
   policy   175
Novak, D.   213
Nov Nueve   169 n.5
NuArt   170 n.13
Nunca   150
Nuria   155
'Nyaki'. *See* Tsana, Nyakonzima

Obrist, Hans Ulrich   3, 4, 6, 179
Ocora   214

*Of Africa: Histories, Collections,
   Reflections*   63–4, 67, 68 n.4
Ogboh, Emeka   47
O'Hare, Patrick   177
On Africa   10–11
online ethnography   195
*The Only Emergency is the Absence of
   Emergency*   165
Ono, Yoko   129 n.11
open-access archive   99, 112
open-endedness   43, 64, 143, 188–9
Orientalism   18
ornamental   149, 151, 155, 166, 167
Ornament and Order (Schacter)   151,
   169 n.5
Orton, Fred   125
Os Gemeos   150, 156
Out of Sight, Out of Mind (1993)   117
overpainting   164

Pacific Standard Time   26
Pagonis, Ilyas   118
painting   23, 99, 164
Palace of the Republic   39
Palazzo Ducale   76, 81–2
Palazzo Lucarini Contemporary   91
Palestine Remix   199
Palimpsests and Remnants (2017)   137–8
Pan-African arts   223–4
'para-site' (2000)   5, 8–9, 19, 76, 98
Parikka, J.   204
Paris   160–1
Paris Triennale (2012)   37
Paris Verticale (2015)   159
Parodi da Passano, Giovanna   76, 80
participant-observation   18, 23, 26, 44–5,
   48, 82
participation   8, 9, 45–7, 51, 93, 137, 147,
   201–2, 207
'participative' films   198
participatory approaches   45–6
participatory art
   movements   22
   projects   11
participatory curation   3–4, 44
'participatory' iDocs   199
participatory media production   202–4
Parzinger, Hermann   174
Passamaquoddy First Nations   214

240   *Index*

patronage 38, 90
Patterson, Simon 130 n.11
Pavilion Zero 73
'pay-to-play' 183
Paz, Octavio 27
Peace and Love (PAL) 164, 170 n.17
Pedersen, Morten Axel 43
Pereira, Marie Hélène 48
performance art 104, 168
permanent museum collections 75, 90
Pernice, Manfred 126
'perpetual decolonization' 9, 18
Pester, Holly 109
Peters, Erin 106
Petros, Dawit L. 65, 68 n.6
Philip, NourbeSe 61, 65–6
philosophical aesthetics 135
phonograph recordings 214
photographic documentation 117, 122
photographic practice 176
photographs/photography 30, 92, 120, 148, 182, 200, 207
Picasso, Pablo 130 n.13
Pink, Sarah 141
Pirelli Hangar Bicocca art centre 8
Pitt Rivers Museum (PRM) 127, 219–20
Plaatje, Sol 221
A Plan for Escape 123
Plato 83, 142
Podcast Series 30
political demagogues 165
political modernism 23
politics and aesthetics 124
Pollock, Griselda 125
Polanyi, Michael 139
polyphonic approach 85
polyvalence of spatiality 183–4
Pop 16 220
popular music 220
postcolonialism 3
postcolonial theory 39, 67, 142
Postlewait, Thomas 41
'post-Mexican condition' 23
postmodern approach 61
postmodern condition 74
postmodern critiques 10
post-socialist society 6
post-studio art 115

Potlatch: A Strict law Bids Us Dance (1975) 129 n.4
Potlatch ceremony 124
Potosí Principle. How Can We Sing the Song of the Lord in an Alien Land?, The 181
Prenowitz, E. 204
presentialism 12, 176
primitive art 84
Primitivism in 20th Century Art: Affinity of the Modern and the Tribal (1984) 180
Pringle, Emily 173
printed matter 119
Printed Matter 129 n.6
printmaking 135
Prison Valley 199
private museums 87, 89
privatization 165
process art 119, 126, 129 n.5
processual difference 181–4
professional art 123
professional artists 12, 140
professional identities 139–40
Promenades (2015) 158
Prospect 68 119
proto-*cartonera* 185
prototypes 11, 99, 104, 108
provisionality 107, 110–11
pseudo-factory system 119
psychogeography 158
public art 148, 155, 166
   practice 23
   works 28
public discourses 39
public gallery 59, 122
public institutions 44, 62, 129 n.11
public library 183, 217
public programmes 64, 185–7
public sculpture 26–8
public space 31, 64, 99, 123, 165, 185
public transcript 90–1
public works 149, 155

Qashqai, Nissan 156
Que Viva México! (1931–32) 5

Rabinow, Paul 19–20, 21, 23, 29, 144
racial inequality 68 n.2

Index

racism 61–2, 68 n.2, 68 n.5, 184
Radio Fields (Ginsburg) 213
Radio Ndjoku 220
Ramirez Vasquez, Pablo 27, 156
Rammert, W. 207
Rancière, J. 10, 140–1, 189, 191
Ravetz, A. 136, 142
Read, Ben 130 n.12
Read, Benedict 122
Read, Herbert 130 n.12
ready-mades 119, 142
reappropriation and reuse 163
recursive curatorial fields 44–50
recursivity 9–10, 13, 37, 38, 40–4, 47, 49, 50–3
Red de Mujeres de La Sabana 187
reflexive anthropology 43
reflexivity 10, 36, 38, 42, 61, 147, 173–5
'rehearsed improvisations' 49
Reina Sofia museum 181
relational aesthetics 22, 24
relational art 4
releituras (rereadings) 184–9
relexification 47
'Relexification Dialogues' project 9, 47, 50, 51–2
Rembrandt (Simmel) 27, 29
reparation 65
repertoires 81
representation 3, 9, 10, 14, 64, 92, 109, 111, 115, 120, 134–5, 143, 147, 173, 184, 201. *See also* cartographic representation
Research Foundation Flanders (FWO) 208 n.1
research-led curating 147
research methodology 124–7, 195–6
Residência Artística Cambridge 176
restitution 38, 138, 147, 174, 190–1
Return of the Real, The (Foster) 175
'Return to Alaska' 174
Revenues and Customs 156
RFI Planète Radio 220
Rhodes University 216
Rice Circle 29
ricochet effects 38, 43
riverbank ecology 136
Riverside Studios 122, 129 n.11
Rizote 164

Robinson, Walter 129 n.6
Rockefeller, Nelson 175
Rogoff, Irit 6, 35–6, 40–1, 50, 53, 54 n.5, 108, 134, 179
Rosler, Martha 181
Roth, Moira 120
Royal Anthropological Institute 173
Royal College of Art 115
Royal Ontario Museum (ROM) 10, 59–60, 62–4, 66–7, 68 n.5
Rubin, William 180
Ruta de la Amistad 27
Ryan, Virginia 91–2, 93

Saeio 164
Said, Edward 18
Sakakeeny, M. 213
Sakakibara, Chie 215
Sandström, U. 191 n.4
Sansi, Roger 37, 40, 44, 49, 53, 139–41, 148
Sargentini, Bruno 120
Sargentini, Fabio 120
Sarno, Louis 218–19, 220
Savage Mind, The (Lévi-Strauss) 24
SAVVY Contemporary 39, 48, 52
scenography 22, 27
Schacter, Rafael 12, 14, 176
Schneider, Arnd 40, 176, 181
Schuping, Mpotseng 221
Schwarcz, Lilia 174
Schweinfurth, Georg 60
science and technology studies (STS) 20, 21
Scottish Enlightenment 137
sculpture 117, 126–7
  map 158
  park 123
  presentation 182
Sculpture Studies Programme 130 n.12
Seattle Art Museum 128 n.3
Seattle World 128 n.3
Second Boer War 227 n.20
self-creation 139–40
self-reflexivity 59, 61, 76–7, 140
self-supporting galleries 149
sensory ethnography 99, 203
Sesc Ipiranga cultural centre 176
Shadrach, Gordon 65

shared space 2, 127, 186
Shearman, Zoe 122, 129 n.11
shebeens 216
Shelemay, Kay Kaufman 214
signs 26
Signs 68 n.6, 151, 154, 155
Silverman, Raymond 66
Silver Sehnsucht (2017) 161
Simmel, Georg 27, 28–30
Simon, Nina 46–7
Simpson, Audra 100
Simpson, Leanne Betasamosake 180
Sin Fronteira Cartonera 187
site-specific installations 22, 135, 151, 163
Situationist International (SI) 126
Sixe Paredes 150
Six Years: The Dematerialization of the Art Object (Lippard) 118
Skotnes, Pippa 215
Skulptur Projekte Münster 119
Skype 102
small narrative units (SNUs) 200, 205
Smith, Linda Tuhiwai 180
Smith, Terry 51, 144 n.1
Smith, Trudi Lynn 98
Smithson, Robert 116–21, 128 n.2
Smithsonian Folkways 214
smoke performance 164–5
social art practice 23–4
social identity 88
social inequality 92
social media 38, 177
social practice 3, 4, 14, 133
social sciences 25, 176
social-scientific methods 147
social theory 21
socio-epistemic exchange 43
'Somagwaza' 217
Somerset House 156, 162
Sonic Boom 213
sonic engagement 213
Sortais, Ken 160
sound archives 214–15, 216
sound art 227
sound curation 12, 13, 211–13, 222
   anthropologists and artists 213–16, 220
sound curator 213, 214, 215, 223

sound elicitation in Xhosa townships 216–20
sound galleries 218–20
'Sound Galleries' 220
sound repatriation 214–15
sound studies 211
sound waves 213
South African Audio Archive Flat International 221
South African National Congress 221
Speculative Ground (2014) 135–6
speculative practice 4, 11
Spies, Paul 46, 52
Spinoza, Baruch 123
Spivak, Gayatri Chakravorty 126
Spok 150
sponsorship 156
Ssorin-Chaikov, Nikolai 5, 44, 53, 176
Staatliche Museen zu Berlin 174
Stanley, Mike 126
Starn, Randolph 109–10
Steir, Pat 129 n.6
Stencil Festival 170 n.13
Stengers, I. 12
stereotypes 61, 76–7, 86–7
Stewart, Kathleen 97
Stiegler, B. 203
Stiftung Preußischer Kulturbesitz (SPK) 174
Stoler, Ann 112
street art 12, 148–9, 150–1, 154–5, 156
Street Art (2008) 150–1, 154–7, 170 n.13
Street Art Festivals 155–6
street artists 12
street theatre 217, 227
Street to Studio (Schacter) 167
Strelow, Hans 119
Strohm, Kiven 10, 182, 189
studio practice 19, 21, 115, 149
Sublime Frequencies 214
Suck Teeth Composition (After Rashaad Newsome) 65
Sun Ra Repatriation Project 216
Szeemann, Harald 130 n.13, 179, 183
Szöke, Anna 54 n.9

Takaragawa, Stephanie 98
Talking Contemporary Curating (Smith) 51

Index

Tate Britain 173
Tate Modern 150, 154–7, 170 nn.7, 8, 173–5
Taussig, Michael 121, 124
Teal, Eugenie 119
Tekam, Wabo 85
'telephone pictures' 121
temporary exhibitions 75
temporary monument 123–4
Teratoma 5
Terrace Rooms 162
Tetlapayac 5
text as gallery guide 104–5
textual anecdotes 108
theatricality 41
theoretical framing 60–2
Theory Is More Than It Used to Be (Boyer, Faubion and Marcus) 20
Theunissen, Eva 12, 14, 208 n.1
Thinking Contemporary Curating (Smith) 51
This is Not Art (Jelinek) 141
3D environment 201
3TTMan 150, 167
Tim Rollins + K.O.S 130 n.11
Tinius, Jonas 9, 45, 47–52, 148
Toguo, Barthelemy 89
Toop, David 213
'top-down' approach 46
Torres Satellite 28
Torres Strait expedition 182
touring exhibition 126
Tracey, Hugh 216–17, 224
traditional African art 76, 83, 86
traditional art gallery 106
trans-Atlantic slave trade 66
transcultural identities 214
transcultural montage 28
transcultural practices 87
transformative alterity 190
Transmitting Contentious Cultural Heritages with the Arts: From Intervention to Co-Production (TRACES) 54 n.9
transnational culture 80
trauma 66
Trower, Shelley 211
Trudeau, Pierre 68 n.2
Tsana, Nyakonzima 217–18, 222

Turner, Victor 150
tutorial videos 185
Tutti 126–7
two-dimensional maps 159
2015 Milan Expo 73

UNAM 27
Uncertain Curature (Hamilton and Skotnes) 215
Under Siege: Four African Cities 123
UNESCO 190
uneven hermeneutics 10
unintentional beauty 28
University College London (UCL) 147, 184
University of Aberdeen 11
University of California 26
University of Chicago Press 29
University of Deusto 208 n.1
University of Leeds 122
University of Oxford 219
University of Pennsylvania 29
University of São Paulo 174
University of the Witwatersrand 221
un-learning 122–4, 126, 141
UnMute Dance Company 221
(*Untitled*) *Dreamcatchers* (2016) 163
urban aesthetics 148, 150
urban environment 157–8
urban regeneration 74
urban space 157
Uricchio, W. 206
utopia 162–5

values 7, 13, 74, 76, 108, 136, 140–1, 151, 155–6, 180, 218, 223–4
Vancouver Art Gallery 117
van den Besselaar, P. 191 n.4
van Doorn, N. 207
'Variações do Corpo Selvagem: Eduardo Viveiros de Castro, fotógrafo' 176
Vazquez, Rolando 64
Vélez, Humberto 99
Vellem, Andile 221–2
Venturing Beyond (2016) 162–6
Vindication of the Rights of Woman, A (Wollstonecraft) 137
virtual archive 112, 205
virtual ethnography 195

244   *Index*

Virtual Reality (VR) documentaries 199
visual activities 150
visual aesthetics 82, 164, 182
visual anthropologists 13
visual anthropology 120, 141, 195
visual arts 13, 147
visual ethnography 195–6, 202, 203
visual identity 177
visual imagining 144 n.1
visuality 158
visual languages 136
visual practice 166
visual representation 165, 195
visual researcher 12–13
Vitruvius 121
Viveiros de Castro, Eduardo 176
Voegelin, Salomé 213
Vogel, Susan 180
'Voltairean sarcasm' 120
von Humboldt, Alexander 54 n.6
von Oswald, Margareta 60, 67
von Zahn, Irena 129 n.6
Von Zinnenburg, Khadija 148
'voodoo doll' 85

Wade, Stephen 215
Wagner, Roy 11, 116, 127–8
Walking Tour 150–1, 155, 166
Walsh, Victoria 178
Warhol, Andy 119
waste material 186
weak theory 110
Weltkulturen Museum 94
Western catalogues 91
Western collection 83
Western culture 82
Western museological conventions 62
Western museums 86–7

Western taxonomies 62
Wheeler, Dennis 118, 129 n.4
Wheeler, Mimi 129 n.6
White, Robin 129 n.6
The Whitney Museum of American
    Art 115, 119
William Cullen Library 221
Winter, Judith 11
Wittgenstein, Ludwig 87
Wollstonecraft, Mary 137
Wonders of Africa: African Arts in
    Italian Collections 11, 73, 76–7,
    79, 81
Wright, Chris 176
writing culture 8, 17

Xhosa
    artists 223
    arts archives 222–4
    history 223
    instruments 217
    music 216–17
Xhosa Chronicles 223

Yandoumbé 219
Yiyi Jambo 187
Yoruba maternity statue 79
'Yo soy Mexico' 5
'Your Square' 201
YouTube 196

Zabala, Santiago 165
Zaidi, Ali 208 n.1
Zaya, Octavio 123
Zong massacre 66
Zong! (Philip) 65–6
Zonophone 221
Zylinska, J. 207

Printed in the United States
by Baker & Taylor Publisher Services